CW00435529

READING FOOTBALL CLUB
EST. 1871

READING

FOOTBALL CLUB OFFICIAL YEARBOOK 2006/07

Editorial
Andy West, Mark Bradley, Simon Heggie

Sidan Press Team
Simon Rosen, Julian Hill-Wood, Marc Fiszman, Mark Peters, Karim Biria, Rob Cubbon, Anette Lundebye, Marina Kravchenko, Gareth Peters, Janet Callcott, Trevor Scimes, John Fitzroy, Jenny Middlemarch, Anders Rasmussen, Lim Wai-Lee, Lex Badia, Charles Grove, Zoe Westbourne

Photography
Craig Mortimer, Mark Bradley, Richard Claypole, Gareth Davies, Jason Dawson, Gary Hynard, Gerry McManus, Ian Morsman

Copyright © 2006 Reading Football Club

SIDAN PRESS
Passionate about sport

Sidan Press, 63-64 Margaret St, London W1W 8SW
Tel: 020 7580 0200
Email: info@sidanpress.com

sidanpress.com

Copyright © 2006 Sidan Press Ltd

Maps redrawn and based on Collins Town and Country series
Copyright © 2006 Bartholomew Ltd
Reproduced by permission of Harpercollins Publishers

Club Directory

READING FOOTBALL CLUB
EST. 1871

Chairman and Directors

Chairman
John Madejski OBE, DL
Chief Executive
Nigel Howe
Directors
Ian Wood-Smith

First Team Management

Manager
Steve Coppell
Director of Football
Nick Hammond
First Team Coaches
Kevin Dillon, Wally Downes & Nigel Gibbs
Reserve Team Manager & Chief Scout
Brian McDermott
Goalkeeping Coach
Sal Bibbo
Head Physiotherapist
Jon Fearn
Sports Scientist
Jon Goodman
Masseur
Andy Stanbury
Prozone Analyst
Stephen Brown
Kit Manager
Ron Grant
Assistant Kit Manager
Selby Armstrong

Club Management

Financial Controller
Bryan Stabler
Sales & Marketing Manager
Boyd Butler
Stadium Manager
Ray Booth
Club Secretary
Sue Hewett
Customer Services Manager
Jackie Evans
Head of Communications
Andy West

Contacts

Address
Reading Football Club
Madejski Stadium
Junction 11, M4
Reading
Berkshire RG2 0FL

For online tickets, merchandise, betting, video highlights, live commentary and all the latest news, visit **www.readingfc.co.uk**

Sales Centre: 0870 999 1871
salescentre@readingfc.co.uk

Megastore: 0118 968 1234
merchandise@readingfc.co.uk

Customer Service: 0118 968 1211
customerservice@readingfc.co.uk

Press office: 0118 968 1052
press@readingfc.co.uk

Community: 0118 968 1415
community@readingfc.co.uk

Promotions: 0118 968 1480
mkearney@readingfc.co.uk

Commercial: 0118 968 1302/3
hospitality@readingfc.co.uk

Training Centre: 0118 968 1202
thedome@readingfc.co.uk

Conference Centre: 0118 968 1333

Millennium Madejski Hotel
0118 925 3500

Switchboard: 0118 968 1100

Fax: 0118 968 1101

Contents

READING FOOTBALL CLUB
EST. 1871

READING FOOTBALL CLUB
EST. 1871

Reading FC Official Partners

KYOCERA

PUMA

QUINTILES

COURAGE

UNDER ARMOUR

vodafone

Chupa Chups

John Madejski

Chairman

After the euphoria of last season's stunning achievements, everybody at Reading Football Club is now greatly relishing our first season in the top flight of English football.

We are approaching our first foray into the Premiership with a combination of optimism and realism. We have every intention of maintaining our status in this division for many years to come, but we also have to appreciate that it will be a difficult task. We will be competing against top-class performers on a weekly basis, in a league that is widely regarded as the best in the world.

For our players, of course, the coming season offers a massive opportunity. Having displayed their abilities at a consistently high level to win last season's Football League title with a record points tally, they now have the chance to prove themselves at the very highest level of club football.

Almost without exception, our players have no prior experience of playing in the Premiership. That should give them added incentive to prove their value, and I have every confidence in their ability to succeed and flourish at this level. I know they can't wait for the action to begin, and likewise the manager, his coaching staff and the backroom team at Madejski Stadium are equally excited by the challenges that lie ahead.

As I have said on many occasions in the past, supporters also have a crucial role to play in determining the team's success, and that will certainly be the case this season as we seek to cement our position in the Premiership.

There may be stages of the season or periods in games where things are tough, and that is when your support will be more important than ever. Last season we were spoiled by the kind of success that comes along once in a lifetime. Clearly we cannot expect to enjoy similar results again this year, but it is absolutely imperative that our supporters continue to generate the positive, vibrant atmosphere that we enjoyed last season.

As we enter the Premiership for the very first time as the oldest club in the top flight, I believe that everybody connected with Reading Football Club can feel immense pride. Considering the huge worldwide interest in the Premiership it is no exaggeration to say that the whole world is now scrutinising our progress. This is our chance to make a mark – not just for Reading Football Club, but for the town and region as a whole – and we are approaching the new season with purpose and determination.

I am delighted that we have been able to include this new yearbook within your season ticket package, and hope that you enjoy studying it as we enter the most exciting season in Reading Football Club's long history.

Best wishes

John Madejski OBE, DL
Reading FC Chairman

Steve Coppell

Manager

We've known for almost five months that the start of Reading Football Club's long-awaited Premier League life will begin in August 2006, and now the time has arrived.

If not quite from day one last season, virtually everything we tried worked. And nearly everything we did, we did well. There was no evident dip in form, no anticipated lull in performance levels and the points continued to tot up. Each and every player strove hard to improve, refusing to rest on their laurels or settle for a certain level of achievement. As a result, we hit new heights and as reward we saw wonderful scenes of celebration.

So many fantastic memories from last season will live with me for the rest of my life but it's now apt that we lock them tidily away into a box labelled 'Last season's success'. We worked very hard to earn enormous respect from our Championship peers last season. Now we have a new set of peers of world class calibre, with humbling histories and very high expectations.

In our first ever Premiership season we will face a completely contrasting set of challenges in what I expect will be very testing circumstances. Our astonishing success last year came courtesy of skill, desire, ability, physical fitness and team ethic but also as a consequence of flourishing and unwavering confidence.

In our promotion-clinching campaign we only lost twice, both narrow defeats by a single goal and both were followed up with league wins. This season we have to understand and accept that we are not going to win 31 games and that we will have to deal quickly and effectively with defeat.

Being beaten breaks a footballer's spirit and can rapidly undermine players' confidence or eat away at a team's self-belief. Last season, my players' confidence needed no nurturing, but a testing Premiership campaign may demand it. As the squad of players proved in emphatic style last season though, we certainly possess the collective mentality to rise to those new standards and achieve a fresh set of goals at the highest level.

We'll only know next May how vast the step up to Premier League football actually was, and learning how to bridge the gap, hopefully we'll be in a qualified position to build and push further forward in the future. At Reading, our aim has been to build on success in a sensible, stable and constructive way and we must not take this one sizeable step forward only to then be forced to take two steps back.

It often goes unmentioned, but we'll also ask a lot of our fans this season. It's imperative that our supporters stay supportive and perform at Premiership level. The tag that will follow us throughout our top flight fight will focus on how happy we'd be to finish fourth from bottom, and how avoiding relegation can be our only realistic aim. Although many will undoubtedly agree, religiously watching a struggling side is not easy and supporting a team that winds up in 17th spot would inevitably involve disappointment and heartache. It might sound strange after such success and jubilation last summer, but I urge the players and our supporters to try to enjoy this season as you did the last.

We walk into the start of this season as part of an elite collection of teams taking part in one of the most gifted, attractive and exhilarating leagues in world football. I'm exceptionally excited and privileged to lead Reading Football Club into their inaugural Premiership adventure.

Best wishes,
Steve Coppell

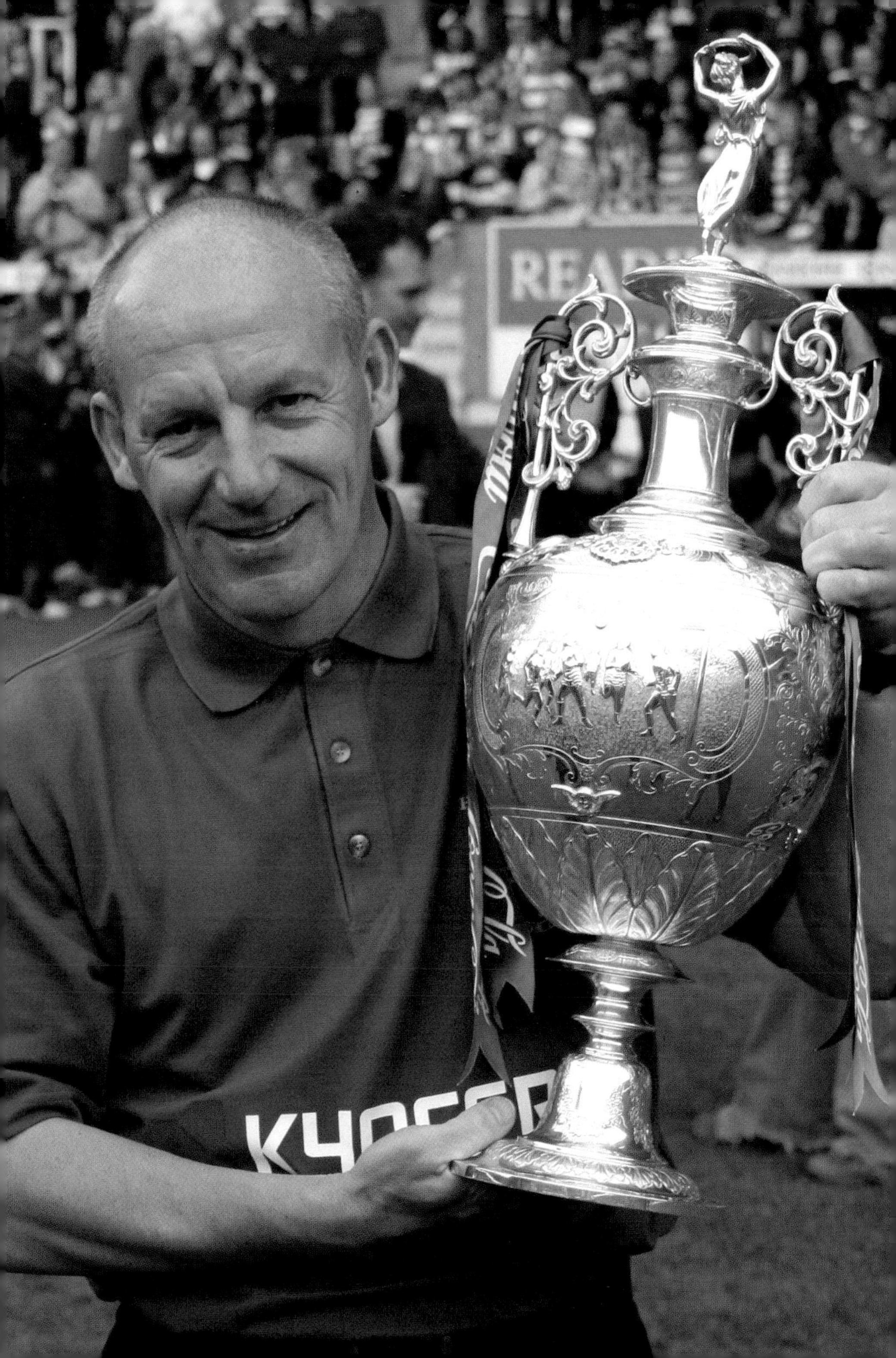

How to Read the Stats

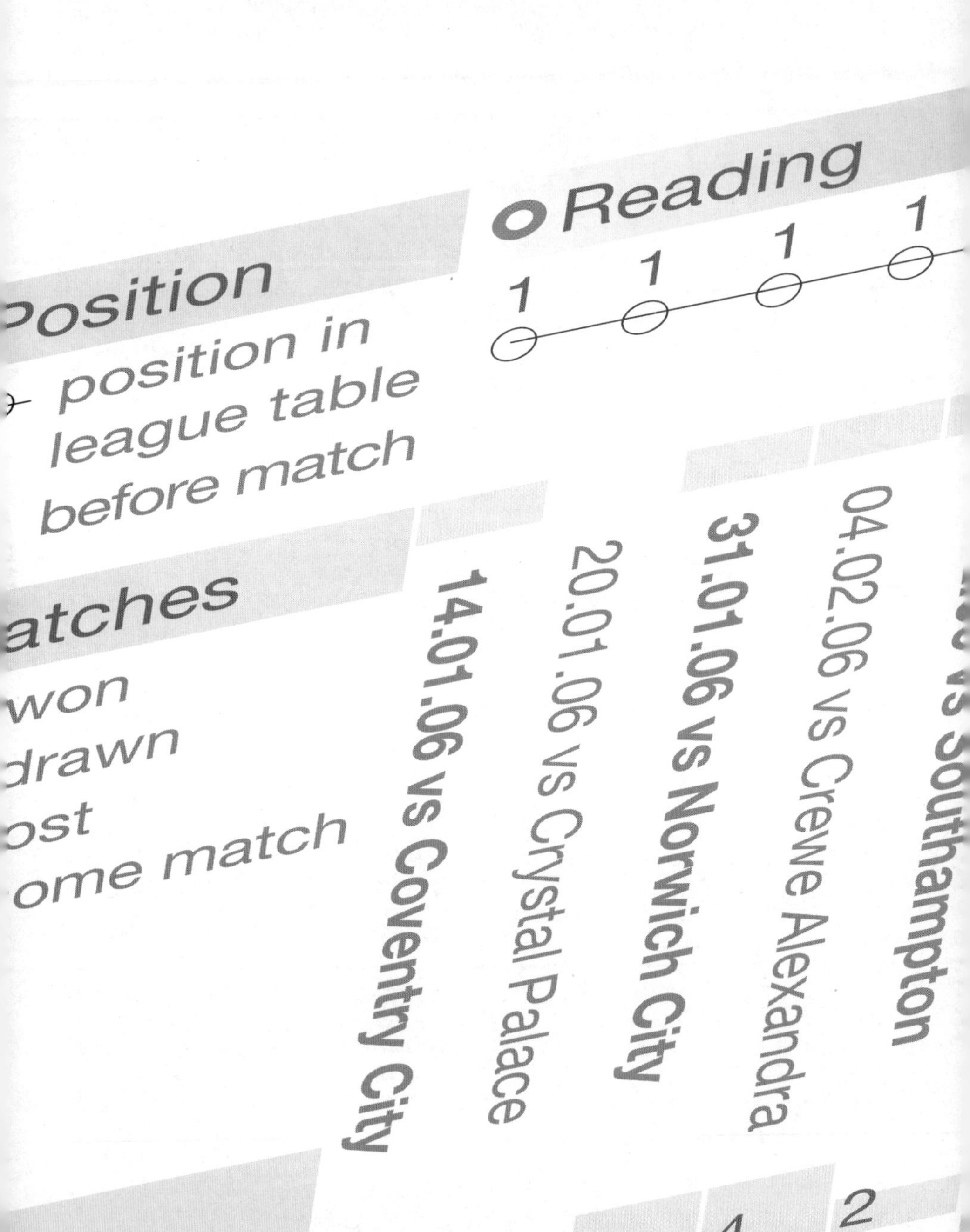

Reading
osition
position in
league table
before match
1
1
1
1
1
atches
won
drawn
ost
ome match
14.01.06 vs Coventry City
20.01.06 vs Crystal Palace
31.01.06 vs Norwich City
04.02.06 vs Crewe Alexandra
vs Southampton
s
ored
2
1
1
4
0
4
3
2
0

Preston
vs
31.01.06 vs Crystal Palace
2 0
04.02.06 vs Stoke City
2 0
11.02.06 vs Luton Town
0 0
15.02.06 vs Southampton
5 1
0 0
17.02.06 vs Luton Town
14.02.06 vs Sheffield
2 3

How to Read the Stats

This year's review is better than ever, packed with the sort of in-depth stats which really get you close to the action. If you'd like to know why a particular match turned out the way it did, how a player's form varied over the course of the season, or how Reading have fared against their biggest rivals, you'll find all the info inside.

To make sure you're getting the most out of the stats, we're including this section to highlight the information presented by some of the charts and tables.

Colours

Reading vs Opposition

There are lots of comparisons between Reading and our opponents throughout the book. Reading stats are shown in blue; opponents are shown in grey:

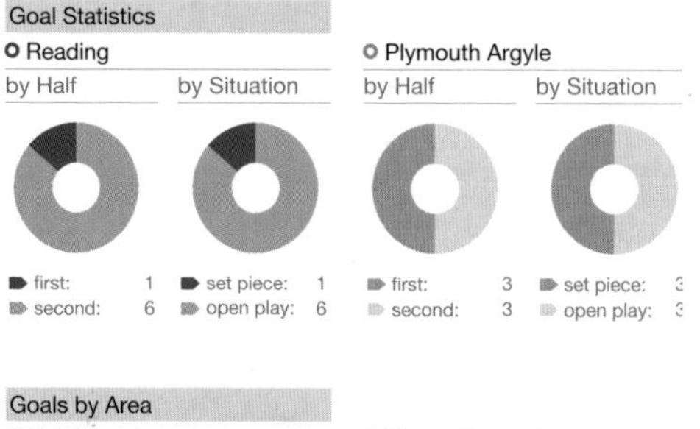

Goal Statistics
Reading
Plymouth Argyle
by Half
by Situation
by Half
by Situation
first: 1
second: 6
set piece: 1
open play: 6
first: 3
second: 3
set piece:
open play:

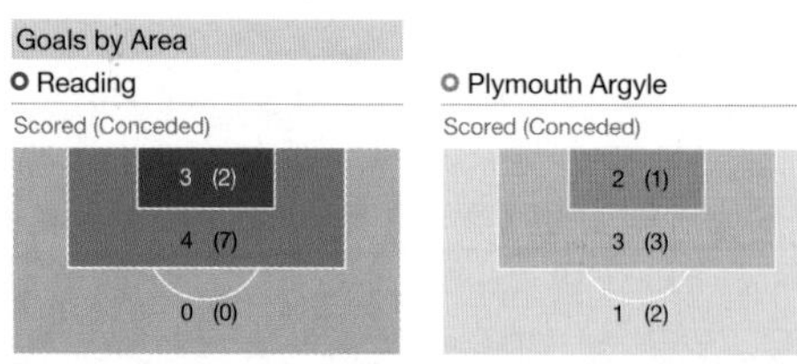

Goals by Area
Reading
Plymouth Argyle
Scored (Conceded)
Scored (Conceded)
3 (2)
4 (7)
0 (0)
2 (1)
3 (3)
1 (2)

Figure 1: Reading stats are in blue; opposition stats are grey.

WDL, Scored, Conceded

When reviewing match results, wins, draws and losses are indicated by green, grey and orange blocks, respectively. For goals, green blocks indicate goals scored; orange blocks show goals conceded:

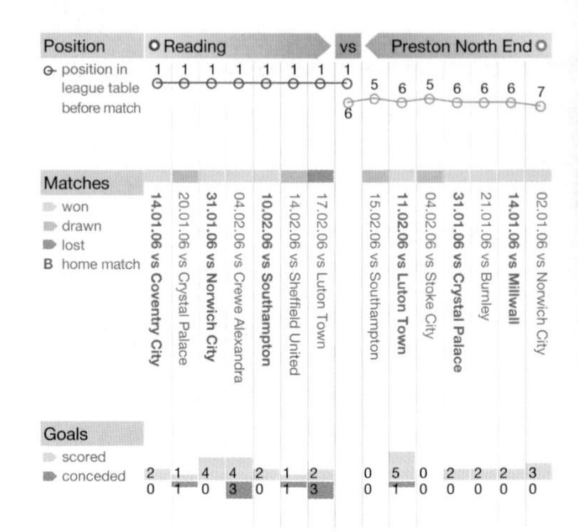

Position
Reading
vs
Preston North End
position in league table before match
Matches
won
drawn
lost
B home match
14.01.06 vs Coventry City
20.01.06 vs Crystal Palace
31.01.06 vs Norwich City
04.02.06 vs Crewe Alexandra
10.02.06 vs Southampton
14.02.06 vs Sheffield United
17.02.06 vs Luton Town
15.02.06 vs Southampton
11.02.06 vs Luton Town
04.02.06 vs Stoke City
31.01.06 vs Crystal Palace
21.01.06 vs Burnley
14.01.06 vs Millwall
02.01.06 vs Norwich City
Goals
scored
conceded

Figure 2: Wins, draws, losses and goals are clearly colour-coded.

Match Reports

The Match Report section contains reports, quotes, facts and stats from every Reading match of the 2005/06 season.

Event Line

Each match has an event line detailing goals, substitutions and bookings. For every goal, the event line describes the point of contact, situation and area using the following abbreviations:

Contact	Situation	Area
H: Header	**IFK:** Indirect Free Kick	**6Y:** 6-Yard Box
LF: Left Foot	**DFK:** Direct Free Kick	**IA:** Inside Area
RF: Right Foot	**OP:** Open Play	**OA:** Outside Area
OG: Own Goal	**C:** Corner	
	P: Penalty	

Stats Order (Home and Away)

The order of the stats varies depending on whether a match was home or away: for home matches, Reading stats are shown on the left, for away matches they're on the right:

Championship Totals	Reading	Plymouth
Championship Appearances	389	278
Team Appearances	389	258
Goals Scored	34	27
Assists	26	25
Clean Sheets (goalkeepers)	19	4
Yellow Cards	30	31
Red Cards	0	2
Full Internationals	4	3

Figure 3: For home matches, Reading stats appear on the left.

Championship Totals	Brighton	Reading
Championship Appearances	262	434
Team Appearances	258	402
Goals Scored	19	37
Assists	17	30
Clean Sheets (goalkeepers)	0	19
Yellow Cards	25	32
Red Cards	2	0
Full Internationals	0	5

Figure 4: For away matches, Reading stats appear on the right.

Form coming into fixture

Stats are from the previous seven league games. For the first few matches, these stats include games from the end of the previous season.

Team Statistics

Stats are for starters and playing subs. The "Championship Totals" chart measures performance within the Championship (with the exception of "Full Internationals").

Championship Totals	Reading	Plymouth
Championship Appearances	389	278
Team Appearances	389	258
Goals Scored	34	27
Assists	26	25
Clean Sheets (goalkeepers)	19	4
Yellow Cards	30	31
Red Cards	0	2
Full Internationals	4	3

Age/Height	
Reading Age	Plymouth Argyle Age
25 yrs, 7 mo	27 yrs, 4 mo
Reading Height	Plymouth Argyle Height
5'11"	5'11"

Figure 5: Team statistics are for starters and playing subs.

Player Profiles

The Player Profile section provides season reviews and comprehensive stats for Reading's players. The section is organised by position, starting with goalkeepers. Ages are as of May, 2006.

Pitch Diagram

The diagram shows all positions the player played during 2005/06. Main and alternative positions are denoted by dark and light blue circles respectively.

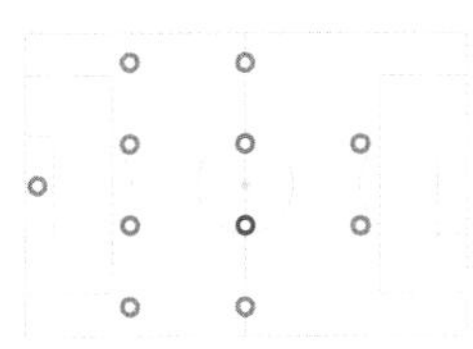

Figure 6: Major positions are shown in dark blue; minor positions are shown in light blue.

Player Performance

All stats show league performance, with the exception of the "Cup Games" table. The "League Performance" chart provides an excellent overview of the player's performance over the course of the season. At a glance, you can see when and how much he played, and see how he contributed to the team's overall performance at different stages of the season.

Career History

Due to the difficulties involved in obtaining reliable stats for international clubs, the "Clubs" table is incomplete for players who have played for non-English clubs. The names of all clubs have been included for the reader's interest, but international stats have been left blank.

The Opposition

The Opposition section shows how Reading sizes up against the other 19 teams in the Premiership.

Points / Position

The points / position chart is a snapshot of the last 10 years' league performance of Reading and the opponent. For any season when the two teams met in the league, the results of their clashes are shown at the bottom of the chart.

Season Review 2005/06

Coca-Cola
KYOCERA
KYOCERA

1-2 Reading Plymouth Argyle

Championship

06.08.05

KYOCER

Leroy Lita shields the ball from danger

Event Line	
12	Doyle
21	Evans / LF / OP / IA
	Assist: Brevett
43	Little
Half time 0-1	
54	Lita / H / IFK / IA
	Assist: Murty
76	Kitson > Little
78	Hunt > Convey
83	Wotton
85	Chadwick > Evans
90	Chadwick / RF / IFK / IA
	Assist: Wotton
90	Djordjic > Buzsaky
Full time 1-2	

Renewed hope and expectation took an injury time nose-dive when the visiting Pilgrims stole three fortuitous points to spread opening day disappointment throughout Madejski Stadium.

Bobby Williamson's Plymouth side took the lead in the 21st minute when Rufus Brevett's fizzed cross was turned home by Micky Evans at Marcus Hahnemann's near post to stun the Royals crowd.

Hahnemann had to stretch to his brilliant best to deny Hungarian midfielder Akos Buzsaky moments before the home side restored parity with their first goal of 2005/6. £1m summer signing Leroy Lita began to pay off his record transfer fee when he headed Graeme Murty's searching cross forcefully into the top corner for 1-1.

Lita was almost celebrating a deflected winner which was scrambled off Argyle's line, before seeing another effort disallowed for offside. But the bitter blow was dealt when Paul Wotton's scuffed strike fell to substitute Nick Chadwick, who sharply converted for a last gasp winner.

Quote

Steve Coppell

After we equalised I thought the momentum was with us and that we were more likely to score, but lazy defending caught us out.

Championship Milestone

First Goal

Leroy Lita marked his Championship debut with a first goal in the competition.

Venue:	Madejski Stadium	Referee:	P.Taylor - 05/06	**Reading**
Attendance:	16,836	Matches:	0	**Plymouth Argyle**
Capacity:	24,200	Yellow Cards:	0	
Occupancy:	70%	Red Cards:	0	

Form Coming into Fixture

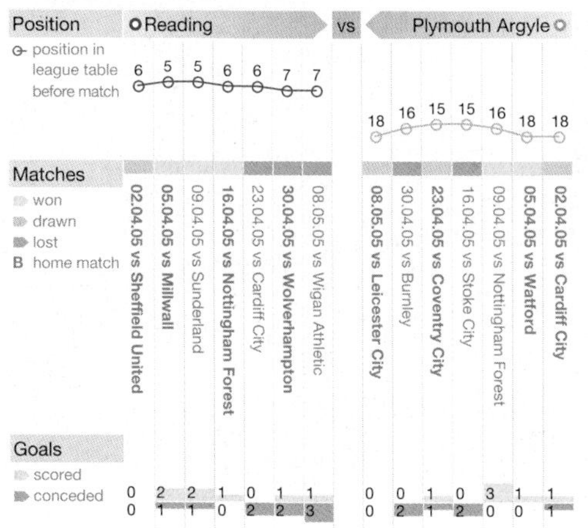

Position
Reading
vs
Plymouth Argyle
position in league table before match
6 5 5 6 6 7 7
18 16 15 15 16 18 18
Matches
won
drawn
lost
B home match
02.04.05 vs Sheffield United
05.04.05 vs Millwall
09.04.05 vs Sunderland
16.04.05 vs Nottingham Forest
23.04.05 vs Cardiff City
30.04.05 vs Wolverhampton
08.05.05 vs Wigan Athletic
08.05.05 vs Leicester City
30.04.05 vs Burnley
23.04.05 vs Coventry City
16.04.05 vs Stoke City
09.04.05 vs Nottingham Forest
05.04.05 vs Watford
02.04.05 vs Cardiff City
Goals
scored
conceded

	02.04.05 vs Sheffield United	05.04.05 vs Millwall	09.04.05 vs Sunderland	16.04.05 vs Nottingham Forest	23.04.05 vs Cardiff City	30.04.05 vs Wolverhampton	08.05.05 vs Wigan Athletic
Reading scored	0	2	2	1	0	1	1
Reading conceded	0	1	1	0	2	2	3

	08.05.05 vs Leicester City	30.04.05 vs Burnley	23.04.05 vs Coventry City	16.04.05 vs Stoke City	09.04.05 vs Nottingham Forest	05.04.05 vs Watford	02.04.05 vs Cardiff City
Plymouth scored	0	0	1	0	3	1	1
Plymouth conceded	0	2	1	2	0	0	1

Goal Statistics

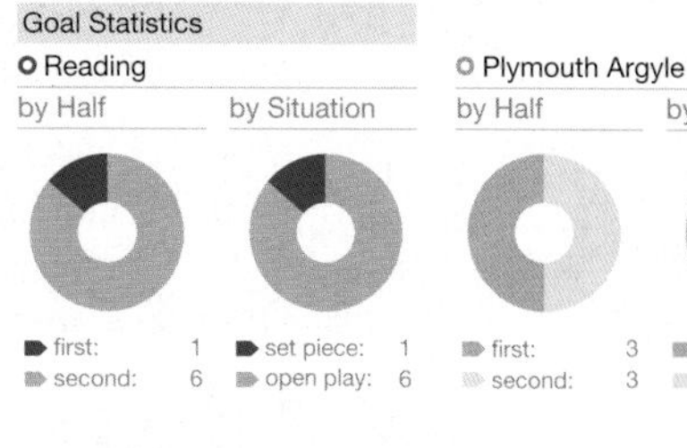

Reading
by Half
by Situation
Plymouth Argyle
by Half
by Situation

Reading

by Half		by Situation	
first:	1	set piece:	1
second:	6	open play:	6

Plymouth Argyle

by Half		by Situation	
first:	3	set piece:	3
second:	3	open play:	3

Goals by Area

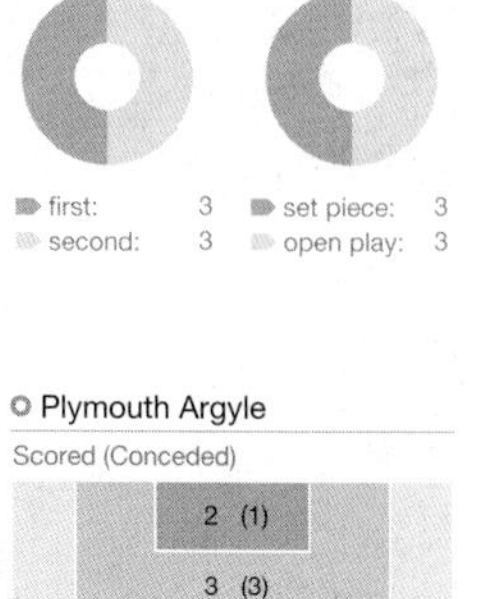

Plymouth Argyle
Scored (Conceded)
2 (1)
3 (3)
1 (2)

Reading — Scored (Conceded): 3 (2); 4 (7); 0 (0)

Plymouth Argyle — Scored (Conceded): 2 (1); 3 (3); 1 (2)

Team Statistics

Starting Line-Ups

Shorey
Convey
Hunt
Ingimarsson
Harper
Hahnemann
Doyle
Evans
Chadwick
Lita
Sonko
Sidwell
Murty
Little
Kitson
Norris
Barness
Gudjonsson
Doumbe
Wotton
Larrieu
Aljofree
Buzsaky
Djordjic
Capaldi
Brevett

4/4/2

Unused Sub: Stack, Makin, Oster

4/5/1

Unused Sub: McCormick, Connolly, Taylor

Championship Totals	Reading	Plymouth
Championship Appearances	389	278
Team Appearances	389	258
Goals Scored	34	27
Assists	26	25
Clean Sheets (goalkeepers)	19	4
Yellow Cards	30	31
Red Cards	0	2
Full Internationals	4	3

Age/Height

Reading Age	Plymouth Argyle Age
25 yrs, 7 mo	27 yrs, 4 mo

Reading Height	Plymouth Argyle Height
5'11"	5'11"

Match Statistics

League Table after Fixture

	Played	Won	Drawn	Lost	For	Against	Pts
4 Plymouth	1	1	0	0	2	1	3
...	...	...	...	...	...	...	...
18 Millwall	0	0	0	0	0	0	0
19 Burnley	1	0	0	1	1	2	0
20 Crystal Palace	1	0	0	1	1	2	0
21 Reading	1	0	0	1	1	2	0
22 Watford	1	0	0	1	1	2	0
23 Cardiff	1	0	0	1	0	1	0
24 Leicester	1	0	0	1	1	4	0

Statistics	Reading	Plymouth
Goals	1	2
Shots on Target	4	4
Shots off Target	5	5
Hit Woodwork	0	0
Possession %	51	49
Corners	4	5
Offsides	2	2
Fouls	20	22
Disciplinary Points	8	4

0-2

Brighton & Hove Albion
Reading

Championship

09.08.05

HAM
VEHICLE
AUCTIONS
VANS. PLANT
BLOCK D
MISHON
MACKAY
BLOCK E
PLANT
HIRE
sdowne
w.lansdownebuilding.co.uk

Glen Little's free-kick evades everyone to fly in

Event Line	
15	Little / RF / DFK / OA Assist: Kitson
Half time 0-1	
58	Sidwell
61	Oster > Little
61	Turienzo > Dodd
63	Kitson / H / OP / 6Y Assist: Shorey
67	Kitson
72	Oster
75	Hunt > Convey
81	Reid
82	Doyle > Lita
84	Robinson > Kazim-Richards
Full time 0-2	

Ex-Albion boss Steve Coppell returned to the Withdean to lead his Royals side to their first three points of the campaign and banish lingering memories of opening day defeat with an impressive away win the following Tuesday night.

A dominant and determined Reading outfit took the lead after just 15 minutes, when goal-starved Glen Little notched his first for the Royals since signing his summer 2004 contract.

The winger wickedly floated a 40-yard free kick dangerously between bodies to see it elude everyone in the box and drift past the helpless Wayne Henderson to nestle inside the right upright for the opener.

Aston Villa loanee Henderson was kept busy throughout, saving well from Leroy Lita and Steve Sidwell, but he couldn't quite keep out Dave Kitson's header just after the hour – last season's top scorer opening his Championship account when connecting well with Nicky Shorey's pinpoint cross to clinch maximum points.

Quote

Steve Coppell

It was a really difficult decision for me to start with Dave Kitson after Kevin Doyle did so well last Saturday.

Championship Milestone

First Goal

Glen Little netted his first goal in the Championship.

Venue:	Withdean Stadium	Referee:	K.Friend - 05/06
Attendance:	6,676	Matches:	1
Capacity:	7,999	Yellow Cards:	2
Occupancy:	83%	Red Cards:	0

Brighton & Hove Albion
Reading

Form Coming into Fixture

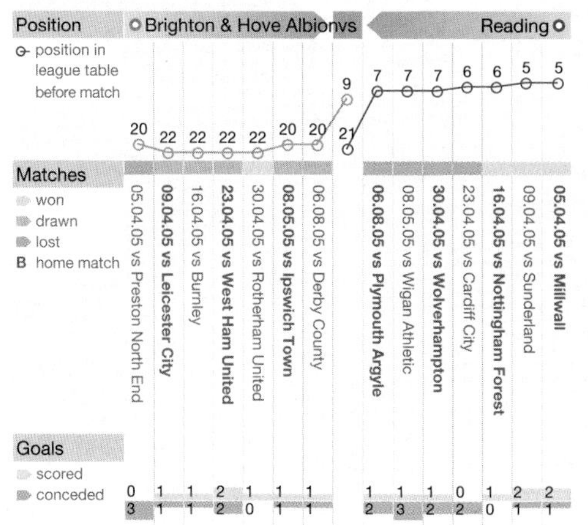

Position
Brighton & Hove Albion
vs
Reading
position in league table before match
20 22 22 22 22 20 20 21
9 7 7 7 6 6 5 5
Matches
won
drawn
lost
B home match
05.04.05 vs Preston North End
09.04.05 vs Leicester City
16.04.05 vs Burnley
23.04.05 vs West Ham United
30.04.05 vs Rotherham United
08.05.05 vs Ipswich Town
06.08.05 vs Derby County
06.08.05 vs Plymouth Argyle
08.05.05 vs Wigan Athletic
30.04.05 vs Wolverhampton
23.04.05 vs Cardiff City
16.04.05 vs Nottingham Forest
09.04.05 vs Sunderland
05.04.05 vs Millwall
Goals
scored
conceded
0 1 1 2 1 1 1
3 1 1 2 0 1 1
1 1 1 0 1 2 2
2 3 2 2 0 1 1

Goal Statistics

Brighton & Hove Albion
by Half
by Situation
first: 3
second: 4
set piece: 3
open play: 3
own goals: 1
Reading
by Half
by Situation
first: 1
second: 7
set piece: 2
open play: 6

Goals by Area

Brighton & Hove Albion

Scored (Conceded)

4 (3)
3 (6)
0 (0)

Reading

Scored (Conceded)

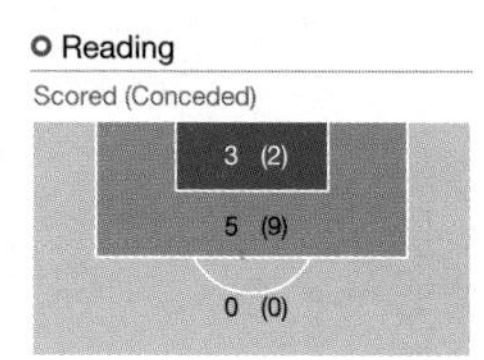

3 (2)
5 (9)
0 (0)

Team Statistics

Starting Line-Ups

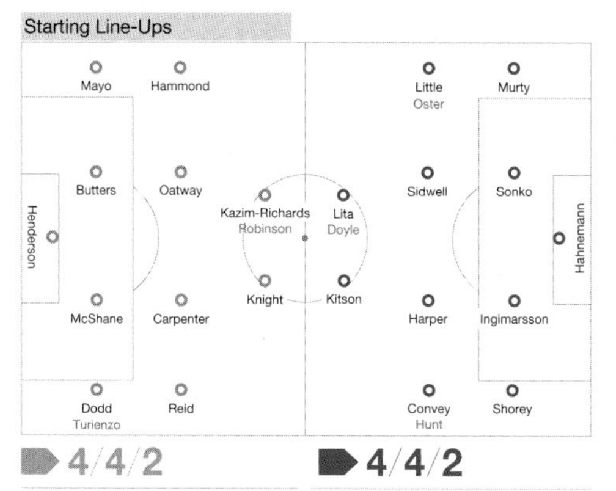

Mayo
Hammond
Butters
Oatway
Kazim-Richards
Robinson
Lita
Doyle
Henderson
McShane
Carpenter
Knight
Kitson
Dodd
Turienzo
Reid
Little
Oster
Murty
Sidwell
Sonko
Hahnemann
Harper
Ingimarsson
Convey
Hunt
Shorey

4/4/2

Unused Sub: Martin, El-Abd, Nicolas

4/4/2

Unused Sub: Stack, Makin

Championship Totals	Brighton	Reading
Championship Appearances	262	434
Team Appearances	258	402
Goals Scored	19	37
Assists	17	30
Clean Sheets (goalkeepers)	0	19
Yellow Cards	25	32
Red Cards	2	0
Full Internationals	0	5

Age/Height

Brighton & Hove Albion Age

25 yrs, 10 mo

Reading Age

25 yrs, 8 mo

Brighton & Hove Albion Height

5'11"

Reading Height

5'11"

Match Statistics

League Table after Fixture

		Played	Won	Drawn	Lost	For	Against	Pts
↑ 2	Luton	2	2	0	0	5	3	6
↑ 3	Plymouth	2	1	1	0	5	4	4
↓ 4	Crewe	2	1	1	0	3	2	4
↓ 5	Preston	2	1	1	0	3	2	4
↑ 6	QPR	2	1	1	0	2	1	4
↑ 7	Wolverhampton	2	1	1	0	2	1	4
↑ 8	Reading	2	1	0	1	3	2	3
...		...	...	...	...	...	...	...
↓ 22	Brighton	2	0	1	1	1	3	1

Statistics	Brighton	Reading
Goals	0	2
Shots on Target	3	5
Shots off Target	6	4
Hit Woodwork	0	0
Possession %	30	70
Corners	9	2
Offsides	0	5
Fouls	15	20
Disciplinary Points	4	12

0-3

Preston North End
Reading

Championship

13.08.05

KYOCEF

Glen Little celebrates making sure of the points

Event Line

34	Lita / RF / OP / IA
	Assist: Convey
Half time 0-1	
46	Lita / RF / OP / IA
	Assist: Convey
54	Davidson
57	Little / H / OP / 6Y
	Assist: Shorey
58	Dichio > McKenna
64	Cresswell
82	Neal L > Cresswell
82	Jones D > Sedgwick
84	Hunt > Convey
87	Oster > Little
Full time 0-3	

Play-off finalists Preston were taught a stern lesson in front of their Deepdale faithful by a Reading side quickly finding fifth gear to condemn Billy Davies' men to their first home league defeat since early November.

North End were hit hard by a resurgent Bobby Convey, who soon began to direct proceedings. The US winger intercepted Youl Mawene's pass before sliding through to Leroy Lita, who smashed a 34th minute bullet high into the roof of the net for 1-0.

Soon after the interval, Convey bettered that by finding Lita again with a breathtaking 50-yard crossfield ball landing into the striker's path. Lita duly obliged by coolly slotting past Carlo Nash for a stunning second.

The visitors were enjoying themselves in the Lancashire sunshine and when Glen Little, with a new-found penchant for scoring goals, latched onto another superb Nicky Shorey cross to head home a third, the travelling fans went wild. Heads were starting to turn!

Quote

Steve Coppell

This time last Saturday the end of the world was nigh, but in the two games since then it's been delayed a bit.

Venue:	Deepdale
Attendance:	13,154
Capacity:	22,225
Occupancy:	59%

Referee:	L.Probert - 05/06
Matches:	2
Yellow Cards:	10
Red Cards:	0

Preston North End
Reading

Form Coming into Fixture

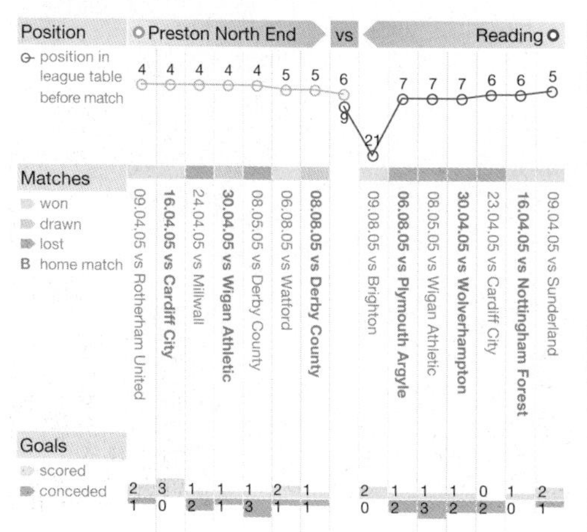

Position
Preston North End
vs
Reading
position in league table before match
Matches
won
drawn
lost
B home match
09.04.05 vs Rotherham United
16.04.05 vs Cardiff City
24.04.05 vs Millwall
30.04.05 vs Wigan Athletic
08.05.05 vs Derby County
06.08.05 vs Watford
08.08.05 vs Derby County
09.08.05 vs Brighton
06.08.05 vs Plymouth Argyle
08.05.05 vs Wigan Athletic
30.04.05 vs Wolverhampton
23.04.05 vs Cardiff City
16.04.05 vs Nottingham Forest
09.04.05 vs Sunderland
Goals
scored
conceded

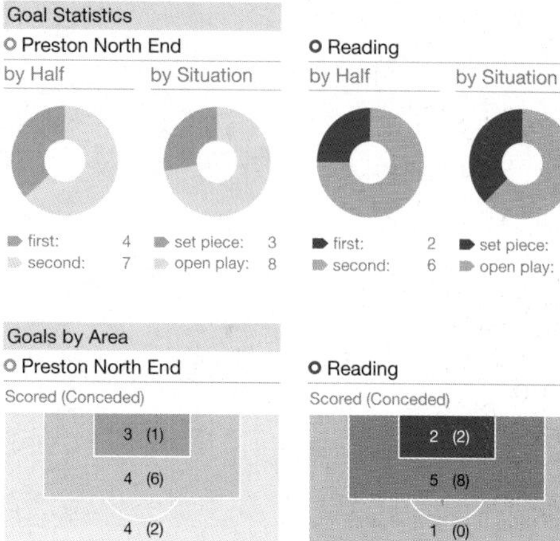

Goal Statistics
Preston North End
by Half
by Situation
first: 4
second: 7
set piece: 3
open play: 8
Reading
by Half
by Situation
first: 2
second: 6
set piece: 3
open play: 5
Goals by Area
Preston North End
Scored (Conceded)
3 (1)
4 (6)
4 (2)
Reading
Scored (Conceded)
2 (2)
5 (8)
1 (0)

Team Statistics

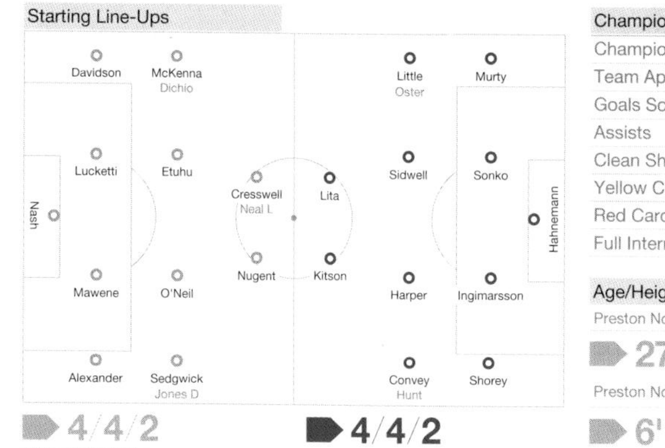

Starting Line-Ups
Davidson
McKenna
Dichio
Nash
Lucketti
Etuhu
Cresswell
Neal L
Nugent
Mawene
O'Neil
Alexander
Sedgwick
Jones D
Little
Oster
Murty
Lita
Kitson
Sidwell
Sonko
Hahnemann
Harper
Ingimarsson
Convey
Hunt
Shorey

4/4/2

Unused Sub: Davis, Agyemang

4/4/2

Unused Sub: Stack, Makin, Doyle

Championship Totals	Preston	Reading
Championship Appearances	459	446
Team Appearances	385	414
Goals Scored	66	39
Assists	51	32
Clean Sheets (goalkeepers)	2	20
Yellow Cards	53	34
Red Cards	4	0
Full Internationals	3	5

Age/Height

Preston North End Age: **27 yrs, 8 mo**

Reading Age: **25 yrs, 11 mo**

Preston North End Height: **6'**

Reading Height: **5'11"**

Match Statistics

League Table after Fixture

		Played	Won	Drawn	Lost	For	Against	Pts
↑ 1	Luton	3	2	1	0	5	3	7
↑ 2	QPR	3	2	1	0	4	2	7
↑ 3	Wolverhampton	3	2	1	0	3	1	7
↑ 4	Reading	3	2	0	1	6	2	6
↓ 5	Sheff Utd	3	2	0	1	7	4	6
↑ 6	Derby	3	1	2	0	4	2	5
↓ 7	Crewe	3	1	2	0	5	4	5
...		...	...	...	...	...	...	...
↓ 15	Preston	3	1	1	1	3	5	4

Statistics	Preston	Reading
Goals	0	3
Shots on Target	5	3
Shots off Target	9	4
Hit Woodwork	0	0
Possession %	50	50
Corners	10	1
Offsides	2	0
Fouls	15	8
Disciplinary Points	8	0

5-0 Reading ○ Millwall ○

Championship

20.08.05

James Harper celebrates his goal with a hug from Ivar Ingimarsson

Event Line
6 ⚽ Convey / LF / OP / OA
15 ⇄ Robinson P > Lawrence
23 ■ Marshall
Handball
23 ⇄ Elliott > Hayles
25 ⚽ Convey / LF / DFK / OA
Assist: Lita
35 ■ Morris
38 ⚽ Harper / H / IFK / IA
43 ⚽ Kitson / LF / P / IA
Half time 4-0
46 ⇄ Serioux > Simpson
57 ⇄ Hunt > Convey
61 ⇄ Doyle > Kitson
68 ■ Robinson P
70 ■ Phillips
79 ⚽ Sidwell / H / C / 6Y
Assist: Little
80 ⇄ Oster > Little
88 ■ Sidwell
Full time 5-0

The Royals heartlessly disposed of 10-man Millwall to storm to the top of the table with a ruthless five-goal thrashing of former Reading coach Colin Lee's Lions.

The rout began when Bobby Convey marked his spectacular start to the season with a magnificent sixth minute solo goal. Breaking from a Millwall corner, he skipped past two men before ending his 50-yard burst with a calm curling finish around the advancing Andy Marshall.

Soon after Marshall instinctively saved Leroy Lita's 30-yard snapshot whilst outside his area. Shown red and without a keeper on the bench, captain Mark Phillips donned the gloves. Convey took full advantage by curling the resulting free-kick low inside the right upright for a second.

Before the half was out James Harper looped home a headed third and Dave Kitson converted from the spot after ex-Royal Sammy Igoe had handled inside the box. Steve Sidwell headed a fifth to deny the Lions' third glovesman, Adrian Serioux, a second half clean sheet. The Lions went home wounded and with their pride badly hurt.

Quote

Steve Coppell

I'm not too excited about being top of the league at this stage of the season.

Championship Milestone

50

Marcus Hahnemann made his 50th appearance in the Championship.

Venue:	Madejski Stadium	Referee:	S.Tanner - 05/06
Attendance:	14,225	Matches:	2
Capacity:	24,200	Yellow Cards:	8
Occupancy:	59%	Red Cards:	0

Reading
Millwall

Form Coming into Fixture

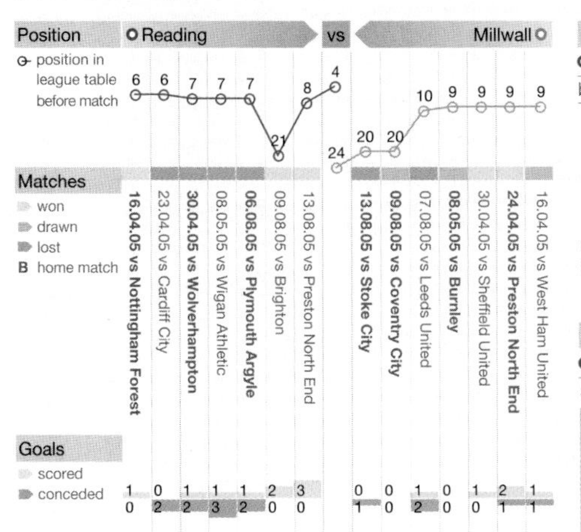

Position
Reading
vs
Millwall
position in league table before match
Matches
won
drawn
lost
B home match
16.04.05 vs Nottingham Forest
23.04.05 vs Cardiff City
30.04.05 vs Wolverhampton
08.05.05 vs Wigan Athletic
06.08.05 vs Plymouth Argyle
09.08.05 vs Brighton
13.08.05 vs Preston North End
13.08.05 vs Stoke City
09.08.05 vs Coventry City
07.08.05 vs Leeds United
08.05.05 vs Burnley
30.04.05 vs Sheffield United
24.04.05 vs Preston North End
16.04.05 vs West Ham United
Goals
scored
conceded

Goal Statistics

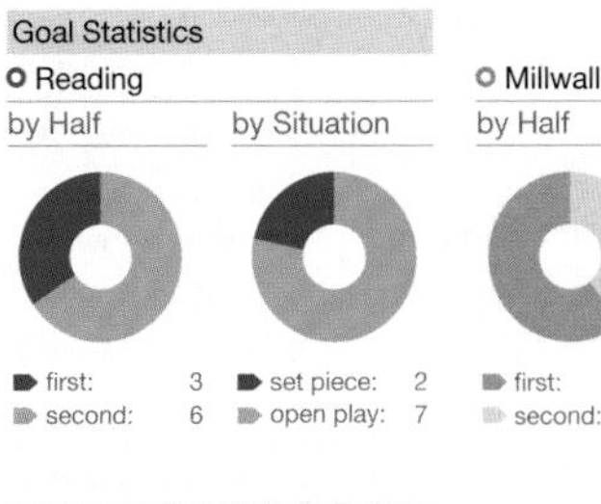

Reading
by Half
by Situation
first: 3
second: 6
set piece: 2
open play: 7

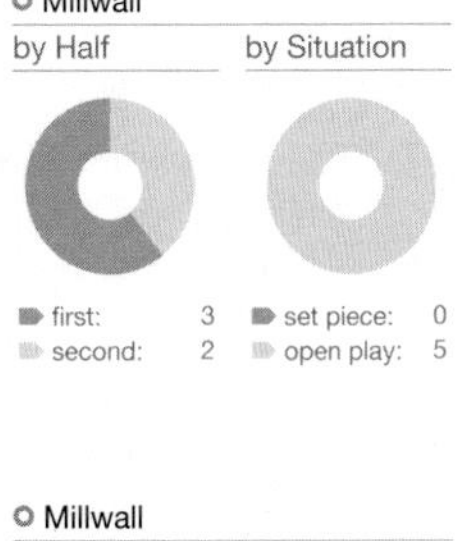

Millwall
by Half
by Situation
first: 3
second: 2
set piece: 0
open play: 5

Goals by Area

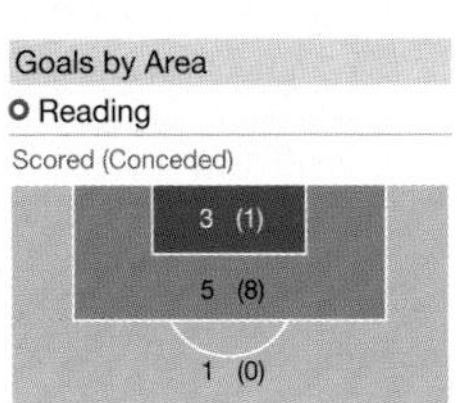

Reading
Scored (Conceded)
3 (1)
5 (8)
1 (0)

Millwall
Scored (Conceded)
0 (1)
5 (3)
0 (1)

Team Statistics

Starting Line-Ups

Shorey
Convey
Hunt
Ingimarsson
Harper
Hahnemann
Kitson
Doyle
May
Lita
Hayles
Elliott
Sonko
Sidwell
Murty
Little
Oster
Igoe
Dunne
Morris
Phillips
Marshall
Livermore
Lawrence
Robinson P
Simpson
Serioux
Vincent

4/4/2 — Unused Sub: Stack, Makin

4/4/2 — Unused Sub: Hutchison, Fangueiro

Championship Totals	Reading	Millwall
Championship Appearances	461	377
Team Appearances	429	358
Goals Scored	42	28
Assists	35	23
Clean Sheets (goalkeepers)	21	7
Yellow Cards	35	50
Red Cards	0	7
Full Internationals	5	3

Age/Height

Reading Age: **25 yrs, 8 mo**

Millwall Age: **26 yrs, 3 mo**

Reading Height: **5'11"**

Millwall Height: **5'11"**

Match Statistics

League Table after Fixture

	Played	Won	Drawn	Lost	For	Against	Pts
↑ 1 Reading	4	3	0	1	11	2	9
↑ 2 Sheff Utd	4	3	0	1	9	5	9
↑ 3 Derby	4	2	2	0	6	3	8
↑ 4 Watford	4	2	1	1	10	7	7
↑ 5 Leeds	4	2	1	1	5	3	7
↓ 6 Luton	4	2	1	1	6	5	7
↑ 7 Ipswich	4	2	1	1	4	3	7
...	...	...	...	...	...	...	...
● 24 Millwall	4	0	1	3	1	8	1

Statistics	Reading	Millwall
Goals	5	0
Shots on Target	10	6
Shots off Target	6	3
Hit Woodwork	1	0
Possession %	59	41
Corners	7	7
Offsides	5	1
Fouls	14	12
Disciplinary Points	4	24

3-1 Reading / Swansea City

Carling Cup

23.08.05

LITA
8
RADIO BERKSH

Leroy Lita secures a place in Round Two

Event Line
14 Kitson / RF / OP / OA
Assist: Doyle
14 Little > Oster
36 Tudor-Jones
45 Harper
Half time 1-0
46 Anderson > Austin
53 Martinez
55 Kitson
71 Gunnarsson > Doyle
73 Gunnarsson
80 Akinfenwa / H / OP / IA
Assist: Anderson
82 Lita > Little
85 Anderson
2nd Bookable Offence
95 Kitson / LF / OP / IA
Assist: Harper
101 MacDonald > Tudor-Jones
114 Lita / LF / OP / IA
Assist: Harper
Full time 3-1

The Royals shattered Swansea's Carling Cup dreams in the opening cup fixture of the campaign, but the League One high-flyers proved tough opposition for Steve Coppell's cup hopefuls, who needed extra time to seal a Second Round berth.

Reading started brightly and went close after five minutes when John Oster's cross was headed wide by Steve Sidwell. The home side didn't have to wait long for the lead though, as Dave Kitson raced onto the end of a direct ball over the top with only 14 minutes played to lift an excellent effort over the onrushing Willy Gueret.

Swansea offered little threat and early in the second period they were on the ropes as Kevin Doyle and Glen Little went close from dangerous crosses whipped in by Stephen Hunt.

As the Royals continued to search for a decisive second goal Kitson hit the bar, Doyle was thwarted by Gueret and Sidwell saw a goal disallowed, but although the second goal wouldn't come it never looked likely that Swansea would manage to conjure an equaliser.

Despite presenting little threat on Graham Stack's goal throughout the previous 80 minutes, though, in the final stages Adebayo Akinfenwa headed substitute Ijah Anderson's cross beyond Stack's stretch with for a shock leveller.

Before the 90 minutes were up, Anderson's untidy challenge on Kitson earned him his marching orders and reduced the Swans to ten men, but the visitors held on to send the game into extra time. With just ten men, though, the League One side

Venue:	Madejski Stadium	Referee:	K.Stroud - 05/06
Attendance:	7,603	Matches:	3
Capacity:	24,200	Yellow Cards:	15
Occupancy:	31%	Red Cards:	1

Reading
Swansea City

BBC
104.4 FM

Lita and Hunt celebrate

Match Statistics

Starting Line-Ups

Shorey
Oster
Little
Ingimarsson
Harper
Stack
Sonko
Sidwell
Makin
Hunt
Kitson
Britton
Doyle
Gunnarsson
Akinfenwa
Connor
Tate
Martinez
Edwards
Gueret
Tudor-Jones
MacDonald
Austin
Anderson
McLeod
Ricketts

4/4/2

Unused Sub: Hahnemann, Convey

4/4/1/1

Unused Sub: Murphy, Goodfellow, Thorpe

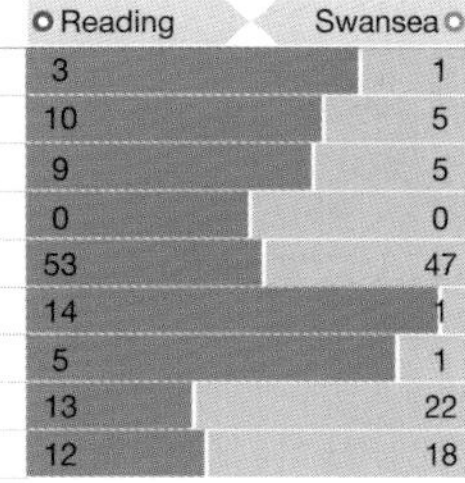

Statistics	Reading	Swansea
Goals	3	1
Shots on Target	10	5
Shots off Target	9	5
Hit Woodwork	0	0
Possession %	53	47
Corners	14	1
Offsides	5	1
Fouls	13	22
Disciplinary Points	12	18

Age/Height

Reading Age

25 yrs, 8 mo

Reading Height

5'11"

Swansea City Age

26 yrs, 1 mo

Swansea City Height

6'

always looked up against it in the extra period and Reading re-established their lead when Kitson latched onto James Harper's throughball to comfortably round Gueret after 95 minutes.

Paul Connor tested Stack with a 20-yard effort as the Swans continued to battle, but after visiting boss Kenny Jackett was sent to the stands for dissent, the result was left in no doubt when Harper burst into space down the right hand side and delivered a precise low cross into the path of substitute Leroy Lita, who fired home a first-time effort to end City's brave but brief attempt at an upset.

Quote

11 Chris Makin

We knew Swansea would come here and make it difficult, but in the end we were able to win comfortably.

0-0 Watford Reading

Championship

27.08.05

KYOCERA

Nicky Shorey assesses his options

Event Line
Half time 0-0
70 ⇄ Bouazza > Henderson
88 ⇄ Doyle > Lita
Full time 0-0

Failing to score for the first time this season, the Royals were held to a goalless draw at Vicarage Road in a largely uneventful affair that only showed glimpses of sparking into life.

Both Ibrahima Sonko and James Harper had to scramble efforts off their own line as former Royals striker Darius Henderson caused problems for the visiting defence, while the threat at the other end stemmed from the wide men – Glen Little and Bobby Convey both forcing Ben Foster into tidy saves.

James Harper was unlucky not to break the deadlock when Convey's corner was only cleared as far as the midfielder, who unleashed a rasping 25-yard second half volley which was expertly tipped over by Foster.

And in the final minutes, Sonko connected with Convey's near post corner but the points were destined to be shared, as the centre-back's header skimmed just over the crossbar.

Quote

Steve Coppell

We could have lost or won, but we probably cancelled each other out and we've got to be happy with a point.

Venue:	**Vicarage Road**	**Referee:**	**R.J.Beeby - 05/06**
Attendance:	12,152	Matches:	4
Capacity:	22,100	Yellow Cards:	8
Occupancy:	55%	Red Cards:	0

Watford
Reading

Form Coming into Fixture

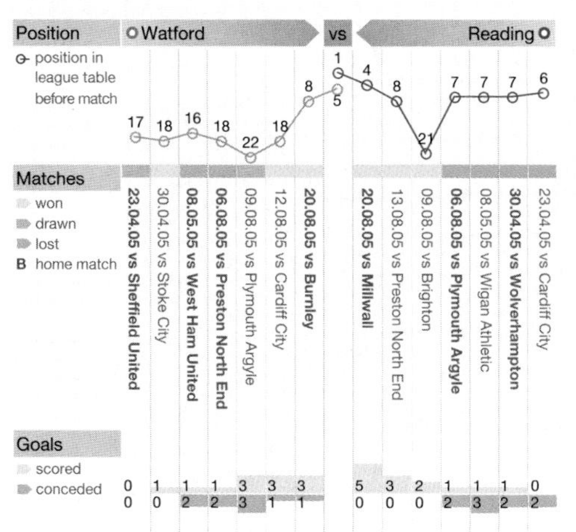

Position
Watford
vs
Reading
position in league table before match
Matches
won
drawn
lost
B home match
23.04.05 vs Sheffield United
30.04.05 vs Stoke City
08.05.05 vs West Ham United
06.08.05 vs Preston North End
09.08.05 vs Plymouth Argyle
12.08.05 vs Cardiff City
20.08.05 vs Burnley
20.08.05 vs Millwall
13.08.05 vs Preston North End
09.08.05 vs Brighton
06.08.05 vs Plymouth Argyle
08.05.05 vs Wigan Athletic
30.04.05 vs Wolverhampton
23.04.05 vs Cardiff City
Goals
scored
conceded

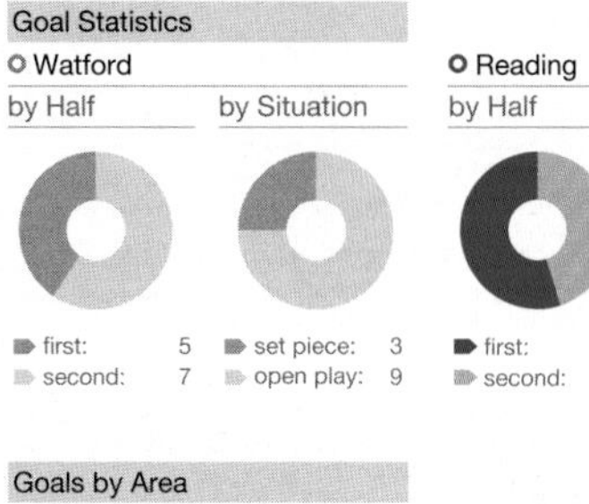

Goal Statistics
Watford
by Half
by Situation
first: 5
second: 7
set piece: 3
open play: 9

Reading

by Half | by Situation

first: 7
second: 6
set piece: 6
open play: 7

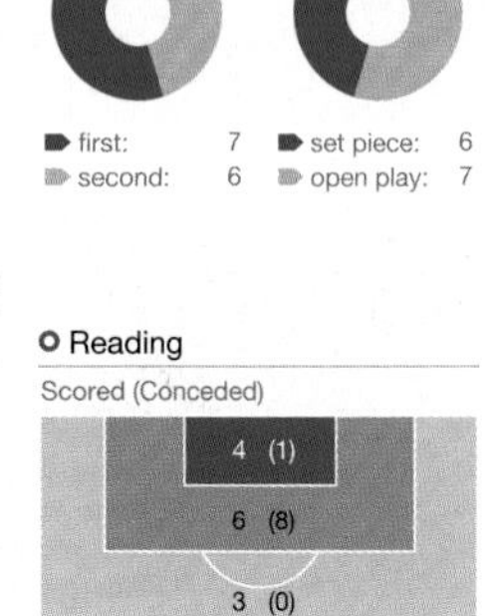

Goals by Area
Watford
Scored (Conceded)
2 (1)
6 (6)
4 (2)
Reading
Scored (Conceded)
4 (1)
6 (8)
3 (0)

Team Statistics

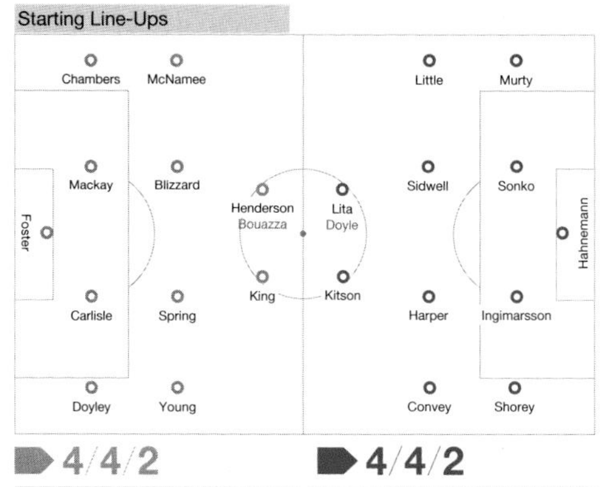

Starting Line-Ups
Chambers
McNamee
Mackay
Blizzard
Foster
Henderson
Bouazza
Lita
Doyle
King
Kitson
Carlisle
Spring
Doyley
Young
Little
Murty
Sidwell
Sonko
Hahnemann
Harper
Ingimarsson
Convey
Shorey
4/4/2
4/4/2

Unused Sub: Chamberlain, DeMerit, Stewart, Bangura

Unused Sub: Stack, Makin, Gunnarsson, Hunt

Championship Totals	Watford	Reading
Championship Appearances	332	436
Team Appearances	199	436
Goals Scored	32	45
Assists	19	34
Clean Sheets (goalkeepers)	0	22
Yellow Cards	33	35
Red Cards	2	0
Full Internationals	2	4

Age/Height

Watford Age: **24 yrs, 1 mo**

Reading Age: **25 yrs, 9 mo**

Watford Height: **6'**

Reading Height: **5'11"**

Match Statistics

League Table after Fixture

		Played	Won	Drawn	Lost	For	Against	Pts
↑ 1	Sheff Utd	5	4	0	1	11	6	12
↓ 2	Reading	5	3	1	1	11	2	10
↑ 3	Luton	5	3	1	1	8	5	10
↑ 4	Leeds	5	3	1	1	6	3	10
↑ 5	Southampton	5	3	1	1	6	3	10
↑ 6	Ipswich	5	3	1	1	6	4	10
↓ 7	Derby	5	2	3	0	8	5	9
↓ 8	Watford	5	2	2	1	10	7	8
↑ 9	Hull	5	2	2	1	4	2	8

Statistics	Watford	Reading
Goals	0	0
Shots on Target	10	7
Shots off Target	10	3
Hit Woodwork	0	0
Possession %	52	48
Corners	13	8
Offsides	6	5
Fouls	9	10
Disciplinary Points	0	0

2-1 Reading Burnley

Championship

29.08.05

KYOCERA

Kevin Doyle celebrates his winner with provider Bobby Convey

Event Line	
7	Lita / RF / OP / IA
	Assist: Kitson
22	Harley
39	Doyle > Kitson
42	Akinbiyi / RF / OP / IA
	Assist: Noel-Williams
Half time 1-1	
46	Makin > Shorey
70	Doyle / H / C / 6Y
	Assist: Convey
72	Sidwell
73	Spicer > Hyde
85	O'Connor G
86	Lowe > Thomas
90	O'Connor G
	Violent Conduct
Full time 2-1	

Kevin Doyle burst from the bench to score his first goal in English football and the winner against Burnley on Bank Holiday Monday. But post-match joy was tinged with worry as Dave Kitson, Nicky Shorey and Steve Sidwell were all injury victims in a robust end-of-August encounter.

Leroy Lita had craftily edged Reading into the lead when an instinctive Michael Owen v Portugal-esque flick from just inside the area surprised Danny Coyne in the Clarets goal, but Steve Cotterill's side struck back before the break.

Ade Akinbiyi buried his fifth of the season low past Marcus Hahnemann to level before a cursed few seconds saw Shorey and Sidwell collect nasty knee knocks and Doyle replaced ankle-bashed Kitson.

The change worked in the home side's favour as Doyle introduced himself as a match-winner. Having missed a great chance earlier, the Irishman nodded home Bobby Convey's pinpoint cross from close range. Frustrated Garreth O'Connor was needlessly sent off after lashing out at playmaker Convey in the dying stages.

Quote

Steve Coppell

I thought Kevin Doyle gave us an injection of mobility. He is strong when he gets the ball and can operate right across the field.

Championship Milestone

50

Ivar Ingimarsson, Nicky Shorey and Steve Sidwell all made their 50th appearances in the Championship.

Venue:	Madejski Stadium	Referee:	R.J.Olivier - 05/06	**Reading**
Attendance:	14,027	Matches:	3	**Burnley**
Capacity:	24,200	Yellow Cards:	12	
Occupancy:	58%	Red Cards:	0	

Form Coming into Fixture

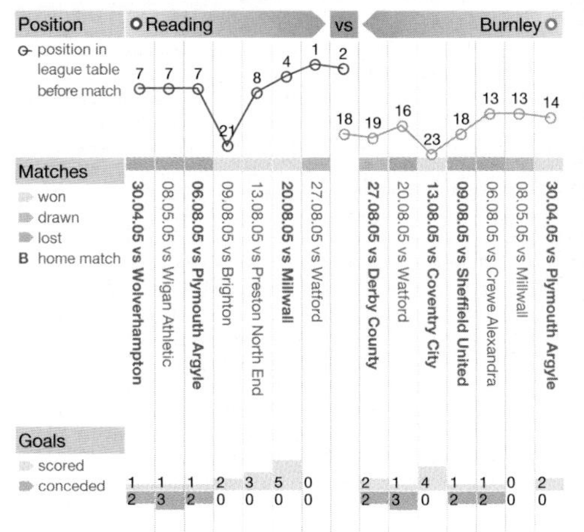

Position
Reading
vs
Burnley
position in league table before match
7 7 7 21 8 4 1 2
18 19 16 23 18 13 13 14
Matches
won
drawn
lost
B home match
30.04.05 vs Wolverhampton
08.05.05 vs Wigan Athletic
06.08.05 vs Plymouth Argyle
09.08.05 vs Brighton
13.08.05 vs Preston North End
20.08.05 vs Millwall
27.08.05 vs Watford
27.08.05 vs Derby County
20.08.05 vs Watford
13.08.05 vs Coventry City
09.08.05 vs Sheffield United
06.08.05 vs Crewe Alexandra
08.05.05 vs Millwall
30.04.05 vs Plymouth Argyle
Goals
scored
conceded
1 1 1 2 3 5 0
2 3 2 0 0 0 0
2 1 4 1 1 0 2
2 3 0 2 2 0 0

Goal Statistics

Reading

by Half / by Situation

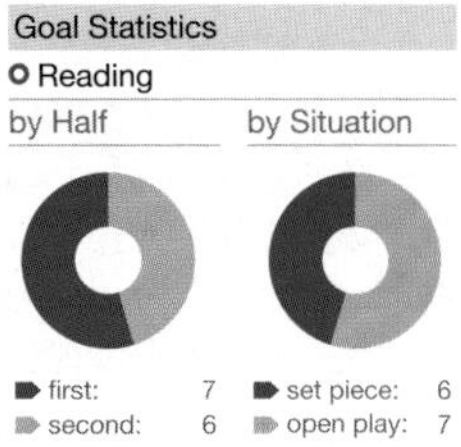

by Half		by Situation	
first:	7	set piece:	6
second:	6	open play:	7

Burnley

by Half / by Situation

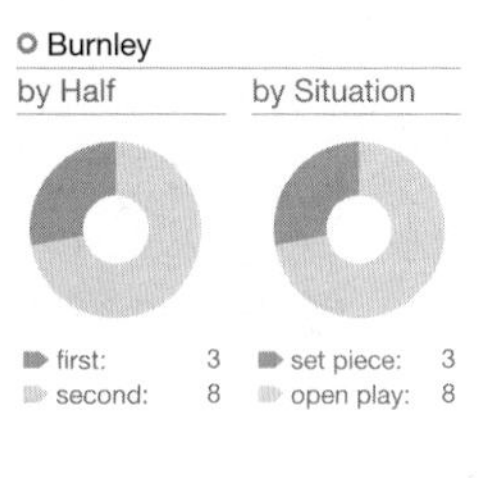

by Half		by Situation	
first:	3	set piece:	3
second:	8	open play:	8

Goals by Area

Reading

Scored (Conceded)

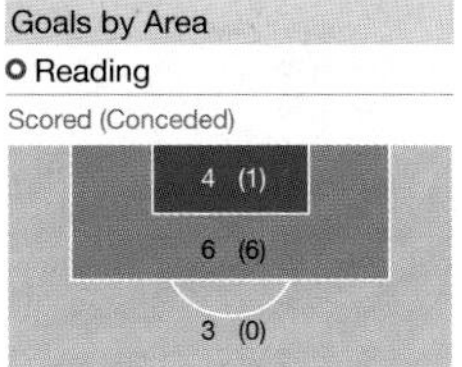

4 (1)
6 (6)
3 (0)

Burnley

Scored (Conceded)

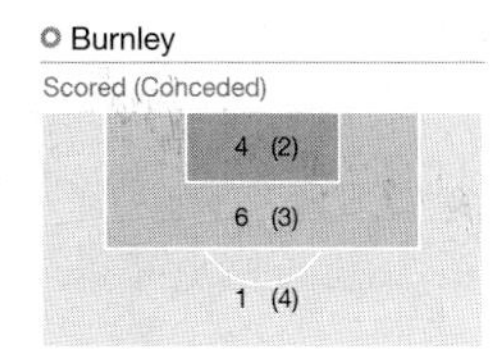

4 (2)
6 (3)
1 (4)

Team Statistics

Starting Line-Ups

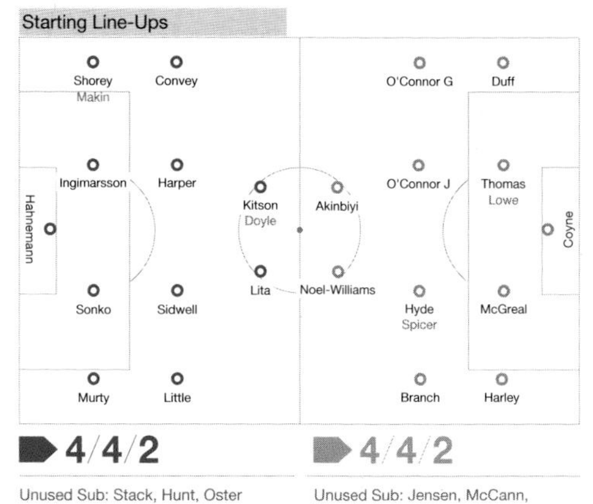

Shorey
Makin
Convey
Ingimarsson
Harper
Hahnemann
Kitson
Doyle
Akinbiyi
Sonko
Sidwell
Lita
Noel-Williams
Murty
Little
O'Connor G
Duff
O'Connor J
Thomas
Lowe
Coyne
Hyde
Spicer
McGreal
Branch
Harley

4/4/2

Unused Sub: Stack, Hunt, Oster

4/4/2

Unused Sub: Jensen, McCann, Bermingham

Championship Totals	Reading	Burnley
Championship Appearances	482	428
Team Appearances	448	259
Goals Scored	45	44
Assists	37	36
Clean Sheets (goalkeepers)	23	8
Yellow Cards	35	54
Red Cards	1	6
Full Internationals	4	4

Age/Height

Reading Age

26 yrs, 3 mo

Burnley Age

27 yrs, 8 mo

Reading Height

5'11"

Burnley Height

6'

Match Statistics

League Table after Fixture

		Played	Won	Drawn	Lost	For	Against	Pts
● 1	Sheff Utd	6	5	0	1	14	7	15
● 2	Reading	6	4	1	1	13	3	13
● 3	Luton	6	4	1	1	10	6	13
↑ 4	Watford	6	3	2	1	12	8	11
● 5	Southampton	6	3	2	1	7	4	11
↓ 6	Leeds	5	3	1	1	6	3	10
↑ 7	Stoke	6	3	1	2	8	8	10
...		...	...	...	...	...	...	...
↓ 19	Burnley	6	1	1	4	10	11	4

Statistics	Reading	Burnley
Goals	2	1
Shots on Target	3	3
Shots off Target	2	2
Hit Woodwork	0	0
Possession %	41	59
Corners	5	2
Offsides	2	2
Fouls	9	15
Disciplinary Points	4	20

1-1 Coventry City Reading

Championship

10.09.05

Coca-Cola

Bobby Convey contemplates Coventry's late leveller

Event Line
23 Jorgensen
36 Page
Half time 0-0
59 Whing > Duffy
63 Shaw
66 Morrell > Flood
68 Doyle / RF / OP / IA Assist: Little
77 Wood > Jorgensen
81 Doyle
87 Page / H / C / 6Y Assist: McSheffrey
88 Oster > Little
89 Obinna > Lita
Full time 1-1

Kevin Doyle starred in an entertaining draw at Coventry's two game-old Ricoh Arena. The Irish strike star was dragged to ground when trying to apply the crucial connection to Graeme Murty's dangerous cross just before half time, but Leroy Lita's spot kick was expertly saved by Stephen Bywater.

Doyle truly made his mark after the interval though. Glen Little sharply spotted the striker's run into space and quickly fed a right-sided throw into his path. Doyle's instinctive first time strike was parried but it fell back to his feet and with a second bite at the cherry he made no mistake.

Marcus Hahnemann looked like he was going to render Doyle's strike the matchwinner, athletically tipping Andy Morrell's bulleted strike over the crossbar before miraculously clawing the same player's close range header wide.

But Robert Page headed home an 87th minute Gary McSheffrey corner for his first goal in over two years, preserving the Sky Blues' unbeaten new home status.

Quote

Steve Coppell

Leroy's taken a few and he's missed a few, but he fancied this one and it was a good hit. It was also a magnificent save.

Championship Milestone

25

Bobby Convey made his 25th appearance in the Championship.

Venue:	Ricoh Arena	Referee:	A.R.Hall - 05/06
Attendance:	22,074	Matches:	5
Capacity:	32,000	Yellow Cards:	13
Occupancy:	69%	Red Cards:	4

Coventry City
Reading

Form Coming into Fixture

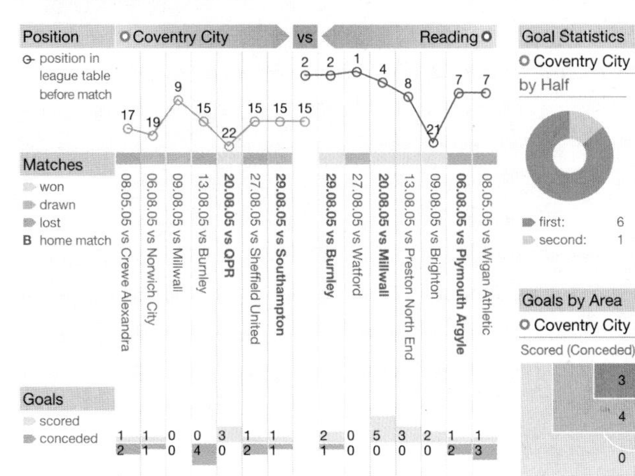

Position
Coventry City
vs
Reading
position in league table before match
17 19 9 15 22 15 15 15
2 2 1 4 8 21 7 7
Matches
won
drawn
lost
B home match
08.05.05 vs Crewe Alexandra
06.08.05 vs Norwich City
09.08.05 vs Millwall
13.08.05 vs Burnley
20.08.05 vs QPR
27.08.05 vs Sheffield United
29.08.05 vs Southampton
29.08.05 vs Burnley
27.08.05 vs Watford
20.08.05 vs Millwall
13.08.05 vs Preston North End
09.08.05 vs Brighton
06.08.05 vs Plymouth Argyle
08.05.05 vs Wigan Athletic
Goals
scored
conceded
1 1 0 0 3 1 1 2 0 5 3 2 1 1
2 1 0 4 0 2 1 1 0 0 0 0 2 3

Goal Statistics

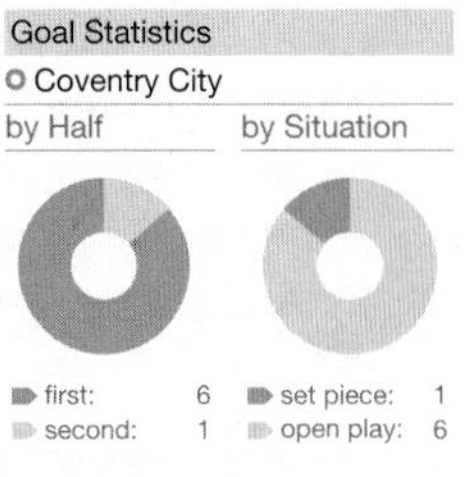

Coventry City
by Half
by Situation
first: 6
second: 1
set piece: 1
open play: 6

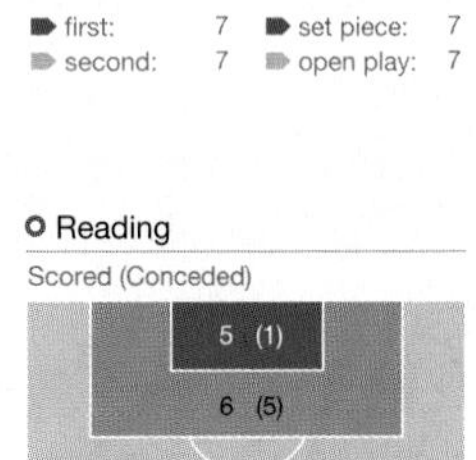

Reading
by Half
by Situation
first: 7
second: 7
set piece: 7
open play: 7

Goals by Area

Coventry City — Scored (Conceded)

3 (3)
4 (6)
0 (1)

Reading — Scored (Conceded)

5 (1)
6 (5)
3 (0)

Team Statistics

Starting Line-Ups

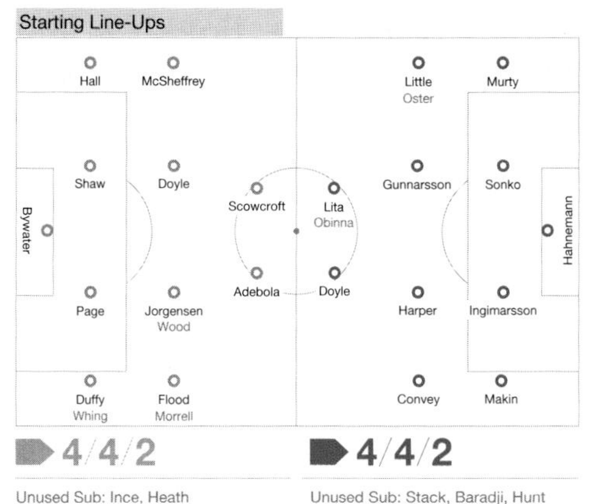

Hall
McSheffrey
Shaw
Doyle
Scowcroft
Bywater
Page
Jorgensen
Wood
Adebola
Duffy
Whing
Flood
Morrell
Lita
Obinna
Doyle
Little
Oster
Murty
Gunnarsson
Sonko
Hahnemann
Harper
Ingimarsson
Convey
Makin

4/4/2 | 4/4/2

Unused Sub: Ince, Heath

Unused Sub: Stack, Baradji, Hunt

Championship Totals	Coventry	Reading
Championship Appearances	428	423
Team Appearances	316	321
Goals Scored	41	22
Assists	33	28
Clean Sheets (goalkeepers)	13	23
Yellow Cards	54	22
Red Cards	0	2
Full Internationals	4	6

Age/Height

Coventry City Age: **26 yrs, 8 mo**

Reading Age: **26 yrs, 11 mo**

Coventry City Height: **5'11"**

Reading Height: **6'**

Match Statistics

League Table after Fixture

		Played	Won	Drawn	Lost	For	Against	Pts
● 1	Sheff Utd	7	6	0	1	16	7	18
● 2	Reading	7	4	2	1	14	4	14
↑ 3	Watford	7	4	2	1	15	8	14
↓ 4	Luton	7	4	2	1	11	7	14
● 5	Southampton	7	3	3	1	8	5	12
● 6	Wolverhampton	7	3	3	1	9	7	12
● 7	Leeds	6	3	2	1	9	6	11
...		...	...	...	...	...	...	...
↓ 17	Coventry	7	1	4	2	7	9	7

Statistics	Coventry	Reading
Goals	1	1
Shots on Target	13	11
Shots off Target	5	8
Hit Woodwork	1	0
Possession %	42	58
Corners	12	3
Offsides	3	4
Fouls	18	16
Disciplinary Points	16	0

3-2 Reading ○ Crystal Palace ○

Championship

13.09.05

▶ Kevin Doyle goes on the attack

Event Line	
26 ○ ⊕	Doyle / LF / OP / OA
29 ○ ⊕	Johnson / RF / OP / IA
	Assist: Morrison
31 ○ ▪	Gunnarsson
33 ○ ▪	Hall F
37 ○ ⇄	Macken > Johnson
44 ○ ▪	Soares
Half time 1-1	
47 ○ ⊕	Morrison / RF / OP / 6Y
	Assist: Ward
58 ○ ▪	Morrison
68 ○ ⊕	Lita / RF / OP / 6Y
69 ○ ▪	Lita
87 ○ ⊕	Sonko / H / IFK / IA
	Assist: Little
88 ○ ⇄	Andrews > Riihilahti
88 ○ ⇄	Hunt > Convey
Full time 3-2	

Voted the best match ever seen at Madejski Stadium, recently relegated Crystal Palace were dramatically foiled by Ibrahima Sonko's last gasp winner on an electric Tuesday night.

Kevin Doyle scored the best of his three in three games by squeezing a low left-footed drive between Gabor Kiraly and the right upright, but the ever-threatening Andy Johnson sped clear to level two minutes later.

Soon after the break, Clinton Morrison silenced the home support by stabbing home Darren Ward's knock down for the lead. But Leroy Lita conjured a moment of sheer brilliance, burying a stupendous overhead scissor kick to make it 2-2.

As at Coventry three days earlier, Doyle earned a penalty which Lita saw saved – this time illegally by Kiraly who crept off his line. The Hungarian stopper then denied Glen Little's retaken penalty to keep the thrilling clash level, but Reading were to take the points with centre-back Sonko's powerful header sealing a stunning comeback.

Quote

Steve Coppell

We wanted to have a go at them and we did a lot of good things that will hold us in good stead for the rest of the season.

Venue: Madejski Stadium
Attendance: 17,562
Capacity: 24,200
Occupancy: 73%

Referee: B.Curson - 05/06
Matches: 4
Yellow Cards: 8
Red Cards: 1

Reading
Crystal Palace

Form Coming into Fixture

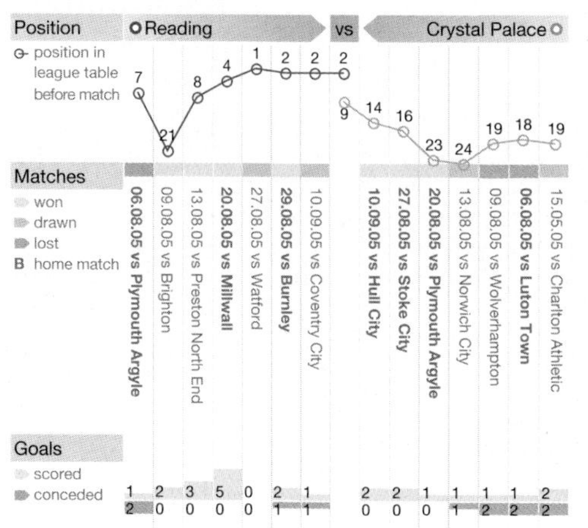

Position
Reading
vs
Crystal Palace
position in league table before match
7 21 8 4 1 2 2 2
9 14 16 23 24 19 18 19
Matches
won
drawn
lost
B home match
06.08.05 vs Plymouth Argyle
09.08.05 vs Brighton
13.08.05 vs Preston North End
20.08.05 vs Millwall
27.08.05 vs Watford
29.08.05 vs Burnley
10.09.05 vs Coventry City
10.09.05 vs Hull City
27.08.05 vs Stoke City
20.08.05 vs Plymouth Argyle
13.08.05 vs Norwich City
09.08.05 vs Wolverhampton
06.08.05 vs Luton Town
15.05.05 vs Charlton Athletic
Goals
scored
conceded
1 2 3 5 0 2 1
2 0 0 0 0 1 1
2 2 1 1 1 1 2
0 0 0 1 2 2 2

Goal Statistics

Reading

by Half | by Situation

first: 7 | set piece: 7
second: 7 | open play: 7

Crystal Palace

by Half | by Situation

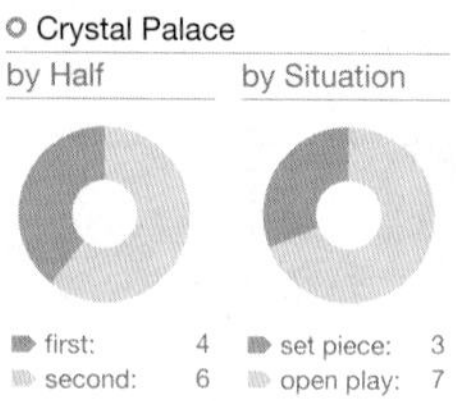

first: 4 | set piece: 3
second: 6 | open play: 7

Goals by Area

Reading

Scored (Conceded)

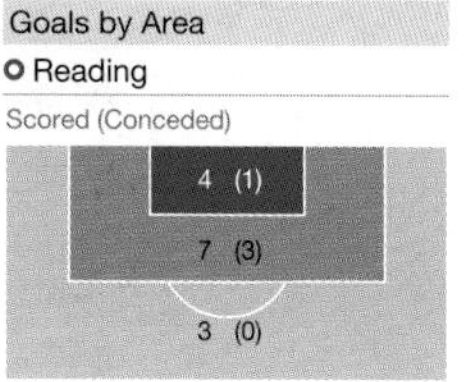

4 (1)
7 (3)
3 (0)

Crystal Palace

Scored (Conceded)

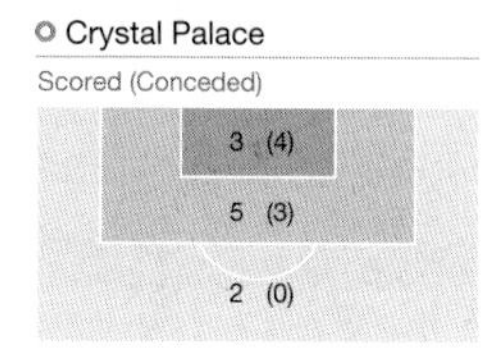

3 (4)
5 (3)
2 (0)

Team Statistics

Starting Line-Ups

Makin
Convey
Hunt
Ingimarsson
Harper
Hahnemann
Doyle
Morrison
Sonko
Gunnarsson
Lita
Johnson
Macken
Murty
Little
Soares
Boyce
Riihilahti
Andrews
Hall F
Kiraly
Watson
Ward
Hughes
Borrowdale

4/4/2

Unused Sub: Stack, Baradji, Oster, Obinna

4/4/2

Unused Sub: Speroni, Butterfield, Popovic

Championship Totals

Championship Totals	Reading	C. Palace
Championship Appearances	403	109
Team Appearances	333	66
Goals Scored	21	7
Assists	26	7
Clean Sheets (goalkeepers)	23	3
Yellow Cards	21	12
Red Cards	2	0
Full Internationals	5	6

Age/Height

Reading Age

26 yrs, 11 mo

Reading Height

5'11"

Crystal Palace Age

25 yrs, 11 mo

Crystal Palace Height

5'11"

Match Statistics

League Table after Fixture

		Played	Won	Drawn	Lost	For	Against	Pts
● 1	Sheff Utd	8	7	0	1	17	7	21
● 2	Reading	8	5	2	1	17	6	17
● 3	Watford	8	5	2	1	17	9	17
● 4	Luton	8	4	2	2	11	8	14
● 5	Southampton	8	3	4	1	10	7	13
↑ 6	Stoke	8	4	1	3	9	11	13
↑ 7	Preston	8	3	3	2	10	8	12
...		...	...	...	...	...	...	...
↓ 12	Crystal Palace	7	3	1	3	10	8	10

Statistics	Reading	C. Palace
Goals	3	2
Shots on Target	11	8
Shots off Target	2	5
Hit Woodwork	0	0
Possession %	43	57
Corners	5	1
Offsides	3	4
Fouls	10	15
Disciplinary Points	8	12

1-0 Reading ○ Crewe Alexandra ○

Championship

17.09.05

ww.masrecruitment.co.uk
Working to keep you working...
KYOCERA
TURTON
0118

Eric Obinna bursts forward

Event Line
Half time 0-0
78 ○ ⇄ Obinna > Lita
79 ○ ⇄ Oster > Little
80 ○ ⇄ Rivers > Vaughan
81 ○ ⚽ Ingimarsson / H / C / 6Y
Assist: Oster
83 ○ ⇄ Hunt > Convey
84 ○ ⇄ Suhaj > Higdon
84 ○ ⇄ Ugarte > Jones S
Full time 1-0

Icelander Ivar Ingimarsson became the ninth player to score in Reading's Championship campaign to extend his side's unbeaten run to nine games with the only goal against gutsy Crewe.

The home side began the better and strike duo Leroy Lita and Kevin Doyle were causing the main threat to Ross Turnbull's goal. Marcus Hahnemann was called into the most urgent action though, pushing Michael Higdon's headed effort wide as Crewe grew in confidence.

Steve Jones saw an effort controversially ruled out for offside while Higdon beat the US keeper only to see his header cannon off the crossbar. But Alex ironically came closest through Royals skipper Graeme Murty, whose skewed clearance almost looped into his own net – James Harper clearing off his goalline to spare the right-back's blushes.

Two minutes into his late substitute appearance, John Oster created the decisive cross which Ingimarsson just managed to force beyond Turnbull with a far post header, stealing maximum points from a tightly-fought encounter.

Quote

Steve Coppell

I thought that was the best opening 15 minutes we have played since I have been in charge of the team.

Championship Milestone

50

Both Graeme Murty and James Harper made their 50th appearances in the Championship.

Venue:	Madejski Stadium	Referee:	A.Woolmer - 05/06
Attendance:	17,668	Matches:	6
Capacity:	24,200	Yellow Cards:	10
Occupancy:	73%	Red Cards:	1

Reading
Crewe Alexandra

Form Coming into Fixture

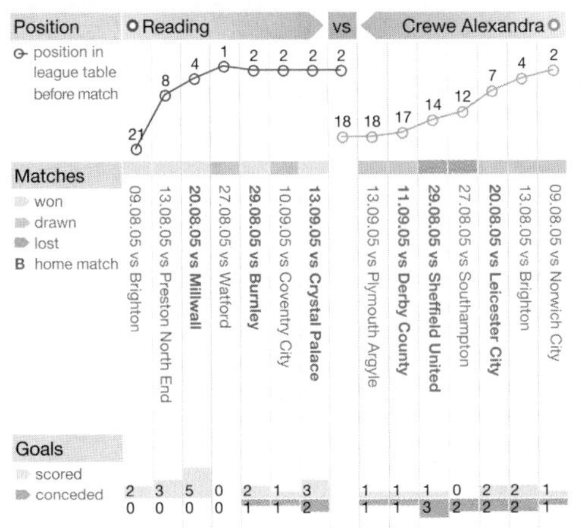

Position
Reading
vs
Crewe Alexandra
position in league table before match
Matches
won
drawn
lost
B home match
09.08.05 vs Brighton
13.08.05 vs Preston North End
20.08.05 vs Millwall
27.08.05 vs Watford
29.08.05 vs Burnley
10.09.05 vs Coventry City
13.09.05 vs Crystal Palace
13.09.05 vs Plymouth Argyle
11.09.05 vs Derby County
29.08.05 vs Sheffield United
27.08.05 vs Southampton
20.08.05 vs Leicester City
13.08.05 vs Brighton
09.08.05 vs Norwich City
Goals
scored
conceded

Goal Statistics

Reading

by Half | by Situation

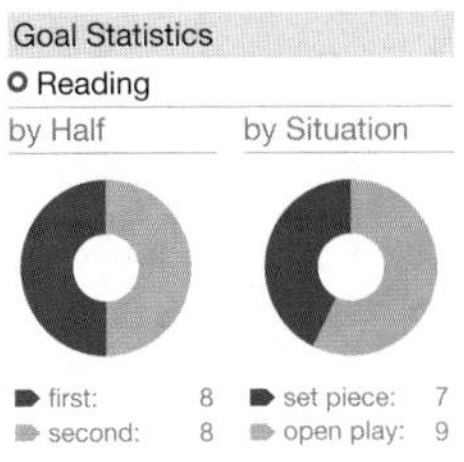

first: 8 | set piece: 7
second: 8 | open play: 9

Crewe Alexandra

by Half | by Situation

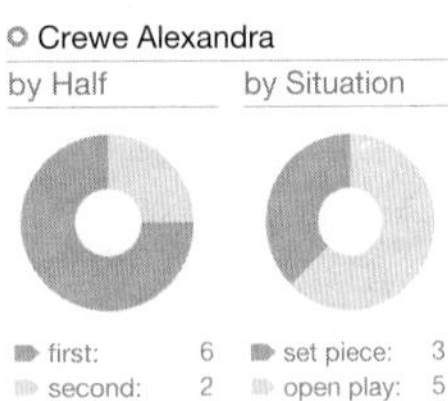

first: 6 | set piece: 3
second: 2 | open play: 5

Goals by Area

Reading — Scored (Conceded)

Crewe Alexandra — Scored (Conceded)

5 (2)
7 (2)
4 (0)
2 (6)
4 (4)
2 (2)

Team Statistics

Starting Line-Ups

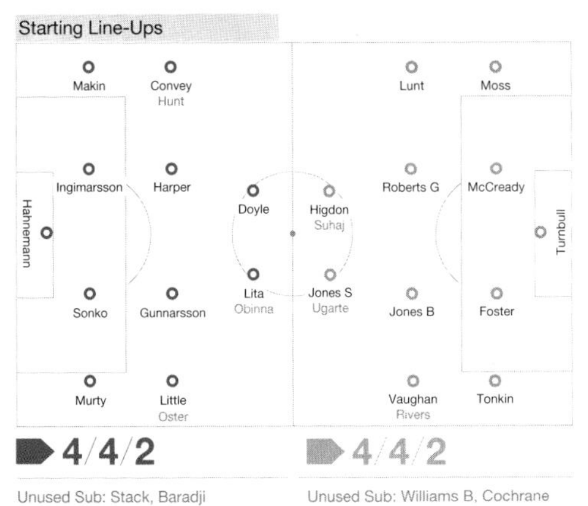

Makin
Convey
Hunt
Lunt
Moss
Ingimarsson
Harper
Doyle
Higdon
Suhaj
Roberts G
McCready
Hahnemann
Turnbull
Lita
Obinna
Jones S
Ugarte
Sonko
Gunnarsson
Jones B
Foster
Murty
Little
Oster
Vaughan
Rivers
Tonkin

4/4/2 | 4/4/2

Unused Sub: Stack, Baradji

Unused Sub: Williams B, Cochrane

Championship Totals	Reading	Crewe
Championship Appearances	452	373
Team Appearances	350	373
Goals Scored	26	39
Assists	30	44
Clean Sheets (goalkeepers)	23	0
Yellow Cards	24	21
Red Cards	2	1
Full Internationals	6	2

Age/Height

Reading Age: **26 yrs, 9 mo**

Crewe Alexandra Age: **23 yrs, 11 mo**

Reading Height: **5'11"**

Crewe Alexandra Height: **5'11"**

Match Statistics

League Table after Fixture

		Played	Won	Drawn	Lost	For	Against	Pts
● 1	Sheff Utd	9	8	0	1	20	9	24
● 2	Reading	9	6	2	1	18	6	20
● 3	Watford	9	5	2	2	19	12	17
↑ 4	Luton	9	5	2	2	12	8	17
↓ 5	Stoke	9	5	1	3	10	11	16
↑ 6	Leeds	8	4	2	2	10	7	14
↓ 7	Southampton	8	3	4	1	10	7	13
...		...	...	...	...	...	...	...
↓ 19	Crewe	9	1	5	3	10	14	8

Statistics	Reading	Crewe
Goals	1	0
Shots on Target	5	4
Shots off Target	2	1
Hit Woodwork	0	1
Possession %	58	42
Corners	12	8
Offsides	3	4
Fouls	10	3
Disciplinary Points	0	0

1-0 Reading Luton Town

Carling Cup

20.09.05

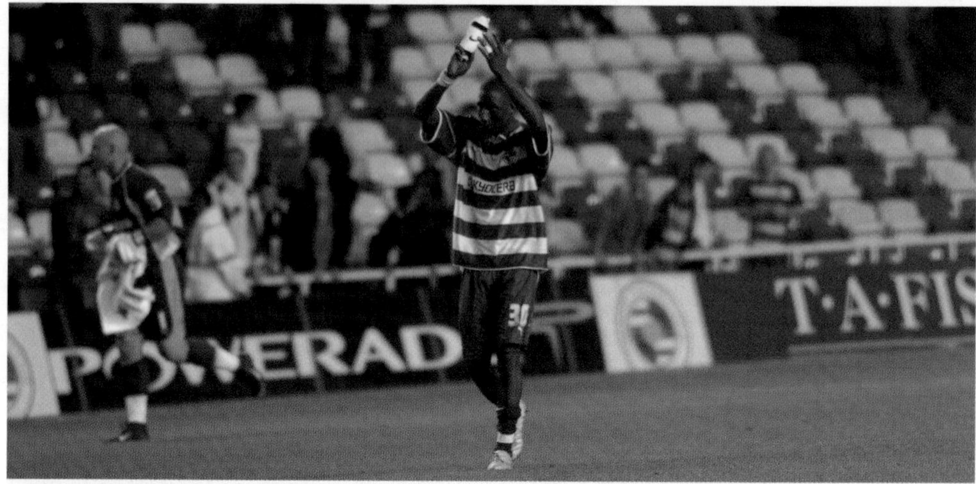
ERAD
T·A·FIS

Sekou Baradji looks forward to Round Three

Event Line
Half time 0-0
55 Keane > Barnett
57 Lita > Doyle
80 Oster / RF / DFK / OA
85 Cox > Obinna
90 Howard
Full time 1-0

Steve Coppell once again rang the changes for the Carling Cup visit of Luton Town, with Graham Stack, Sekou Baradji, John Oster, Stephen Hunt and Eric Obinna all being handed starting berths. And it was one of those changes, Oster, who provided the decisive moment of a dreary cup tie with a fortunate second-half winner.

In a game with very little goalmouth incident, Hatters winger Dean Morgan was keen to impress his former employers but a host of long-range efforts failed to trouble Marcus Hahnemann.

Warren Feeney did test the US keeper with a rare strike on target, while Hunt and Obinna came closest for the Royals. Indeed, Obinna often looked the most likely threat for the Royals.

Luton enjoyed the better of the opening period in terms of possession, but struggled to create the openings some of their approach play had merited.

The opening stages of the second half were more even, with neither side able to play with any fluency or force opportunities on goal.

With 20 minutes remaining, though, the game suddenly livened up as Obinna produced some good forward play to find substitute Leroy Lita, but the substitute's effort was blocked as the stalemate continued. But the best chance of the evening was then created by Luton, as Feeney broke forward and crossed for strike partner

Venue:	Madejski Stadium	Referee:	M.Fletcher - 05/06
Attendance:	6,941	Matches:	7
Capacity:	24,200	Yellow Cards:	31
Occupancy:	29%	Red Cards:	1

KYOCERA
CARLING

Simon Cox gets a taste of the action

Match Statistics

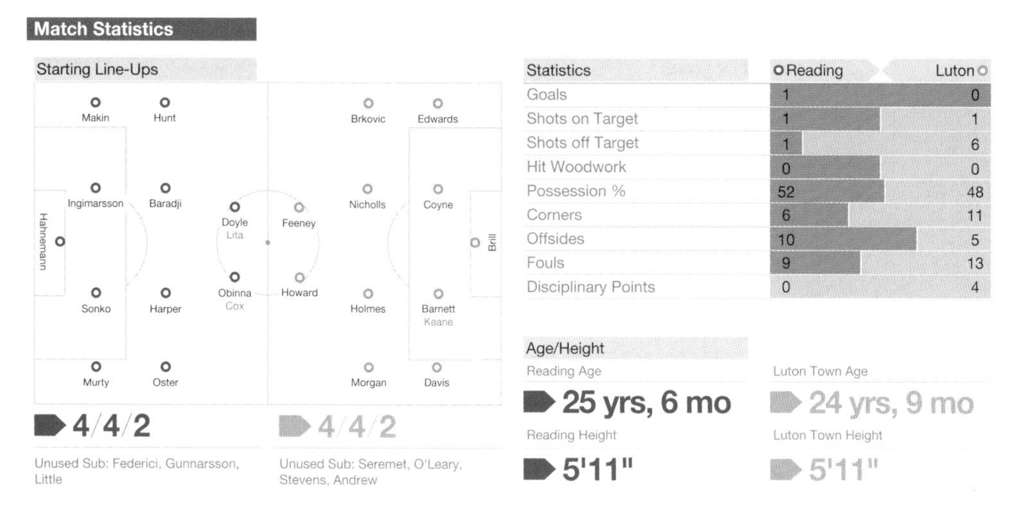

Starting Line-Ups

Reading: Hahnemann; Makin, Ingimarsson, Sonko, Murty; Hunt, Baradji, Harper, Oster; Doyle (Lita), Obinna (Cox)

4/4/2

Unused Sub: Federici, Gunnarsson, Little

Luton: Brill; Edwards, Coyne, Barnett (Keane), Davis; Brkovic, Nicholls, Holmes, Morgan; Feeney, Howard

4/4/2

Unused Sub: Seremet, O'Leary, Stevens, Andrew

Statistics	Reading	Luton
Goals	1	0
Shots on Target	1	1
Shots off Target	1	6
Hit Woodwork	0	0
Possession %	52	48
Corners	6	11
Offsides	10	5
Fouls	9	13
Disciplinary Points	0	4

Age/Height

Reading Age
25 yrs, 6 mo

Luton Town Age
24 yrs, 9 mo

Reading Height
5'11"

Luton Town Height
5'11"

Steve Howard, who wasted the clear opening by shooting wide from ten yards.

As time began to run short and an unwanted period of extra time loomed large, Obinna won a free kick just left of centre which Oster stepped up to take. Starting only his second game since signing for the club in the summer, Oster curled his 40-yard set piece dangerously into the six yard box. Evading Lita's outstretched leg and onlooking Hatters defenders, the ball drifted tamely past visiting keeper Dean Brill to bounce inside the far post for the winner that had hardly looked likely.

The game ended on a positive note for the Royals as local youngster Simon Cox was introduced to the action, replacing Obinna for the final five minutes and impressing with a lively cameo performance.

Quote

Steve Coppell

We were disappointed with ourselves going forward in certain respects, which put us under extra pressure.

0-1 Norwich City Reading

Championship

24.09.05

NORWICH UNION

Glen Little embarks upon a dangerous run

Event Line

20	Hughes
Half time 0-0	
57	Murty
61	Harper / LF / OP / IA
	Assist: Doyle
62	Huckerby > McVeigh
74	Henderson > Brennan
79	Obinna > Lita
86	Fleming > Colin
90	Makin
Full time 0-1	

A determined Reading side survived a last minute penalty to hold on and snatch all three points from Carrow Road thanks to James Harper's second half drive.

A groggy Dean Ashton recovered from an early clash of heads to cause a constant threat for the Canaries, but the striker scooped Youssef Safri's curling free kick over the crossbar before the break and saw a header cleared off the line by Ibrahima Sonko after the interval.

With the game in the balance, Kevin Doyle masterfully muscled Calum Davenport off the ball to cut back to the onrushing Harper. The midfielder's first shot was blocked but he was first to the rebound to stroke left-footed past Robert Green for the lead.

It seemed the points might be contentiously shared though, when referee Trevor Kettle changed his mind in the dying seconds. After booking Davenport for a dive, he consulted his linesman and awarded a penalty for Bobby Convey's challenge on the centre-back. But Ashton dragged the spot-kick wide to the Royals' relief and 1-0 it stayed.

Quote

Steve Coppell

We were a bit lucky to take all three points, but we battled away and that's why we got the win.

Venue:	Carrow Road	Referee:	T.Kettle - 05/06
Attendance:	24,850	Matches:	9
Capacity:	27,470	Yellow Cards:	42
Occupancy:	90%	Red Cards:	2

Norwich City
Reading

Form Coming into Fixture

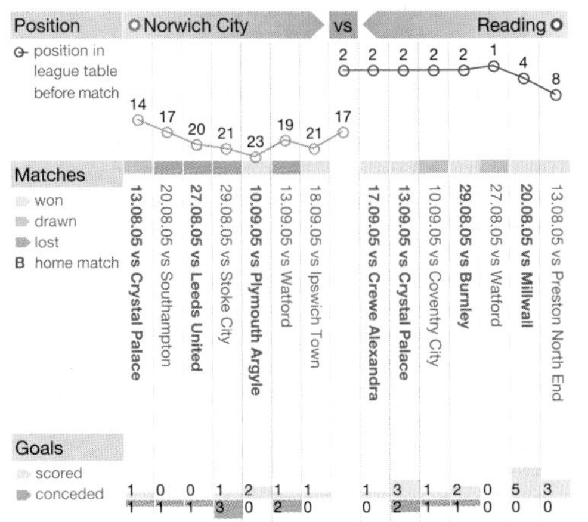

Position
Norwich City
vs
Reading
position in league table before match
14 17 20 21 23 19 21 17
2 2 2 2 2 1 4 8
Matches
won
drawn
lost
B home match
13.08.05 vs Crystal Palace
20.08.05 vs Southampton
27.08.05 vs Leeds United
29.08.05 vs Stoke City
10.09.05 vs Plymouth Argyle
13.09.05 vs Watford
18.09.05 vs Ipswich Town
17.09.05 vs Crewe Alexandra
13.09.05 vs Crystal Palace
10.09.05 vs Coventry City
29.08.05 vs Burnley
27.08.05 vs Watford
20.08.05 vs Millwall
13.08.05 vs Preston North End
Goals
scored
conceded
1 0 0 1 2 1 1
1 1 1 3 0 2 0
1 3 1 2 0 5 3
0 2 1 1 0 0 0

Goal Statistics

Norwich City

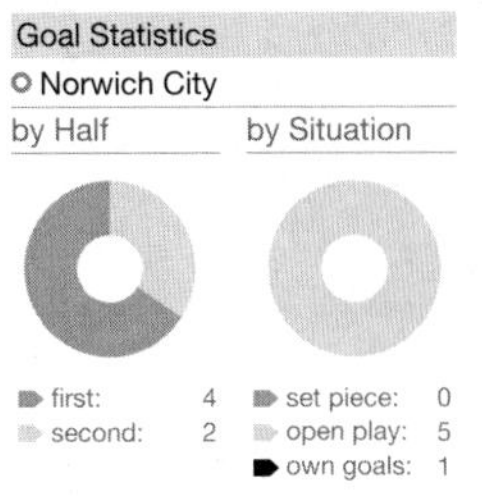

by Half
by Situation
first: 4
second: 2
set piece: 0
open play: 5
own goals: 1

Reading

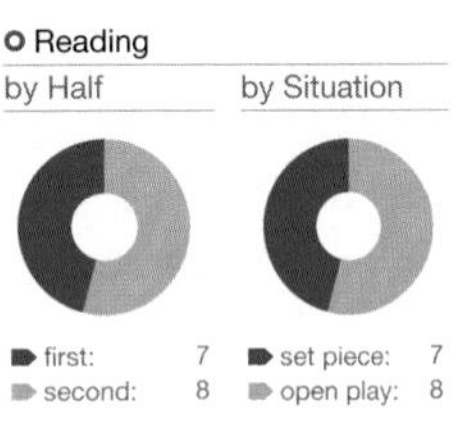

by Half
by Situation
first: 7
second: 8
set piece: 7
open play: 8

Goals by Area

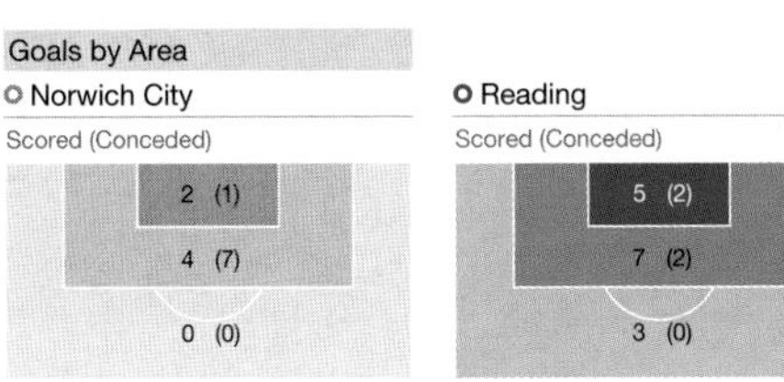

Norwich City
Scored (Conceded)
2 (1)
4 (7)
0 (0)
Reading
Scored (Conceded)
5 (2)
7 (2)
3 (0)

Team Statistics

Starting Line-Ups

Drury
Brennan
Henderson
Davenport
Green
Safri
Ashton
McVeigh
Huckerby
Lisbie
Doherty
Hughes
Colin
Fleming
Lita
Obinna
Doyle
Little
Murty
Gunnarsson
Sonko
Hahnemann
Harper
Ingimarsson
Convey
Makin

4/4/2 (Diamond)

Unused Sub: Ward, Marney

4/4/2

Unused Sub: Federici, Cox, Hunt, Oster

Championship Totals	Norwich	Reading
Championship Appearances	165	423
Team Appearances	84	353
Goals Scored	24	25
Assists	18	27
Clean Sheets (goalkeepers)	2	24
Yellow Cards	14	23
Red Cards	1	2
Full Internationals	6	5

Age/Height

Norwich City Age

26 yrs, 6 mo

Norwich City Height

6'

Reading Age

26 yrs, 11 mo

Reading Height

6'

Match Statistics

League Table after Fixture

		Played	Won	Drawn	Lost	For	Against	Pts
●	1 Sheff Utd	10	9	0	1	22	10	27
●	2 Reading	10	7	2	1	19	6	23
↑	3 Watford	10	5	3	2	19	12	18
↓	4 Luton	10	5	3	2	14	10	18
↑	5 Wolverhampton	10	4	4	2	13	10	16
↓	6 Stoke	10	5	1	4	11	14	16
↓	7 Southampton	10	3	6	1	12	9	15
...		...	...	...	...	...	...	...
↓	18 Norwich	10	2	3	5	8	11	9

Statistics	Norwich	Reading
Goals	0	1
Shots on Target	6	3
Shots off Target	7	5
Hit Woodwork	0	0
Possession %	51	49
Corners	7	4
Offsides	9	3
Fouls	14	10
Disciplinary Points	4	8

0-0 Southampton Reading

Championship

28.09.05

Glen Little is put under pressure by Nigel Quashie

Event Line
15 Little
23 Quashie
27 Doyle
37 Hunt > Murty
Half time 0-0
71 Pahars > Kosowski
82 Obinna > Lita
88 Ormerod > Jones
Full time 0-0

Facing the third side relegated from the Premiership, a goalless draw with Southampton led the Royals out of a daunting September schedule unbeaten and with confidence unscathed.

A tempestuous encounter at St Mary's was played in torrential midweek rain, and the tone was set when Nigel Quashie raced onto Kenwyne Jones' knock down to squander a glorious chance in front of goal after just 35 seconds.

Top flight referee Graham Poll failed to see Darren Powell's off-the-ball elbow which left Kevin Doyle needing dental repair work and later earned Powell a deserved suspension. But Poll had plenty to keep him busy with penalty claims and good chances at both ends in an entertaining stalemate.

The outstanding Ibrahima Sonko and Ivar Ingimarsson denied the dominant home side on countless occasions, the best chance falling to long-term injury victim Marian Pahars, who saw a late close-range effort defiantly blocked at the near post. Marcus Hahnemann also made a series of excellent saves as the draw took Reading's unbeaten league streak into double figures.

Quote

Steve Coppell

We were under pressure most of the game, but it's a tremendous compliment to my lads that we held in there and came away with a point.

Championship Milestone

50

Ibrahima Sonko made his 50th appearance in the Championship.

Venue:	St Mary's Stadium
Attendance:	24,946
Capacity:	32,251
Occupancy:	77%

Referee:	G.Poll - 05/06
Matches:	7
Yellow Cards:	25
Red Cards:	1

Southampton
Reading

Form Coming into Fixture

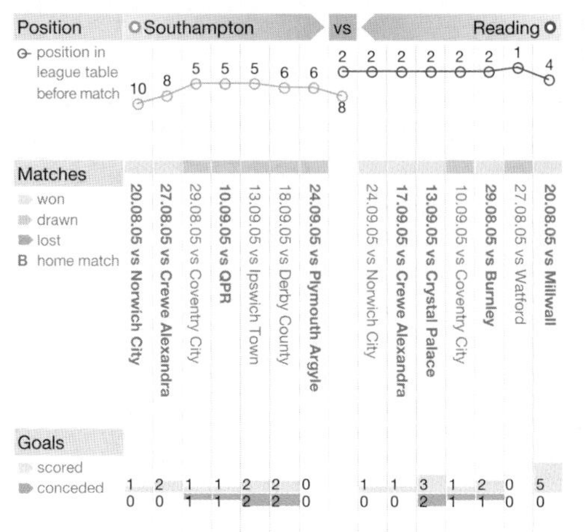

Position
Southampton
vs
Reading
position in league table before match
10 8 5 5 5 6 6 8
2 2 2 2 2 2 1 4
Matches
won
drawn
lost
B home match
20.08.05 vs Norwich City
27.08.05 vs Crewe Alexandra
29.08.05 vs Coventry City
10.09.05 vs QPR
13.09.05 vs Ipswich Town
18.09.05 vs Derby County
24.09.05 vs Plymouth Argyle
24.09.05 vs Norwich City
17.09.05 vs Crewe Alexandra
13.09.05 vs Crystal Palace
10.09.05 vs Coventry City
29.08.05 vs Burnley
27.08.05 vs Watford
20.08.05 vs Millwall
Goals
scored
conceded
1 2 1 1 2 2 0
0 0 1 1 2 2 0
1 1 3 1 2 0 5
0 0 2 1 1 0 0

Goal Statistics

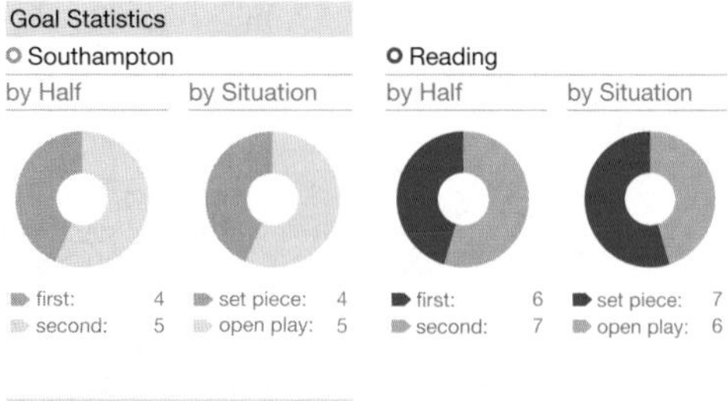

Southampton
by Half
by Situation
Reading
by Half
by Situation

Southampton		Southampton	
first:	4	set piece:	4
second:	5	open play:	5

Reading		Reading	
first:	6	set piece:	7
second:	7	open play:	6

Goals by Area

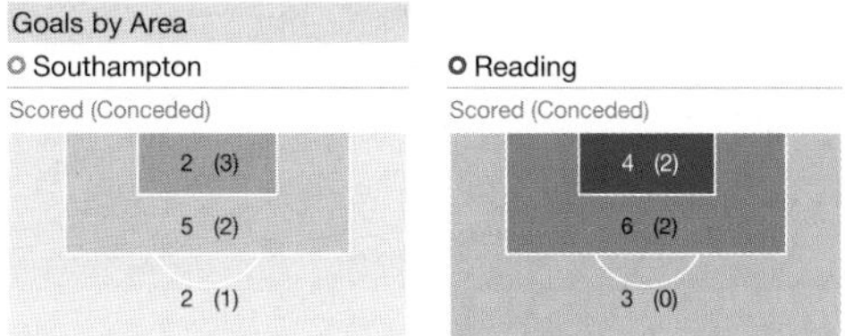

Southampton
Scored (Conceded)
2 (3)
5 (2)
2 (1)
Reading
Scored (Conceded)
4 (2)
6 (2)
3 (0)

Team Statistics

Starting Line-Ups

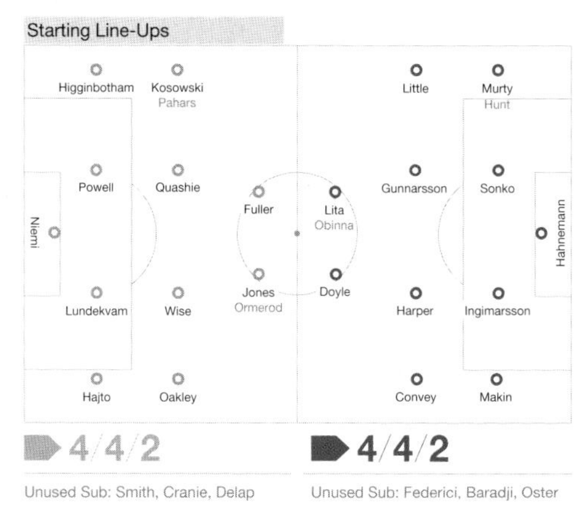

Higginbotham
Kosowski
Pahars
Powell
Quashie
Fuller
Lita
Obinna
Niemi
Lundekvam
Wise
Jones
Ormerod
Doyle
Hajto
Oakley
Little
Murty
Hunt
Gunnarsson
Sonko
Hahnemann
Harper
Ingimarsson
Convey
Makin
4/4/2
4/4/2

Unused Sub: Smith, Cranie, Delap

Unused Sub: Federici, Baradji, Oster

Championship Totals

Championship Totals	Southampton	Reading
Championship Appearances	159	441
Team Appearances	102	371
Goals Scored	21	26
Assists	13	28
Clean Sheets (goalkeepers)	5	25
Yellow Cards	29	25
Red Cards	2	2
Full Internationals	9	5

Age/Height

Southampton Age: **29 yrs, 5 mo**

Reading Age: **26 yrs, 9 mo**

Southampton Height: **6'**

Reading Height: **6'**

Match Statistics

League Table after Fixture

		Played	Won	Drawn	Lost	For	Against	Pts
● 1	Sheff Utd	11	10	0	1	24	10	30
● 2	Reading	11	7	3	1	19	6	24
● 3	Luton	11	6	3	2	17	10	21
● 4	Wolverhampton	11	5	4	2	17	10	19
● 5	Watford	11	5	3	3	20	15	18
↑ 6	Leeds	10	5	2	3	13	10	17
↑ 7	Southampton	11	3	7	1	12	9	16
↓ 8	QPR	11	4	4	3	10	12	16
↓ 9	Stoke	11	5	1	5	11	17	16

Statistics

Statistics	Southampton	Reading
Goals	0	0
Shots on Target	5	5
Shots off Target	12	4
Hit Woodwork	0	0
Possession %	61	39
Corners	10	4
Offsides	3	2
Fouls	8	11
Disciplinary Points	4	8

2-1

Reading ○
Sheffield United ○

Championship

01.10.05

RABBITS

➡ Brynjar Gunnarsson is mobbed by exuberant teammates

Event Line	
3 ○	⚽ Gunnarsson / RF / C / IA
	Assist: Little
12 ○	▪ Quinn A
15 ○	⚽ Kabba / H / OP / 6Y
	Assist: Quinn A
33 ○	▪ Kenny
Half time 1-1	
46 ○	⇄ Oster > Little
67 ○	⇄ Gillespie > Ifill
67 ○	⇄ Baradji > Convey
78 ○	⇄ Obinna > Lita
89 ○	⚽ Gunnarsson / H / IFK / IA
	Assist: Baradji
90 ○	▪ Morgan
90 ○	⇄ Webber > Quinn A
90 ○	⇄ Pericard > Shipperley
Full time 2-1	

First versus second at Madejski Stadium saw the hard-chasing Royals close the gap at the top thanks to Brynjar Gunnarsson's 88th minute header.

Icelandic midfielder Gunnarsson had notched his first for the Club when he swept Glen Little's corner beyond Paddy Kenny in the Blades' goal for a 3rd minute lead, but free-scoring Steve Kabba nodded Alan Quinn's low cross past Marcus Hahnemann for a swift reply.

With the game level, two hotly disputed refereeing decisions by Grant Hegley riled both sets of supporters. First Kenny handled outside his area to prevent Kevin Doyle capitalising on Nick Montgomery's half-hearted header back, but only a yellow card was the outcome. Then James Harper was fortunate not to concede a late penalty when clattering into Keith Gillespie.

But the game was decided when Gunnarsson glanced substitute Sekou Baradji's floated free kick inches wide of Kenny's desperate dive for a dramatic winner – to Neil Warnock's all too obvious disgust!

Quote

Steve Coppell

I hope we have a bit more firepower from different areas now. Brynjar Gunnarsson ghosted in very nicely for both goals.

Championship Milestone

➡ First Goal

Brynjar Gunnarsson netted his first goals in the Championship for Reading.

Venue:	Madejski Stadium	Referee:	G.K.Hegley - 05/06
Attendance:	22,068	Matches:	8
Capacity:	24,200	Yellow Cards:	16
Occupancy:	91%	Red Cards:	1

Reading
Sheffield United

Form Coming into Fixture

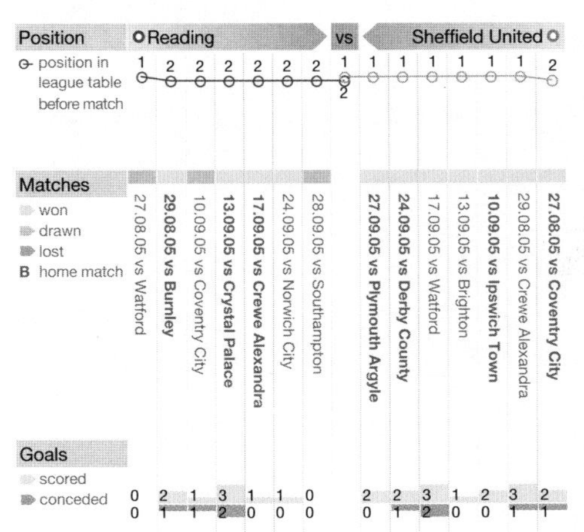

Position
Reading
vs
Sheffield United
position in league table before match
Matches
won
drawn
lost
B home match
27.08.05 vs Watford
29.08.05 vs Burnley
10.09.05 vs Coventry City
13.09.05 vs Crystal Palace
17.09.05 vs Crewe Alexandra
24.09.05 vs Norwich City
28.09.05 vs Southampton
27.09.05 vs Plymouth Argyle
24.09.05 vs Derby County
17.09.05 vs Watford
13.09.05 vs Brighton
10.09.05 vs Ipswich Town
29.08.05 vs Crewe Alexandra
27.08.05 vs Coventry City
Goals
scored
conceded

Goal Statistics

Reading — by Half / by Situation

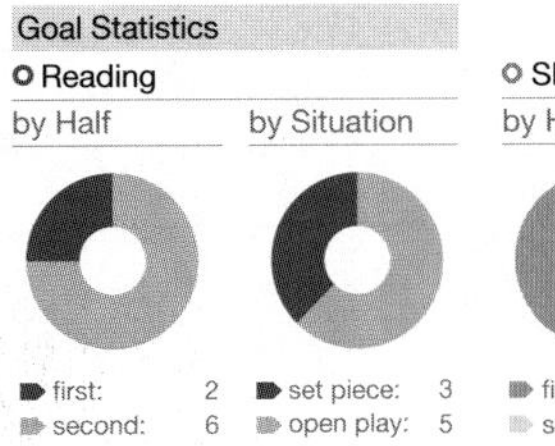

first: 2 — second: 6 — set piece: 3 — open play: 5

Sheffield United — by Half / by Situation

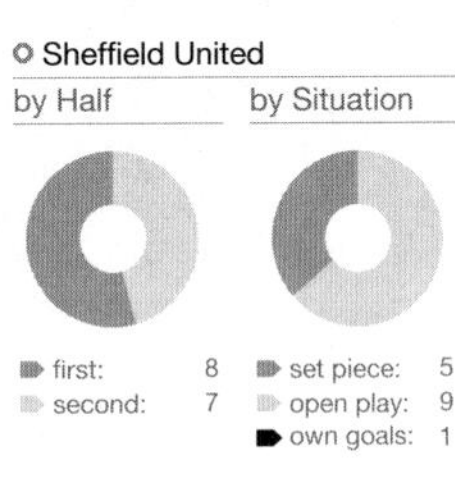

first: 8 — second: 7 — set piece: 5 — open play: 9 — own goals: 1

Goals by Area

Reading — Scored (Conceded)

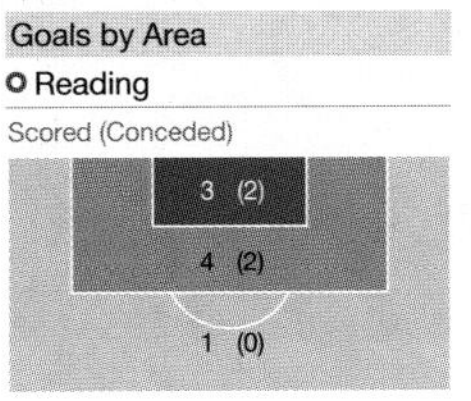

3 (2)
4 (2)
1 (0)

Sheffield United — Scored (Conceded)

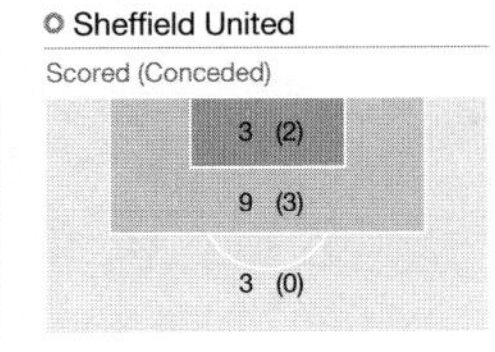

3 (2)
9 (3)
3 (0)

Team Statistics

Starting Line-Ups

Hunt
Convey
Baradji
Ingimarsson
Harper
Hahnemann
Sonko
Gunnarsson
Makin
Little
Oster
Doyle
Kabba
Lita
Obinna
Shipperley
Pericard
Ifill
Gillespie
Kozluk
Montgomery
Bromby
Kenny
Jagielka
Morgan
Quinn A
Webber
Unsworth
4/4/2
4/4/2

Unused Sub: Federici, Osano

Unused Sub: Geary, Tonge

Championship Totals	Reading	Sheff Utd
Championship Appearances	439	490
Team Appearances	337	397
Goals Scored	28	61
Assists	30	47
Clean Sheets (goalkeepers)	26	15
Yellow Cards	25	44
Red Cards	2	5
Full Internationals	5	5

Age/Height

Reading Age: **26 yrs, 1 mo**

Sheffield United Age: **26 yrs, 8 mo**

Reading Height: **6'**

Sheffield United Height: **5'11"**

Match Statistics

League Table after Fixture

		Played	Won	Drawn	Lost	For	Against	Pts
1	Sheff Utd	12	10	0	2	25	12	30
2	Reading	12	8	3	1	21	7	27
3	Luton	12	7	3	2	19	11	24
4	Wolverhampton	12	5	4	3	17	11	19
5	Watford	12	5	4	3	20	15	19
6	Leeds	11	5	3	3	13	10	18
7	Southampton	12	3	8	1	13	10	17
↑ 8	Ipswich	12	5	2	5	12	17	17
↓ 9	QPR	11	4	4	3	10	12	16

Statistics	Reading	Sheff Utd
Goals	2	1
Shots on Target	2	3
Shots off Target	5	4
Hit Woodwork	0	0
Possession %	48	52
Corners	4	7
Offsides	1	2
Fouls	8	19
Disciplinary Points	0	12

2-0 Reading Ipswich Town

Championship

16.10.05

Kevin Doyle is the hero for Reading

Event Line

4		De Vos
18	⚽	Naylor / LF / OG / 6Y
		Assist: Doyle
19		Naylor
Half time 1-0		
46	⇄	Proudlock > De Vos
47	⚽	Doyle / H / OP / IA
		Assist: Little
64	⇄	Kitson > Doyle
69	⇄	Garvan > Forster
71		Wilnis
72	⇄	Oster > Little
77		McEveley
81	⇄	Hunt > Convey
83	⇄	Bowditch > Currie
86		Bowditch
Full time 2-0		

Steve Coppell's side laid on a scintillating exhibition for Sky Sports' Sunday afternoon cameras in calmly disposing of visitors Ipswich.

From the opening whistle the Royals produced fluent and fast-moving attacking football, and Town defender Jason de Vos was a little lucky not to see red early on after dragging back the quickly breaking Kevin Doyle on the edge of the visitors' area.

Irishman Doyle was soon causing more problems, fizzing a low cross in to Leroy Lita, who could only stab wide. Two minutes later a similar move allowed Doyle to fashion another searching centre, which this time didn't reach Lita as Richard Naylor's outstretched leg intercepted only to divert over the line for an own goal opener.

Shortly after the interval, provider turned goalscorer when Doyle headed home Glen Little's excellent cross for a second. Both Doyle and Lita hammered the woodwork in the space of seconds as Reading looked for more with waves of relentless pressure, but a warranted third did not materialise and Ibrahima Sonko had to make a miraculous goalline clearance to deny Sam Parkin as ex-Royals favourite Nicky Forster saw his return end in comprehensive defeat.

Quote

Steve Coppell

Kevin Doyle has come from nowhere and the nice thing is he's what I call a low maintenance player.

Venue:	Madejski Stadium	Referee:	S.Tanner - 05/06
Attendance:	17,581	Matches:	9
Capacity:	24,200	Yellow Cards:	33
Occupancy:	73%	Red Cards:	3

Reading
Ipswich Town

Form Coming into Fixture

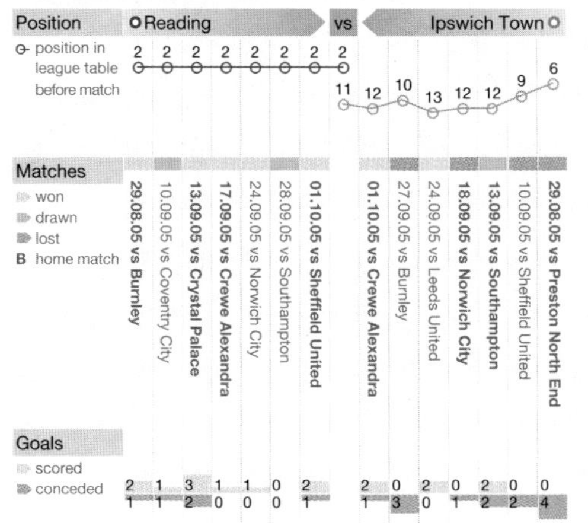

Position
Reading
vs
Ipswich Town
position in league table before match
2 2 2 2 2 2 2 2
11 12 10 13 12 12 9 6
Matches
won
drawn
lost
B home match
29.08.05 vs Burnley
10.09.05 vs Coventry City
13.09.05 vs Crystal Palace
17.09.05 vs Crewe Alexandra
24.09.05 vs Norwich City
28.09.05 vs Southampton
01.10.05 vs Sheffield United
01.10.05 vs Crewe Alexandra
27.09.05 vs Burnley
24.09.05 vs Leeds United
18.09.05 vs Norwich City
13.09.05 vs Southampton
10.09.05 vs Sheffield United
29.08.05 vs Preston North End
Goals
scored
conceded
2 1 3 1 1 0 2
1 1 2 0 0 0 1
2 0 2 0 2 0 0
1 3 0 1 2 2 4

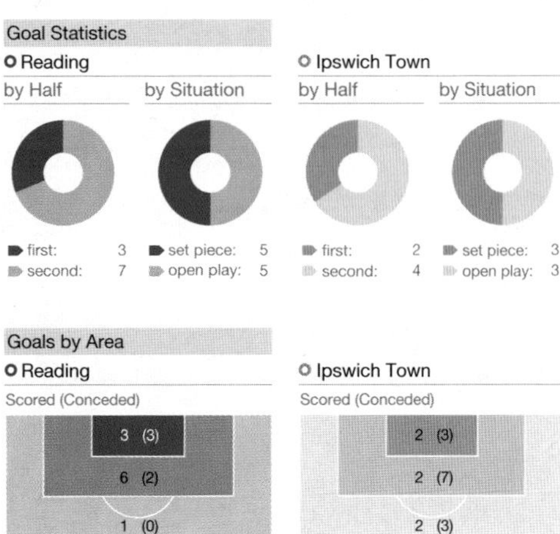

Goal Statistics
Reading
by Half
by Situation
first: 3
second: 7
set piece: 5
open play: 5
Ipswich Town
by Half
by Situation
first: 2
second: 4
set piece: 3
open play: 3
Goals by Area
Reading
Scored (Conceded)
3 (3)
6 (2)
1 (0)
Ipswich Town
Scored (Conceded)
2 (3)
2 (7)
2 (3)

Team Statistics

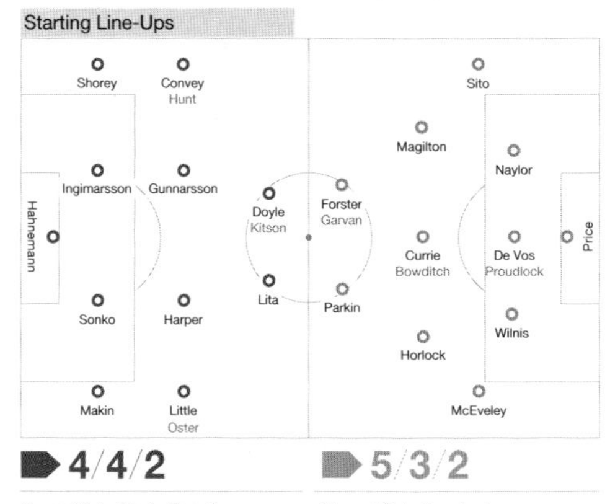

Starting Line-Ups
Shorey
Convey
Hunt
Ingimarsson
Gunnarsson
Hahnemann
Doyle
Kitson
Forster
Garvan
Lita
Parkin
Sonko
Harper
Makin
Little
Oster
Sito
Magilton
Naylor
Currie
Bowditch
De Vos
Proudlock
Price
Wilnis
Horlock
McEveley

4/4/2
Unused Sub: Stack, Baradji

5/3/2
Unused Sub: Supple, Juan

Championship Totals	Reading	Ipswich
Championship Appearances	540	463
Team Appearances	438	385
Goals Scored	54	40
Assists	46	57
Clean Sheets (goalkeepers)	26	3
Yellow Cards	32	47
Red Cards	2	4
Full Internationals	5	3

Age/Height

Reading Age	Ipswich Town Age
26 yrs, 5 mo	27 yrs, 3 mo
Reading Height	Ipswich Town Height
5'11"	6'

Match Statistics

League Table after Fixture

		Played	Won	Drawn	Lost	For	Against	Pts
1	Sheff Utd	13	11	0	2	26	12	33
2	Reading	13	9	3	1	23	7	30
3	Luton	13	7	3	3	20	14	24
4	Leeds	12	6	3	3	15	11	21
5	Crystal Palace	12	6	2	4	20	12	20
6	Wolverhampton	13	5	4	4	17	12	19
7	Watford	13	5	4	4	21	17	19
...		...	...	...	...	...	...	...
11	Ipswich	13	5	2	6	12	19	17

Statistics	Reading	Ipswich
Goals	2	0
Shots on Target	7	2
Shots off Target	12	1
Hit Woodwork	0	0
Possession %	57	43
Corners	8	4
Offsides	4	8
Fouls	6	15
Disciplinary Points	0	20

1-1 Hull City Reading

Championship

18.10.05

Ivar Ingimarsson shakes hands at the final whistle

Event Line
23 Woodhouse
Half time 0-0
56 Brown / LF / C / 6Y
Assist: Woodhouse
70 Oster > Convey
70 Kitson > Lita
74 Little / H / OP / IA
Assist: Shorey
76 Elliott > Green
79 Burgess > Fagan
Full time 1-1

The Royals made their KC Stadium debut as they took on promoted Hull City for the first time in more than a decade.

In-form forwards Kevin Doyle and Leroy Lita were both thwarted in the first half by Tigers' goalkeeper Boaz Myhill, parrying Lita's fierce volley and palming Doyle's header as Steve Coppell's side started strongly.

But Hull gradually got back into the game, and took the lead when on-loan Sunderland striker Chris Brown netted his first and only goal for Peter Taylor's men, converting from close range shortly after Leon Cort's floated header had struck the Royals crossbar.

City began to frustrate Coppell's previously dominant troops, but with 15 minutes remaining Glen Little got on the end of left-back Nicky Shorey's far post cross to equalise with a well-taken downward header.

Brynjar Gunnarsson, enjoying his extended and impressive spell in the first team, almost snatched a late winner but could only glance his injury time header wide and Hull hung on for a point.

Quote

Steve Coppell

When we went behind we responded in the right way - we didn't panic, we continued to pass the ball and continued to create chances.

Championship Milestone

75

Glen Little's goal was the 75th scored in the Championship by Reading.

Venue: KC Stadium
Attendance: 17,698
Capacity: 25,504
Occupancy: 69%

Referee: G.Laws - 05/06
Matches: 10
Yellow Cards: 37
Red Cards: 1

Hull City
Reading

Form Coming into Fixture

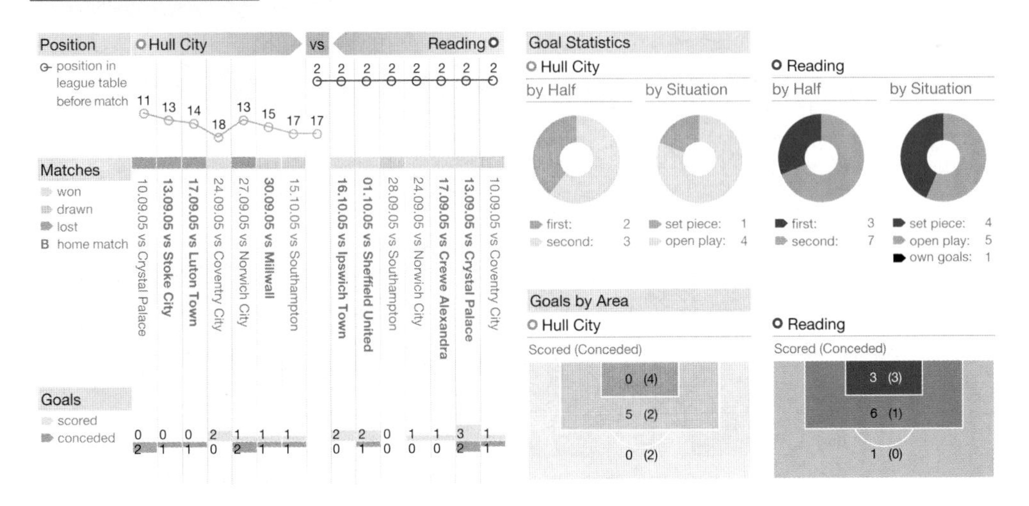

Position
Hull City
vs
Reading
position in league table before match
11 13 14 18 13 15 17 17
2 2 2 2 2 2 2 2
Matches
won
drawn
lost
B home match
10.09.05 vs Crystal Palace
13.09.05 vs Stoke City
17.09.05 vs Luton Town
24.09.05 vs Coventry City
27.09.05 vs Norwich City
30.09.05 vs Millwall
15.10.05 vs Southampton
16.10.05 vs Ipswich Town
01.10.05 vs Sheffield United
28.09.05 vs Southampton
24.09.05 vs Norwich City
17.09.05 vs Crewe Alexandra
13.09.05 vs Crystal Palace
10.09.05 vs Coventry City
Goals
scored
conceded
0 0 0 2 1 1 1
2 1 1 0 2 1 1
2 2 0 1 1 3 1
0 1 0 0 0 2 1
Goal Statistics
Hull City
by Half
by Situation
first: 2
second: 3
set piece: 1
open play: 4
Reading
by Half
by Situation
first: 3
second: 7
set piece: 4
open play: 5
own goals: 1
Goals by Area
Hull City
Scored (Conceded)
0 (4)
5 (2)
0 (2)
Reading
Scored (Conceded)
3 (3)
6 (1)
1 (0)

Team Statistics

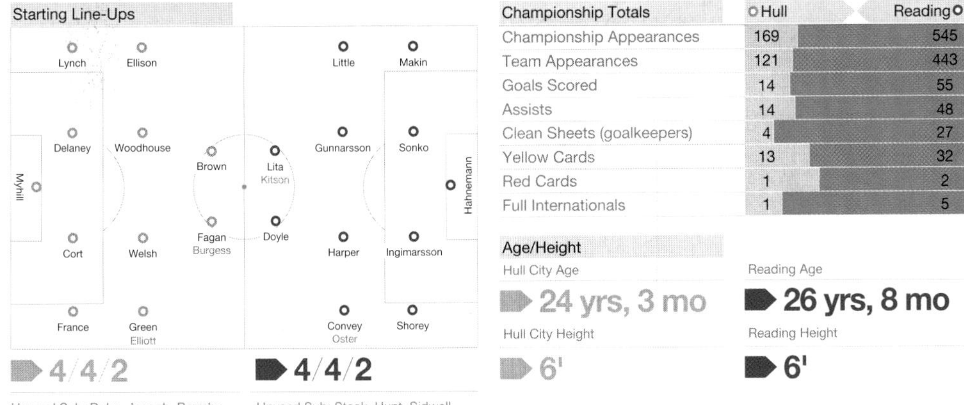

Starting Line-Ups
Lynch
Ellison
Delaney
Woodhouse
Myhill
Cort
Welsh
France
Green
Elliott
Brown
Lita
Kitson
Fagan
Burgess
Doyle
Little
Makin
Gunnarsson
Sonko
Hahnemann
Harper
Ingimarsson
Convey
Oster
Shorey
4/4/2
4/4/2

Championship Totals	Hull	Reading
Championship Appearances	169	545
Team Appearances	121	443
Goals Scored	14	55
Assists	14	48
Clean Sheets (goalkeepers)	4	27
Yellow Cards	13	32
Red Cards	1	2
Full Internationals	1	5

Unused Sub: Duke, Joseph, Barmby

Unused Sub: Stack, Hunt, Sidwell

Age/Height

Hull City Age
24 yrs, 3 mo

Hull City Height
6'

Reading Age
26 yrs, 8 mo

Reading Height
6'

Match Statistics

League Table after Fixture

	Played	Won	Drawn	Lost	For	Against	Pts
1 Sheff Utd	14	12	0	2	30	12	36
2 Reading	14	9	4	1	24	8	31
3 Luton	14	8	3	3	24	16	27
4 Leeds	13	7	3	3	17	12	24
5 Crystal Palace	13	6	2	5	20	13	20
6 Wolverhampton	14	5	5	4	18	13	20
7 Watford	14	5	5	4	22	18	20
...	...	...	...	...	...	...	...
17 Hull	14	3	6	5	11	12	15

Statistics	Hull	Reading
Goals	1	1
Shots on Target	6	5
Shots off Target	7	5
Hit Woodwork	0	0
Possession %	54	46
Corners	3	13
Offsides	6	3
Fouls	5	10
Disciplinary Points	4	0

0-1

Stoke City
Reading

Championship

22.10.05

Dave Kitson returns with a bang for Reading

Event Line
17 Makin
35 Little
Half time 0-0
46 Sidibe > Chadwick
46 Sweeney > Kolar
53 Sidwell > Makin
69 Hoefkens
73 Oster > Little
76 Buxton
77 Kitson / LF / P / IA Assist: Kitson
87 Wilkinson > Taggart
90 Bangoura
90 Hunt > Convey
Full time 0-1

Dave Kitson marked his return to the starting line-up after injury with a crucial penalty that earned the high-flying Royals three more points at Stoke City's Britannia Stadium.

Ex-Potters midfielder Brynjar Gunnarsson came desperately close to giving his new side the lead on three occasions in the first half. A 20 yard drive whistled just wide of one post, before the Icelander volleyed Bobby Convey's corner wide of the other upright and agonisingly sliced Glen Little's cut back over the crossbar before the half was up.

Home goalkeeper Steve Simonsen had to act quickly to prevent Bobby Convey's curling set piece from dipping underneath his bar after the break, and the Royals had to wait until the 76th minute to break the deadlock.

Convey danced between City defenders to thread an accurate pass through to Kitson, who was tripped by Lewis Buxton as he prepared to pull the trigger. After dusting himself down, Kitson fired the spot kick home to open up a six point gap on third-placed Luton.

Quote

Steve Coppell

In the second half they had a go at us and we had to defend a little harder, but it also meant that we had more space to play into.

Championship Milestone

50

Glen Little made his 50th appearance in the Championship.

Venue:	Britannia Stadium	Referee:	G.Salisbury - 05/06
Attendance:	13,484	Matches:	11
Capacity:	28,218	Yellow Cards:	26
Occupancy:	48%	Red Cards:	2

Stoke City
Reading

Form Coming into Fixture

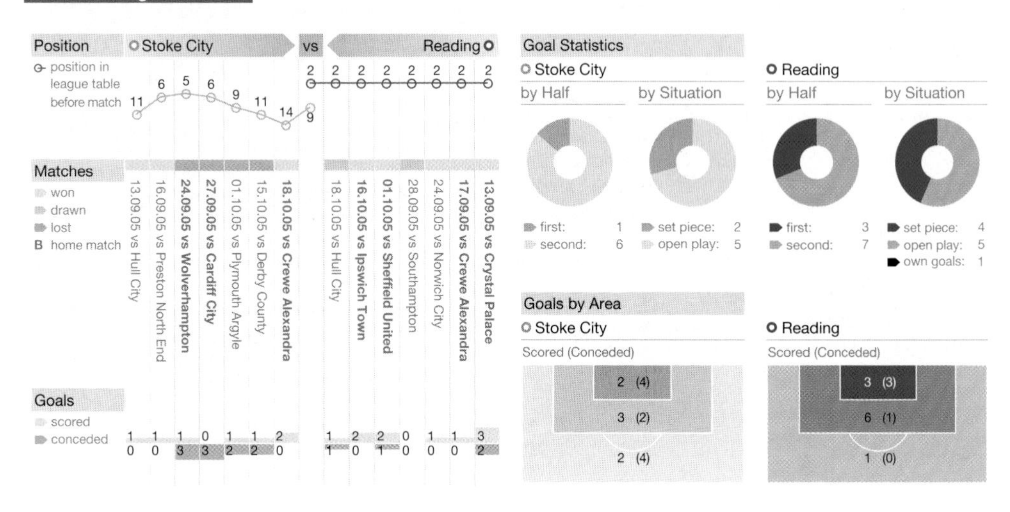

Position
Stoke City
vs
Reading
position in league table before match
11 6 5 6 9 11 14 9
2 2 2 2 2 2 2 2
Matches
won
drawn
lost
B home match
13.09.05 vs Hull City
16.09.05 vs Preston North End
24.09.05 vs Wolverhampton
27.09.05 vs Cardiff City
01.10.05 vs Plymouth Argyle
15.10.05 vs Derby County
18.10.05 vs Crewe Alexandra
18.10.05 vs Hull City
16.10.05 vs Ipswich Town
01.10.05 vs Sheffield United
28.09.05 vs Southampton
24.09.05 vs Norwich City
17.09.05 vs Crewe Alexandra
13.09.05 vs Crystal Palace
Goals
scored
conceded
1 1 1 0 1 1 2
0 0 3 3 2 2 0
1 2 2 0 1 1 3
1 0 1 0 0 0 2
Goal Statistics
Stoke City
by Half
by Situation
first: 1
second: 6
set piece: 2
open play: 5
Reading
by Half
by Situation
first: 3
second: 7
set piece: 4
open play: 5
own goals: 1
Goals by Area
Stoke City
Scored (Conceded)
2 (4)
3 (2)
2 (4)
Reading
Scored (Conceded)
3 (3)
6 (1)
1 (0)

Team Statistics

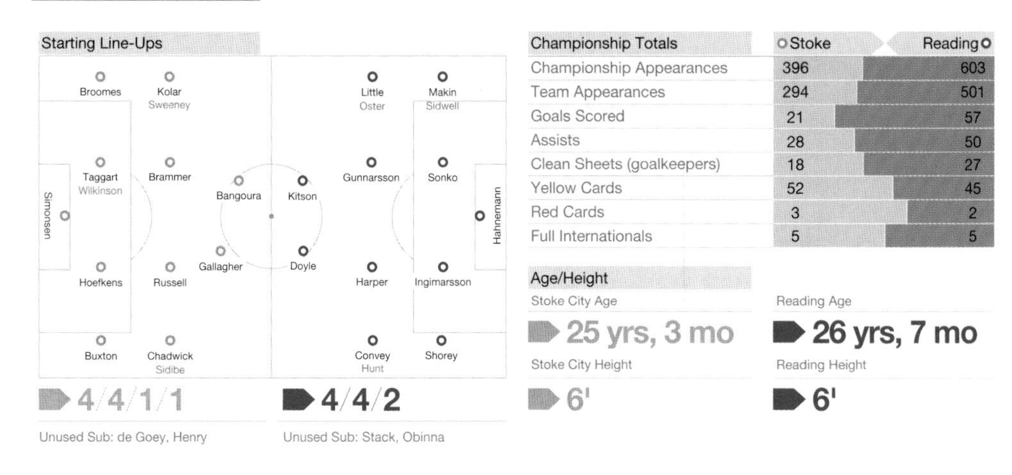

Starting Line-Ups
Broomes
Kolar
Sweeney
Taggart
Wilkinson
Brammer
Simonsen
Bangoura
Kitson
Hoefkens
Russell
Gallagher
Doyle
Buxton
Chadwick
Sidibe
Little
Oster
Makin
Sidwell
Gunnarsson
Sonko
Hahnemann
Harper
Ingimarsson
Convey
Hunt
Shorey
4/4/1/1
4/4/2
Unused Sub: de Goey, Henry
Unused Sub: Stack, Obinna
Age/Height
Stoke City Age
25 yrs, 3 mo
Reading Age
26 yrs, 7 mo
Stoke City Height
6'
Reading Height
6'

Championship Totals	Stoke	Reading
Championship Appearances	396	603
Team Appearances	294	501
Goals Scored	21	57
Assists	28	50
Clean Sheets (goalkeepers)	18	27
Yellow Cards	52	45
Red Cards	3	2
Full Internationals	5	5

Match Statistics

League Table after Fixture

		Played	Won	Drawn	Lost	For	Against	Pts
● 1	Sheff Utd	15	12	1	2	31	13	37
● 2	Reading	15	10	4	1	25	8	34
● 3	Luton	15	8	4	3	25	17	28
● 4	Leeds	14	7	4	3	18	13	25
● 5	Crystal Palace	14	7	2	5	22	13	23
↑ 6	Watford	15	6	5	4	23	18	23
↑ 7	Cardiff	14	6	4	4	25	18	22
...		...	...	...	...	...	...	...
↓ 11	Stoke	15	6	1	8	15	22	19

Statistics	Stoke	Reading
Goals	0	1
Shots on Target	5	8
Shots off Target	2	9
Hit Woodwork	0	0
Possession %	49	51
Corners	5	6
Offsides	5	2
Fouls	14	9
Disciplinary Points	12	8

2-0

Reading ○
Sheffield United ○

Carling Cup

25.10.05

ROSS
a.c.beck

Steve Sidwell gets a foot to the ball

Event Line

Half time 0-0
54 ○ ⚽ Kitson / LF / IFK / IA
Assist: Ingimarsson
58 ○ ⇄ Law > Marrison
67 ○ ▪ Kitson
75 ○ ⚽ Kitson / LF / OP / 6Y
Assist: Obinna
78 ○ ⇄ Cox > Kitson
81 ○ ⇄ Nix > Webber
82 ○ ⇄ Horwood > Francis
85 ○ ⇄ Little > Hunt
Full time 2-0

As was becoming customary for cup competitions, Steve Coppell made seven changes from his league line-up when Sheffield United visited Madejski Stadium for the second time in October. Blades boss Neil Warnock also used 'squad rotation', even going so far as to suggest to his own supporters that they should stay at home rather than making the trip south!

Reading dominated proceedings from the opening whistle, and after ten minutes lively Nigerian striker Eric Obinna showed good trickery to create an opportunity for himself but shot straight at visiting keeper Phil Barnes. Steve Sidwell then had a decent penalty appeal waved away as the Royals continued to press, but the remainder of the opening period offered little goalmouth action.

The second half got underway with Jonathan Forte creating danger with an impressive run into the Reading penalty area, but after 54 minutes the home side took the lead as Stephen Hunt's excellent left-wing cross was flicked on by Sidwell and the lurking Dave Kitson impressively swept home on the half-volley.

Hunt then crossed for Obinna to head narrowly wide and Kitson touched just past the post from Ivar Ingimarsson's delivery as Steve Coppell's side threatened to put the game beyond the visitors.

The Blades had rarely threatened Graham Stack's goal, but did go close when substitute Nicky Law latched onto Danny Webber's flick-on and found space inside the penalty area, but blazed his shot well wide from 12 yards.

Venue:	Madejski Stadium	Referee:	R.Styles - 05/06
Attendance:	11,607	Matches:	11
Capacity:	24,200	Yellow Cards:	33
Occupancy:	48%	Red Cards:	2

Reading
Sheffield United

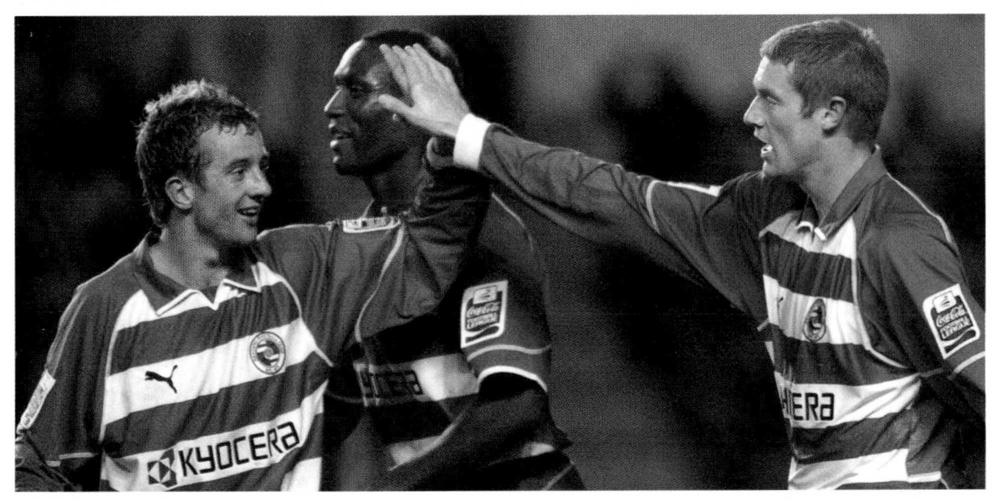

KYOCERA

High Fives for double goalscorer Kitson

Match Statistics

Starting Line-Ups

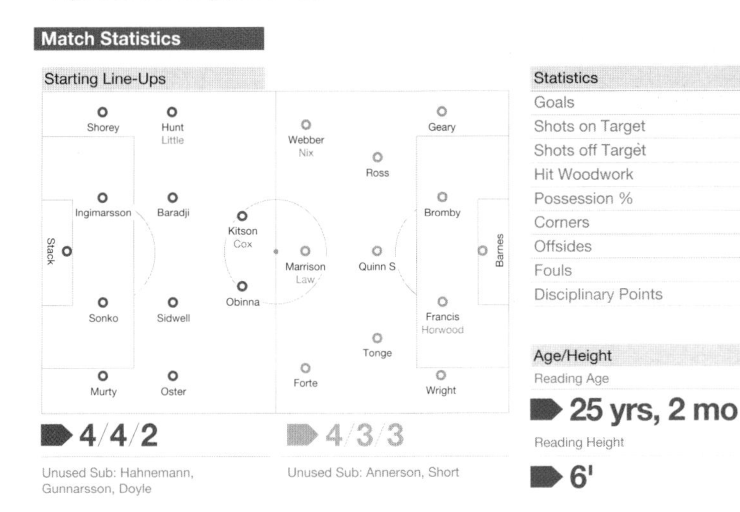

Shorey
Hunt
Little
Ingimarsson
Baradji
Stack
Kitson
Cox
Obinna
Sonko
Sidwell
Murty
Oster
Webber
Nix
Ross
Geary
Marrison
Law
Quinn S
Bromby
Barnes
Francis
Horwood
Tonge
Forte
Wright

4/4/2

Unused Sub: Hahnemann, Gunnarsson, Doyle

4/3/3

Unused Sub: Annerson, Short

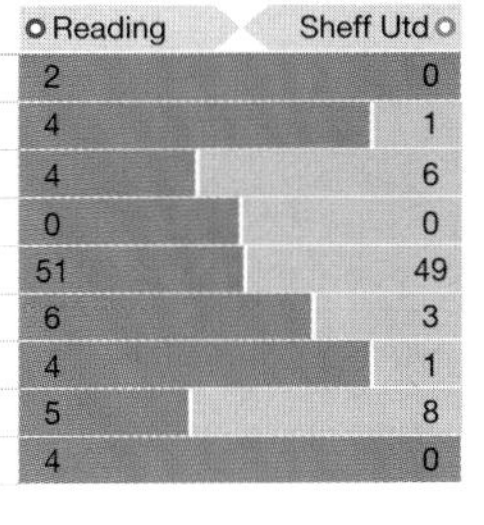

Statistics	Reading	Sheff Utd
Goals	2	0
Shots on Target	4	1
Shots off Target	4	6
Hit Woodwork	0	0
Possession %	51	49
Corners	6	3
Offsides	4	1
Fouls	5	8
Disciplinary Points	4	0

Age/Height

Reading Age

25 yrs, 2 mo

Sheffield United Age

22 yrs, 10 mo

Reading Height

6'

Sheffield United Height

5'10"

Warnock's men were left to rue that miss with 74 minutes played, when Hunt was again the creator as Kitson doubled his tally. Obinna did well to nod the Irish winger's delivery back into the middle where the unmarked marksman stretched and prodded an instinctive close range second past Barnes.

United finally mustered a meaningful shot on target with Stephen Quinn's 88th minute drive, but former Arsenal keeper Stack saved with comfort.

The home victory set up a mouth-watering Fourth Round tie with Premiership giants Arsenal in the last 16 of the competition, and also made club history by equalling Reading Football Club's best ever unbeaten run in all competitions, matching a 17-game streak that had been racked up in 1973.

Quote

Steve Coppell

Physically, the extra matches are not taking much out of us at the moment.

1-1 Reading Leeds United

Championship

29.10.05

Kevin Doyle fires agonisingly wide

Event Line
Half time 0-0
63 Gunnarsson / RF / C / IA Assist: Convey
65 Butler
66 Healy > Blake
68 Moore > Richardson
75 Healy / RF / OP / IA
82 Gunnarsson
84 Sidwell > Gunnarsson
87 Hunt > Convey
90 Pugh > Lewis
Full time 1-1

Despite a superb performance in the opening hour, the Royals had to settle for a point against Leeds to set a new club record unbeaten run by recording an 18th consecutive match without defeat.

The first half ended with honours even, but just after the hour Brynjar Gunnarsson put Reading into the lead. Collecting Bobby Convey's cross, the midfield maestro took a touch onto his right foot and drove low inside Neil Sullivan's right upright.

After falling behind, the introduction of substitute David Healy seemed to spark United into life and minutes after taking to the field Healy found Jonathan Douglas, who squandered a great chance by firing wide.

It took an uncharacteristic error from Ivar Ingimarsson to allow Kevin Blackwell's side a route back. Our Iceland international cleared blindly to Healy's feet before unluckily deflecting the Northern Irishman's strike past Marcus Hahnemann.

Dave Kitson forced Sullivan into an astonishing last minute save low at his near post, ensuring that the points were shared.

Quote

Steve Coppell

That was a tough test for us, particularly to discover whether we could reproduce our first half form in the second half.

Venue:	Madejski Stadium	Referee:	P.J.Joslin - 05/06	**Reading**
Attendance:	22,012	Matches:	13	**Leeds United**
Capacity:	24,200	Yellow Cards:	42	
Occupancy:	91%	Red Cards:	2	

Form Coming into Fixture

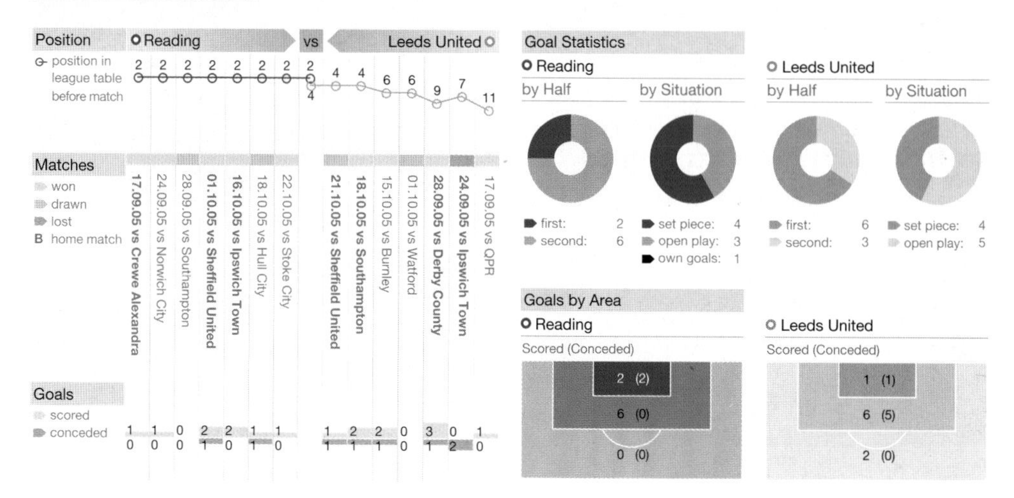

Position
Reading
vs
Leeds United
position in league table before match
2 2 2 2 2 2 2 2
4 4 4 6 6 9 7 11
Matches
won
drawn
lost
B home match
17.09.05 vs Crewe Alexandra
24.09.05 vs Norwich City
28.09.05 vs Southampton
01.10.05 vs Sheffield United
16.10.05 vs Ipswich Town
18.10.05 vs Hull City
22.10.05 vs Stoke City
21.10.05 vs Sheffield United
18.10.05 vs Southampton
15.10.05 vs Burnley
01.10.05 vs Watford
28.09.05 vs Derby County
24.09.05 vs Ipswich Town
17.09.05 vs QPR
Goals
scored
conceded
1 1 0 2 2 1 1
0 0 0 1 0 1 0
1 2 2 0 3 0 1
1 1 1 0 1 2 0
Goal Statistics
Reading
by Half
by Situation
first: 2
second: 6
set piece: 4
open play: 3
own goals: 1
Leeds United
by Half
by Situation
first: 6
second: 3
set piece: 4
open play: 5
Goals by Area
Reading
Scored (Conceded)
2 (2)
6 (0)
0 (0)
Leeds United
Scored (Conceded)
1 (1)
6 (5)
2 (0)

Team Statistics

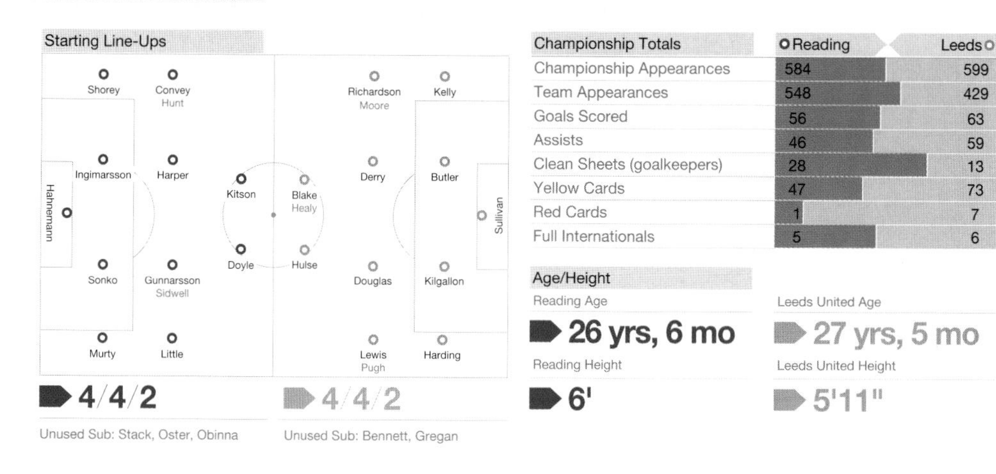

Starting Line-Ups
Shorey
Convey
Hunt
Ingimarsson
Harper
Hahnemann
Kitson
Blake
Healy
Sonko
Gunnarsson
Sidwell
Doyle
Hulse
Murty
Little
Richardson
Moore
Kelly
Derry
Butler
Sullivan
Douglas
Kilgallon
Lewis
Pugh
Harding
4/4/2
4/4/2
Unused Sub: Stack, Oster, Obinna
Unused Sub: Bennett, Gregan
Championship Totals
Reading
Leeds
Championship Appearances 584 599
Team Appearances 548 429
Goals Scored 56 63
Assists 46 59
Clean Sheets (goalkeepers) 28 13
Yellow Cards 47 73
Red Cards 1 7
Full Internationals 5 6
Age/Height
Reading Age
26 yrs, 6 mo
Leeds United Age
27 yrs, 5 mo
Reading Height
6'
Leeds United Height
5'11"

Match Statistics

League Table after Fixture

		Played	Won	Drawn	Lost	For	Against	Pts
● 1	Sheff Utd	16	12	2	2	31	13	38
● 2	Reading	16	10	5	1	26	9	35
● 3	Luton	16	8	4	4	25	18	28
↑ 4	Watford	16	7	5	4	26	19	26
↓ 5	Leeds	15	7	5	3	19	14	26
↓ 6	Crystal Palace	15	7	3	5	24	15	24
↑ 7	Southampton	16	5	9	2	19	13	24
↑ 8	QPR	16	6	6	4	18	18	24
↓ 9	Cardiff	15	6	5	4	25	18	23

Statistics	Reading	Leeds
Goals	1	1
Shots on Target	7	6
Shots off Target	10	7
Hit Woodwork	0	0
Possession %	49	51
Corners	5	4
Offsides	1	2
Fouls	8	11
Disciplinary Points	4	4

2-0

Reading
Sheffield Wednesday

Championship

01.11.05

KYOCE

Dave Kitson keeps a close eye on the ball

Event Line

38 Whelan / LF / OG / IA
Assist: Doyle

Half time 1-0

63 Eagles > Partridge

64 Kitson / RF / OP / IA
Assist: Little

71 Peacock

72 Hunt > Convey

81 O'Brien > Peacock

81 Oster > Little

89 Graham > Hills

Full time 2-0

Sheffield mourned as three more points and a twelfth clean sheet saw Reading defeat Wednesday and keep up the race with United for top spot.

The opener came directly after an impressive smothering save from Marcus Hahnemann at the feet of Richie Partridge. The keeper immediately launched a counter attack via Kevin Doyle, who sped down the left before squaring. Glenn Whelan intercepted ahead of Dave Kitson but the ball sliced off the Owls skipper's right leg and beat David Lucas to gift the Royals an opener.

Into the second half, uproar ensued when Kevin Doyle was only given a free kick after being brought down by Graeme Lee yards inside the box, but the lead was soon doubled. A rampant Glen Little beat numerous tackles to successfully pick out Kitson, who drove low under Lucas for a 64th minute second.

Bobby Convey hit the post, Kitson and Steve Sidwell were deprived by desperate defending and Lucas stopped Doyle adding to the scoreline, while Chris Brunt came closest for Wednesday.

Quote

Steve Coppell

Credit to them, they came to have a go and the game was a lot more open than we have had recently.

Venue:	Madejski Stadium
Attendance:	16,188
Capacity:	24,200
Occupancy:	67%

Referee:	M.Thorpe - 05/06
Matches:	12
Yellow Cards:	27
Red Cards:	1

Reading
Sheffield Wednesday

Form Coming into Fixture

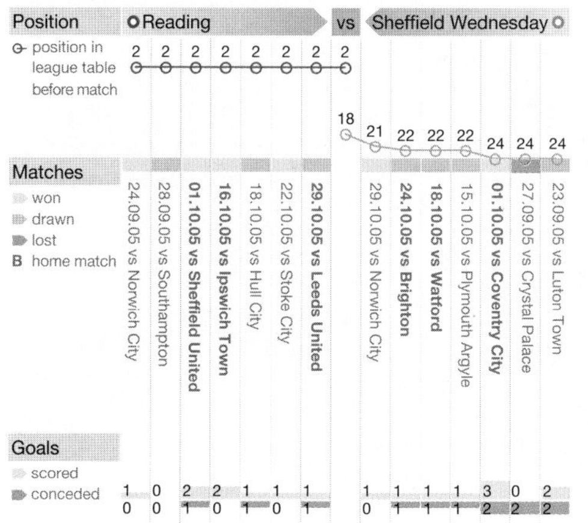

Position
Reading
vs
Sheffield Wednesday
position in league table before match
2 2 2 2 2 2 2 2
18 21 22 22 22 24 24 24
Matches
won
drawn
lost
B home match
24.09.05 vs Norwich City
28.09.05 vs Southampton
01.10.05 vs Sheffield United
16.10.05 vs Ipswich Town
18.10.05 vs Hull City
22.10.05 vs Stoke City
29.10.05 vs Leeds United
29.10.05 vs Norwich City
24.10.05 vs Brighton
18.10.05 vs Watford
15.10.05 vs Plymouth Argyle
01.10.05 vs Coventry City
27.09.05 vs Crystal Palace
23.09.05 vs Luton Town
Goals
scored
conceded

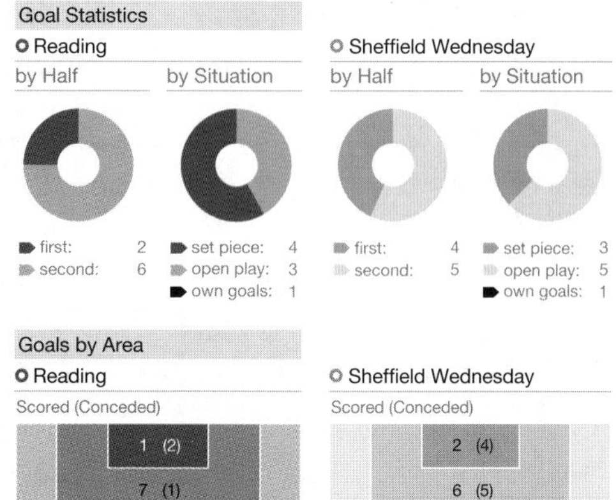

Goal Statistics
Reading
by Half
by Situation
Sheffield Wednesday
by Half
by Situation

Reading			
first:	2	set piece:	4
second:	6	open play:	3
		own goals:	1

Sheffield Wednesday			
first:	4	set piece:	3
second:	5	open play:	5
		own goals:	1

Goals by Area

Reading — Scored (Conceded): 1 (2); 7 (1); 0 (0)

Sheffield Wednesday — Scored (Conceded): 2 (4); 6 (5); 1 (0)

Team Statistics

Starting Line-Ups

Shorey
Convey
Hunt
Partridge
Eagles
Simek
Ingimarsson
Sidwell
Doyle
Agbonlahor
Whelan
Lee
Hahnemann
Lucas
Kitson
Peacock
O'Brien
Sonko
Harper
Rocastle
Wood
Murty
Little
Oster
Brunt
Hills
Graham

4/4/2

Unused Sub: Stack, Osano, Obinna

4/4/2

Unused Sub: Bullen, Heckingbottom

Championship Totals	Reading	Sheff Wed
Championship Appearances	592	246
Team Appearances	560	173
Goals Scored	53	11
Assists	48	19
Clean Sheets (goalkeepers)	28	4
Yellow Cards	41	26
Red Cards	0	1
Full Internationals	5	1

Age/Height

Reading Age
26 yrs, 3 mo

Sheffield Wednesday Age
24 yrs

Reading Height
5'11"

Sheffield Wednesday Height
6'

Match Statistics

League Table after Fixture

		Played	Won	Drawn	Lost	For	Against	Pts
● 1	Sheff Utd	17	13	2	2	35	13	41
● 2	Reading	17	11	5	1	28	9	38
↑ 3	Watford	17	8	5	4	29	20	29
↓ 4	Luton	17	8	4	5	25	22	28
● 5	Leeds	16	7	5	4	19	15	26
● 6	Crystal Palace	15	7	3	5	24	15	24
● 7	Southampton	16	5	9	2	19	13	24
...		...	...	...	...	...	...	...
↓ 21	Sheff Wed	16	3	7	6	13	19	16

Statistics	Reading	Sheff Wed
Goals	2	0
Shots on Target	3	2
Shots off Target	6	0
Hit Woodwork	0	0
Possession %	54	46
Corners	6	2
Offsides	6	5
Fouls	6	10
Disciplinary Points	0	4

1-2 Queens Park Rangers ○ Reading ○

Championship

05.11.05

➡ Kevin Doyle applauds the travelling fans

Event Line	
10 ○ ⚽	Harper / LF / OP / IA
	Assist: Kitson
28 ○ ▪	Gallen
44 ○ ⇄	Ainsworth > Sturridge
Half time 0-1	
47 ○ ⚽	Cook / LF / OP / OA
57 ○ ▪	Little
63 ○ ⇄	Oster > Little
66 ○ ⚽	Ingimarsson / H / C / IA
	Assist: Oster
71 ○ ⇄	Hunt > Convey
84 ○ ▪	Kitson
Full time 1-2	

Taking their unbeaten record to 20 consecutive games, the second placed Royals extended the gap over third spot with a determined 2-1 win at QPR.

Kevin Doyle's pace almost stunned Loftus Road in the opening seconds, but home keeper Simon Royce smartly narrowed the angle to prevent the Irish striker scoring a first minute opener.

But it wasn't long before James Harper pounced on Dave Kitson's bright flick to thunder the Royals into the lead with another well-taken left-footed drive. As the game progressed Rangers began to impart a threat and early in the second half Lee Cook fizzed a leveller brushing past Marcus Hahnemann's fingertips and in off the far post.

But Steve Coppell's men rose to the challenge and Ivar Ingimarsson supplied the match winner, forcefully heading John Oster's outswinging corner through Royce's attempted parry and high into net. Dave Kitson picked up his fifth booking of the season and a one-match suspension, but the Royals went into a two-week break in winning style.

Quote

Steve Coppell

It was hard work, but the characteristic of a good team is one that does not play well and still wins.

Venue:	Loftus Road
Attendance:	15,347
Capacity:	18,500
Occupancy:	83%

Referee:	A.R.Leake - 05/06
Matches:	14
Yellow Cards:	36
Red Cards:	2

Queens Park Rangers
Reading

Form Coming into Fixture

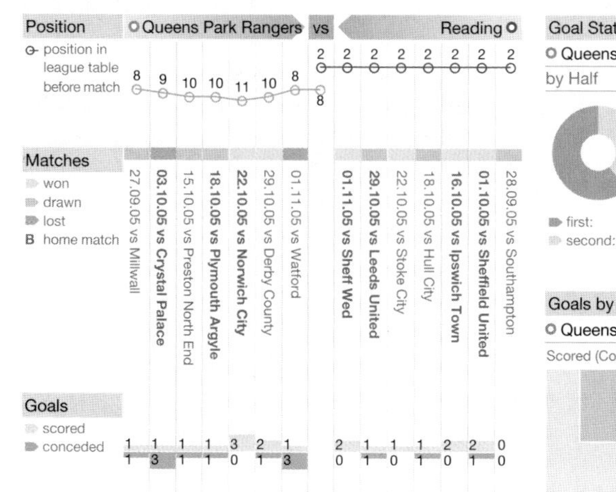

Position
Queens Park Rangers
vs
Reading
position in league table before match
8 9 10 10 11 10 8
8
2 2 2 2 2 2 2 2
Matches
won
drawn
lost
B home match
27.09.05 vs Millwall
03.10.05 vs Crystal Palace
15.10.05 vs Preston North End
18.10.05 vs Plymouth Argyle
22.10.05 vs Norwich City
29.10.05 vs Derby County
01.11.05 vs Watford
01.11.05 vs Sheff Wed
29.10.05 vs Leeds United
22.10.05 vs Stoke City
18.10.05 vs Hull City
16.10.05 vs Ipswich Town
01.10.05 vs Sheffield United
28.09.05 vs Southampton
Goals
scored
conceded
1 1 1 1 3 2 1
1 3 1 1 0 1 3
2 1 1 1 2 2 0
0 1 0 1 0 1 0

Goal Statistics

Queens Park Rangers

by Half / by Situation

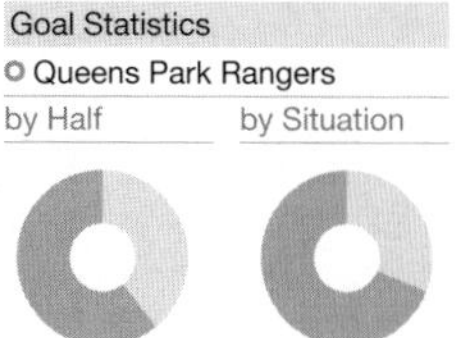
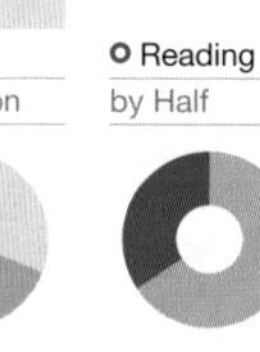

by Half		by Situation	
first:	6	set piece:	7
second:	4	open play:	3

Reading

by Half / by Situation

by Half		by Situation	
first:	3	set piece:	4
second:	6	open play:	3
		own goals:	2

Goals by Area

Queens Park Rangers

Scored (Conceded)

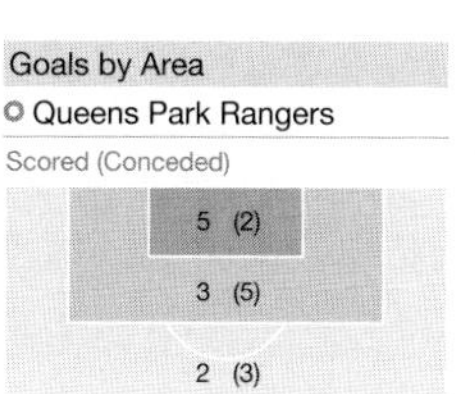

5 (2)
3 (5)
2 (3)

Reading

Scored (Conceded)

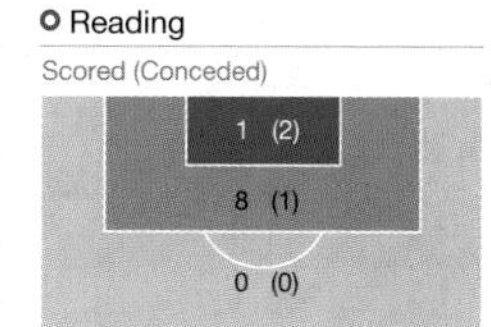

1 (2)
8 (1)
0 (0)

Team Statistics

Starting Line-Ups

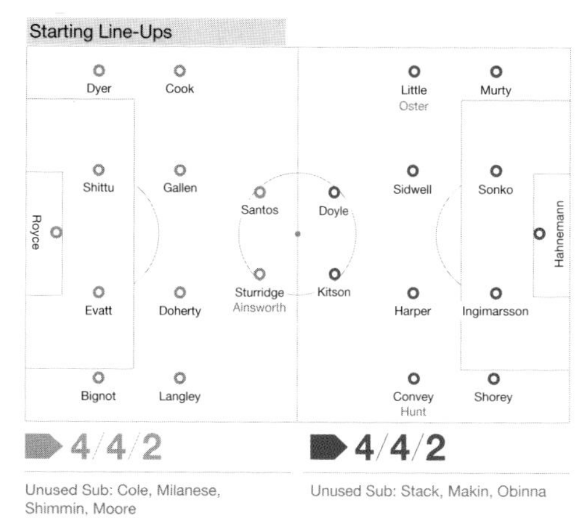

Dyer
Cook
Shittu
Gallen
Royce
Santos
Doyle
Evatt
Doherty
Sturridge
Ainsworth
Kitson
Bignot
Langley
Little
Oster
Murty
Sidwell
Sonko
Hahnemann
Harper
Ingimarsson
Convey
Hunt
Shorey
4/4/2
4/4/2

Unused Sub: Cole, Milanese, Shimmin, Moore

Unused Sub: Stack, Makin, Obinna

Championship Totals

Championship Totals	QPR	Reading
Championship Appearances	435	605
Team Appearances	393	573
Goals Scored	37	54
Assists	48	50
Clean Sheets (goalkeepers)	10	29
Yellow Cards	54	41
Red Cards	3	0
Full Internationals	4	5

Age/Height

Queens Park Rangers Age

28 yrs, 8 mo

Reading Age

26 yrs, 3 mo

Queens Park Rangers Height

5'11"

Reading Height

5'11"

Match Statistics

League Table after Fixture

		Played	Won	Drawn	Lost	For	Against	Pts
● 1	Sheff Utd	18	14	2	2	38	15	44
● 2	Reading	18	12	5	1	30	10	41
● 3	Watford	18	9	5	4	31	21	32
● 4	Luton	18	8	4	6	27	25	28
● 5	Leeds	17	7	6	4	19	15	27
↑ 6	Southampton	17	5	10	2	19	13	25
↑ 7	Wolverhampton	18	6	7	5	23	18	25
...		...	...	...	...	...	...	...
↓ 11	QPR	18	6	6	6	20	23	24

Statistics

Statistics	QPR	Reading
Goals	1	2
Shots on Target	2	3
Shots off Target	9	2
Hit Woodwork	0	0
Possession %	52	48
Corners	3	6
Offsides	1	4
Fouls	10	10
Disciplinary Points	4	8

3-1

Reading
Hull City

Championship

19.11.05

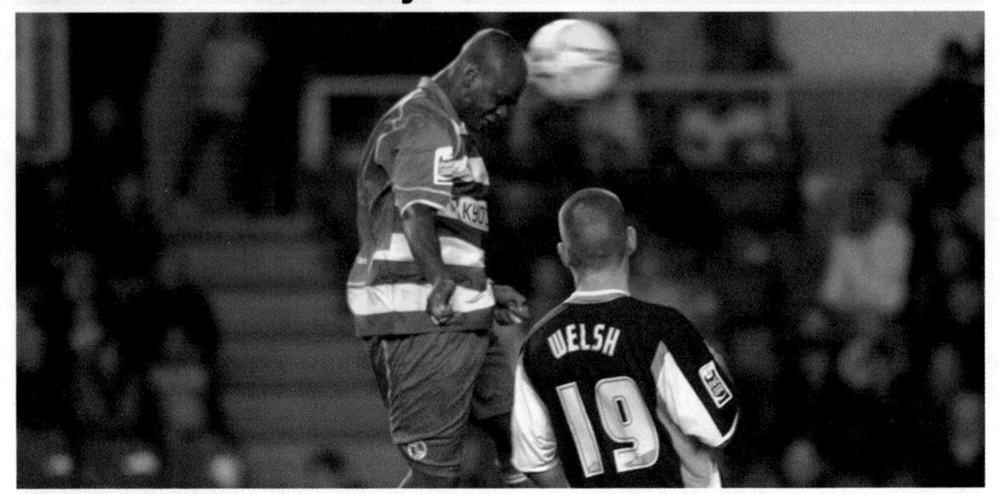
WELSH
19

Leroy Lita makes good aerial contact

Event Line	
7	Convey / LF / OP / IA Assist: Doyle
Half time 1-0	
55	Barmby / H / OP / 6Y Assist: Burgess
69	Doyle / RF / OP / IA Assist: Little
70	Little / RF / OP / IA Assist: Convey
72	Fagan
73	Fry > Elliott
76	Hunt > Convey
76	Oster > Little
77	Ellison > Barmby
77	Paynter > Burgess
84	Obinna > Doyle
Full time 3-1	

The Royals and the Tigers met for the second time in just over a month, with the home side ending up with a comprehensive 3-1 scoreline, even if the result at times looked in the balance.

Bobby Convey was instrumental throughout and calmly stroked home the opener with just seven minutes on the clock after Kevin Doyle had neatly slotted the American winger in.

Peter Taylor's side almost restored parity before the break when Marcus Hahnemann had to tidily save from Leon Cort, and soon after Nick Barmby's headed effort grazed the outside of the right post.

Former England man Barmby made no mistake with his head ten minutes after the interval to snaffle the equaliser, but two goals in a minute quelled City's challenge. Doyle effortlessly hooked an impressive high volley in off the underside of the crossbar from 15 yards, and immediately after the restart Glen Little demonstrated quick feet to deftly steer Convey's precise pass past Boaz Myhill for the third. Kingsley was mobbed by the arm-wheeling Little and the points were safely in the bag.

Quote

Steve Coppell

We looked good going forward but there were moments when we were vulnerable. After they scored there was a five or ten-minute period when we got anxious.

Venue: Madejski Stadium
Attendance: 17,864
Capacity: 24,200
Occupancy: 74%

Referee: C.Penton - 05/06
Matches: 15
Yellow Cards: 50
Red Cards: 3

Reading
Hull City

Form Coming into Fixture

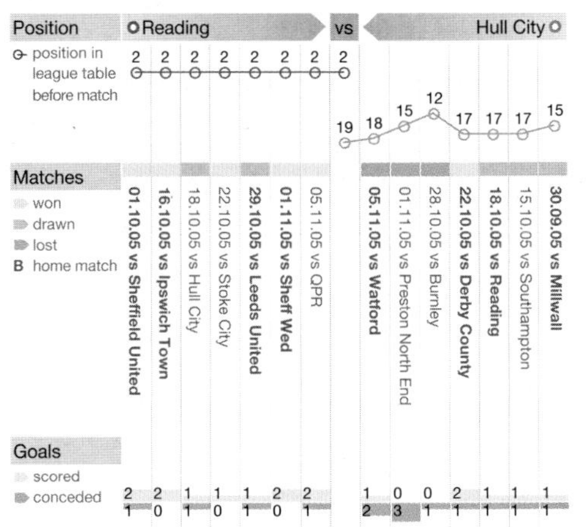

Position
Reading
vs
Hull City
position in league table before match
2 2 2 2 2 2 2 2
19 18 15 12 17 17 17 15
Matches
won
drawn
lost
B home match
01.10.05 vs Sheffield United
16.10.05 vs Ipswich Town
18.10.05 vs Hull City
22.10.05 vs Stoke City
29.10.05 vs Leeds United
01.11.05 vs Sheff Wed
05.11.05 vs QPR
05.11.05 vs Watford
01.11.05 vs Preston North End
28.10.05 vs Burnley
22.10.05 vs Derby County
18.10.05 vs Reading
15.10.05 vs Southampton
30.09.05 vs Millwall
Goals
scored
conceded
2 2 1 1 1 2 2
1 0 1 0 1 0 1
1 0 0 2 1 1 1
2 3 1 1 1 1 1

Goal Statistics
Reading
by Half
by Situation
first: 4
second: 7
set piece: 5
open play: 4
own goals: 2
Hull City
by Half
by Situation
first: 2
second: 4
set piece: 2
open play: 4
Goals by Area
Reading
Scored (Conceded)
1 (2)
10 (1)
0 (1)
Hull City
Scored (Conceded)
1 (1)
5 (6)
0 (3)

Team Statistics

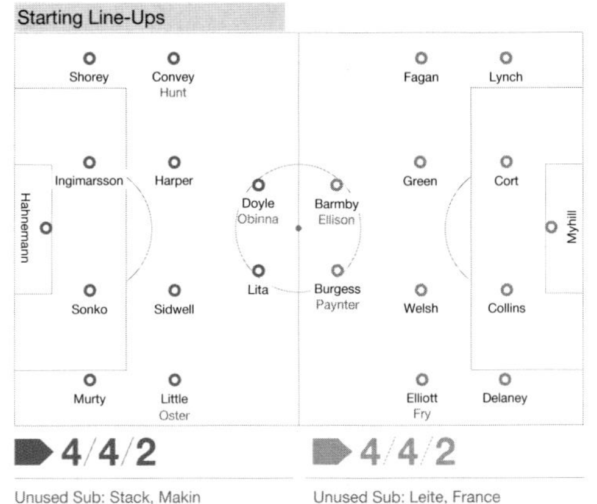

Starting Line-Ups
Shorey
Convey
Hunt
Ingimarsson
Harper
Hahnemann
Sonko
Sidwell
Murty
Little
Oster
Doyle
Obinna
Barmby
Ellison
Lita
Burgess
Paynter
Fagan
Lynch
Green
Cort
Myhill
Welsh
Collins
Elliott
Fry
Delaney
4/4/2
4/4/2

Unused Sub: Stack, Makin

Unused Sub: Leite, France

Championship Totals	Reading	Hull
Championship Appearances	588	166
Team Appearances	556	155
Goals Scored	38	12
Assists	46	6
Clean Sheets (goalkeepers)	29	4
Yellow Cards	38	11
Red Cards	0	1
Full Internationals	5	2

Age/Height

Reading Age

25 yrs, 10 mo

Hull City Age

24 yrs, 9 mo

Reading Height

5'11"

Hull City Height

6'

Match Statistics

League Table after Fixture

		Played	Won	Drawn	Lost	For	Against	Pts
●	1 Sheff Utd	19	14	3	2	40	17	45
●	2 Reading	19	13	5	1	33	11	44
●	3 Watford	19	10	5	4	33	22	35
↑	4 Leeds	18	8	6	4	23	18	30
↓	5 Wolverhampton	19	7	7	5	26	18	28
↑	6 Burnley	19	8	4	7	27	23	28
↓	7 Luton	19	8	4	7	27	27	28
...		...	...	...	...	...	...	...
↓	22 Hull	19	4	6	9	15	22	18

Statistics	Reading	Hull
Goals	3	1
Shots on Target	10	4
Shots off Target	8	1
Hit Woodwork	0	1
Possession %	58	42
Corners	9	2
Offsides	3	6
Fouls	9	6
Disciplinary Points	0	4

0-3 Ipswich Town Reading

Championship

22.11.05

OWERGEN
ERGEN
e.on

Glen Little takes control at Portman Road

Event Line
18 Forster > Parkin
29 Sidwell / LF / OP / IA
Assist: Doyle
34 Wilnis > Horlock
Half time 0-1
53 Lita / RF / OP / IA
Assist: Doyle
60 Westlake > Juan
77 Doyle / LF / C / 6Y
Assist: Lita
78 Hunt > Convey
78 Oster > Little
Full time 0-3

Joe Royle's Town were taught a second stern lesson by another awesome Reading display at Portman Road which took the Royals top, a position they weren't willing to relinquish for the rest of the 2005/6 season.

Steve Sidwell had already forced Lewis Price into a stunning fingertip save after letting rip with a fearsome drive in the early stages, and as the home side struggled to stem the incessant tide of pressure raining in on their goal – changes of personnel and formation providing little respite for Royle's men – Sidwell finally snatched the first by stroking home Price's parry from a Kevin Doyle effort.

Doyle teed up Leroy Lita for a bulleted second half strike which whistled past Price for 2-0 and after the Town keeper had sharply prevented Fabian Wilnis from deflecting Bobby Convey's low cross into his own net, Lita returned the favour to link up with Doyle, who tapped home a close-range third. It capped off a mesmerising display that warranted the title of league leaders.

Quote

Steve Coppell

Being top means nothing to me at this stage of the season. I have said we don't want the highlight of our season to be in October or November.

Venue:	Portman Road	Referee:	P.Melin - 05/06
Attendance:	22,621	Matches:	14
Capacity:	30,300	Yellow Cards:	42
Occupancy:	75%	Red Cards:	5

Ipswich Town
Reading

Form Coming into Fixture

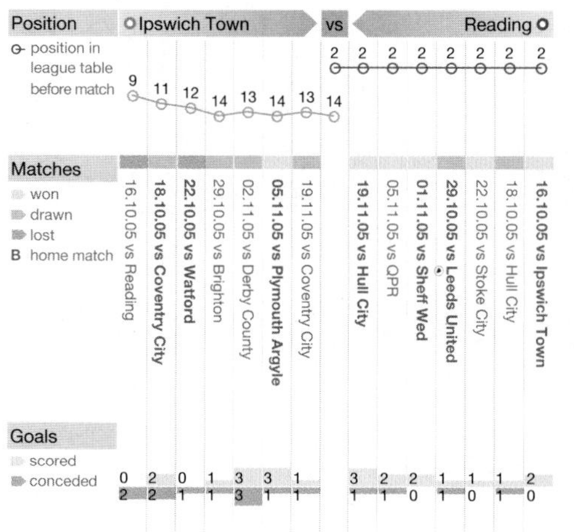

Position
Ipswich Town
vs
Reading
position in league table before match
9 11 12 14 13 14 13 14
2 2 2 2 2 2 2 2
Matches
won
drawn
lost
B home match
16.10.05 vs Reading
18.10.05 vs Coventry City
22.10.05 vs Watford
29.10.05 vs Brighton
02.11.05 vs Derby County
05.11.05 vs Plymouth Argyle
19.11.05 vs Coventry City
19.11.05 vs Hull City
05.11.05 vs QPR
01.11.05 vs Sheff Wed
29.10.05 vs Leeds United
22.10.05 vs Stoke City
18.10.05 vs Hull City
16.10.05 vs Ipswich Town
Goals
scored
conceded
0 2 0 1 3 3 1
2 2 1 1 3 1 1
3 2 2 1 1 1 2
1 1 0 1 0 1 0

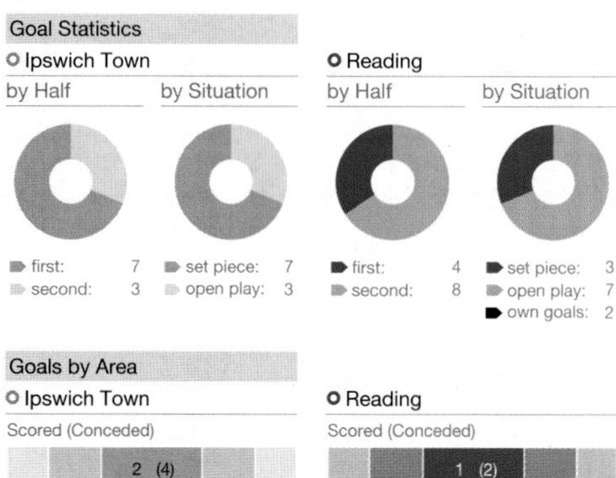

Goal Statistics
Ipswich Town
by Half
by Situation
Reading
by Half
by Situation
first: 7
second: 3
set piece: 7
open play: 3
first: 4
second: 8
set piece: 3
open play: 7
own goals: 2

Goals by Area

Ipswich Town — Scored (Conceded): 2 (4), 5 (5), 3 (2)

Reading — Scored (Conceded): 1 (2), 11 (1), 0 (1)

Team Statistics

Starting Line-Ups

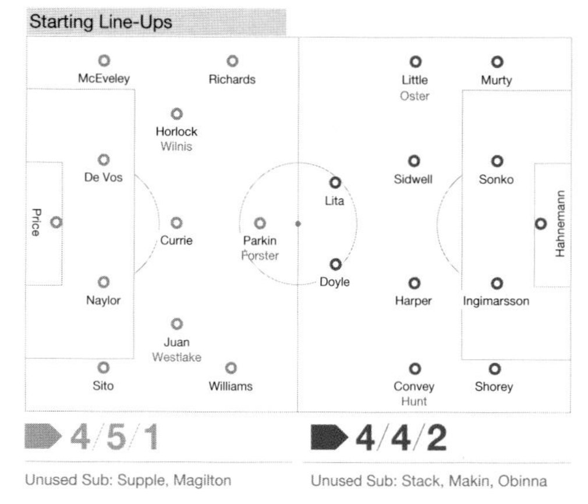

McEveley
Richards
Horlock
Wilnis
De Vos
Price
Currie
Parkin
Forster
Lita
Doyle
Naylor
Juan
Westlake
Sito
Williams
Little
Oster
Murty
Sidwell
Sonko
Hahnemann
Harper
Ingimarsson
Convey
Hunt
Shorey

4/5/1 — 4/4/2

Unused Sub: Supple, Magilton

Unused Sub: Stack, Makin, Obinna

Championship Totals	Ipswich	Reading
Championship Appearances	532	596
Team Appearances	460	564
Goals Scored	51	41
Assists	61	49
Clean Sheets (goalkeepers)	3	29
Yellow Cards	59	38
Red Cards	4	0
Full Internationals	4	5

Age/Height

Ipswich Town Age: **26 yrs, 10 mo**

Reading Age: **25 yrs, 11 mo**

Ipswich Town Height: **6'**

Reading Height: **5'11"**

Match Statistics

League Table after Fixture

		Played	Won	Drawn	Lost	For	Against	Pts
↑ 1	Reading	20	14	5	1	36	11	47
↓ 2	Sheff Utd	20	14	4	2	40	17	46
• 3	Watford	20	10	6	4	35	24	36
• 4	Leeds	19	9	6	4	25	18	33
↑ 5	Luton	20	9	4	7	31	28	31
↑ 6	Crystal Palace	18	9	3	6	31	20	30
↓ 7	Wolverhampton	20	7	8	5	26	18	29
...		...	...	...	...	...	...	...
• 14	Ipswich	20	6	6	8	22	31	24

Statistics	Ipswich	Reading
Goals	0	3
Shots on Target	1	12
Shots off Target	6	7
Hit Woodwork	0	0
Possession %	45	55
Corners	3	14
Offsides	3	5
Fouls	10	8
Disciplinary Points	0	0

0-2 Plymouth Argyle / Reading

Championship

26.11.05

HARPER

Glen Little celebrates his goal with James Harper

Event Line
20 Little / RF / OP / IA
22 Sidwell
24 Buzsaky
Half time 0-1
46 Djordjic > Buzsaky
57 Doyle / RF / OP / 6Y
Assist: Convey
58 Doyle
73 Aljofree
81 Derbyshire > Evans
82 Oster > Little
84 Hunt > Convey
90 Cox > Doyle
Full time 0-2

Wing wizard Glen Little stole the show with an exquisite chip that stunned Home Park and rivalled Leroy Lita's overhead thriller against Palace for the honour of Royals goal of the season.

A minute before Little's opener, Madejski Stadium's opening day spoilsport Nick Chadwick forced an excellent save from Marcus Hahnemann.

Then came Little's moment of magic. Latching onto a loose ball 25 yards from goal, and with three Argyle defenders in close attendance, the Royals winger found space to audaciously loft a classy chip over the surprised six foot four Romain Larrieu and inside the far post for a marvellous goal. George Best's life had been remembered with a minute's applause before the game, and many observers noted that Little's strike was a fitting tribute to the former Manchester United great.

Just before the hour, Leroy Lita's deflected strike was bobbling wide before Kevin Doyle raced in to get a decisive close range touch to add a second, and although Chadwick came close again by heading onto Hahnemann's crossbar, the unbeaten run stretched to a 23rd game with a result that rarely looked threatened.

Quote

Steve Coppell

Glen Little scored a terrific individual goal that shone out like a beacon in a scrappy first 45 minutes.

Championship Milestone

Debut

Simon Cox made his Championship debut.

Venue:	Home Park
Attendance:	14,020
Capacity:	20,922
Occupancy:	67%

Referee:	K.Wright - 05/06
Matches:	13
Yellow Cards:	49
Red Cards:	4

Plymouth Argyle
Reading

Form Coming into Fixture

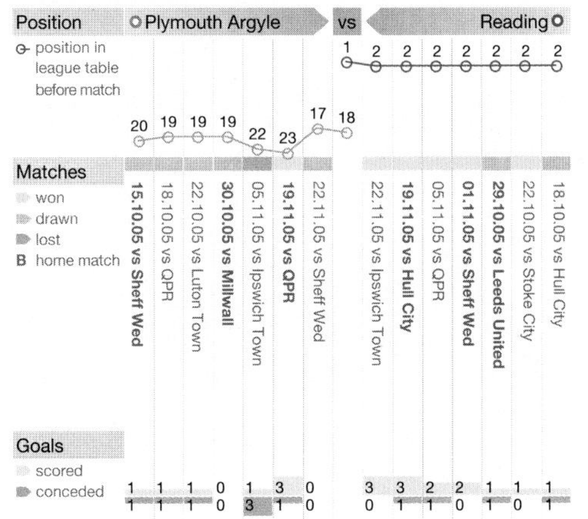

Position
Plymouth Argyle
vs
Reading
position in league table before match
20 19 19 19 22 23 17 18
1 2 2 2 2 2 2 2
Matches
won
drawn
lost
B home match
15.10.05 vs Sheff Wed
18.10.05 vs QPR
22.10.05 vs Luton Town
30.10.05 vs Millwall
05.11.05 vs Ipswich Town
19.11.05 vs QPR
22.11.05 vs Sheff Wed
22.11.05 vs Ipswich Town
19.11.05 vs Hull City
05.11.05 vs QPR
01.11.05 vs Sheff Wed
29.10.05 vs Leeds United
22.10.05 vs Stoke City
18.10.05 vs Hull City
Goals
scored
conceded
1 1 1 0 1 3 0 3 3 2 2 1 1 1
1 1 1 0 3 1 0 0 1 1 0 1 0 1

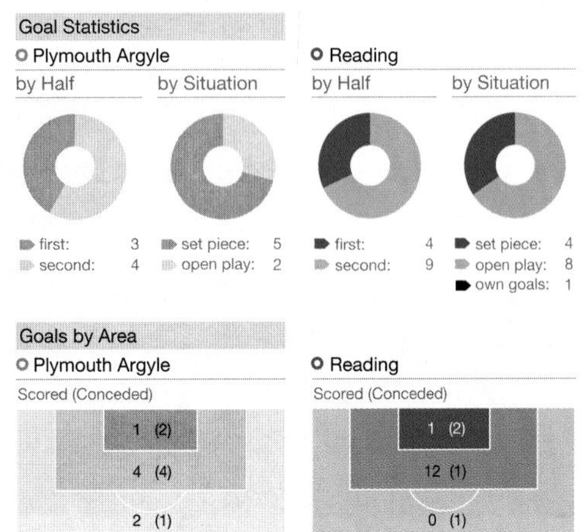

Goal Statistics
Plymouth Argyle
by Half
by Situation
first: 3
second: 4
set piece: 5
open play: 2
Reading
by Half
by Situation
first: 4
second: 9
set piece: 4
open play: 8
own goals: 1
Goals by Area
Plymouth Argyle
Scored (Conceded)
1 (2)
4 (4)
2 (1)
Reading
Scored (Conceded)
1 (2)
12 (1)
0 (1)

Team Statistics

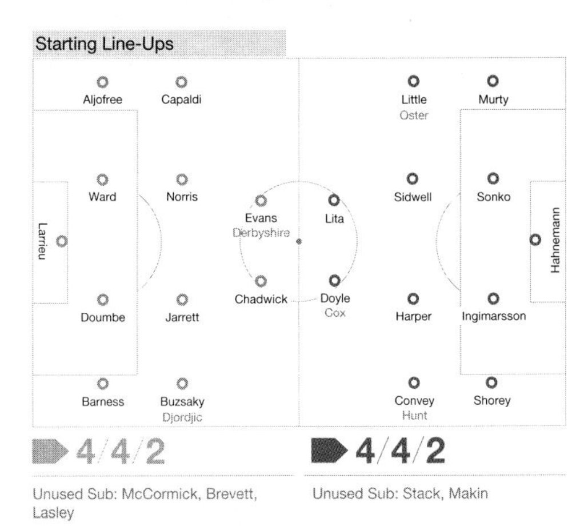

Starting Line-Ups
Aljofree
Capaldi
Ward
Norris
Larrieu
Evans
Derbyshire
Lita
Chadwick
Doyle
Cox
Doumbe
Jarrett
Barness
Buzsaky
Djordjic
Little
Oster
Murty
Sidwell
Sonko
Hahnemann
Harper
Ingimarsson
Convey
Hunt
Shorey
4/4/2
4/4/2

Unused Sub: McCormick, Brevett, Lasley

Unused Sub: Stack, Makin

Championship Totals	Plymouth	Reading
Championship Appearances	420	609
Team Appearances	385	577
Goals Scored	25	44
Assists	31	52
Clean Sheets (goalkeepers)	8	30
Yellow Cards	42	38
Red Cards	1	0
Full Internationals	3	5

Age/Height

Plymouth Argyle Age
25 yrs, 9 mo

Reading Age
25 yrs, 5 mo

Plymouth Argyle Height
5'11"

Reading Height
5'11"

Match Statistics

League Table after Fixture

	Played	Won	Drawn	Lost	For	Against	Pts
● 1 Reading	21	15	5	1	38	11	50
● 2 Sheff Utd	21	14	4	3	42	21	46
● 3 Watford	21	10	7	4	36	25	37
● 4 Leeds	20	10	6	4	26	18	36
● 5 Luton	21	10	4	7	33	28	34
↑ 6 Burnley	21	9	4	8	30	25	31
↑ 7 Stoke	21	10	1	10	25	28	31
...	...	...	...	...	...	...	...
↓ 19 Plymouth	20	4	8	8	16	25	20

Statistics	Plymouth	Reading
Goals	0	2
Shots on Target	4	6
Shots off Target	7	7
Hit Woodwork	1	0
Possession %	52	48
Corners	9	7
Offsides	2	4
Fouls	14	23
Disciplinary Points	8	8

3-0 Arsenal Reading

Carling Cup

29.11.05

KYOCERA
KYOCERA
Arsenal

Smiles all round during the pre-match formalities

Event Line
12 Reyes / LF / OP / IA
Assist: Owusu-Abeyie
42 van Persie / LF / OP / OA
Assist: Reyes
Half time 2-0
59 Makin > Shorey
63 Lupoli > van Persie
65 Lupoli / RF / OP / 6Y
72 Doyle > Lita
75 Cygan > Reyes
83 Bendtner > Owusu-Abeyie
83 Hahnemann > Stack
86 Cygan
Full time 3-0

Cup fever was rife and an unparalleled ticket rush saw Reading fans scramble for a chance to follow their team to Premiership giants Arsenal, but the Royals bid their farewell to Highbury by bowing out of the Carling Cup as Arsene Wenger's pacy youngsters out-finished the Championship league-leaders.

Half expecting the Gunners to field a seriously under strength outfit, with Premiership and Champions League matters more of an Arsenal concern, Arsene Wenger instead listed a host of first team names amongst his starting line-up. While Steve Coppell rested his two World Cup-bound stars (Marcus Hahnemann and Bobby Convey), Arsenal boasted five who were to book their summer tickets to Germany – Emmanuel Eboue (Ivory Coast), Phillippe Senderos, Johan Djourou (Switzerland), Jose Antonio Reyes (Spain) and Robin Van Persie (Holland).

And although Dave Kitson and Leroy Lita had early chances to spark an upset, the Royals hotshots found Manuel Almunia in inspired form. When Quincy Owusu-Abeyie stroked a pass through to Reyes, ex-Gunners goalkeeper Graham Stack was tidily rounded and Arsenal had the lead.

Another ex-Highbury resident James Harper was denied a dream return and an all-important equaliser by the impressive Almunia and Stephen Hunt too brought the best from the Spanish keeper as Reading searched for a reply. But before the break Van Persie doubled the home side's advantage. A speedy break characteristic of Wenger's Arsenal era was ended with a clinical finish from the Dutchman, who swept past Stack for 2-0.

Venue:	Highbury
Attendance:	36,167
Capacity:	38,419
Occupancy:	94%

Referee:	L.Mason - 05/06
Matches:	13
Yellow Cards:	38
Red Cards:	2

Arsenal
Reading

Stephen Hunt surges forward at Highbury

Match Statistics

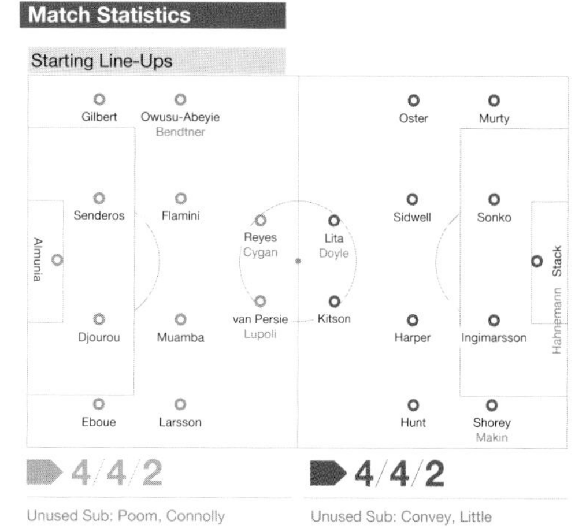

Starting Line-Ups
Gilbert
Owusu-Abeyie
Bendtner
Senderos
Flamini
Almunia
Reyes
Cygan
Lita
Doyle
van Persie
Lupoli
Kitson
Djourou
Muamba
Eboue
Larsson
Oster
Murty
Sidwell
Sonko
Stack
Hahnemann
Harper
Ingimarsson
Hunt
Shorey
Makin
4/4/2
4/4/2

Unused Sub: Poom, Connolly

Unused Sub: Convey, Little

Statistics	Arsenal	Reading
Goals	3	0
Shots on Target	6	6
Shots off Target	5	4
Hit Woodwork	0	0
Possession %	48	52
Corners	9	8
Offsides	2	3
Fouls	10	4
Disciplinary Points	4	0

Age/Height

Arsenal Age
21 yrs, 7 mo

Arsenal Height
6'

Reading Age
26 yrs, 3 mo

Reading Height
5'11"

The third ex-Arsenal youngster in Reading's side, Steve Sidwell, struck a 35-yard volley just over the bar and dragged another snapshot wide of Almunia's woodwork after the break as the undeterred Royals continued to press.

But it was Stack who had to save acrobatically from a spectacular Kerrea Gilbert strike that seemed destined to curl into the top corner and minutes later, young Italian striker Arturo Lupoli evaded Ibrahima Sonko's challenge and Stack's sprawling dive to calmly notch a third and end the Royals' resistance.

It also put a cap on the record-breaking Reading run, which entered the history books at 23 consecutive games, but despite the emphatic scoreline the Royals went home with heads held high having tasted the Highbury experience.

Quote

Steve Coppell

I wanted us to try and have a go and I wasn't overly concerned with the result.

3-0 Reading / Luton Town

Championship

03.12.05

KYOCERA
Electrolux

Dave Kitson makes it 2-0

Event Line
44 Sidwell / RF / OP / OA
Half time 1-0
62 Kitson > Lita
66 Hunt > Convey
69 Barnett > Heikkinen
73 Howard > Vine
76 Kitson / H / IFK / IA Assist: Little
83 Feeney > Morgan
88 Doyle / H / OP / IA Assist: Little
90 Oster > Little
Full time 3-0

Any questions being asked about how Steve Coppell's side would react to defeat at Arsenal were answered when Luton arrived hoping to avenge their Carling Cup exit inflicted earlier in the season.

Any doubts about Reading's character were dismissed when Steve Sidwell's confident drive from distance took a wicked deflection to deceive Marlon Beresford and open the scoring just before half time.

Marcus Hahnemann twice had to deny Dean Morgan a goalscoring return to Madejski Stadium and without the comfort of a second goal, an edgy home crowd knew the points weren't safely secured. But in the 74th minute Dave Kitson stole in ahead of the Hatters' keeper to confidently glance Glen Little's inswinging free kick over the line.

Little chalked another assist up in the dying stages, planting an excellent cross onto Kevin Doyle's head which coolly powered the ball home for a well-taken third, and the Royals were quickly back into winning ways.

Quote

M. Hahnemann

Luton are a good side and we had our hands full. I don't think the scoreline reflected the way the game went.

Championship Milestone

50

Dave Kitson made his 50th appearance in the Championship.

Venue:	Madejski Stadium	Referee:	M.J.Jones - 05/06
Attendance:	19,478	Matches:	14
Capacity:	24,200	Yellow Cards:	47
Occupancy:	80%	Red Cards:	2

Reading
Luton Town

Form Coming into Fixture

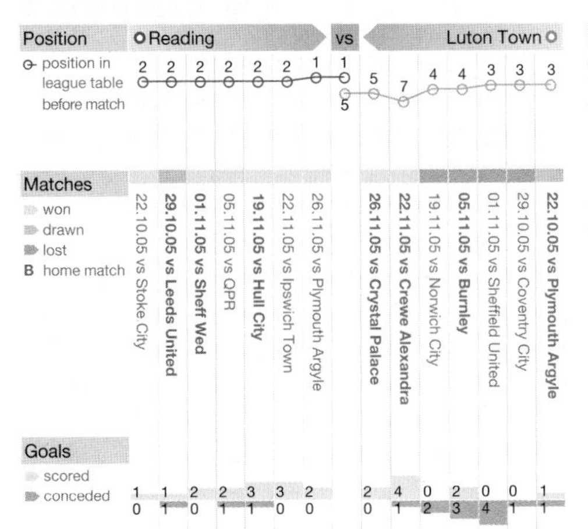

Position
Reading
vs
Luton Town
position in league table before match
2 2 2 2 2 2 1 1
5 5 7 4 4 3 3 3
Matches
won
drawn
lost
B home match
22.10.05 vs Stoke City
29.10.05 vs Leeds United
01.11.05 vs Sheff Wed
05.11.05 vs QPR
19.11.05 vs Hull City
22.11.05 vs Ipswich Town
26.11.05 vs Plymouth Argyle
26.11.05 vs Crystal Palace
22.11.05 vs Crewe Alexandra
19.11.05 vs Norwich City
05.11.05 vs Burnley
01.11.05 vs Sheffield United
29.10.05 vs Coventry City
22.10.05 vs Plymouth Argyle
Goals
scored
conceded
1 1 2 2 3 3 2
0 1 0 1 1 0 0
2 4 0 2 0 0 1
0 1 2 3 4 1 1

Goal Statistics

Reading

by Half | by Situation

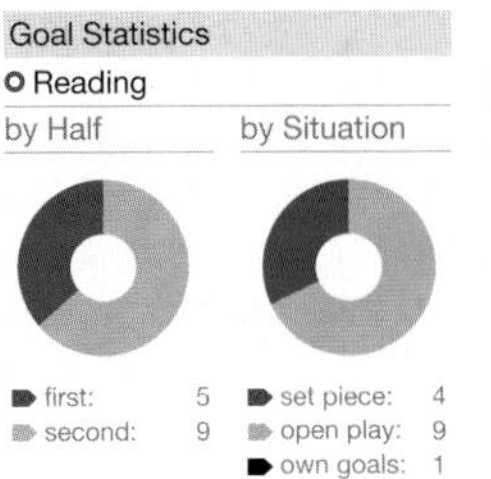

by Half		by Situation	
first:	5	set piece:	4
second:	9	open play:	9
		own goals:	1

Luton Town

by Half | by Situation

by Half		by Situation	
first:	3	set piece:	4
second:	6	open play:	5

Goals by Area

Reading

Scored (Conceded)

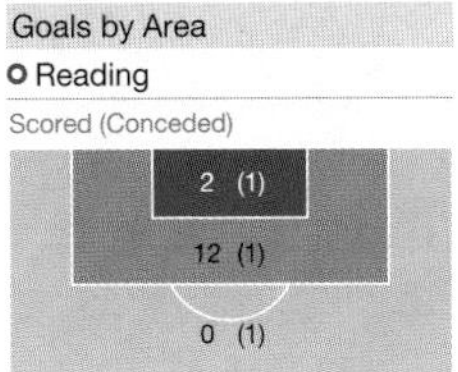

2 (1)
12 (1)
0 (1)

Luton Town

Scored (Conceded)

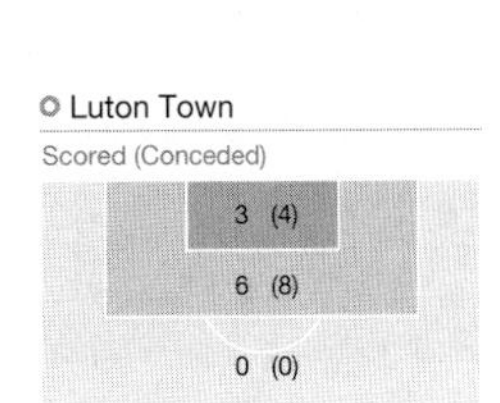

3 (4)
6 (8)
0 (0)

Team Statistics

Starting Line-Ups

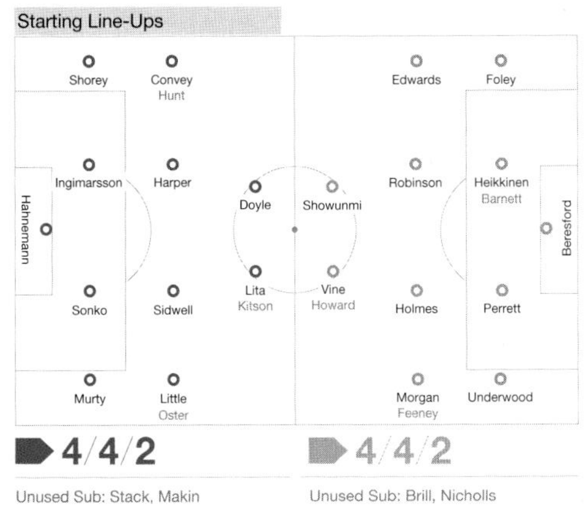

Shorey
Convey
Hunt
Ingimarsson
Harper
Doyle
Showunmi
Edwards
Foley
Robinson
Heikkinen
Barnett
Hahnemann
Beresford
Sonko
Sidwell
Lita
Kitson
Vine
Howard
Holmes
Perrett
Murty
Little
Oster
Morgan
Feeney
Underwood

4/4/2 | **4/4/2**

Unused Sub: Stack, Makin

Unused Sub: Brill, Nicholls

Championship Totals	Reading	Luton
Championship Appearances	671	225
Team Appearances	639	207
Goals Scored	69	27
Assists	60	25
Clean Sheets (goalkeepers)	31	4
Yellow Cards	46	13
Red Cards	0	2
Full Internationals	5	5

Age/Height

Reading Age

26 yrs

Luton Town Age

26 yrs, 10 mo

Reading Height

5'11"

Luton Town Height

6'

Match Statistics

League Table after Fixture

		Played	Won	Drawn	Lost	For	Against	Pts
● 1	Reading	22	16	5	1	41	11	53
● 2	Sheff Utd	22	15	4	3	43	21	49
↑ 3	Leeds	21	11	6	4	28	19	39
↓ 4	Watford	22	10	8	4	37	26	38
● 5	Luton	22	10	4	8	33	31	34
↑ 6	Preston	22	7	11	4	26	20	32
● 7	Burnley	22	9	5	8	31	26	32
↑ 8	Crystal Palace	20	9	4	7	32	23	31
↑ 9	Wolverhampton	22	7	10	5	27	19	31

Statistics	Reading	Luton
Goals	3	0
Shots on Target	6	4
Shots off Target	4	6
Hit Woodwork	0	0
Possession %	49	51
Corners	11	5
Offsides	1	4
Fouls	10	11
Disciplinary Points	0	0

5-1 Reading / Brighton & Hove Albion

Championship

10.12.05

SHOREY
SODKO

Reading celebrate a five-star performance

Event Line

26 Hammond

27 Oatway / RF / OG / 6Y
Assist: Little

42 Shorey

45 Knight

Half time 1-0

48 Elphick G
2nd Bookable Offence

51 Kitson / LF / P / IA
Assist: Kitson

54 Kazim-Richards > Carole

65 Robinson > Reid

71 Kitson / H / OP / 6Y
Assist: Shorey

73 Hunt > Doyle

73 Gunnarsson > Harper

73 Elphick T > Knight

76 Hunt / H / OP / 6Y
Assist: Shorey

79 Oster > Little

84 Kazim-Richards / RF / OP / O

90 Kitson / H / OP / IA
Assist: Sidwell

Full time 5-1

Mark McGhee's struggling Albion triggered their own downfall as Dave Kitson wreaked havoc to fire the only hat-trick of the Royals' league campaign.

Visiting captain Charlie Oatway steered Glen Little's low cross over his own goalline to offer the Royals a charitable opener, and when Gary Elphick dragged Kitson back early into the second half to receive a red card the home side took command.

Kitson earned and dispatched a penalty, then quickly positioned himself to nod home Nicky Shorey's deflected strike at the far post for 3-0. Stephen Hunt added another with his first for the Club four minutes later, but Colin Kazim-Richards struck a spectacular 25-yard bullet, borne largely from frustration, to pull one back.

Kitson had the last word though, scrambling Steve Sidwell's cutback cross through the hands of the desperately recovering Seagulls keeper. Hunt raced in to make sure and set the net rippling but the ball was already over the line so Kitson was not to be denied his treble, nor the Royals one of five five-goal hauls during the campaign.

Quote

Steve Coppell

We've won here and we are in a strong position, but we will not get carried away.

Championship Milestone

25

Dave Kitson's first goal was his 25th in the Championship.

Venue:	Madejski Stadium	Referee:	P.Taylor - 05/06
Attendance:	18,546	Matches:	15
Capacity:	24,200	Yellow Cards:	43
Occupancy:	77%	Red Cards:	3

Reading
Brighton & Hove Albion

Form Coming into Fixture

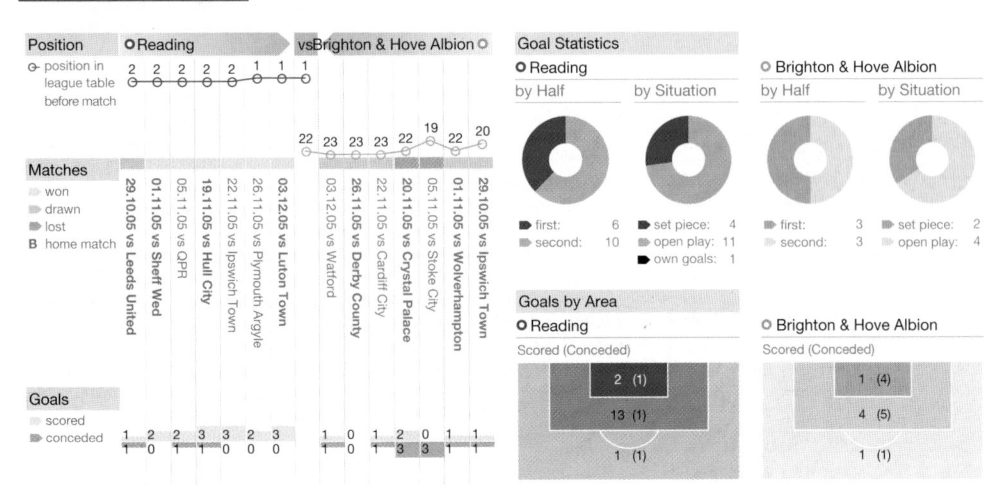

Position
Reading
vs
Brighton & Hove Albion
position in league table before match
2 2 2 2 2 1 1 1
22 23 23 23 22 19 22 20
Matches
won
drawn
lost
B home match
29.10.05 vs Leeds United
01.11.05 vs Sheff Wed
05.11.05 vs QPR
19.11.05 vs Hull City
22.11.05 vs Ipswich Town
26.11.05 vs Plymouth Argyle
03.12.05 vs Luton Town
03.12.05 vs Watford
26.11.05 vs Derby County
22.11.05 vs Cardiff City
20.11.05 vs Crystal Palace
05.11.05 vs Stoke City
01.11.05 vs Wolverhampton
29.10.05 vs Ipswich Town
Goals
scored
conceded
1 2 2 3 3 2 3
1 0 1 1 0 0 0
1 0 1 2 0 1 1
1 0 1 3 3 1 1
Goal Statistics
Reading
by Half
by Situation
first: 6
second: 10
set piece: 4
open play: 11
own goals: 1
Brighton & Hove Albion
by Half
by Situation
first: 3
second: 3
set piece: 2
open play: 4
Goals by Area
Reading
Scored (Conceded)
2 (1)
13 (1)
1 (1)
Brighton & Hove Albion
Scored (Conceded)
1 (4)
4 (5)
1 (1)

Team Statistics

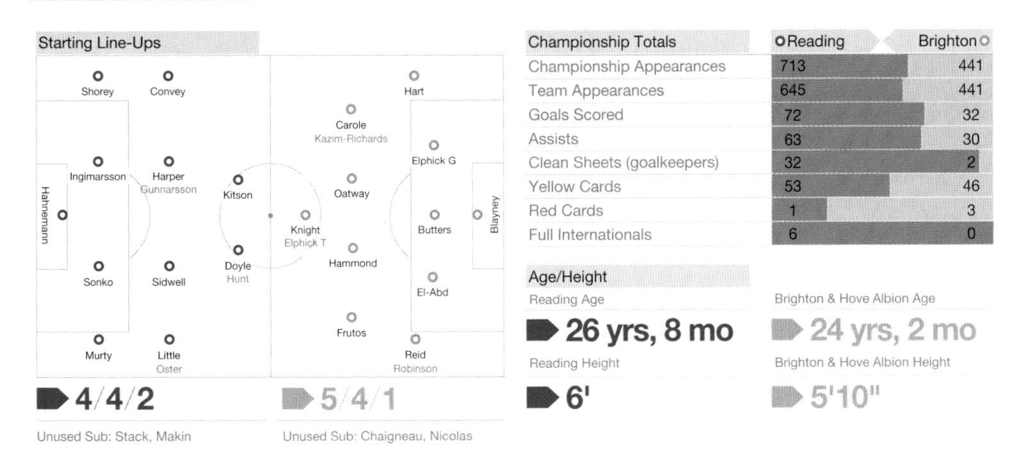

Starting Line-Ups
Shorey
Convey
Ingimarsson
Harper
Gunnarsson
Kitson
Hahnemann
Sonko
Sidwell
Doyle
Hunt
Murty
Little
Oster
Hart
Carole
Kazim-Richards
Elphick G
Oatway
Knight
Elphick T
Butters
Blayney
Hammond
El-Abd
Frutos
Reid
Robinson
4/4/2
5/4/1
Unused Sub: Stack, Makin
Unused Sub: Chaigneau, Nicolas
Championship Totals
Reading
Brighton
Championship Appearances 713 441
Team Appearances 645 441
Goals Scored 72 32
Assists 63 30
Clean Sheets (goalkeepers) 32 2
Yellow Cards 53 46
Red Cards 1 3
Full Internationals 6 0
Age/Height
Reading Age
26 yrs, 8 mo
Reading Height
6'
Brighton & Hove Albion Age
24 yrs, 2 mo
Brighton & Hove Albion Height
5'10"

Match Statistics

League Table after Fixture

	Played	Won	Drawn	Lost	For	Against	Pts
● 1 Reading	23	17	5	1	46	12	56
● 2 Sheff Utd	23	16	4	3	46	21	52
↑ 3 Watford	23	10	9	4	38	27	39
↓ 4 Leeds	22	11	6	5	28	20	39
↑ 5 Cardiff	23	9	7	7	33	26	34
↓ 6 Luton	22	10	4	8	33	31	34
↓ 7 Stoke	23	11	1	11	29	32	34
...	...	...	...	...	...	...	...
● 22 Brighton	23	2	13	8	22	35	19

Statistics

Statistics	Reading	Brighton
Goals	5	1
Shots on Target	7	1
Shots off Target	2	1
Hit Woodwork	0	0
Possession %	61	39
Corners	8	0
Offsides	4	1
Fouls	11	19
Disciplinary Points	4	18

0-2 Millwall Reading

Championship

17.12.05

KYOCERA
BEKO
BEKO

Graeme Murty leads the team into battle

Event Line	
37	Sidwell
37	Dunne
40	Sidwell / RF / OP / IA
	Assist: Doyle
Half time 0-1	
47	Craig
	Foul
59	Braniff > Dyer
68	Doyle / LF / OP / IA
	Assist: Shorey
80	Gunnarsson > Sidwell
82	Oster > Little
88	Hunt > Doyle
Full time 0-2	

An eighth consecutive league win was earned at the New Den as lowly Millwall shipped two more goals to the rampant Royals, who surged six points clear at the top to open up an astonishing 20 point advantage over third-placed Watford.

Belying their respective league positions, rock-bottom Millwall began the brighter and were unlucky not to take the lead when Alan Dunne's header cannoned against the crossbar before Graeme Murty could clear the danger.

Shortly before the break, though, Steve Sidwell ran onto Kevin Doyle's cross to unleash a blistering 15-yard volley which the Lions' keeper Colin Doyle barely saw.

Doyle's pace was again causing panic for the opposing defence – so much so that Tony Craig was forced to manhandle the Irishman to the ground inside the box, for which he was issued with his marching orders.

Kitson's penalty was saved but Doyle eventually wrapped up the points, finishing Nicky Shorey's foraging run by neatly placing a well-taken left-footed drive beyond his namesake in the Lions goal.

Quote

Steve Coppell

It wasn't very good, but it was effective. We have got to the stage where people are judging us on more than results.

Venue:	The New Den
Attendance:	12,920
Capacity:	20,146
Occupancy:	64%

Referee:	A.R.Hall - 05/06
Matches:	17
Yellow Cards:	65
Red Cards:	6

Millwall
Reading

Form Coming into Fixture

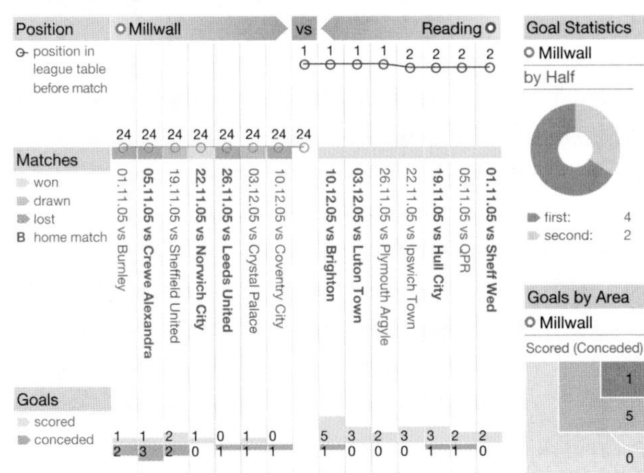

Position
Millwall
vs
Reading
position in league table before match
1 1 1 1 2 2 2 2
24 24 24 24 24 24 24 24
Matches
won
drawn
lost
B home match
01.11.05 vs Burnley
05.11.05 vs Crewe Alexandra
19.11.05 vs Sheffield United
22.11.05 vs Norwich City
26.11.05 vs Leeds United
03.12.05 vs Crystal Palace
10.12.05 vs Coventry City
10.12.05 vs Brighton
03.12.05 vs Luton Town
26.11.05 vs Plymouth Argyle
22.11.05 vs Ipswich Town
19.11.05 vs Hull City
05.11.05 vs QPR
01.11.05 vs Sheff Wed
Goals
scored
conceded
1 1 2 1 0 1 0
2 3 2 0 1 1 1
5 3 2 3 3 2 2
1 0 0 0 1 1 0

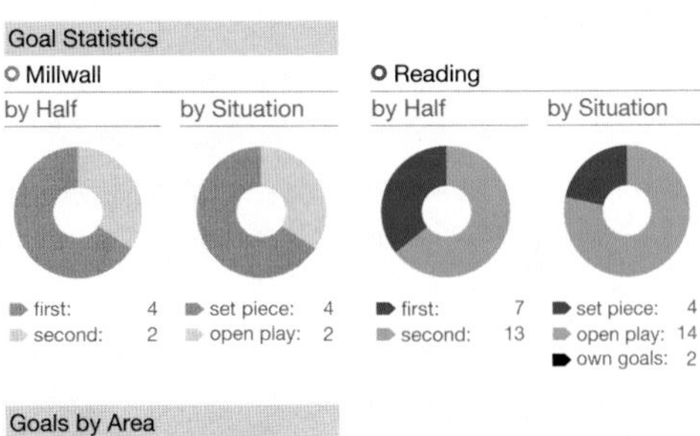

Goal Statistics
Millwall
by Half
by Situation
first: 4
second: 2
set piece: 4
open play: 2
Reading
by Half
by Situation
first: 7
second: 13
set piece: 4
open play: 14
own goals: 2

Goals by Area

Millwall

Scored (Conceded)

1 (1)
5 (8)
0 (1)

Reading

Scored (Conceded)

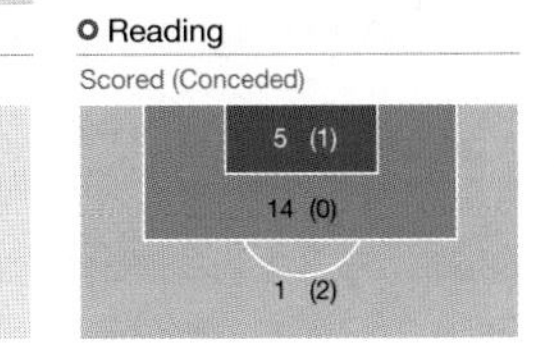

5 (1)
14 (0)
1 (2)

Team Statistics

Starting Line-Ups

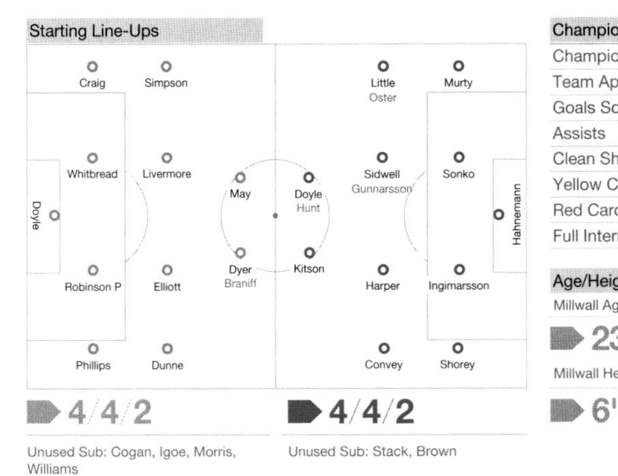

Craig
Simpson
Whitbread
Livermore
Doyle
Robinson P
Elliott
Phillips
Dunne
May
Dyer
Braniff
Doyle
Hunt
Kitson
Little
Oster
Murty
Sidwell
Gunnarsson
Sonko
Hahnemann
Harper
Ingimarsson
Convey
Shorey

4/4/2

Unused Sub: Cogan, Igoe, Morris, Williams

4/4/2

Unused Sub: Stack, Brown

Championship Totals	Millwall	Reading
Championship Appearances	366	727
Team Appearances	317	659
Goals Scored	25	76
Assists	29	68
Clean Sheets (goalkeepers)	1	32
Yellow Cards	49	54
Red Cards	5	1
Full Internationals	1	6

Age/Height

Millwall Age	Reading Age
23 yrs, 2 mo	26 yrs, 8 mo
Millwall Height	**Reading Height**
6'	6'

Match Statistics

League Table after Fixture

		Played	Won	Drawn	Lost	For	Against	Pts
● 1	Reading	24	18	5	1	48	12	59
● 2	Sheff Utd	24	16	5	3	46	21	53
● 3	Watford	24	10	9	5	39	31	39
● 4	Leeds	23	11	6	6	28	21	39
↑ 5	Stoke	24	12	1	11	32	34	37
↑ 6	Wolverhampton	24	8	11	5	29	20	35
↓ 7	Cardiff	24	9	8	7	33	26	35
...		...	...	...	...	...	...	...
● 24	Millwall	24	3	8	13	17	37	17

Statistics	Millwall	Reading
Goals	0	2
Shots on Target	7	7
Shots off Target	6	5
Hit Woodwork	0	0
Possession %	50	50
Corners	4	6
Offsides	3	1
Fouls	11	18
Disciplinary Points	16	4

0-2 Wolves Reading

Championship

26.12.05

KITSON
12

Dave Kitson and Kevin Doyle celebrate with Bobby Convey

Event Line
29 Kitson / H / OP / 6Y Assist: Little
Half time 0-1
47 Oster > Little
61 Cameron > Ricketts
64 Convey / LF / OP / OA
69 Ndah > Anderton
73 Craddock > Gyepes
82 Hunt > Convey
Full time 0-2

A hectic Christmas period began in extremely impressive fashion at Molineux with Wolves well beaten by a determined and stylish Reading performance. Early mayhem ensued when Dave Kitson amazingly struck the woodwork twice in a matter of seconds with quick-fire headers.

Kitson made sure he hit the back of the net with half an hour gone though, after Glen Little had conjured a delightful piece of skill to skip clear of three men and arc an inch-perfect cross onto the striker's head for the far post opener.

Kitson had the ball in the back of the net for a second time on the hour mark, but was adjudged to have clambered over Rob Edwards and his header was ruled out. South Korean forward Ki-Hyeon Seol powered Darren Anderton's cross against the Royals crossbar but Bobby Convey, Hoddle's target when boss at Spurs, rifled a driven left-footed strike past Stefan Postma to cement a 2-0 scoreline.

Colin Cameron hammered Marcus Hahnemann's woodwork with a 25-yard piledriver but the result was never in doubt and the Boxing Day points were Reading's reward.

Quote

Steve Coppell

We have more of a cutting edge this season and are not just reliant on Dave Kitson for goals.

Championship Milestone

100

Dave Kitson's goal was the 100th scored in the Championship by Reading.

Venue: Molineux
Attendance: 27,980
Capacity: 29,400
Occupancy: 95%

Referee: S.Tanner - 05/06
Matches: 17
Yellow Cards: 73
Red Cards: 6

Wolverhampton Wanderers
Reading

Form Coming into Fixture

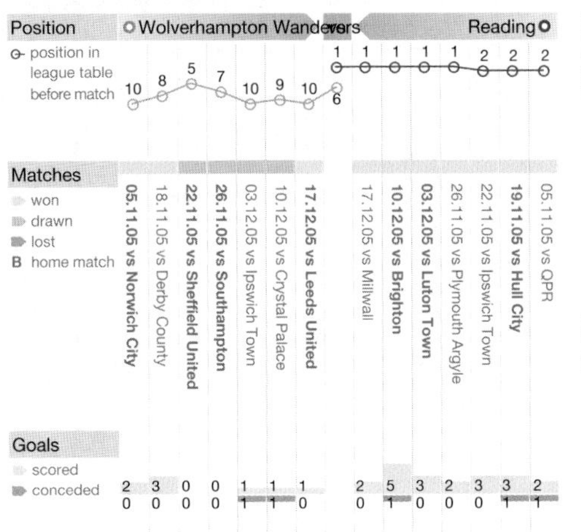

Position
Wolverhampton Wanderers
Reading
position in league table before match
10 8 5 7 10 9 10 6
1 1 1 1 1 2 2 2
Matches
won
drawn
lost
B home match
05.11.05 vs Norwich City
18.11.05 vs Derby County
22.11.05 vs Sheffield United
26.11.05 vs Southampton
03.12.05 vs Ipswich Town
10.12.05 vs Crystal Palace
17.12.05 vs Leeds United
17.12.05 vs Millwall
10.12.05 vs Brighton
03.12.05 vs Luton Town
26.11.05 vs Plymouth Argyle
22.11.05 vs Ipswich Town
19.11.05 vs Hull City
05.11.05 vs QPR
Goals
scored
conceded

	05.11.05	18.11.05	22.11.05	26.11.05	03.12.05	10.12.05	17.12.05	17.12.05	10.12.05	03.12.05	26.11.05	22.11.05	19.11.05	05.11.05
scored	2	3	0	0	1	1	1	2	5	3	2	3	3	2
conceded	0	0	0	0	1	1	0	0	1	0	0	0	1	1

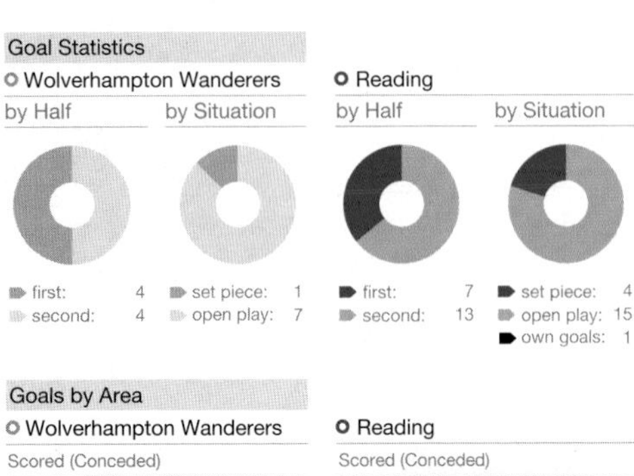

Goal Statistics
Wolverhampton Wanderers
by Half
by Situation
Reading
by Half
by Situation

Wolverhampton Wanderers

by Half		by Situation	
first:	4	set piece:	1
second:	4	open play:	7

Reading

by Half		by Situation	
first:	7	set piece:	4
second:	13	open play:	15
		own goals:	1

Goals by Area

Wolverhampton Wanderers — Scored (Conceded): 1 (0); 4 (2); 3 (0)

Reading — Scored (Conceded): 5 (1); 14 (0); 1 (2)

Team Statistics

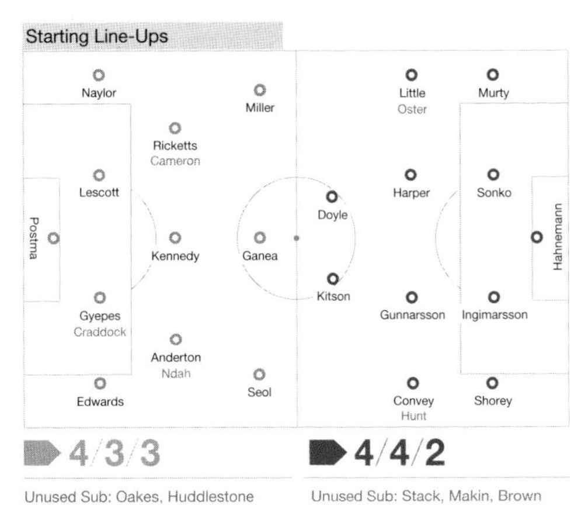

Starting Line-Ups
Naylor
Miller
Ricketts
Cameron
Lescott
Postma
Kennedy
Ganea
Doyle
Kitson
Gyepes
Craddock
Anderton
Ndah
Edwards
Seol
Little
Oster
Murty
Harper
Sonko
Hahnemann
Gunnarsson
Ingimarsson
Convey
Hunt
Shorey

4/3/3

Unused Sub: Oakes, Huddlestone

4/4/2

Unused Sub: Stack, Makin, Brown

Championship Totals	Wolves	Reading
Championship Appearances	525	681
Team Appearances	519	613
Goals Scored	50	69
Assists	57	67
Clean Sheets (goalkeepers)	5	33
Yellow Cards	51	39
Red Cards	2	1
Full Internationals	8	6

Age/Height

Wolverhampton Wanderers Age: 28 yrs

Reading Age: 27 yrs

Wolverhampton Wanderers Height: 6'

Reading Height: 6'

Match Statistics

League Table after Fixture

		Played	Won	Drawn	Lost	For	Against	Pts
● 1	Reading	25	19	5	1	50	12	62
● 2	Sheff Utd	25	16	5	4	47	24	53
● 3	Watford	25	11	9	5	42	31	42
● 4	Leeds	24	12	6	6	31	22	42
↑ 5	Burnley	25	11	5	9	36	30	38
↓ 6	Stoke	25	12	1	12	32	35	37
↑ 7	Crystal Palace	23	10	5	8	35	26	35
↓ 8	Wolverhampton	25	8	11	6	29	22	35
● 9	Preston	25	7	14	4	27	21	35

Statistics	Wolves	Reading
Goals	0	2
Shots on Target	3	6
Shots off Target	9	4
Hit Woodwork	0	2
Possession %	47	53
Corners	3	5
Offsides	4	5
Fouls	8	13
Disciplinary Points	0	0

2-0 Reading Leicester City

Championship

28.12.05

Kevin Doyle helps the ball on

Event Line	
Half time 0-0	
50	Sonko
60	Doyle / LF / OP / IA Assist: Kitson
71	Hunt > Convey
72	Gudjonsson
73	Stearman > Gerrbrand
73	Smith > Hamill
73	Hammond > Hughes
79	McCarthy
79	Kitson
80	Long > Kitson
83	Gunnarsson > Oster
87	Gunnarsson / H / IFK / IA Assist: Shorey
89	Gunnarsson
90	Hunt
Full time 2-0	

Only two days after the excellent victory at Wolves, Steve Coppell's men had to work incredibly hard for their tenth successive Championship win against a gutsy Foxes outfit at Madejski Stadium.

Dave Kitson was denied a penalty after seemingly being tripped by Leicester keeper Rab Douglas while at the other end Mark de Vries was testing Marcus Hahnemann, and the league leaders had to wait for an hour for the opener.

Kitson opted not to spread the play to John Oster, making his first league start for the Royals, and aware of Kevin Doyle's central position the striker instead laid a perfect ball through to the fleet-footed Irishman. Bursting beyond the back line and keeping his feet at pace, Doyle maturely passed wide of the onrushing Douglas and into the right-hand corner.

But Leicester kept battling and only when substitute Brynjar Gunnarsson nodded Nicky Shorey's 88th minute cross into the top right hand corner could Madejski Stadium breathe a sigh of relief in the knowledge that three more points were sealed.

Quote

Steve Coppell

There is no jealousy when I make changes as players realise this is not about individuals but the team.

Championship Milestone

50

Brynjar Gunnarsson made his 50th appearance in the Championship.

Venue:	Madejski Stadium	Referee:	A.G.Wiley - 05/06
Attendance:	22,061	Matches:	22
Capacity:	24,200	Yellow Cards:	64
Occupancy:	91%	Red Cards:	4

Reading
Leicester City

Form Coming into Fixture

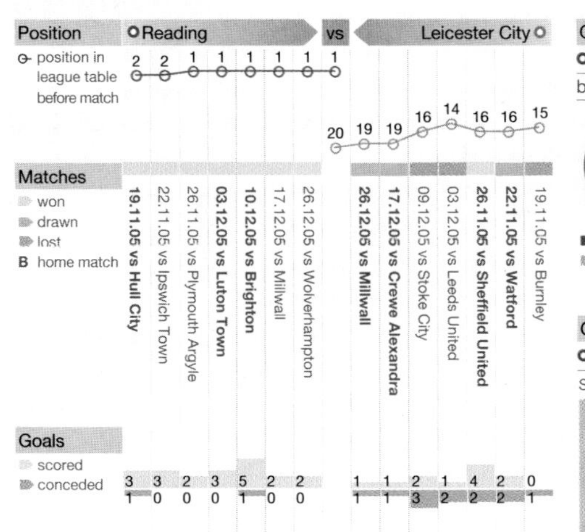

Position
Reading
vs
Leicester City
position in league table before match
2 2 1 1 1 1 1 1
20 19 19 16 14 16 16 15
Matches
won
drawn
lost
B home match
19.11.05 vs Hull City
22.11.05 vs Ipswich Town
26.11.05 vs Plymouth Argyle
03.12.05 vs Luton Town
10.12.05 vs Brighton
17.12.05 vs Millwall
26.12.05 vs Wolverhampton
26.12.05 vs Millwall
17.12.05 vs Crewe Alexandra
09.12.05 vs Stoke City
03.12.05 vs Leeds United
26.11.05 vs Sheffield United
22.11.05 vs Watford
19.11.05 vs Burnley
Goals
scored
conceded
3 3 2 3 5 2 2
1 0 0 0 1 0 0
1 1 2 1 4 2 0
1 1 3 2 2 2 1

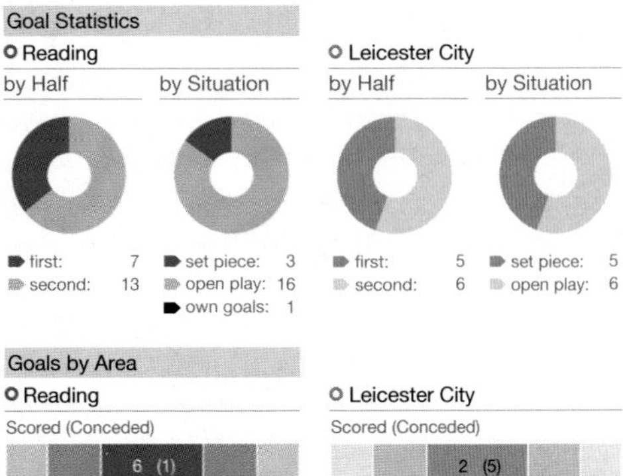

Goal Statistics
Reading
by Half
by Situation
first: 7
second: 13
set piece: 3
open play: 16
own goals: 1
Leicester City
by Half
by Situation
first: 5
second: 6
set piece: 5
open play: 6

Goals by Area

Reading

Scored (Conceded)

6 (1)
12 (0)
2 (1)

Leicester City

Scored (Conceded)

2 (5)
8 (5)
1 (2)

Team Statistics

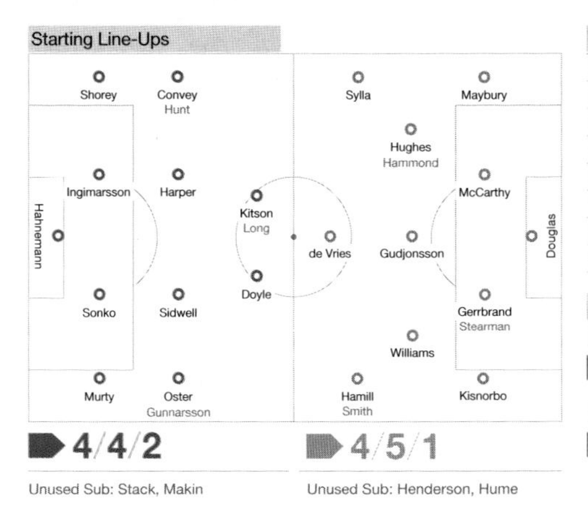

Starting Line-Ups
Shorey
Convey
Hunt
Ingimarsson
Harper
Hahnemann
Kitson
Long
Doyle
Sonko
Sidwell
Murty
Oster
Gunnarsson
Sylla
Maybury
Hughes
Hammond
McCarthy
de Vries
Gudjonsson
Douglas
Gerrbrand
Stearman
Williams
Hamill
Smith
Kisnorbo
4/4/2
4/5/1

Unused Sub: Stack, Makin

Unused Sub: Henderson, Hume

Championship Totals	Reading	Leicester
Championship Appearances	694	376
Team Appearances	626	376
Goals Scored	75	26
Assists	51	27
Clean Sheets (goalkeepers)	34	5
Yellow Cards	47	65
Red Cards	1	3
Full Internationals	6	6

Age/Height

Reading Age: 25 yrs, 11 mo

Leicester City Age: 25 yrs

Reading Height: 5'11"

Leicester City Height: 6'

Match Statistics

League Table after Fixture

		Played	Won	Drawn	Lost	For	Against	Pts
● 1	Reading	26	20	5	1	52	12	65
● 2	Sheff Utd	26	17	5	4	48	24	56
↑ 3	Leeds	25	13	6	6	32	22	45
↓ 4	Watford	26	11	10	5	42	31	43
↑ 5	Crystal Palace	24	11	5	8	37	26	38
↑ 6	Wolverhampton	26	9	11	6	31	22	38
↓ 7	Burnley	26	11	5	10	37	32	38
...		...	...	...	...	...	...	...
● 20	Leicester	25	5	11	9	27	32	26

Statistics	Reading	Leicester
Goals	2	0
Shots on Target	3	1
Shots off Target	2	1
Hit Woodwork	0	0
Possession %	54	46
Corners	4	3
Offsides	7	2
Fouls	13	14
Disciplinary Points	16	8

2-2 Derby County Reading

Championship

31.12.05

Brynjar Gunnarsson stretches to retain possession

Event Line

32 Johnson S / LF / OP / IA
Assist: Smith

34 Doyle / H / OP / 6Y
Assist: Little

Half time 1-1

62 Johnson S / LF / IFK / OA
Assist: Bolder

70 Long > Convey

71 Davies
2nd Bookable Offence

71 Johnson M > Smith

77 Thirlwell > Holmes

81 Oster > Hunt

86 Peschisolido > Graham

86 Harper > Murty

88 Long / H / C / 6Y
Assist: Sidwell

Full time 2-2

Summer-long scouting sessions in Ireland proved their true worth as a last gasp leveller from an 18 year-old Emerald Isle starlet kept the Royals' unbeaten run alive on New Year's Eve.

Seth Johnson swept home his first goal at Pride Park when a suspiciously offside-looking Tommy Smith squared for the ex-England man to give the Rams the lead. But just seconds after the restart, Kevin Doyle equalised as his near-post run culminated in heading Glen Little's dinked right-sided cross firmly into the net.

Johnson doubled his tally when Reading failed to clear just after the hour, and Derby briefly looked likely to add to their advantage.

Enter Shane Long. Within seconds on-loan Middlesbrough defender Andrew Davies scythed down the young Irishman and was ordered off with a second yellow card brandished. The visitors pressed to make full use of the numerical ascendancy, but it wasn't until the 88th minute that the levelling goal finally arrived – Long leaping high to nod home Steve Sidwell's cross-goal header and earn an immediate place in Royals' fans hearts.

Quote

Steve Coppell

Derby can play and made us work hard. We found it difficult to find our tempo and rhythm.

Championship Milestone

First Goal

Shane Long netted his first goal in the Championship.

Venue:	Pride Park	Referee:	B.Curson - 05/06	**Derby County**
Attendance:	21,434	Matches:	19	**Reading**
Capacity:	33,597	Yellow Cards:	43	
Occupancy:	64%	Red Cards:	2	

Form Coming into Fixture

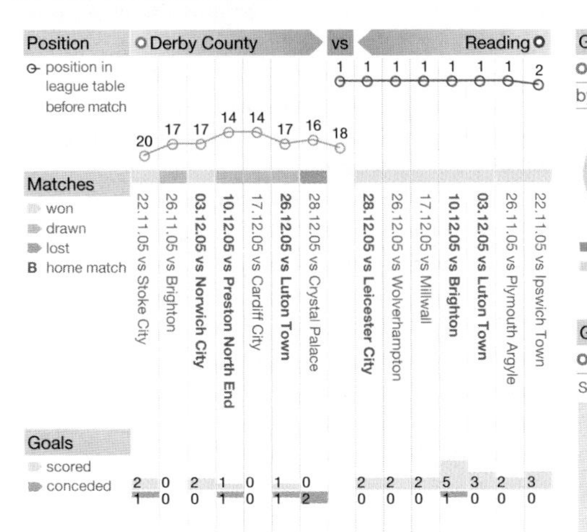

Position
Derby County
vs
Reading
position in league table before match
20 17 17 14 14 17 16 18
1 1 1 1 1 1 1 2
Matches
won
drawn
lost
B home match
22.11.05 vs Stoke City
26.11.05 vs Brighton
03.12.05 vs Norwich City
10.12.05 vs Preston North End
17.12.05 vs Cardiff City
26.12.05 vs Luton Town
28.12.05 vs Crystal Palace
28.12.05 vs Leicester City
26.12.05 vs Wolverhampton
17.12.05 vs Millwall
10.12.05 vs Brighton
03.12.05 vs Luton Town
26.11.05 vs Plymouth Argyle
22.11.05 vs Ipswich Town
Goals
scored
conceded
2 0 2 1 0 1 0
1 0 0 1 0 1 2
2 2 2 5 3 2 3
0 0 0 1 0 0 0

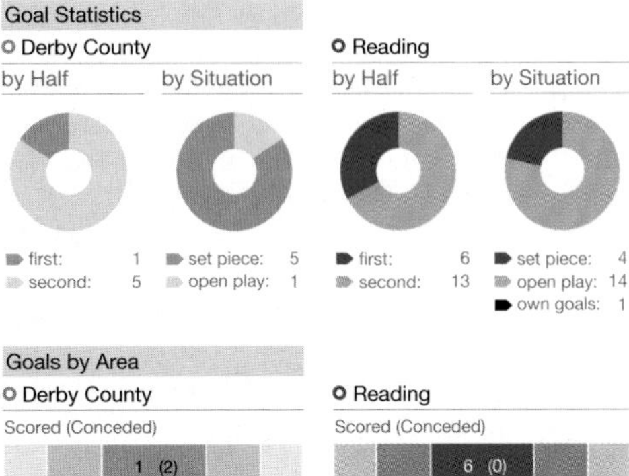

Goal Statistics
Derby County
by Half
by Situation
first: 1
second: 5
set piece: 5
open play: 1
Reading
by Half
by Situation
first: 6
second: 13
set piece: 4
open play: 14
own goals: 1

Goals by Area

Derby County — Scored (Conceded): 1 (2), 4 (3), 1 (0)

Reading — Scored (Conceded): 6 (0), 11 (0), 2 (1)

Team Statistics

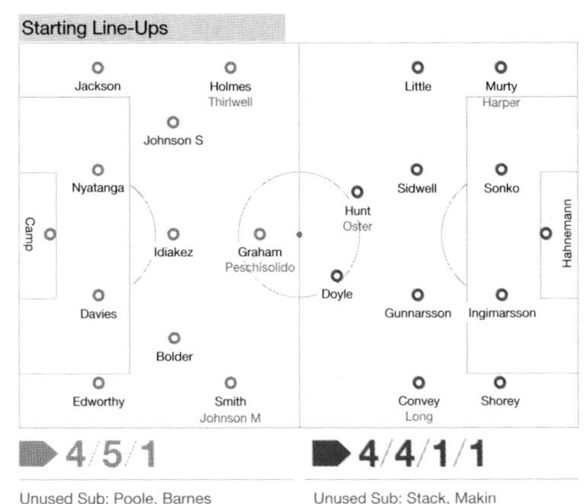

Starting Line-Ups
Jackson
Holmes
Thirlwell
Johnson S
Nyatanga
Camp
Idiakez
Graham
Peschisolido
Davies
Bolder
Edworthy
Smith
Johnson M
Little
Murty
Harper
Hunt
Oster
Sidwell
Sonko
Hahnemann
Doyle
Gunnarsson
Ingimarsson
Convey
Long
Shorey
4/5/1
4/4/1/1

Unused Sub: Poole, Barnes

Unused Sub: Stack, Makin

Championship Totals	Derby	Reading
Championship Appearances	524	714
Team Appearances	479	646
Goals Scored	50	54
Assists	51	64
Clean Sheets (goalkeepers)	17	35
Yellow Cards	65	52
Red Cards	5	1
Full Internationals	3	6

Age/Height

Derby County Age: **25 yrs, 10 mo**

Reading Age: **26 yrs, 2 mo**

Derby County Height: **5'10"**

Reading Height: **5'11"**

Match Statistics

League Table after Fixture

	Played	Won	Drawn	Lost	For	Against	Pts
1 Reading	27	20	6	1	54	14	66
2 Sheff Utd	27	18	5	4	50	25	59
3 Leeds	26	14	6	6	34	22	48
4 Watford	27	11	10	6	43	33	43
5 Crystal Palace	25	12	5	8	39	27	41
6 Wolverhampton	27	9	12	6	32	23	39
↑ 7 Preston	26	8	14	4	30	22	38
...	...	...	...	...	...	...	...
↑ 17 Derby	27	5	14	8	33	38	29

Statistics	Derby	Reading
Goals	2	2
Shots on Target	5	7
Shots off Target	4	5
Hit Woodwork	0	0
Possession %	49	51
Corners	2	7
Offsides	2	2
Fouls	14	9
Disciplinary Points	10	0

5-1 Reading Cardiff City

Championship

02.01.06

KYOCERA
HUNT
10

Dave Kitson completes the scoring from the penalty spot

Event Line
11 Sidwell / H / OP / IA
Assist: Little
32 Sonko / H / IFK / IA
Assist: Shorey
Half time 2-0
51 Kitson / LF / OP / 6Y
Assist: Little
52 Alexander
58 Ardley > Cooper
62 Jerome / RF / OP / OA
Assist: Koumas
71 Sidwell / H / IFK / IA
Assist: Shorey
72 Hunt > Convey
76 Kitson / LF / P / IA
76 Long > Kitson
76 Oster > Little
82 Darlington > Weston
Full time 5-1

Bouncing back from a below-par Pride Park performance, Steve Coppell's Royals destroyed Dave Jones' Bluebirds with a five-star display.

As so often was the case, a positive Reading reaction was sparked by an impressive Marcus Hahnemann save. Alan Lee was the Cardiff striker denied in the ninth minute by an expert stop from the USA international, and seconds later Steve Sidwell's diving header opened proceedings before Ibrahima Sonko powered Nicky Shorey's in-swinging free-kick past Neil Alexander for two.

Dave Kitson and Kevin Doyle were denied before half time, but Kitson converted Glen Little's probing cross from close range soon after the interval. Cameron Jerome's swerving 25-yard strike deceived Hahnemann on the hour to make it 3-1, but Sidwell completed his brace with a second header and Kitson also tallied two, punishing Darren Purse's handball with a driven fifth from the penalty spot.

Sidwell came agonisingly close to his first ever professional hat-trick only to see the left upright stand in the way of his sliding effort in the final minute, but five goals was more than enough to demonstrate the home side's majestic superiority.

Quote

Steve Coppell

When they scored it could still have got hairy, but we weathered their five-minute storm and over the 90 minutes we played some good stuff.

Championship Milestone

10

Steve Sidwell's first goal was his tenth in the Championship.

Venue:	Madejski Stadium	Referee:	R.J.Olivier - 05/06
Attendance:	22,061	Matches:	19
Capacity:	24,200	Yellow Cards:	58
Occupancy:	91%	Red Cards:	4

Reading
Cardiff City

Form Coming into Fixture

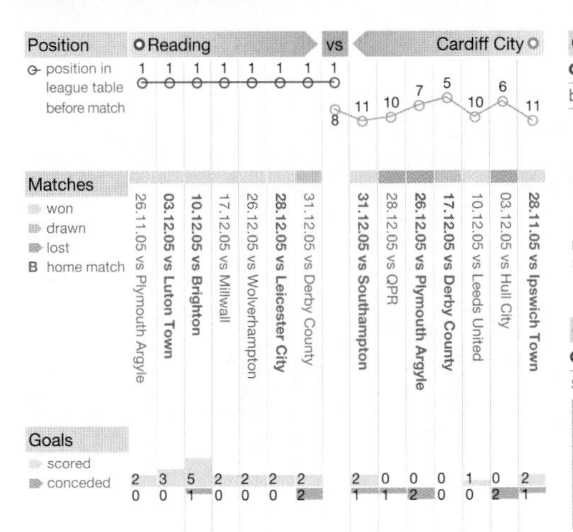

Position
Reading
vs
Cardiff City
position in league table before match
1 1 1 1 1 1 1 1
8 11 10 7 5 10 6 11
Matches
won
drawn
lost
B home match
26.11.05 vs Plymouth Argyle
03.12.05 vs Luton Town
10.12.05 vs Brighton
17.12.05 vs Millwall
26.12.05 vs Wolverhampton
28.12.05 vs Leicester City
31.12.05 vs Derby County
31.12.05 vs Southampton
28.12.05 vs QPR
26.12.05 vs Plymouth Argyle
17.12.05 vs Derby County
10.12.05 vs Leeds United
03.12.05 vs Hull City
28.11.05 vs Ipswich Town
Goals
scored
conceded
2 3 5 2 2 2 2
0 0 1 0 0 0 2
2 0 0 0 1 0 2
1 1 2 0 0 2 1

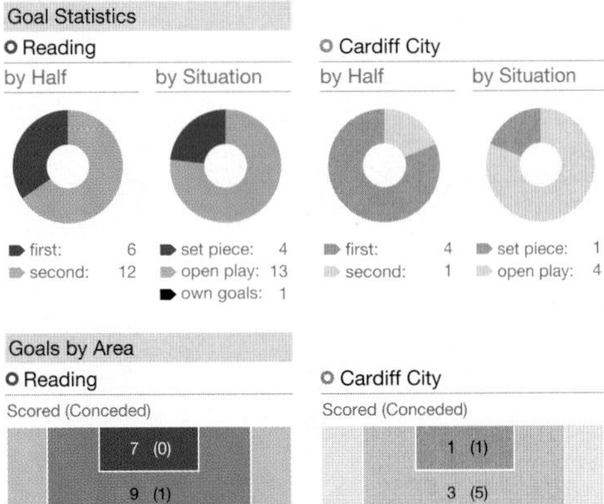

Goal Statistics
Reading
by Half
by Situation
first: 6
second: 12
set piece: 4
open play: 13
own goals: 1
Cardiff City
by Half
by Situation
first: 4
second: 1
set piece: 1
open play: 4
Goals by Area
Reading
Scored (Conceded)
7 (0)
9 (1)
2 (2)
Cardiff City
Scored (Conceded)
1 (1)
3 (5)
1 (1)

Team Statistics

Starting Line-Ups
Shorey
Convey
Hunt
Ingimarsson
Harper
Hahnemann
Doyle
Kitson
Long
Sonko
Sidwell
Murty
Little
Oster
Cooper
Ardley
Weston
Darlington
Whitley
Purse
Lee
Jerome
Alexander
Ledley
Loovens
Koumas
Barker

4/4/2

Unused Sub: Stack, Gunnarsson

4/4/2

Unused Sub: Margetson, Cox, Ricketts

Championship Totals	Reading	Cardiff
Championship Appearances	731	595
Team Appearances	699	470
Goals Scored	77	55
Assists	72	55
Clean Sheets (goalkeepers)	35	13
Yellow Cards	50	61
Red Cards	0	4
Full Internationals	5	5

Age/Height

Reading Age

25 yrs, 11 mo

Reading Height

5'11"

Cardiff City Age

26 yrs, 6 mo

Cardiff City Height

5'11"

Match Statistics

League Table after Fixture

	Played	Won	Drawn	Lost	For	Against	Pts
1 Reading	28	21	6	1	59	15	69
2 Sheff Utd	27	18	5	4	50	25	59
3 Leeds	27	15	6	6	37	22	51
4 Watford	28	12	10	6	45	34	46
5 Crystal Palace	26	13	5	8	41	27	44
↑ 6 Preston	27	9	14	4	33	22	41
↓ 7 Wolverhampton	28	9	12	7	32	25	39
...	...	...	...	...	...	...	...
↓ 10 Cardiff	28	10	8	10	36	35	38

Statistics	Reading	Cardiff
Goals	5	1
Shots on Target	10	6
Shots off Target	2	2
Hit Woodwork	1	0
Possession %	64	36
Corners	8	3
Offsides	9	3
Fouls	4	7
Disciplinary Points	0	4

1-1 West Bromwich Albion Reading

FA Cup

07.01.06

KYOCERA
KYOCERA
T-Mobile

Reading earn a late penalty at The Hawthorns

Event Line
28 Makin
Half time 0-0
53 Campbell > Ellington
53 Horsfield > Inamoto
59 Lita > Long
66 Kitson
69 Doyle > Kitson
72 Gera > Greening
82 Gera / RF / P / IA
Assist: Horsfield
84 Doyle / RF / P / IA
86 Little > Hunt
Full time 1-1

A tale of two penalties resulted in FA Cup equality when the Royals took on the second of three top flight opponents in 2005/6.

Bryan Robson might have been excused a first team reshuffle as his Albion side continued to toy with the threat of relegation, but the Premiership side fielded a strong side including the likes of £3m 20 year-old Curtis Davies, former Wigan goal-machine Nathan Ellington and Nigerian legend Nwankwo Kanu.

Steve Coppell remained consistent, treating both cup competitions with respect but a little less priority. Young Irishman Shane Long was rewarded for his dramatic Derby impact with his full Royals debut while Leroy Lita came off the bench to replace him in the second half to return from injury.

The first chance fell to Ellington, who belied his 2004/5 Championship top scorer tag with a horrendous 10th minute gaffe. At centre back Brynjar Gunnarsson tackled robustly but the ball cannoned off Ellington, looped over Graham Stack and onto the right upright. The rebound fell back to Ellington yards out with the goal gaping, but treading on the ball he miscued his tap in and a glorious chance went begging.

The visitors tried to take advantage of their let off and Dave Kitson's low drive was successfully parried by Chris Kirkland's legs minutes later. Stack had to be alert to keep Davies' scuffed effort out but the Championship side were holding their own, with Nicky Shorey forcing Kirkland into a low save from his dipping free-kick.

The game only really sprang into life with nine minutes remaining. Baggies substitute Geoff Horsfield couldn't connect with Martin Albrechtsen's cross and fell to the floor. Controversially Chris Makin was adjudged to have pushed the

Venue:	The Hawthorns	Referee:	M.D.Messias - 05/06
Attendance:	19,197	Matches:	15
Capacity:	28,003	Yellow Cards:	53
Occupancy:	69%	Red Cards:	2

West Bromwich Albion
Reading

Doyle strokes home the penalty

Match Statistics

Starting Line-Ups

Robinson
Carter
Moore
Inamoto
Horsfield
Kirkland
Ellington
Campbell
Kanu
Davies C
Wallwork
Albrechtsen
Greening
Gera
Long
Lita
Kitson
Doyle
Oster
Makin
Sidwell
Gunnarsson
Stack
Harper
Ingimarsson
Hunt
Little
Shorey

4/4/2

Unused Sub: Kuszczak, Chaplow

4/4/2

Unused Sub: Hahnemann, Sonko

Statistics	West Brom	Reading
Goals	1	1
Shots on Target	3	5
Shots off Target	6	1
Hit Woodwork	0	0
Possession %	47	53
Corners	1	2
Offsides	4	0
Fouls	17	16
Disciplinary Points	0	8

Age/Height

West Bromwich Albion Age

27 yrs, 4 mo

West Bromwich Albion Height

6'1"

Reading Age

25 yrs, 7 mo

Reading Height

5'11"

Baggies striker and despite Royals' protests, Hungarian Zoltan Gera stepped up to stroke home from the penalty spot.

Without a dropped head Reading responded. Shorey delivered a dangerous free kick towards Ivar Ingimarsson, whose far post downward header was intercepted by Albrechsten's flailing arm. A second penalty was awarded and Kevin Doyle blocked out the pressure to strike an unstoppable spot-kick past Kirkland for the equaliser.

Both penalties on reflection had looked a little generous, and in a fairly even game maybe it was apt that both had been coolly slotted away and the tie was taken to a Madejski Stadium replay.

Quote

Steve Coppell

We probably deserved a draw. We played a full part in the game and tried to get forward as much as possible.

2-0 Reading Coventry City

Championship
14.01.06

10
KYOCERA
BE FEARLESS

Ibrahima Sonko outmuscles Stern John

Event Line
42 Williams
Half time 0-0
46 Kitson / LF / OP / IA Assist: Convey
57 Murty
59 Hutchison > Whing
71 Hunt > Convey
74 Adebola > Jorgensen
78 Kitson / LF / OP / 6Y Assist: Hunt
81 Impey > Duffy
87 Lita > Doyle
90 Shaw
Full time 2-0

When Championship action resumed, a more familiar line-up welcomed a very familiar face back to Madejski Stadium in ex-Royals skipper Adie Williams, but Dave Kitson took the headlines by sailing to the top of the goalscoring charts with a second half brace.

Goalless at half-time, a minute after the restart Reading broke the deadlock, Kitson controlling Bobby Convey's pinpoint pass from the left before turning his marker and effortlessly touching over the onrushing Martin Fulop.

Marcus Hahnemann, meanwhile, was performing goalkeeping miracles. After pushing away Stern John's downward header in the opening exchanges, the US stopper athletically tipped Don Hutchison's free-kick around his post and from the resulting corner incredibly scooped James Scowcroft's looping header clear.

Marcus Hall did beat Hahnemann to rattle the crossbar with a fierce volley but Kitson capitalised on some clever footwork from Stephen Hunt to tap home his second and take Reading nine points clear of Sheffield United.

Quote

Steve Coppell

Marcus Hahnemann was the biggest factor in our victory, making four top-quality saves.

Championship Milestone

75

Marcus Hahnemann made his 75th appearance in the Championship.

Venue:	Madejski Stadium	Referee:	A.Bates - 05/06
Attendance:	22,813	Matches:	20
Capacity:	24,200	Yellow Cards:	63
Occupancy:	94%	Red Cards:	4

Reading
Coventry City

Form Coming into Fixture

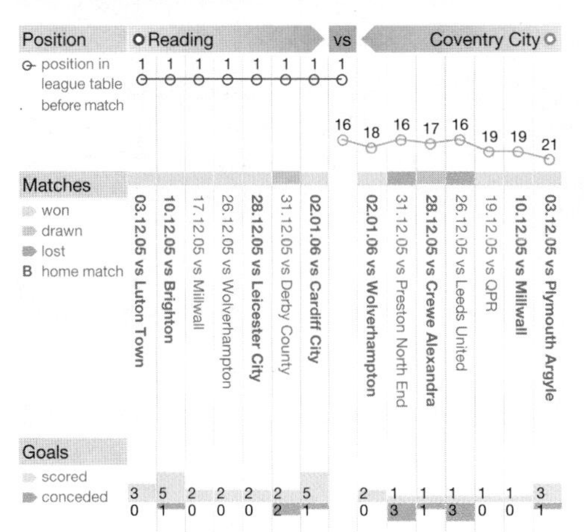

Position
Reading
vs
Coventry City
position in league table before match
1 1 1 1 1 1 1 1
16 18 16 17 16 19 19 21
Matches
won
drawn
lost
B home match
03.12.05 vs Luton Town
10.12.05 vs Brighton
17.12.05 vs Millwall
26.12.05 vs Wolverhampton
28.12.05 vs Leicester City
31.12.05 vs Derby County
02.01.06 vs Cardiff City
02.01.06 vs Wolverhampton
31.12.05 vs Preston North End
28.12.05 vs Crewe Alexandra
26.12.05 vs Leeds United
19.12.05 vs QPR
10.12.05 vs Millwall
03.12.05 vs Plymouth Argyle
Goals
scored
conceded
3 5 2 2 2 2 5
0 1 0 0 0 2 1
2 1 1 1 1 1 3
0 3 1 3 0 0 1

Goal Statistics

Reading

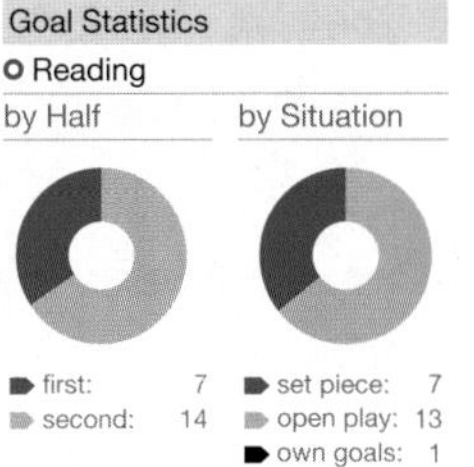

by Half
by Situation
first: 7
second: 14
set piece: 7
open play: 13
own goals: 1

Coventry City

by Half
by Situation
first: 6
second: 4
set piece: 3
open play: 6
own goals: 1

Goals by Area

Reading

Scored (Conceded)

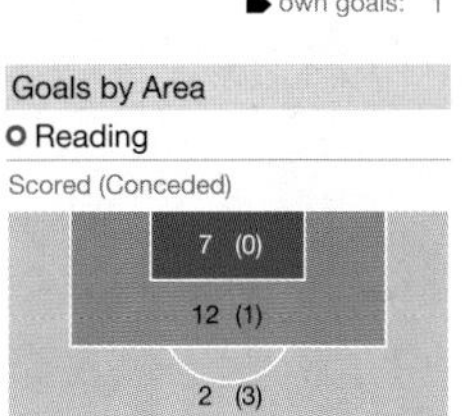

7 (0)
12 (1)
2 (3)

Coventry City

Scored (Conceded)

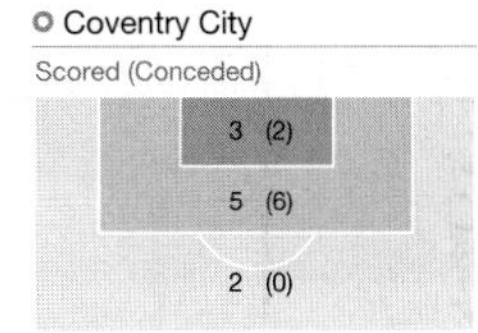

3 (2)
5 (6)
2 (0)

Team Statistics

Starting Line-Ups

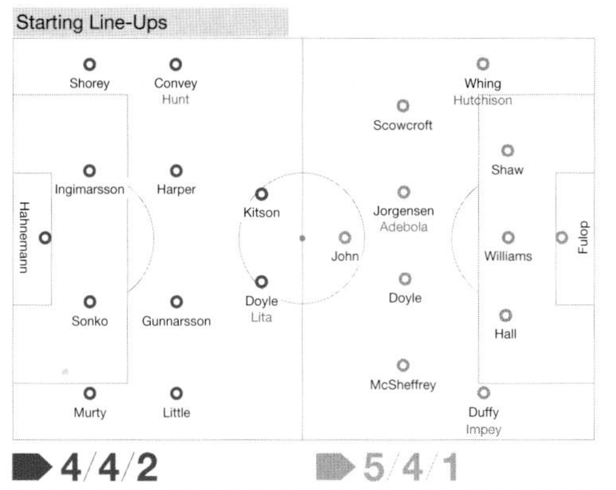

Shorey
Convey
Hunt
Ingimarsson
Harper
Hahnemann
Sonko
Gunnarsson
Murty
Little
Kitson
John
Doyle
Lita
Whing
Hutchison
Scowcroft
Shaw
Jorgensen
Adebola
Williams
Fulop
Doyle
Hall
McSheffrey
Duffy
Impey

4/4/2

Unused Sub: Stack, Makin, Oster

5/4/1

Unused Sub: Ince, Morrell

Championship Totals	Reading	Coventry
Championship Appearances	695	631
Team Appearances	659	493
Goals Scored	81	70
Assists	72	56
Clean Sheets (goalkeepers)	35	5
Yellow Cards	43	89
Red Cards	1	3
Full Internationals	5	7

Age/Height

Reading Age: **26 yrs, 7 mo**

Coventry City Age: **28 yrs, 9 mo**

Reading Height: **5'11"**

Coventry City Height: **6'**

Match Statistics

League Table after Fixture

		Played	Won	Drawn	Lost	For	Against	Pts
● 1	Reading	29	22	6	1	61	15	72
● 2	Sheff Utd	29	19	6	4	54	27	63
● 3	Leeds	28	15	6	7	38	24	51
● 4	Watford	29	13	10	6	46	34	49
● 5	Crystal Palace	27	14	5	8	43	28	47
↑ 6	Preston	28	10	14	4	35	22	44
↓ 7	Wolverhampton	29	10	12	7	34	26	42
...		...	...	...	...	...	...	...
↓ 17	Coventry	29	7	11	11	34	43	32

Statistics	Reading	Coventry
Goals	2	0
Shots on Target	5	2
Shots off Target	4	5
Hit Woodwork	0	1
Possession %	61	39
Corners	7	8
Offsides	2	1
Fouls	10	16
Disciplinary Points	4	8

3-2 Reading ○ West Bromwich Albion ○

FA Cup

17.01.06

Mobile

Stephen Hunt protects the ball well

Event Line
9 ○ ⚽ Chaplow / LF / OP / IA
Assist: Wallwork
32 ○ ⚽ Chaplow / RF / OP / 6Y
Assist: Ellington
38 ○ ▪ Long
Half time 0-2
50 ○ ⚽ Lita / LF / OP / IA
Assist: Oster
65 ○ ⚽ Lita / RF / OP / OA
Assist: Harper
79 ○ ▪ Wallwork
81 ○ ⇄ Dyer > Greening
90 ○ ⇄ Davies R > Inamoto
90 ○ ⇄ Doyle > Long
93 ○ ⚽ Lita / RF / OP / IA
Assist: Harper
94 ○ ▪ Lita
101 ○ ⇄ Cox > Lita
106 ○ ⇄ Nicholson > Wallwork
107 ○ ⇄ Osano > Oster
Full time 3-2

Madejski Stadium witnessed a thrilling Royals comeback which earned the home side a Fourth Round clash with Birmingham City and dumped Bryan Robson's West Bromwich Albion side out of the FA Cup in extra time.

Ex-Burnley midfielder Richard Chaplow seemed to have swung a delicately matched tie into Albion's favour with two early goals that stunned an expectant Royals crowd. The former Claret first beat the offside trap to race onto Ronnie Wallwork's throughball and drill beyond Graham Stack in the 9th minute. After few other openings at either end, Ellington latched onto Darren Carter's cross with half an hour gone to force Stack into a half-stop at his near post, and Chaplow burst onto the rebound to tap the Baggies into a two goal lead and duplicate his name on the scoresheet.

Reading's Cup hopes were fading at half time, but the home side soon had a reply. The outstandingly creative John Oster weaved through bodies soon after the interval to cross low into Leroy Lita, who took a touch and struck low past Chris Kirkland to halve the deficit.

Lita then summoned something special for a 65th minute equaliser. Good work from Shane Long and a canny flick in the middle of the field from James Harper cleverly released Lita in space, and the striker instinctively whipped a breathtaking 25-yard strike over Kirkland and into the top corner, triggering an impromptu celebration with kit man Ron Grant who was sent crashing to the dugout ground in a show of boisterous jubilation.

Venue:	Madejski Stadium	Referee:	P.Taylor - 05/06
Attendance:	16,737	Matches:	20
Capacity:	24,200	Yellow Cards:	52
Occupancy:	69%	Red Cards:	4

Reading
West Bromwich Albion

Kit man Ron Grant congratulates hat-trick hero Leroy Lita

Match Statistics

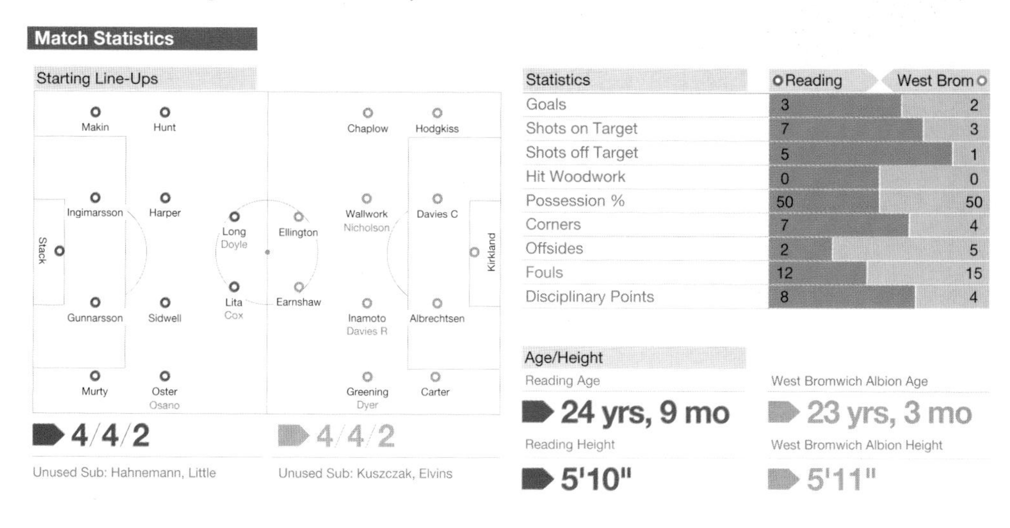

Starting Line-Ups
Makin
Hunt
Ingimarsson
Harper
Stack
Gunnarsson
Sidwell
Murty
Oster
Osano
Long
Doyle
Lita
Cox
Ellington
Earnshaw
Chaplow
Hodgkiss
Wallwork
Nicholson
Davies C
Kirkland
Inamoto
Davies R
Albrechtsen
Greening
Dyer
Carter
4/4/2
4/4/2

Unused Sub: Hahnemann, Little

Unused Sub: Kuszczak, Elvins

Statistics	Reading	West Brom
Goals	3	2
Shots on Target	7	3
Shots off Target	5	1
Hit Woodwork	0	0
Possession %	50	50
Corners	7	4
Offsides	2	5
Fouls	12	15
Disciplinary Points	8	4

Age/Height

Reading Age
24 yrs, 9 mo

West Bromwich Albion Age
23 yrs, 3 mo

Reading Height
5'10"

West Bromwich Albion Height
5'11"

Stack had to parry Ellington's powerful strike four minutes later to keep the comeback alive and take the game beyond 90 minutes and into extra time. And three minutes into the first period, the matchball was Lita's. Oster fed Harper, who prodded through to the goal-hungry frontman who clinically squeezed a low strike beyond on-loan Liverpool keeper Kirkland for his hattrick and to deny Albion a local cup derby with Steve Bruce's Blues, who overcame Torquay at the second attempt.

A dominant Reading side deserved the win and Steve Coppell took the chance to blood two young prospects in extra time, the impressive Curtis Osano making his first team debut and Simon Cox also tasting first team action.

Quote

Steve Coppell

Leroy Lita is one of those players who, when he gets a sight of goal, thinks of nothing else but scoring.

1-1 Crystal Palace ○ Reading ○

Championship

20.01.06

CROYDON

James Harper salvages a point at Selhurst Park

Event Line
Half time 0-0
64 Lita > Kitson
76 Hughes
79 Johnson / RF / P / IA Assist: Johnson
80 Johnson
81 Harper / RF / OP / IA Assist: Lita
Full time 1-1

The unbeaten league run continued as the Royals earned a valuable point from a difficult trip to Selhurst Park.

James Harper almost gifted the lethal Andy Johnson a fourth minute first when his mis-hit backpass inadvertently fell into the England man's path, but Marcus Hahnemann raced from his line to narrow the angle and save well.

Hahnemann was Johnson's nemesis for much of the match, palming wide and parrying a cheeky header to frustrate the nippy striker. Meanwhile Hungarian goalkeeper Gabor Kiraly had to pull off fingertip saves to prevent Glen Little's left-footed volley and Kevin Doyle's testing header.

With just over 10 minutes remaining, the relentlessly searching Johnson penetrated again and nudging past Hahnemann, he tripped over the American's frame. Aptly, Johnson took the resulting spotkick himself and calmly made it 1-0.

Seconds after the restart though, Harper levelled matters. Little fed Lita who teed up the midfield maestro and without breaking stride Harper ferociously drove past Kiraly. The Royals still needed Hahnemann to produce an astonishing double save to deny Johnson and then Tom Soares to seal the point.

Quote

Steve Coppell

I can only compliment the players on a terrific response to going behind.

Venue:	Selhurst Park	Referee:	T.Kettle - 05/06
Attendance:	19,888	Matches:	22
Capacity:	26,309	Yellow Cards:	101
Occupancy:	76%	Red Cards:	7

Crystal Palace
Reading

Form Coming into Fixture

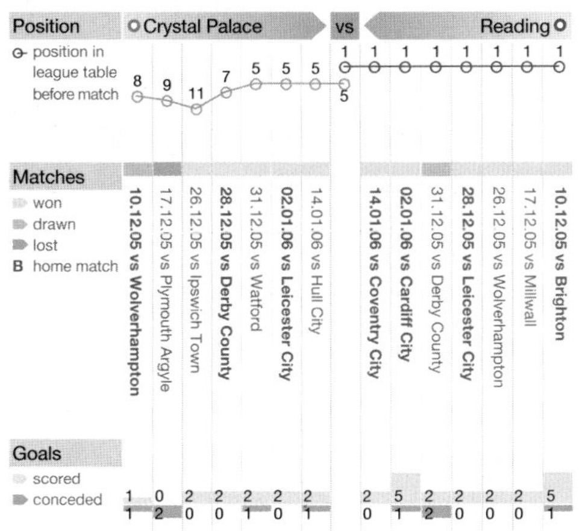

Position
Crystal Palace
vs
Reading
position in league table before match
8
9
11
7
5
5
5
1
1
1
1
1
1
1
1
5
Matches
won
drawn
lost
B home match
10.12.05 vs Wolverhampton
17.12.05 vs Plymouth Argyle
26.12.05 vs Ipswich Town
28.12.05 vs Derby County
31.12.05 vs Watford
02.01.06 vs Leicester City
14.01.06 vs Hull City
14.01.06 vs Coventry City
02.01.06 vs Cardiff City
31.12.05 vs Derby County
28.12.05 vs Leicester City
26.12.05 vs Wolverhampton
17.12.05 vs Millwall
10.12.05 vs Brighton
Goals
scored
conceded
1 0 2 2 2 2 2
1 2 0 0 1 0 1
2 5 2 2 2 2 5
0 1 2 0 0 0 1

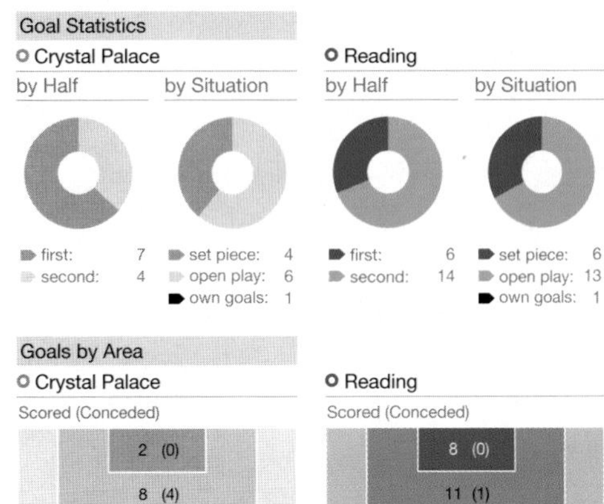

Goal Statistics
Crystal Palace
by Half
by Situation
Reading
by Half
by Situation
first: 7
second: 4
set piece: 4
open play: 6
own goals: 1
first: 6
second: 14
set piece: 6
open play: 13
own goals: 1
Goals by Area
Crystal Palace
Scored (Conceded)
2 (0)
8 (4)
1 (1)
Reading
Scored (Conceded)
8 (0)
11 (1)
1 (3)

Team Statistics

Starting Line-Ups
Boyce
McAnuff
Hudson
Hughes
Kiraly
Macken
Kitson
Lita
Johnson
Doyle
Ward
Watson
Hall F
Soares
Little
Murty
Sidwell
Sonko
Hahnemann
Harper
Ingimarsson
Convey
Shorey

4/4/2

Unused Sub: Speroni, Leigertwood, Andrews, Freedman, Morrison

4/4/2

Unused Sub: Stack, Gunnarsson, Hunt, Oster

Championship Totals	C. Palace	Reading
Championship Appearances	324	695
Team Appearances	237	695
Goals Scored	28	86
Assists	21	74
Clean Sheets (goalkeepers)	9	36
Yellow Cards	50	50
Red Cards	2	0
Full Internationals	5	4

Age/Height

Crystal Palace Age

25 yrs, 10 mo

Reading Age

26 yrs, 2 mo

Crystal Palace Height

5'11"

Reading Height

5'11"

Match Statistics

League Table after Fixture

		Played	Won	Drawn	Lost	For	Against	Pts
1	Reading	30	22	7	1	62	16	73
2	Sheff Utd	29	19	6	4	54	27	63
3	Leeds	28	15	6	7	38	24	51
4	Watford	29	13	10	6	46	34	49
5	Crystal Palace	28	14	6	8	44	29	48
6	Preston	28	10	14	4	35	22	44
7	Wolverhampton	29	10	12	7	34	26	42
8	Cardiff	29	11	8	10	39	35	41
9	Burnley	29	11	6	12	39	38	39

Statistics	C. Palace	Reading
Goals	1	1
Shots on Target	12	6
Shots off Target	3	9
Hit Woodwork	0	0
Possession %	51	49
Corners	7	8
Offsides	5	3
Fouls	13	8
Disciplinary Points	8	0

1-1 Reading Birmingham City

FA Cup

28.01.06

flybe
KYOCERA
PUMA
Shane Long gets a shot away

Event Line

31	Long / RF / OP / IA
	Assist: Harper
Half time 1-0	
57	Dunn > Heskey
57	Kilkenny > Izzet
57	Forssell > Jarosik
67	Dunn / RF / OP / IA
	Assist: Sutton
75	Tebily
87	Oster
88	Sonko
90	Doyle > Long
Full time 1-1	

The FA Cup run was prolonged as another top flight side almost came unstuck at the hands of Steve Coppell's high-flying Royals.

Coppell made no fewer than eight changes to the side that started at Crystal Palace a week earlier, the most significant of which saw new signing John Halls make his Reading debut in place of the rested Graeme Murty at right-back. Brynjar Gunnarsson continued his new-found Cup role which saw him start at centre-back against both the Baggies and the Blues.

Steve Bruce named a strong squad for the Madejski Stadium clash and a starting line-up that included ex-Chelsea men Mario Melchiot and Jiri Jarosik, former England strikers Emile Heskey and Chris Sutton plus creative midfielder Muzzy Izzet. Former Arsenal youngster Jermaine Pennant was given the chance to link up with our collection of ex-Gunners again, while son of the gaffer, Alex Bruce, began at centre-back.

Izzet had the first chance of the game but sent his instinctive header from Melchiot's launched long throw looping over Graham Stack's crossbar. But with half an hour gone it was Shane Long who stole the headlines. John Oster laid off to James Harper, who brilliantly swept a reverse pass to his right and into Long's quick step. The young Irishman had peeled off his marker effectively and, unchallenged, he placed a succulent low fizzer inside Maik Taylor's right hand post for his first goal in front of the home fans.

Blues substitute David Dunn, though, was to take the plaudits after the injury-plagued midfielder was introduced just before the hour. After finding his range with an early volley, Dunn steered Pennant's cross to Stack's right with a diving header from distance to fire a warning of what he could do.

Venue:	Madejski Stadium	Referee:	R.Styles - 05/06	**Reading**
Attendance:	23,762	Matches:	27	**Birmingham City**
Capacity:	24,200	Yellow Cards:	92	
Occupancy:	98%	Red Cards:	3	

KYOCERA

Birmingham City's Emile Heskey challenges Brynjar Gunnarsson

Match Statistics

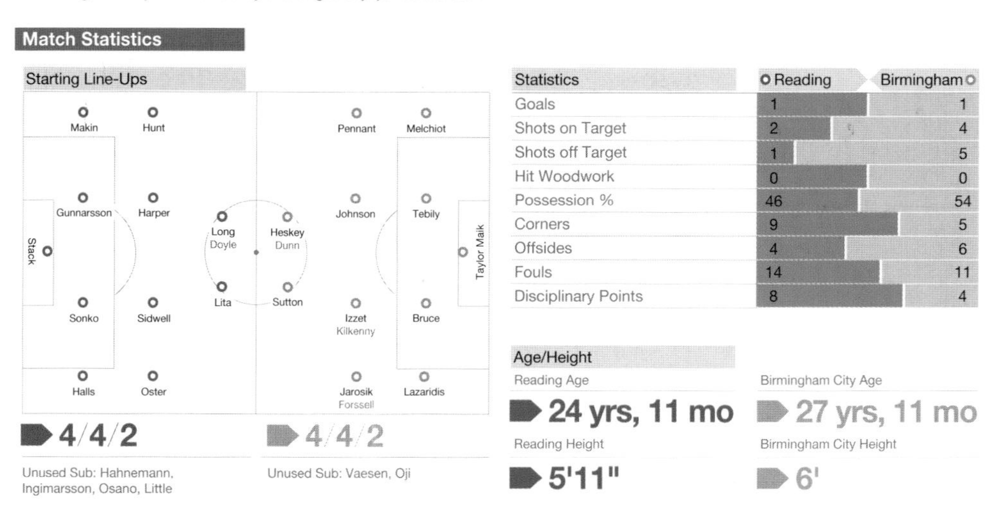

Starting Line-Ups
Makin
Hunt
Gunnarsson
Harper
Stack
Sonko
Sidwell
Halls
Oster
Long
Doyle
Lita
Heskey
Dunn
Sutton
Pennant
Melchiot
Johnson
Tebily
Taylor Maik
Izzet
Kilkenny
Bruce
Jarosik
Forssell
Lazaridis

4/4/2

Unused Sub: Hahnemann, Ingimarsson, Osano, Little

4/4/2

Unused Sub: Vaesen, Oji

Statistics	Reading	Birmingham
Goals	1	1
Shots on Target	2	4
Shots off Target	1	5
Hit Woodwork	0	0
Possession %	46	54
Corners	9	5
Offsides	4	6
Fouls	14	11
Disciplinary Points	8	4

Age/Height

Reading Age

24 yrs, 11 mo

Reading Height

5'11"

Birmingham City Age

27 yrs, 11 mo

Birmingham City Height

6'

It wasn't heeded and less than 10 minutes after taking to the field, Dunn latched onto Sutton's flick on the edge of six yard box, and the midfielder easily swept an equaliser past Stack at the back post.

Stack had to make two important saves to force the eventual replay as a spurred City finished the stronger of the two sides. The first saw Melchiot's close range header cannon luckily off the keeper's chest, while the second saw Stack tip Pennant's free-kick past his post and take the tie to St Andrews.

Quote

Steve Coppell

Once we took the lead, it was almost as though we had settled for a 1-0 win, which was fatal.

4-0 Reading Norwich City

Championship

31.01.06

KYOCERA
AWE

James Harper closes down former teammate Andy Hughes

Event Line	
6	Doherty
6	Shorey / LF / DFK / OA
	Assist: Doyle
17	Sidwell / H / OP / 6Y
	Assist: Little
Half time 2-0	
46	Jarrett > Drury
55	Lita / RF / OP / 6Y
	Assist: Doyle
60	Oster > Little
64	Jarrett
64	Henderson > McVeigh
64	Johansson > Thorne
69	Convey / RF / OP / IA
	Assist: Shorey
71	Gunnarsson > Sidwell
74	Long > Doyle
90	Charlton
Full time 4-0	

Another prolific Reading display humbled the previous season's final day Premiership relegation victims as Steve Coppell's side ended January with four goals and a masterclass in clinical finishing.

An archetypal Kevin Doyle burst left Gary Doherty for dead and forced the ex-Spurs centre-back to pull his fellow Irishman to ground 25 yards from goal. Nicky Shorey stepped up to brilliantly place the left-footed curler inside Robert Green's post for his first of the campaign.

The game was being played at a frantic pace and the mesmeric Glen Little delicately danced between bodies to reach the byline and chip inside where Steve Sidwell stooped to head home a second.

Andy Hughes' Canaries were squandering what chances they had with Dickson Etuhu dragging wide and Jason Jarrett lashing over, and soon it was three. Doyle embarrassed Doherty again and supplied a battling Leroy Lita with a six yard box finish, before a confident Bobby Convey effortlessly raced 40 yards to add an excellent fourth and the rout was complete.

Quote

Steve Coppell

Although we looked good going forward, 4-0 probably flattered us. We'll keep taking it one game at a time and continue to build our season.

Championship Milestone

75

Ivar Ingimarsson made his 75th appearance in the Championship.

Venue:	Madejski Stadium	Referee:	L.Mason - 05/06
Attendance:	21,442	Matches:	19
Capacity:	24,200	Yellow Cards:	49
Occupancy:	89%	Red Cards:	2

Reading
Norwich City

Form Coming into Fixture

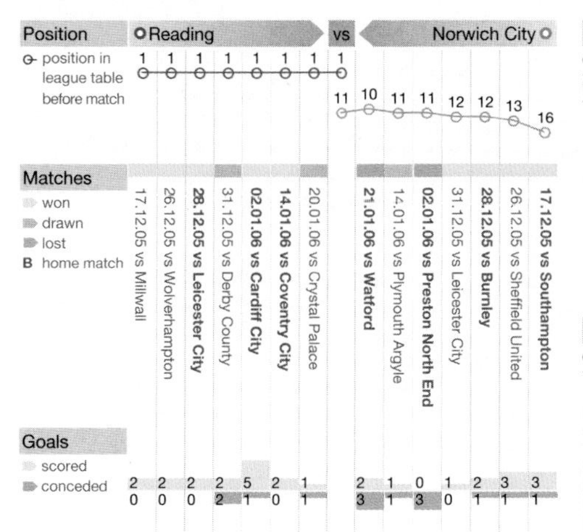

Position
Reading
vs
Norwich City
position in league table before match
1 1 1 1 1 1 1 1
11 10 11 11 12 12 13 16
Matches
won
drawn
lost
B home match
17.12.05 vs Millwall
26.12.05 vs Wolverhampton
28.12.05 vs Leicester City
31.12.05 vs Derby County
02.01.06 vs Cardiff City
14.01.06 vs Coventry City
20.01.06 vs Crystal Palace
21.01.06 vs Watford
14.01.06 vs Plymouth Argyle
02.01.06 vs Preston North End
31.12.05 vs Leicester City
28.12.05 vs Burnley
26.12.05 vs Sheffield United
17.12.05 vs Southampton
Goals
scored
conceded
2 2 2 2 5 2 1 2 1 0 1 2 3 3
0 0 0 2 1 0 1 3 1 3 0 1 1 1

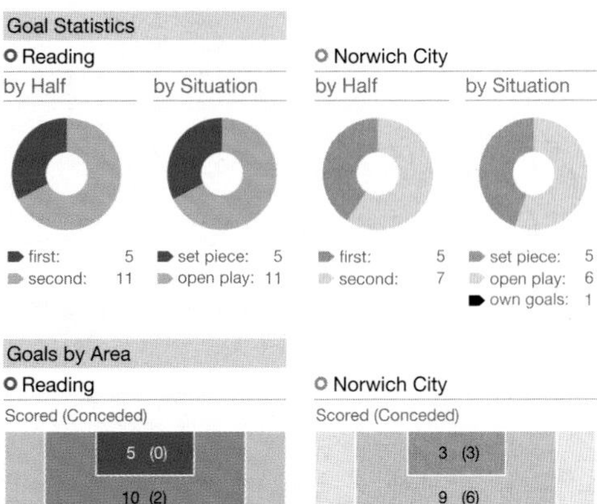

Goal Statistics
Reading
by Half
by Situation
first: 5
second: 11
set piece: 5
open play: 11
Norwich City
by Half
by Situation
first: 5
second: 7
set piece: 5
open play: 6
own goals: 1
Goals by Area
Reading
Scored (Conceded)
5 (0)
10 (2)
1 (2)
Norwich City
Scored (Conceded)
3 (3)
9 (6)
0 (1)

Team Statistics

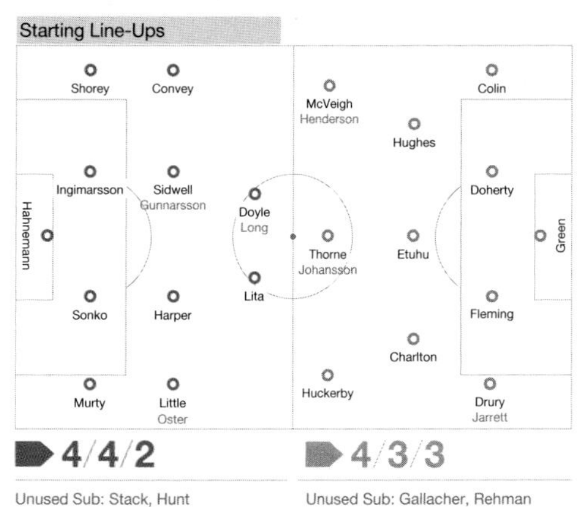

Starting Line-Ups
Shorey
Convey
Ingimarsson
Sidwell
Gunnarsson
Hannemann
Doyle
Long
Lita
Sonko
Harper
Murty
Little
Oster
McVeigh
Henderson
Hughes
Thorne
Johansson
Etuhu
Charlton
Huckerby
Colin
Doherty
Green
Fleming
Drury
Jarrett
4/4/2
4/3/3

Unused Sub: Stack, Hunt

Unused Sub: Gallacher, Rehman

Championship Totals	Reading	Norwich
Championship Appearances	758	408
Team Appearances	690	265
Goals Scored	65	34
Assists	74	25
Clean Sheets (goalkeepers)	36	5
Yellow Cards	53	37
Red Cards	1	2
Full Internationals	6	4

Age/Height

Reading Age	Norwich City Age
26 yrs	28 yrs, 1 mo
Reading Height	Norwich City Height
5'11"	5'11"

Match Statistics

League Table after Fixture

		Played	Won	Drawn	Lost	For	Against	Pts
• 1	Reading	31	23	7	1	66	16	76
• 2	Sheff Utd	30	20	6	4	57	28	66
↑ 3	Leeds	30	16	7	7	42	25	55
↓ 4	Watford	31	15	10	6	53	37	55
↑ 5	Preston	30	12	14	4	39	22	50
↓ 6	Crystal Palace	30	14	7	9	44	31	49
• 7	Cardiff	31	12	9	10	42	37	45
...		...	...	...	...	...	...	...
↓ 12	Norwich	31	11	6	14	35	44	39

Statistics	Reading	Norwich
Goals	4	0
Shots on Target	7	2
Shots off Target	3	4
Hit Woodwork	0	0
Possession %	58	42
Corners	4	1
Offsides	3	3
Fouls	7	13
Disciplinary Points	0	12

3-4 Crewe Alexandra ○ Reading ○

Championship

04.02.06

KYOCERA

Glen Little waltzes through the Crewe defence

Event Line	
14 ○ ⊕ Bell / RF / OP / 6Y	Assist: Rodgers
24 ● ⊕ Shorey / LF / DFK / OA	Assist: Convey
26 ● ⊕ Sidwell / H / OP / 6Y	Assist: Little
43 ● ⊕ Lita / RF / OP / IA	Assist: Shorey
Half time 1-3	
51 ○ ⊕ Taylor / LF / OP / 6Y	Assist: Jones S
53 ● ⊕ Lita / RF / OP / IA	Assist: Convey
68 ○ ⊕ Lunt / RF / P / IA	Assist: Jones S
69 ○ ⇄ McCready > Bell	
79 ● ⇄ Hunt > Convey	
81 ● ⇄ Kitson > Lita	
87 ○ ⇄ Moss > Tonkin	
90 ● ⇄ Gunnarsson > Little	
90 ○ ■ Lunt	Foul
Full time 3-4	

Seven goals were scored when top met bottom in an enthrallingly open and entertaining encounter at Gresty Road.

Early on Kevin Doyle struck the base of Ross Turnbull's far post, but the Railwaymen took the lead five minutes later, when Marcus Hahnemann parried Luke Rodgers' swerving strike into the stride of Luke Bell, who quickly turned the loose ball home.

Leroy Lita peppered a shot against the crossbar before two goals in two minutes saw the lead change hands. Nicky Shorey scored another left-footed free-kick before Glen Little's 26th minute cross was headed back across Turnbull and into the far post by Steve Sidwell.

Before the break, Lita turned to drive an excellently crafted 18-yard third, but soon after the interval Steve Jones' downward header was only pushed into Gareth Taylor's path and Crewe were back in it. Lita settled away day nerves by deftly glancing Bobby Convey's low cross in at the near post and although Shorey's handball allowed Kenny Lunt to make it 4-3 from the spot, Lunt was sent off for pulling back Stephen Hunt in the dying stages and the Royals held on for the points.

Quote

Steve Coppell

If we keep winning games and keep accumulating points, it's going to be hard for others, but it is not about looking at anyone else.

Championship Milestone

50

Bobby Convey made his 50th appearance in the Championship.

Venue:	Gresty Road
Attendance:	6,484
Capacity:	10,066
Occupancy:	64%

Referee:	C.H.Webster - 05/06
Matches:	24
Yellow Cards:	82
Red Cards:	9

Crewe Alexandra
Reading

Form Coming into Fixture

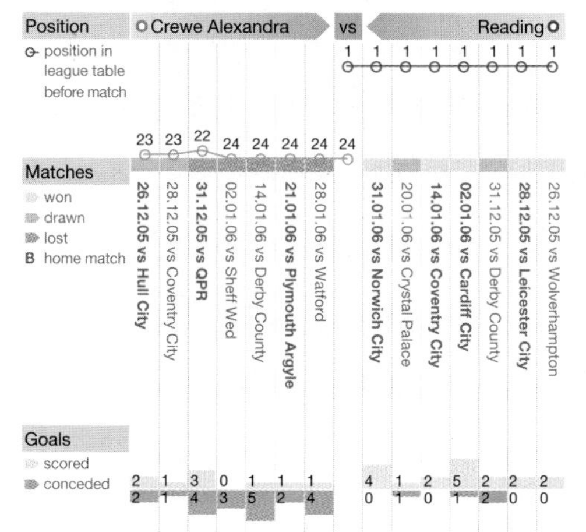

Position
Crewe Alexandra
vs
Reading
position in league table before match
1 1 1 1 1 1 1 1
23 23 22 24 24 24 24 24
Matches
won
drawn
lost
B home match
26.12.05 vs Hull City
28.12.05 vs Coventry City
31.12.05 vs QPR
02.01.06 vs Sheff Wed
14.01.06 vs Derby County
21.01.06 vs Plymouth Argyle
28.01.06 vs Watford
31.01.06 vs Norwich City
20.01.06 vs Crystal Palace
14.01.06 vs Coventry City
02.01.06 vs Cardiff City
31.12.05 vs Derby County
28.12.05 vs Leicester City
26.12.05 vs Wolverhampton
Goals
scored
conceded
2 1 3 0 1 1 1
2 1 4 3 5 2 4
4 1 2 5 2 2 2
0 1 0 1 2 0 0

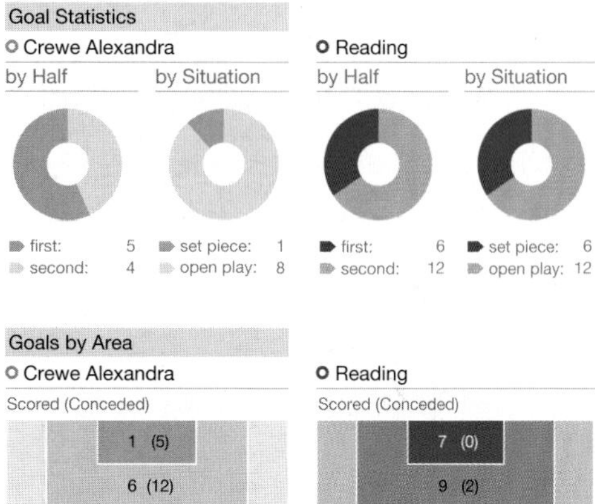

Goal Statistics
Crewe Alexandra
by Half
by Situation
first: 5
second: 4
set piece: 1
open play: 8
Reading
by Half
by Situation
first: 6
second: 12
set piece: 6
open play: 12

Goals by Area

Crewe Alexandra — Scored (Conceded)

1 (5)
6 (12)
2 (4)

Reading — Scored (Conceded)

7 (0)
9 (2)
2 (2)

Team Statistics

Starting Line-Ups

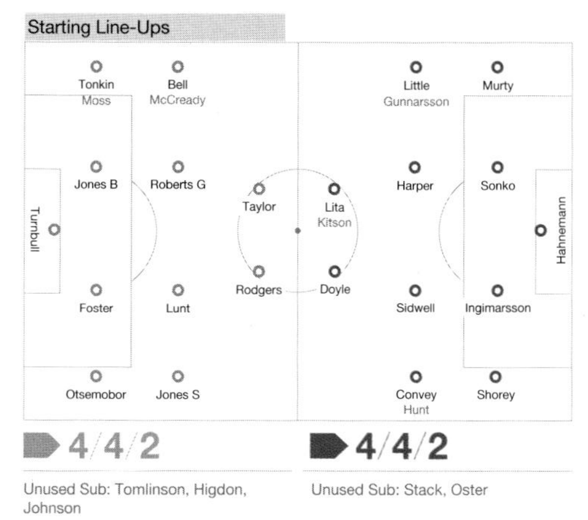

Tonkin
Moss
Bell
McCready
Jones B
Roberts G
Taylor
Lita
Kitson
Turnbull
Foster
Lunt
Rodgers
Doyle
Otsemobor
Jones S
Little
Gunnarsson
Murty
Harper
Sonko
Hahnemann
Sidwell
Ingimarsson
Convey
Hunt
Shorey

4/4/2

Unused Sub: Tomlinson, Higdon, Johnson

4/4/2

Unused Sub: Stack, Oster

Championship Totals	Crewe	Reading
Championship Appearances	511	795
Team Appearances	475	759
Goals Scored	40	99
Assists	57	83
Clean Sheets (goalkeepers)	1	37
Yellow Cards	39	60
Red Cards	4	1
Full Internationals	2	5

Age/Height

Crewe Alexandra Age

24 yrs, 5 mo

Crewe Alexandra Height

5'11"

Reading Age

26 yrs, 4 mo

Reading Height

5'11"

Match Statistics

League Table after Fixture

		Played	Won	Drawn	Lost	For	Against	Pts
● 1	Reading	32	24	7	1	70	19	79
● 2	Sheff Utd	31	21	6	4	58	28	69
● 3	Leeds	31	17	7	7	44	25	58
● 4	Watford	31	15	10	6	53	37	55
↑ 5	Crystal Palace	31	15	7	9	45	31	52
↓ 6	Preston	31	12	15	4	39	22	51
● 7	Cardiff	32	12	9	11	42	38	45
...		...	...	...	...	...	...	...
● 24	Crewe	32	4	10	18	37	71	22

Statistics	Crewe	Reading
Goals	3	4
Shots on Target	9	11
Shots off Target	5	6
Hit Woodwork	1	2
Possession %	49	51
Corners	5	3
Offsides	1	2
Fouls	10	8
Disciplinary Points	12	0

2-1 Birmingham City ○ Reading ○

FA Cup

07.02.06

29
KYOCERA

All eyes on the coin toss

Event Line

30 ○ ⚽ Forssell / LF / OP / 6Y
Assist: Pennant

Half time 1-0

51 ○ ⚽ Hunt / LF / OP / IA
Assist: Oster

59 ○ ⇄ Sadler > Birley

67 ○ ⚽ Gray / H / OP / 6Y
Assist: Jarosik

68 ○ ⇄ Cox > Long

76 ○ Gunnarsson

90 ○ ⇄ Oji > Clemence

Full time 2-1

A fourth tightly contested cup tie in the space of a month saw the Royals finally beaten by Premiership opposition in front of a meek midweek St Andrews crowd.

Steve Coppell named a vastly inexperienced squad as he rested many of his first team stars in favour of a very youthful bench which included Adam Federici, Scott Golbourne, Curtis Osano, Conor Sinnott and Simon Cox. Steve Bruce made changes too, but they were largely forced upon him by a long list of injuries which hamstrung his options.

The Royals had a fantastic chance to take a seventh-minute lead. Brynjar Gunnarsson evaded two challenges in midfield to carve a pass through to Dave Kitson, who beat the offside trap to race at Maik Taylor and in on goal. But the striker dragged his effort just wide of the far post and the game remained goalless.

On the half hour mark, Reading were made to pay. The dangerous Jermaine Pennant passed inside and Finnish striker Mikael Forssell touched it past two defensive challenges to edge into the box. Graham Stack parried the frontman's first effort but it fell kindly back to the ex-Chelsea predator, who made no second mistake and opened the scoring.

Two minutes later Reading could so easily have restored parity. Steve Sidwell blasted a stunning low drive which seemed certain to creep inside the City woodwork for an immediate response, but Maik Taylor tipped it onto his right post. The rebound came quickly at Kitson who instinctively directed it back towards goal but Taylor recovered to save for a second time.

Venue:	St Andrew's	Referee:	P.Walton - 05/06	**Birmingham City**
Attendance:	16,644	Matches:	27	**Reading**
Capacity:	30,016	Yellow Cards:	85	
Occupancy:	55%	Red Cards:	4	

Dave Kitson lines up a shot

Match Statistics

Starting Line-Ups
Gray
Birley
Sadler
Painter
Clemence
Oji
Taylor Maik
Bruce
Clapham
Melchiot
Pennant
Jarosik
Long
Cox
Forssell
Kitson
Oster
Halls
Gunnarsson
Sonko
Stack
Sidwell
Ingimarsson
Hunt
Makin

4/4/2

Unused Sub: Vaesen, Alsop, Allen

4/4/2

Unused Sub: Federici, Golbourne, Osano, Sinnott

Statistics	Birmingham	Reading
Goals	2	1
Shots on Target	5	4
Shots off Target	5	2
Hit Woodwork	0	2
Possession %	43	57
Corners	4	6
Offsides	1	3
Fouls	14	11
Disciplinary Points	0	4

Age/Height

Birmingham City Age	Reading Age
25 yrs, 1 mo	25 yrs, 4 mo

Birmingham City Height	Reading Height
6'	6'

One down at half time, Stephen Hunt equalised soon after the break when a chance sprouted from nowhere. John Oster's direct floated ball wasn't adequately dealt with by Alex Bruce and Hunt wrestled ahead of the Birmingham boss' son to find space and rifle a stunning volley beyond Taylor for 1-1.

The home side responded though, and Stack had to save smartly from Jiri Jarosik before Julian Gray sliced a great chance high over the crossbar just after the hour. But Gray made no mistake four minutes later, ghosting in at the far post to head Jarosik's floated cross home for an insurmountable 2-1 lead. City went on to beat Stoke before crashing out 7-0 in the quarter-finals to Liverpool.

Quote

Steve Coppell

We had good possession and created some decent chances, but it was a difficult night.

2-0 Reading Southampton

Championship

10.02.06

KYOCE

Leroy Lita celebrates opening the scoring

Event Line
16 Lita / RF / OP / 6Y
Assist: Little
19 Ostlund
38 Doyle / LF / IFK / IA
Assist: Hahnemann
Half time 2-0
70 Surman > Dyer
76 Kitson > Lita
81 Jones > Madsen
81 Hunt > Convey
Full time 2-0

Following a thunderous goalless draw at St Mary's in September, the Royals braced themselves for another stern test when George Burley's new look Saints side visited Madejski Stadium. But two first half finishes saw Southampton soundly beaten in front of Sky Sports' Friday night cameras.

Glen Little capitalised on inexperience and hesitation from Nathan Dyer in the 16th minute to dispossess the youngster and square for Leroy Lita, who simply had to direct the low cut back into a gaping net for a deserved opener.

Saints had two great chances to level before the break, Grzegorz Rasiak dragging the best opportunity wide of Marcus Hahnemann's far post before Alexander Ostlund went closer by powering his bullet header against the woodwork.

Kevin Doyle then doubled the lead, controlling Hahnemann's long clearance before drilling low inside the right upright and sealing all three points for the table-toppers. The second half was relatively uneventful, with Saints unable to claw their way back into the game as the Royals rearguard held firm.

Quote

Steve Coppell

We are three points closer, but we just take one game at a time and keep ticking them off.

Championship Milestone

23,845

The attendance of 23,845 was a Championship record at the Madejski Stadium.

Venue:	Madejski Stadium	Referee:	A.P.D'Urso - 05/06
Attendance:	23,845	Matches:	23
Capacity:	24,200	Yellow Cards:	85
Occupancy:	99%	Red Cards:	8

Reading
Southampton

Form Coming into Fixture

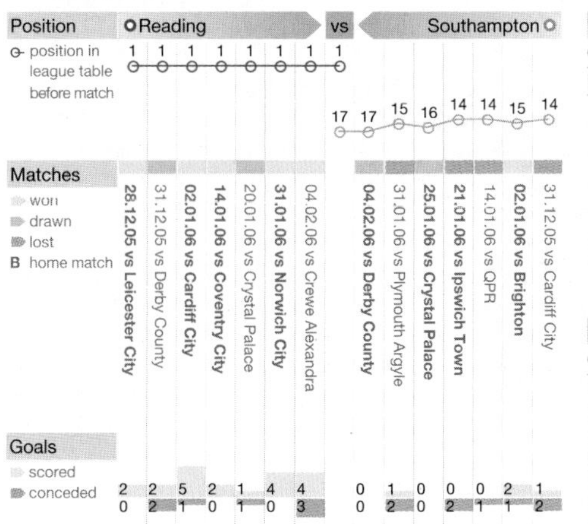

Position
Reading
vs
Southampton
position in league table before match
1 1 1 1 1 1 1 1
17 17 15 16 14 14 15 14
Matches
won
drawn
lost
B home match
28.12.05 vs Leicester City
31.12.05 vs Derby County
02.01.06 vs Cardiff City
14.01.06 vs Coventry City
20.01.06 vs Crystal Palace
31.01.06 vs Norwich City
04.02.06 vs Crewe Alexandra
04.02.06 vs Derby County
31.01.06 vs Plymouth Argyle
25.01.06 vs Crystal Palace
21.01.06 vs Ipswich Town
14.01.06 vs QPR
02.01.06 vs Brighton
31.12.05 vs Cardiff City
Goals
scored
conceded
2 2 5 2 1 4 4
0 2 1 0 1 0 3
0 1 0 0 0 2 1
0 2 0 2 1 1 2

Goal Statistics

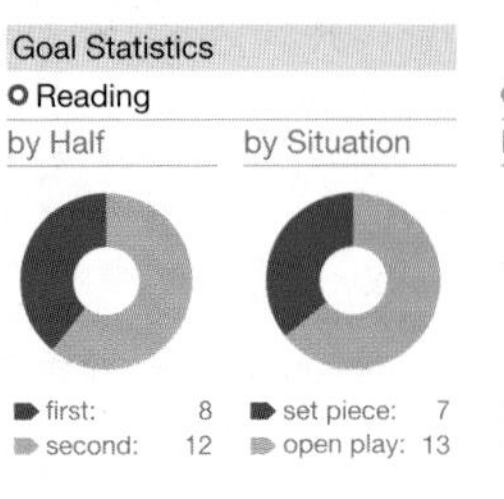

Reading
by Half
by Situation
first: 8
second: 12
set piece: 7
open play: 13

Southampton
by Half
by Situation
first: 2
second: 2
set piece: 0
open play: 4

Goals by Area

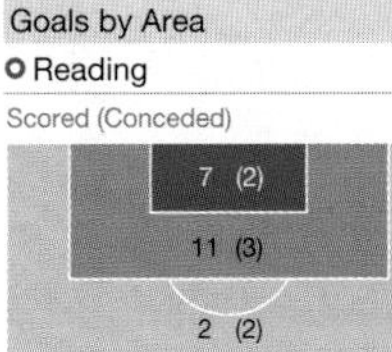

Reading
Scored (Conceded)
7 (2)
11 (3)
2 (2)

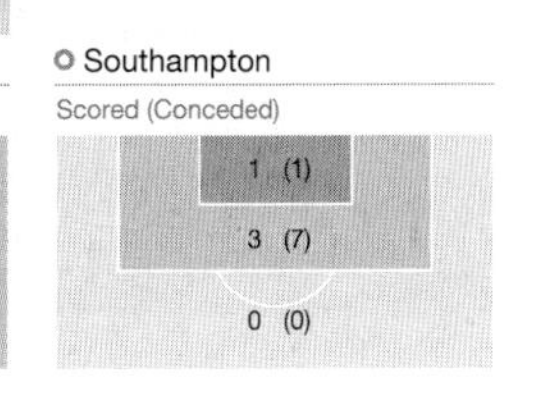

Southampton
Scored (Conceded)
1 (1)
3 (7)
0 (0)

Team Statistics

Starting Line-Ups

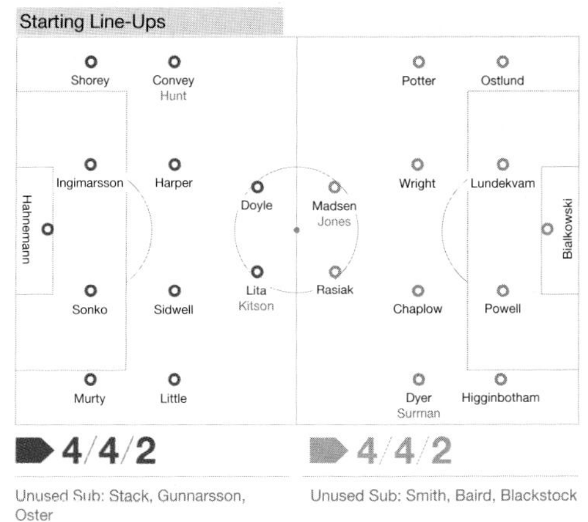

Shorey
Convey
Hunt
Ingimarsson
Harper
Hahnemann
Doyle
Madsen
Jones
Lita
Kitson
Rasiak
Sonko
Sidwell
Murty
Little
Potter
Ostlund
Wright
Lundekvam
Bialkowski
Chaplow
Powell
Dyer
Surman
Higginbotham

4/4/2 — 4/4/2

Unused Sub: Stack, Gunnarsson, Oster

Unused Sub: Smith, Baird, Blackstock

Championship Totals	Reading	Southampton
Championship Appearances	755	249
Team Appearances	755	111
Goals Scored	96	37
Assists	84	36
Clean Sheets (goalkeepers)	37	2
Yellow Cards	51	23
Red Cards	0	1
Full Internationals	4	5

Age/Height

Reading Age	Southampton Age
26 yrs, 1 mo	24 yrs, 9 mo
Reading Height	**Southampton Height**
5'11"	6'1"

Match Statistics

League Table after Fixture

	Played	Won	Drawn	Lost	For	Against	Pts
1 Reading	33	25	7	1	72	19	82
2 Sheff Utd	32	21	6	5	59	32	69
3 Watford	32	16	10	6	57	38	58
4 Leeds	31	17	7	7	44	25	58
5 Crystal Palace	31	15	7	9	45	31	52
6 Preston	31	12	15	4	39	22	51
7 Cardiff	32	12	9	11	42	38	45
...	...	...	...	...	...	...	...
↓ 18 Southampton	33	7	15	11	30	36	36

Statistics	Reading	Southampton
Goals	2	0
Shots on Target	6	4
Shots off Target	4	5
Hit Woodwork	0	1
Possession %	61	39
Corners	8	1
Offsides	0	2
Fouls	6	9
Disciplinary Points	0	4

1-1 Sheffield United Reading

Championship
14.02.06

12
15

Bobby Convey prepares to send over a dangerous cross

Event Line

9	Dyer / RF / OP / IA
	Assist: Akinbiyi
12	Kitson / RF / OP / 6Y
	Assist: Convey
24	Kozluk > Bromby
Half time 1-1	
69	Kabba > Dyer
88	Flitcroft > Short
Full time 1-1	

Little love was lost between first and second on Valentine's Day at Bramall Lane, but points were shared in a frenetic midweek encounter.

Quick touches from Paul Ifill and Ade Akinbiyi turned Leigh Bromby's low cross into Bruce Dyer's sights in the ninth minute, and on his Blades debut the 30 year-old striker fired wide of Marcus Hahnemann to set the top-of-the-table clash alight.

The Royals hit back just three minutes later. Bobby Convey's low cross missed Kevin Doyle at the near post and skimmed through to Dave Kitson, whose outstretched leg smartly flicked the ball past Paddy Kenny from close range.

Chances at either end saw Craig Short, Michael Tonge and Akinbiyi all go close for the home team and both Bobby Convey and Kevin Doyle denied by Kenny. As time wore thin a desperate scramble somehow kept Phil Jagielka's effort out before Steve Kabba's sidefooted sitter was clawed away by Hahnemann.

In injury time though, Kenny dragged Convey back after the American's threatening break caused panic. A last gasp penalty was awarded but Kenny made amends to brilliantly save Kitson's spot-kick and honours ended even.

Quote

Steve Coppell

It would have been a psychological boost for whoever got the points, but the conclusions can only be drawn at the end of the season.

Championship Milestone

75

James Harper made his 75th appearance in the Championship.

Venue:	Bramall Lane	Referee:	M.R.Halsey - 05/06	**Sheffield United**
Attendance:	25,011	Matches:	24	**Reading**
Capacity:	30,558	Yellow Cards:	38	
Occupancy:	82%	Red Cards:	5	

Form Coming into Fixture

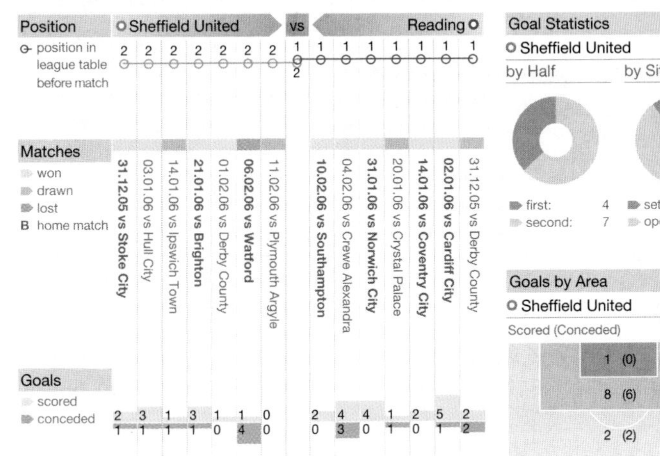

Position
Sheffield United
vs
Reading
position in league table before match
2 2 2 2 2 2 2 2
1 1 1 1 1 1 1 1
Matches
won
drawn
lost
B home match
31.12.05 vs Stoke City
03.01.06 vs Hull City
14.01.06 vs Ipswich Town
21.01.06 vs Brighton
01.02.06 vs Derby County
06.02.06 vs Watford
11.02.06 vs Plymouth Argyle
10.02.06 vs Southampton
04.02.06 vs Crewe Alexandra
31.01.06 vs Norwich City
20.01.06 vs Crystal Palace
14.01.06 vs Coventry City
02.01.06 vs Cardiff City
31.12.05 vs Derby County
Goals
scored
conceded
2 3 1 3 1 1 0
1 1 1 1 0 4 0
2 4 4 1 2 5 2
0 3 0 1 0 1 2

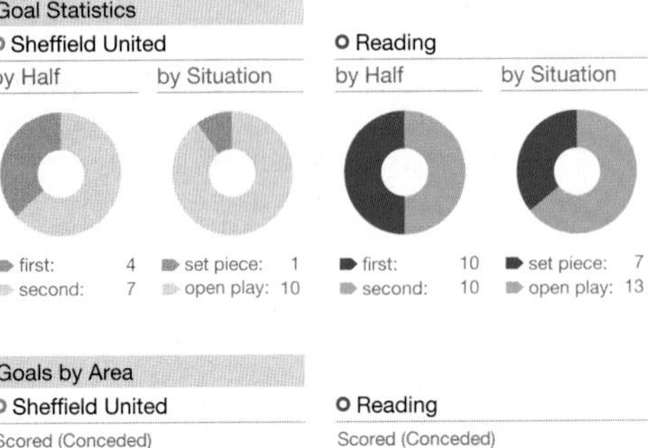

Goal Statistics
Sheffield United
by Half
by Situation
Reading
by Half
by Situation
first: 4
second: 7
set piece: 1
open play: 10
first: 10
second: 10
set piece: 7
open play: 13

Goals by Area

Sheffield United Scored (Conceded)	Reading Scored (Conceded)
1 (0)	8 (2)
8 (6)	10 (3)
2 (2)	2 (2)

Team Statistics

Starting Line-Ups

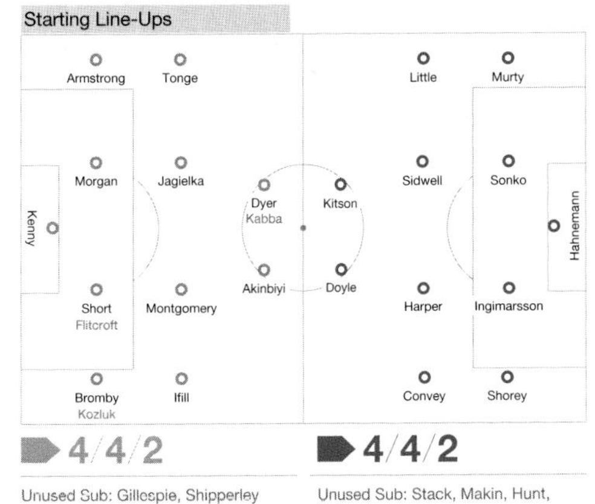

Armstrong
Tonge
Morgan
Jagielka
Kenny
Dyer
Kabba
Kitson
Akinbiyi
Doyle
Short
Flitcroft
Montgomery
Bromby
Kozluk
Ifill
Little
Murty
Sidwell
Sonko
Hahnemann
Harper
Ingimarsson
Convey
Shorey

4/4/2

Unused Sub: Gillespie, Shipperley

4/4/2

Unused Sub: Stack, Makin, Hunt, Oster, Long

Championship Totals	Sheff Utd	Reading
Championship Appearances	674	719
Team Appearances	530	719
Goals Scored	82	87
Assists	69	82
Clean Sheets (goalkeepers)	26	38
Yellow Cards	68	49
Red Cards	5	0
Full Internationals	3	4

Age/Height

Sheffield United Age	Reading Age
27 yrs, 9 mo	26 yrs, 8 mo

Sheffield United Height	Reading Height
5'11"	6'

Match Statistics

League Table after Fixture

		Played	Won	Drawn	Lost	For	Against	Pts
• 1	Reading	34	25	8	1	73	20	83
• 2	Sheff Utd	34	21	8	5	60	33	71
↑ 3	Leeds	33	18	8	7	46	26	62
↓ 4	Watford	34	17	10	7	62	40	61
↑ 5	Crystal Palace	33	16	8	9	47	32	56
↓ 6	Preston	32	13	15	4	44	23	54
• 7	Cardiff	34	13	10	11	48	41	49
• 8	Wolverhampton	33	11	14	8	36	28	47
↑ 9	Ipswich	34	12	11	11	40	47	47

Statistics	Sheff Utd	Reading
Goals	1	1
Shots on Target	11	7
Shots off Target	6	0
Hit Woodwork	0	0
Possession %	49	51
Corners	6	8
Offsides	5	1
Fouls	9	8
Disciplinary Points	0	0

3-2

Luton Town Reading

Championship

17.02.06

GO
er prices
0906
123

John Oster tries to find a way past the Luton defence

Event Line
1 Doyle / LF / OP / IA
Assist: Convey
20 Vine / RF / OP / IA
Assist: Howard
26 Vine / RF / OP / IA
Assist: Foley
Half time 2-1
51 Morgan / RF / OP / OA
Assist: Howard
54 Doyle
56 Vine
58 Kitson
64 Oster
64 Hunt > Convey
77 Beresford
79 Lita > Oster
80 Feeney > Vine
81 Holmes > Davis
83 Showunmi > Morgan
90 Shorey
90 Doyle / H / OP / 6Y
Assist: Hunt
Full time 3-2

Reading's magnificent unbeaten run was finally halted by Luton at Kenilworth Road. Having not tasted defeat since the opening day at home to Plymouth, that run seemed like to continue when Kevin Doyle took advantage of Leon Barnett's slip to fire the Royals into a first minute lead.

Without sign of discouragement though, the Hatters found their feet and Steve Howard supplied a defence-splitting pass to allow Rowan Vine to loft over Marcus Hahnemann and equalise. Luton were on top and Vine latched onto Kevin Foley's low cross to sweep home a second soon after.

For once the Royals seemed rattled and after Howard and Vine had both come close before the interval, ex-Royals forward Dean Morgan expertly drove a low strike past the helpless Hahnemann for a third early in the second half.

The Royals offered signs of a dramatic comeback when Irishman Doyle rose to head home a final minute Stephen Hunt cross and offer late hope. But the surge came too late and the unbeaten streak stopped at 33.

Quote

Steve Coppell

We were beaten, and it hurts. Footballers thrive on not getting beaten, and it's a kick in the groin when you lose.

Championship Milestone

125

Kevin Doyle's first goal was the 125th scored in the Championship by Reading.

Venue:	Kenilworth Road	Referee:	K.Wright - 05/06
Attendance:	8,705	Matches:	22
Capacity:	10,300	Yellow Cards:	73
Occupancy:	85%	Red Cards:	5

Luton Town
Reading

Form Coming into Fixture

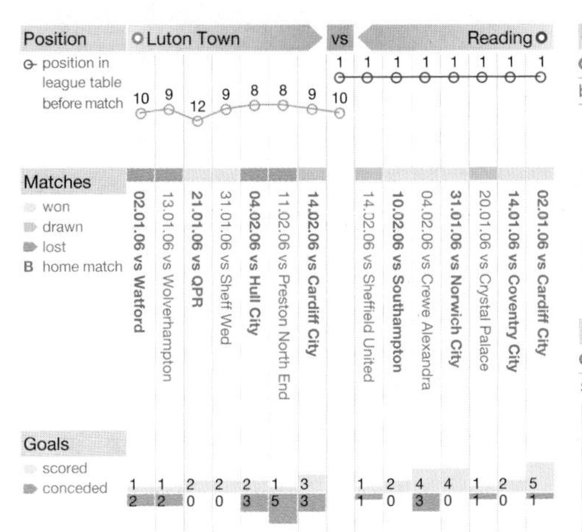

Position
Luton Town
vs
Reading
position in league table before match
10 9 12 9 8 8 9 10
1 1 1 1 1 1 1 1
Matches
won
drawn
lost
B home match
02.01.06 vs Watford
13.01.06 vs Wolverhampton
21.01.06 vs QPR
31.01.06 vs Sheff Wed
04.02.06 vs Hull City
11.02.06 vs Preston North End
14.02.06 vs Cardiff City
14.02.06 vs Sheffield United
10.02.06 vs Southampton
04.02.06 vs Crewe Alexandra
31.01.06 vs Norwich City
20.01.06 vs Crystal Palace
14.01.06 vs Coventry City
02.01.06 vs Cardiff City
Goals
scored
conceded
1 1 2 2 2 1 3
2 2 0 0 3 5 3
1 2 4 4 1 2 5
1 0 3 0 1 0 1

Goal Statistics

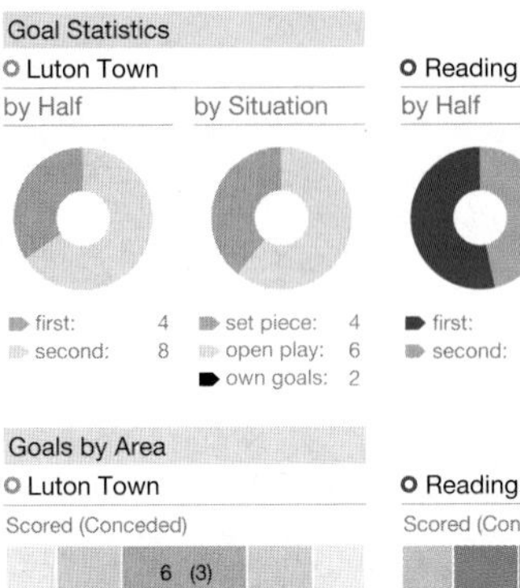

Luton Town
by Half
by Situation
first: 4
second: 8
set piece: 4
open play: 6
own goals: 2
Goals by Area
Luton Town
Scored (Conceded)
6 (3)
5 (8)
1 (4)

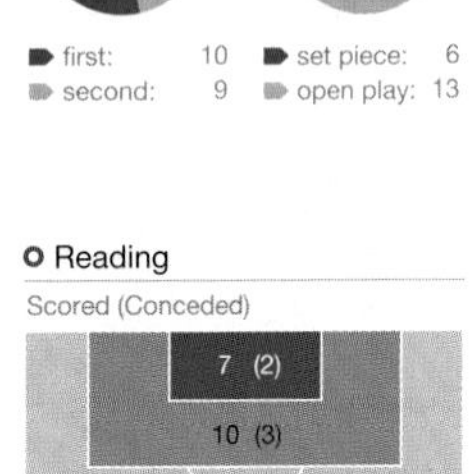

Reading
by Half
by Situation
first: 10
second: 9
set piece: 6
open play: 13

Reading
Scored (Conceded)
7 (2)
10 (3)
2 (1)

Team Statistics

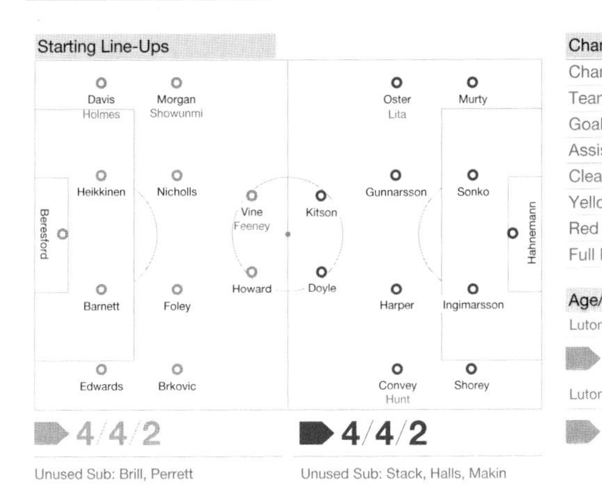

Starting Line-Ups
Davis
Holmes
Morgan
Showunmi
Heikkinen
Nicholls
Beresford
Vine
Feeney
Kitson
Howard
Doyle
Barnett
Foley
Edwards
Brkovic
Oster
Lita
Murty
Gunnarsson
Sonko
Hahnemann
Harper
Ingimarsson
Convey
Hunt
Shorey
4/4/2
4/4/2

Unused Sub: Brill, Perrett

Unused Sub: Stack, Halls, Makin

Championship Totals	Luton	Reading
Championship Appearances	375	751
Team Appearances	357	683
Goals Scored	47	90
Assists	46	65
Clean Sheets (goalkeepers)	7	38
Yellow Cards	32	37
Red Cards	3	1
Full Internationals	4	6

Age/Height

Luton Town Age: 26 yrs, 3 mo

Reading Age: 26 yrs, 5 mo

Luton Town Height: 6'

Reading Height: 5'11"

Match Statistics

League Table after Fixture

		Played	Won	Drawn	Lost	For	Against	Pts
1	Reading	35	25	8	2	75	23	83
2	Sheff Utd	34	21	8	5	60	33	71
3	Leeds	33	18	8	7	46	26	62
4	Watford	34	17	10	7	62	40	61
5	Crystal Palace	33	16	8	9	47	32	56
6	Preston	33	13	16	4	44	23	55
7	Cardiff	34	13	10	11	48	41	49
↑ 8	Luton	35	14	6	15	54	54	48
↓ 9	Wolverhampton	33	11	14	8	36	28	47

Statistics	Luton	Reading
Goals	3	2
Shots on Target	5	3
Shots off Target	5	5
Hit Woodwork	1	0
Possession %	44	56
Corners	4	4
Offsides	6	3
Fouls	21	17
Disciplinary Points	8	16

2-1 Reading Preston North End

Championship

25.02.06

Charters
Defence.com
AWE

Leroy Lita wheels away after netting the winner

Event Line	
6	Sidwell / RF / C / 6Y
	Assist: Ingimarsson
8	Davidson / LF / DFK / OA
	Assist: Davis
18	Davis
37	Hill
40	Lita > Kitson
45	Lita / RF / OP / IA
	Assist: Doyle
Half time 2-1	
55	O'Neil
61	Whaley > Sedgwick
62	Gunnarsson > Sidwell
74	Agyemang > Nugent
81	Dichio > Ormerod
85	Hunt > Oster
Full time 2-1	

Defeat at Luton barely broke the leaders' stride as Preston's 22-match unbeaten run was brought to an abrupt end at Madejski Stadium by substitute Leroy Lita's fine first half finish.

From the kick-off the visitors almost shocked Steve Coppell's side with a very early opener – David Nugent racing clear 10 seconds after the whistle only for Marcus Hahnemann to smother at the frontman's feet.

A thrilling opening 10 minutes saw both sides score. First Ivar Ingimarsson volleyed Bobby Convey's corner viciously across goal and Steve Sidwell battled with keeper Carlo Nash to bundle over the line. But Callum Davidson placed a precise left-footed free kick wide of the unsighted Hahnemann's dive for an eighth-minute equaliser.

A concussed Dave Kitson had to be taken off after suffering worst in an aerial clattering with Nash, but his replacement made a decisive impact before the break. Kevin Doyle's excellent reverse pass found Lita who emphatically rifled low into the far corner. Some dogged defending repressed North End's attempts to fight back and three points saw normal service resumed.

Quote

Steve Coppell

We signed Leroy Lita and Kevin Doyle in the summer to address our goalscoring problems, but we didn't expect either of them to do as well as they have done.

Championship Milestone

10

Leroy Lita marked his 25th appearance in the Championship with a 10th goal in the competition.

Venue:	Madejski Stadium	Referee:	K.Stroud - 05/06
Attendance:	23,011	Matches:	29
Capacity:	24,200	Yellow Cards:	108
Occupancy:	95%	Red Cards:	6

Reading
Preston North End

Form Coming into Fixture

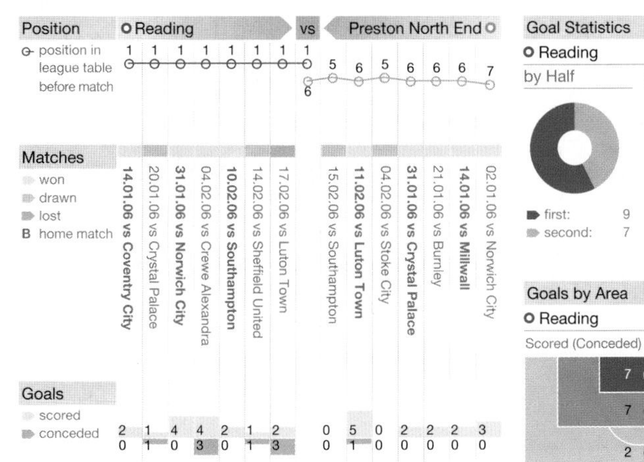

Position
Reading
vs
Preston North End
position in league table before match
1 1 1 1 1 1 1 1
5 6 5 6 6 6 7 6
Matches
won
drawn
lost
B home match
14.01.06 vs Coventry City
20.01.06 vs Crystal Palace
31.01.06 vs Norwich City
04.02.06 vs Crewe Alexandra
10.02.06 vs Southampton
14.02.06 vs Sheffield United
17.02.06 vs Luton Town
15.02.06 vs Southampton
11.02.06 vs Luton Town
04.02.06 vs Stoke City
31.01.06 vs Crystal Palace
21.01.06 vs Burnley
14.01.06 vs Millwall
02.01.06 vs Norwich City
Goals
scored
conceded
2 1 4 4 2 1 2
0 1 0 3 0 1 3
0 5 0 2 2 2 3
0 1 0 0 0 0 0

Goal Statistics

Reading
by Half
by Situation

Reading by Half		Reading by Situation	
first:	9	set piece:	3
second:	7	open play:	13

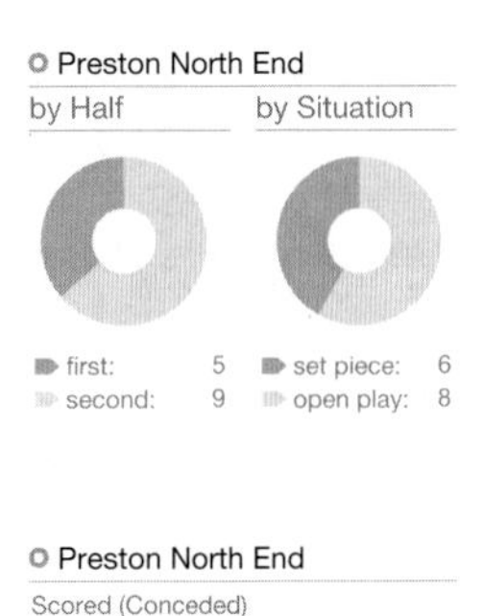

Preston North End
by Half
by Situation

Preston North End by Half		Preston North End by Situation	
first:	5	set piece:	6
second:	9	open play:	8

Goals by Area

Reading — Scored (Conceded)

7 (2)
7 (5)
2 (1)

Preston North End — Scored (Conceded)

1 (1)
12 (0)
1 (0)

Team Statistics

Starting Line-Ups

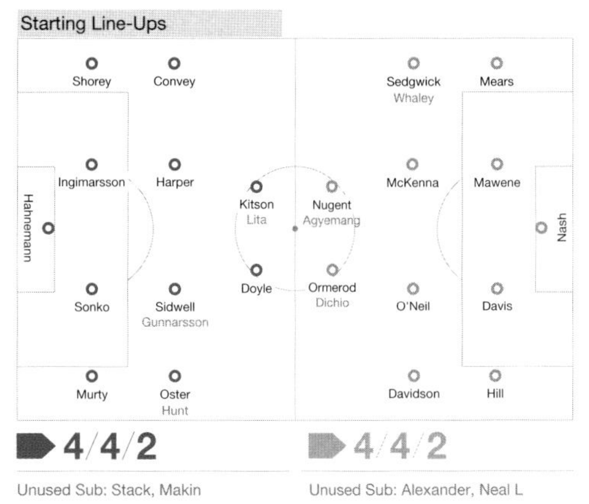

Shorey
Convey
Ingimarsson
Harper
Hahnemann
Kitson
Lita
Nugent
Agyemang
Doyle
Ormerod
Dichio
Sonko
Sidwell
Gunnarsson
Murty
Oster
Hunt
Sedgwick
Whaley
Mears
McKenna
Mawene
Nash
O'Neil
Davis
Davidson
Hill
4/4/2
4/4/2

Unused Sub: Stack, Makin

Unused Sub: Alexander, Neal L

Championship Totals	Reading	Preston
Championship Appearances	832	681
Team Appearances	764	586
Goals Scored	105	71
Assists	71	62
Clean Sheets (goalkeepers)	38	18
Yellow Cards	57	86
Red Cards	1	5
Full Internationals	6	4

Age/Height

Reading Age
26 yrs, 2 mo

Preston North End Age
27 yrs, 1 mo

Reading Height
5'11"

Preston North End Height
6'

Match Statistics

League Table after Fixture

		Played	Won	Drawn	Lost	For	Against	Pts
● 1	Reading	36	26	8	2	77	24	86
● 2	Sheff Utd	36	22	8	6	64	37	74
● 3	Watford	36	19	10	7	65	41	67
● 4	Leeds	35	19	9	7	49	28	66
● 5	Crystal Palace	35	17	9	9	52	34	60
● 6	Preston	34	13	16	5	45	25	55
↑ 7	Wolverhampton	35	13	14	8	40	30	53
↓ 8	Cardiff	36	14	10	12	50	43	52
↑ 9	Ipswich	36	13	11	12	42	48	50

Statistics	Reading	Preston
Goals	2	1
Shots on Target	4	1
Shots off Target	2	4
Hit Woodwork	0	0
Possession %	41	59
Corners	5	8
Offsides	1	1
Fouls	17	16
Disciplinary Points	0	12

0-3 Burnley Reading

Championship

04.03.06

erea
Fine
Na
er Gr

Leroy Lita is stretchered off the pitch

Event Line

10	Convey / LF / OP / OA
45	Kitson > Lita
Half time 0-1	
52	Little > Oster
55	Sonko / H / IFK / IA
	Assist: Little
55	O'Connor J
57	Elliott > Spicer
83	Hunt > Little
90	Kitson / LF / OP / IA
	Assist: Hunt
Full time 0-3	

A dark shadow was cast over three more points and a 14-point gap as star striker Leroy Lita was stretchered off with a broken ankle at Turf Moor. The freak injury came with the Royals leading 1-0 as the disastrous result of the striker's studs getting stuck in the Burnley turf as he fired off a shot on goal from the edge of the box.

Bobby Convey's 10th-minute stunner had deserved the headlines, the American putting the visitors in the lead with a ferocious top corner 25-yard strike.

Glen Little tested his injured groin to come on for a telling cameo against his former club. Early in the second half, the winger's left-sided in-swinger found Ibrahima Sonko's athletic leap and the Senegalese centre-back headed home the second to put the result beyond any real doubt.

Burnley were offering little threat and as the game petered out, Dave Kitson added an injury time third by meeting substitute Stephen Hunt's excellent cut back and sidefooting past Brian Jensen in the Clarets' goal. But Lita's injury meant that celebrations were muted.

Quote

Kevin Dillon

We have three strikers who have scored 35 goals between them this season - and you need that if you want to progress.

Championship Milestone

75

Nicky Shorey made his 75th appearance in the Championship.

Venue:	Turf Moor	Referee:	M.J.Jones - 05/06
Attendance:	12,888	Matches:	29
Capacity:	22,546	Yellow Cards:	86
Occupancy:	57%	Red Cards:	4

Burnley
Reading

Form Coming into Fixture

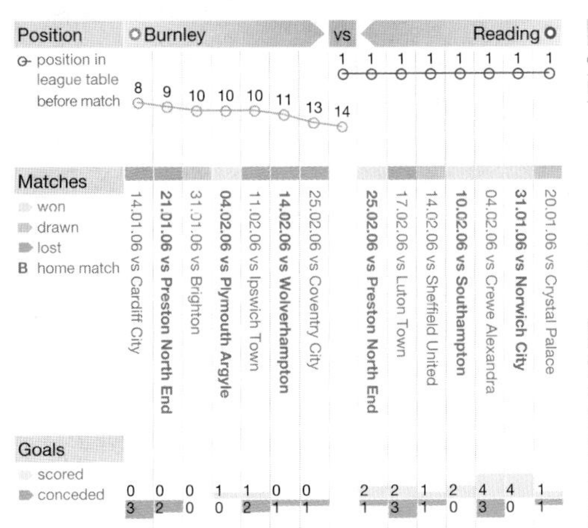

Position
Burnley
vs
Reading
position in league table before match
8 9 10 10 10 11 13 14
1 1 1 1 1 1 1 1
Matches
won
drawn
lost
B home match
14.01.06 vs Cardiff City
21.01.06 vs Preston North End
31.01.06 vs Brighton
04.02.06 vs Plymouth Argyle
11.02.06 vs Ipswich Town
14.02.06 vs Wolverhampton
25.02.06 vs Coventry City
25.02.06 vs Preston North End
17.02.06 vs Luton Town
14.02.06 vs Sheffield United
10.02.06 vs Southampton
04.02.06 vs Crewe Alexandra
31.01.06 vs Norwich City
20.01.06 vs Crystal Palace
Goals
scored
conceded
0 0 0 1 1 0 0
3 2 0 0 2 1 1
2 2 1 2 4 4 1
1 3 1 0 3 0 1

Goal Statistics

Burnley

by Half
by Situation

first: 2 · second: 0 · set piece: 0 · open play: 2

Reading

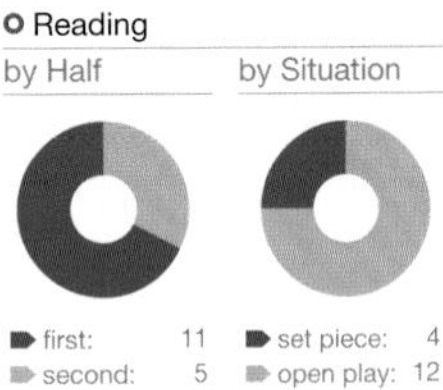

by Half
by Situation

first: 11 · second: 5 · set piece: 4 · open play: 12

Goals by Area

Burnley — Scored (Conceded)

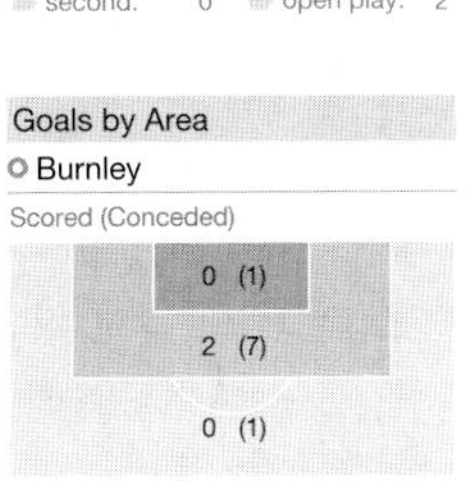

0 (1)
2 (7)
0 (1)

Reading — Scored (Conceded)

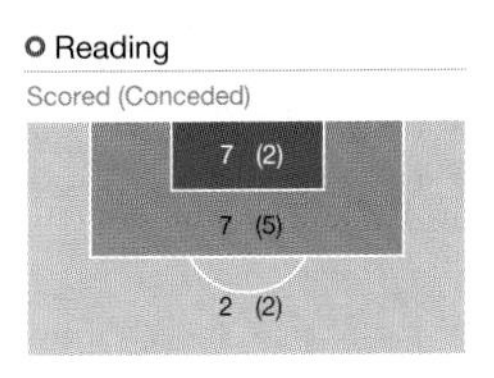

7 (2)
7 (5)
2 (2)

Team Statistics

Starting Line-Ups

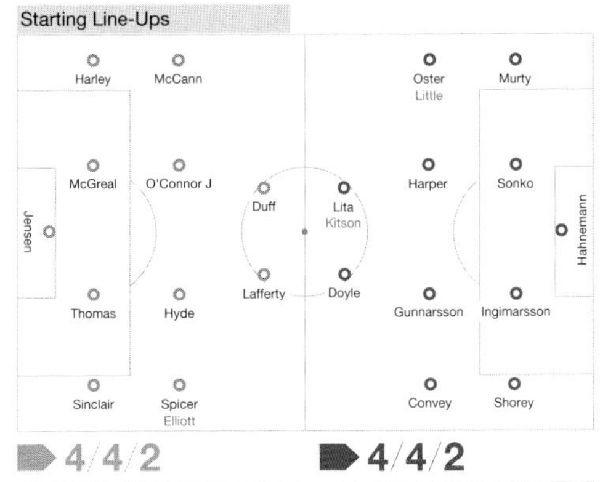

Jensen
Harley
McCann
McGreal
O'Connor J
Thomas
Hyde
Sinclair
Spicer
Elliott
Duff
Lafferty
Lita
Kitson
Doyle
Oster
Little
Murty
Harper
Sonko
Gunnarsson
Ingimarsson
Convey
Shorey
Hahnemann

4/4/2 — Unused Sub: Crossley, Courtney, Karbassiyoon, O'Connor G

4/4/2 — Unused Sub: Stack, Makin

Championship Totals	Burnley	Reading
Championship Appearances	586	845
Team Appearances	503	777
Goals Scored	23	98
Assists	30	95
Clean Sheets (goalkeepers)	20	38
Yellow Cards	90	49
Red Cards	8	1
Full Internationals	3	7

Age/Height

Burnley Age: **27 yrs**

Reading Age: **26 yrs, 9 mo**

Burnley Height: **5'11"**

Reading Height: **5'11"**

Match Statistics

League Table after Fixture

		Played	Won	Drawn	Lost	For	Against	Pts
●	1 Reading	37	27	8	2	80	24	89
●	2 Sheff Utd	37	22	9	6	64	37	75
↑	3 Leeds	36	20	9	7	51	29	69
↓	4 Watford	37	19	11	7	67	43	68
●	5 Crystal Palace	36	17	9	10	53	36	60
●	6 Preston	34	13	16	5	45	25	55
↑	7 Cardiff	37	15	10	12	51	43	55
...		...	...	...	...	...	...	...
↓	15 Burnley	36	12	7	17	41	47	43

Statistics	Burnley	Reading
Goals	0	3
Shots on Target	5	6
Shots off Target	3	3
Hit Woodwork	0	0
Possession %	55	45
Corners	5	3
Offsides	4	5
Fouls	14	11
Disciplinary Points	4	0

0-0 Reading Watford

Championship

11.03.06

DIADORA
loans.co.uk
KYOCERA
17

Bobby Convey fires goalwards

Event Line
36 Convey
Half time 0-0
46 King > McNamee
76 Hunt > Oster
83 Bangura > Young
89 Gunnarsson
Full time 0-0

Astonishingly, the two most prolific goal-happy sides in the country couldn't summon a single goal against each other for the second time in the Coca-Cola Championship this season.

Not for the first time, Kevin Doyle had a seemingly clear penalty claim waved away yet again when Malky Mackay bundled the Irish striker to ground, while Dave Kitson, Bobby Convey and Hornets' midfielder Matthew Spring were all unable to find the target with respective goal attempts.

Nicky Shorey managed to trouble the goalkeeper with a trademark curling free kick, but Ben Foster safely held onto the left-back's strike and Ibrahima Sonko had his header cleared off the line by Mackay. In the latter stages of the half, Kitson touched John Oster's direct ball wide of the onrushing Foster and Doyle directed the loose ball toward the open goal, but Lloyd Doyley speedily backtracked to sensationally block on his line.

After the break Oster probed for a breakthrough and top scorer Marlon King fired wildly over, but the game ended goalless to keep Reading's promotion party on track and Watford's play-off plans intact.

Quote

Steve Coppell

We probably created more clear-cut chances than Watford, but they had opportunities to score as well.

Championship Milestone

75

Graeme Murty made his 75th appearance in the Championship.

Venue:	Madejski Stadium	Referee:	S.Tanner - 05/06
Attendance:	23,724	Matches:	25
Capacity:	24,200	Yellow Cards:	106
Occupancy:	98%	Red Cards:	8

Reading
Watford

Form Coming into Fixture

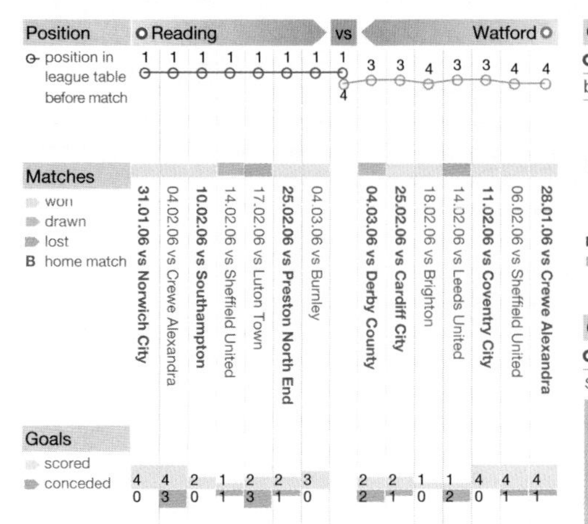

Position
Reading
vs
Watford
position in league table before match
1 1 1 1 1 1 1 1
4
3 3 4 3 3 4 4
Matches
won
drawn
lost
B home match
31.01.06 vs Norwich City
04.02.06 vs Crewe Alexandra
10.02.06 vs Southampton
14.02.06 vs Sheffield United
17.02.06 vs Luton Town
25.02.06 vs Preston North End
04.03.06 vs Burnley
04.03.06 vs Derby County
25.02.06 vs Cardiff City
18.02.06 vs Brighton
14.02.06 vs Leeds United
11.02.06 vs Coventry City
06.02.06 vs Sheffield United
28.01.06 vs Crewe Alexandra
Goals
scored
conceded
4 4 2 1 2 2 3
0 3 0 1 3 1 0
2 2 1 1 4 4 4
2 1 0 2 0 1 1

Goal Statistics

Reading

by Half / by Situation

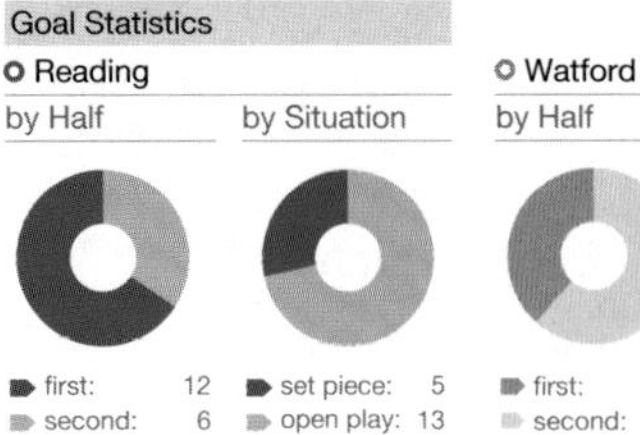

first: 12 — second: 6

set piece: 5 — open play: 13

Watford

by Half / by Situation

first: 7 — second: 11

set piece: 6 — open play: 12

Goals by Area

Reading

Scored (Conceded)

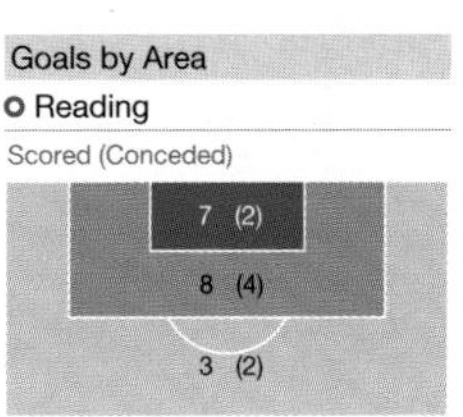

7 (2)
8 (4)
3 (2)

Watford

Scored (Conceded)

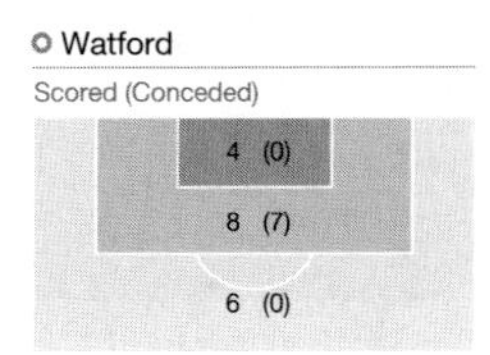

4 (0)
8 (7)
6 (0)

Team Statistics

Starting Line-Ups

Shorey
Convey
Ingimarsson
Gunnarsson
Hahnemann
Sonko
Harper
Murty
Oster
Hunt
Kitson
Henderson
Doyle
Young
Bangura
Eagles
Doyley
Spring
DeMerit
Foster
Mahon
Mackay
McNamee
King
Stewart

4/4/2

Unused Sub: Stack, Halls, Makin, Long

4/4/2

Unused Sub: Chamberlain, Carlisle, Chambers

Championship Totals	Reading	Watford
Championship Appearances	764	679
Team Appearances	696	521
Goals Scored	85	85
Assists	67	65
Clean Sheets (goalkeepers)	39	9
Yellow Cards	40	64
Red Cards	1	7
Full Internationals	7	2

Age/Height

Reading Age

26 yrs, 11 mo

Watford Age

24 yrs, 6 mo

Reading Height

5'11"

Watford Height

5'11"

Match Statistics

League Table after Fixture

		Played	Won	Drawn	Lost	For	Against	Pts
● 1	Reading	38	27	9	2	80	24	90
● 2	Sheff Utd	38	22	9	7	64	39	75
● 3	Leeds	37	20	10	7	53	31	70
● 4	Watford	38	19	12	7	67	43	69
● 5	Crystal Palace	36	17	9	10	53	36	60
↑ 6	Wolverhampton	38	14	16	8	42	30	58
↓ 7	Preston	36	13	18	5	45	25	57
● 8	Cardiff	38	15	10	13	51	45	55
↑ 9	Coventry	38	13	12	13	51	54	51

Statistics	Reading	Watford
Goals	0	0
Shots on Target	1	3
Shots off Target	6	5
Hit Woodwork	0	0
Possession %	59	41
Corners	5	4
Offsides	5	4
Fouls	12	16
Disciplinary Points	8	0

1-1

Reading ○
Wolves ○

Championship

18.03.06

Bobby Convey only has eyes for the ball

Event Line
23 ○ ⚽ Convey / LF / OP / IA
Assist: Oster
25 ○ Harper
Half time 1-0
46 ○ ⇄ Ross > Edwards
64 ○ ⚽ Miller / RF / OP / IA
76 ○ ⇄ Sidwell > Gunnarsson
78 ○ Ricketts
82 ○ Miller
84 ○ ⇄ Cort > Miller
86 ○ Murty
88 ○ ⇄ Hunt > Oster
Full time 1-1

Glenn Hoddle was left cursing his former Spurs target Bobby Convey for a second time this season with a strike that stunted Wolves' play-off ambitions in a hard-fought 1-1 draw at Madejski Stadium.

The home side looked the more dominant early on, and pressure paid in the 23rd minute when John Oster sprayed a low centre across the face of goal for Convey to burst onto and fire high into the roof of the net for the lead. Kevin Doyle then fizzed a shot wide and Ibrahima Sonko almost made his aerial dominance pay but he glanced Oster's cross just wide shortly before the break.

In the second half Wolves started to look dangerous at the other end and just after the hour, Celtic-bound Kenny Miller levelled. Ivar Ingimarsson's challenge fell loose to the Scottish international, who clinically arced a shot first time past Marcus Hahnemann.

The Royals had Hahnemann to thank in the dying stages when the US keeper produced a brilliant save at the feet of Jeremie Aliadiere to secure a point that made a promotion party possible at Leicester the following week.

Quote

Steve Coppell

We spent huge spells of the match on top and had more opportunities, but in the end it was us who had to defend well.

Venue: Madejski Stadium
Attendance: 23,502
Capacity: 24,200
Occupancy: 97%

Referee: P.Walton - 05/06
Matches: 33
Yellow Cards: 100
Red Cards: 6

Reading
Wolverhampton Wanderers

Form Coming into Fixture

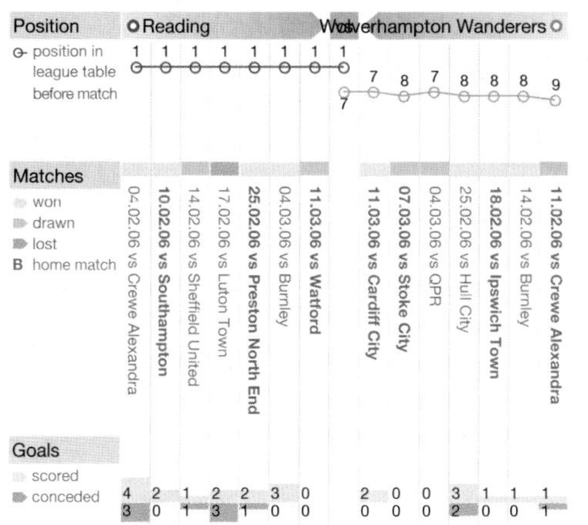

Position
Reading
Wolverhampton Wanderers
position in league table before match
1 1 1 1 1 1 1 1
7 7 8 7 8 8 8 9
Matches
won
drawn
lost
B home match
04.02.06 vs Crewe Alexandra
10.02.06 vs Southampton
14.02.06 vs Sheffield United
17.02.06 vs Luton Town
25.02.06 vs Preston North End
04.03.06 vs Burnley
11.03.06 vs Watford
11.03.06 vs Cardiff City
07.03.06 vs Stoke City
04.03.06 vs QPR
25.02.06 vs Hull City
18.02.06 vs Ipswich Town
14.02.06 vs Burnley
11.02.06 vs Crewe Alexandra
Goals
scored
conceded
4 2 1 2 2 3 0
3 0 1 3 1 0 0
2 0 0 3 1 1 1
0 0 0 2 0 0 1

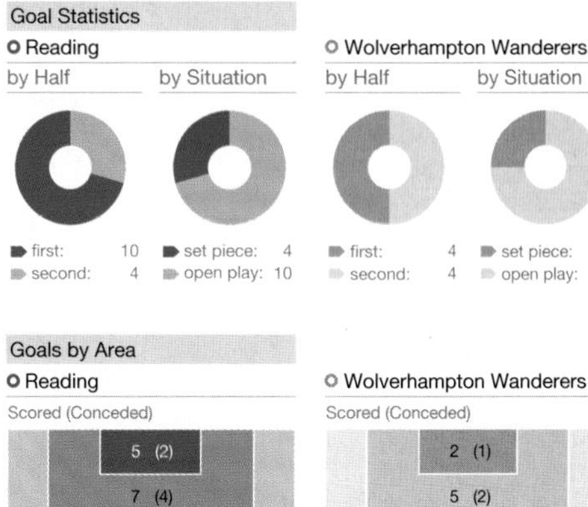

Goal Statistics
Reading
by Half
by Situation
first: 10
second: 4
set piece: 4
open play: 10
Goals by Area
Reading
Scored (Conceded)
5 (2)
7 (4)
2 (2)

Wolverhampton Wanderers
by Half
by Situation
first: 4
second: 4
set piece: 2
open play: 6
Wolverhampton Wanderers
Scored (Conceded)
2 (1)
5 (2)
1 (0)

Team Statistics

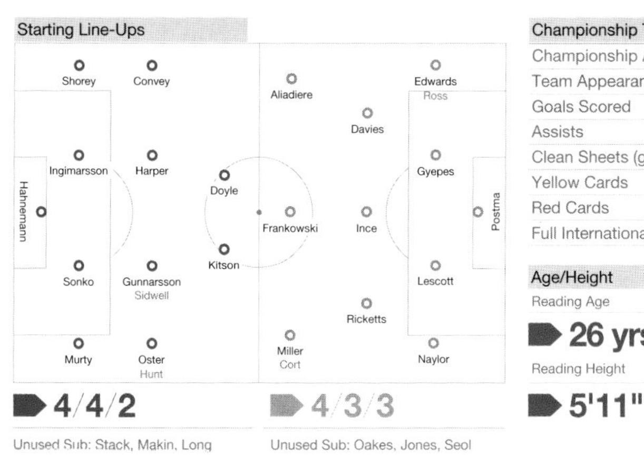

Starting Line-Ups
Shorey
Convey
Ingimarsson
Harper
Hahnemann
Sonko
Gunnarsson
Sidwell
Murty
Oster
Hunt
Doyle
Kitson
Aliadiere
Frankowski
Miller
Cort
Davies
Ince
Ricketts
Edwards
Ross
Gyepes
Lescott
Naylor
Postma

4/4/2

4/3/3

Unused Sub: Stack, Makin, Long

Unused Sub: Oakes, Jones, Seol

Championship Totals	Reading	Wolves
Championship Appearances	845	489
Team Appearances	777	482
Goals Scored	99	67
Assists	71	51
Clean Sheets (goalkeepers)	40	12
Yellow Cards	58	53
Red Cards	1	1
Full Internationals	7	6

Age/Height

Reading Age
26 yrs, 8 mo

Wolverhampton Wanderers Age
26 yrs, 3 mo

Reading Height
5'11"

Wolverhampton Wanderers Height
6'

Match Statistics

League Table after Fixture

		Played	Won	Drawn	Lost	For	Against	Pts
1	Reading	39	27	10	2	81	25	91
2	Sheff Utd	39	22	9	8	65	41	75
3	Leeds	38	20	11	7	54	32	71
4	Watford	38	19	12	7	67	43	69
5	Crystal Palace	38	18	10	10	58	39	64
6	Preston	38	14	18	6	48	28	60
7	Wolverhampton	39	14	17	8	43	31	59
8	Cardiff	39	16	10	13	52	45	58
↑ 9	Norwich	39	15	8	16	49	55	53

Statistics	Reading	Wolves
Goals	1	1
Shots on Target	6	3
Shots off Target	4	4
Hit Woodwork	0	0
Possession %	50	50
Corners	8	2
Offsides	6	4
Fouls	10	6
Disciplinary Points	8	8

1-1 Leicester City Reading

Championship

25.03.06

Kevin Doyle celebrates the goal that secured promotion

Event Line
33 Gunnarsson
38 Hume / RF / OP / OA
Assist: Fryatt
40 Ingimarsson
Half time 1-0
61 Sidwell > Gunnarsson
61 Long > Oster
77 Hume
78 O'Grady > Fryatt
80 Hunt > Convey
84 Welsh > Hume
85 Doyle / H / C / 6Y
Assist: Ingimarsson
Full time 1-1

The party started here! After 135 years of football in the lower levels, Reading Football Club confirmed their place in the top flight with what turned out to be an irrelevant point at the Walkers Stadium.

The Royals went into the game knowing a win would be enough to secure automatic promotion, but when Iain Hume's 38th minute strike gave the home side the lead, it seemed the promotion celebrations might have to wait.

Rob Kelly's Foxes were determined to delay the party and Joey Gudjonsson and Matty Fryatt also went close for an impressive Leicester side, but the Royals again showed their character as Kevin Doyle dramatically equalised with an 85th minute header from James Harper's corner. Stephen Hunt was then denied a dramatic late winner by Paul Henderson, but by now attention was turning to other games.

And with other results going in Reading's favour as Leeds and Watford dropped points, in the end the result at Leicester didn't matter allowing the players and management to celebrate promotion in front of 3,000 overjoyed travelling loyal Royals.

Quote

Steve Coppell

I wish I could can this feeling and open it later – it is absolutely brilliant. This is great for the chairman for all the work he has put in.

Leicester City
Reading

Venue: Walkers Stadium
Attendance: 25,578
Capacity: 32,500
Occupancy: 79%

Referee: C.Penton - 05/06
Matches: 31
Yellow Cards: 97
Red Cards: 9

Form Coming into Fixture

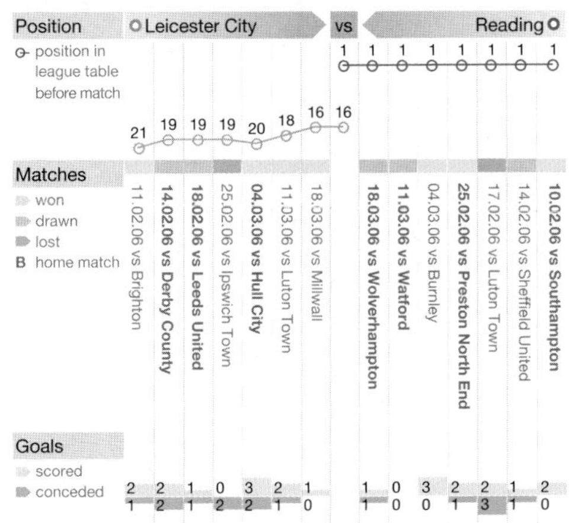

Position
Leicester City
vs
Reading
position in league table before match
21 19 19 19 20 18 16 16
1 1 1 1 1 1 1 1
Matches
won
drawn
lost
B home match
11.02.06 vs Brighton
14.02.06 vs Derby County
18.02.06 vs Leeds United
25.02.06 vs Ipswich Town
04.03.06 vs Hull City
11.03.06 vs Luton Town
18.03.06 vs Millwall
18.03.06 vs Wolverhampton
11.03.06 vs Watford
04.03.06 vs Burnley
25.02.06 vs Preston North End
17.02.06 vs Luton Town
14.02.06 vs Sheffield United
10.02.06 vs Southampton
Goals
scored
conceded
2 2 1 0 3 2 1
1 2 1 2 2 1 0
1 0 3 2 2 1 2
1 0 0 1 3 1 0

Goal Statistics
Leicester City
by Half
by Situation
first: 7
second: 4
set piece: 2
open play: 9
Reading
by Half
by Situation
first: 8
second: 3
set piece: 3
open play: 8

Goals by Area

Leicester City — Scored (Conceded)

1 (4)
8 (4)
2 (1)

Reading — Scored (Conceded)

4 (0)
6 (4)
1 (2)

Team Statistics

Starting Line-Ups

Johansson
Hughes
Kisnorbo
Williams
Henderson
Hume
Welsh
Doyle
Fryatt
O'Grady
Kitson
McCarthy
Gudjonsson
Stearman
Maybury
Oster
Long
Murty
Gunnarsson
Sidwell
Sonko
Hahnemann
Harper
Ingimarsson
Convey
Hunt
Shorey

4/4/2

Unused Sub: Douglas, Gerrbrand, Hammond

4/4/2

Unused Sub: Stack, Makin

Championship Totals	Leicester	Reading
Championship Appearances	435	862
Team Appearances	428	794
Goals Scored	37	101
Assists	34	72
Clean Sheets (goalkeepers)	2	40
Yellow Cards	72	60
Red Cards	4	1
Full Internationals	6	7

Age/Height

Leicester City Age: 23 yrs, 9 mo

Reading Age: 26 yrs, 1 mo

Leicester City Height: 5'11"

Reading Height: 5'11"

Match Statistics

League Table after Fixture

		Played	Won	Drawn	Lost	For	Against	Pts
1	Reading	40	27	11	2	82	26	92
2	Sheff Utd	40	23	9	8	68	41	78
3	Watford	40	20	12	8	70	46	72
4	Leeds	40	20	12	8	54	33	72
5	Crystal Palace	40	19	10	11	60	41	67
6	Preston	39	14	19	6	48	28	61
7	Wolverhampton	40	14	17	9	44	34	59
...		...	...	...	...	...	...	...
16	Leicester	40	11	14	15	45	52	47

Statistics	Leicester	Reading
Goals	1	1
Shots on Target	9	5
Shots off Target	3	3
Hit Woodwork	1	0
Possession %	46	54
Corners	8	6
Offsides	6	2
Fouls	18	16
Disciplinary Points	4	8

5-0

Reading
Derby County

Championship

01.04.06

PUMA

Graeme Murty leads the title-winning celebrations

Event Line
Half time 0-0
59 Harper / RF / OP / IA
Assist: Kitson
65 Doyle / H / OP / 6Y
Assist: Convey
68 Hunt > Convey
69 Oster > Little
70 Oster / RF / OP / IA
72 Bisgaard > Bolder
72 Ainsworth > Peschisolido
72 Long > Doyle
74 Long / H / OP / 6Y
Assist: Murty
83 Long / RF / OP / IA
Assist: Hunt
Full time 5-0

Champions! A stunning display crowned the Royals as the best in the league with five goals flying past helpess County keeper Lee Camp in a euphoric 24-minute spell which sparked ecstatic scenes at Madejski Stadium.

An uneventful first half was decorated with news of Josip Skoko's goal for Stoke against Sheffield United but the Royals needed a win. They had to wait until almost the hour mark when James Harper's opener fast eroded the floodgates.

Kevin Doyle comfortably headed Bobby Convey's cross in for a second and when John Oster netted his first league goal for the Royals the job was done. There was still time for Shane Long to broaden a few smiles, applying a near post header to Graeme Murty's brilliant cross before a firm right-footed effort capped a memorable day. With the Blades only drawing, full time at Madejski Stadium sparked an all-encompassing pitch invasion.

The players were ushered upstairs to launch unforgettable celebrations from the Directors Box, after a stylish display had seen the Royals claim the greatest prize in their long Football League history.

Quote

Steve Coppell

We have led the pack for an awfully long time and the second half performance reflected what we've been about all season.

Championship Milestone

First Goal

John Oster netted his first goal in the Championship for Reading.

Venue: Madejski Stadium
Attendance: 22,981
Capacity: 24,200
Occupancy: 95%

Referee: A.Bates - 05/06
Matches: 28
Yellow Cards: 83
Red Cards: 6

Reading
Derby County

Form Coming into Fixture

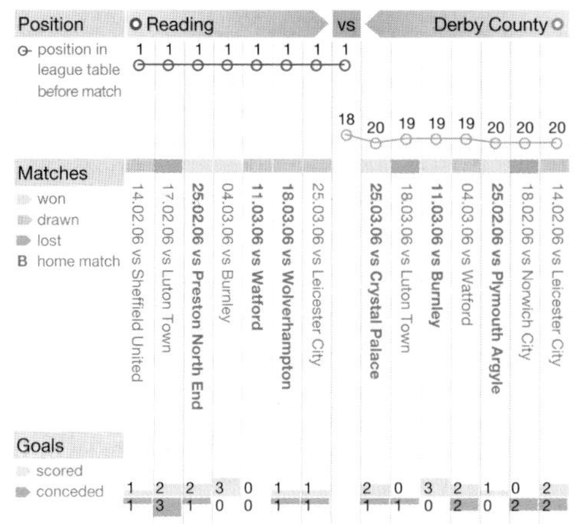

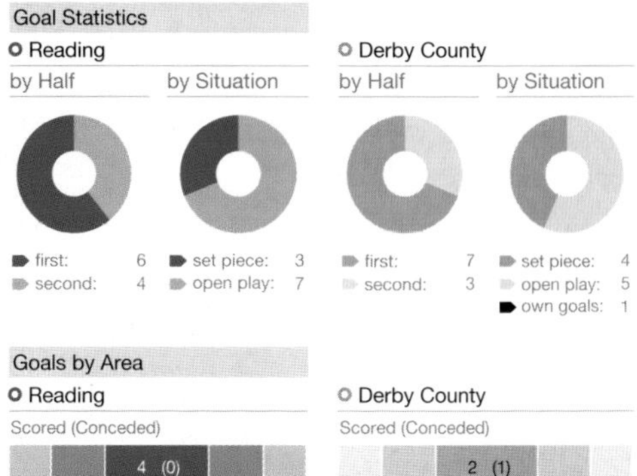

Team Statistics

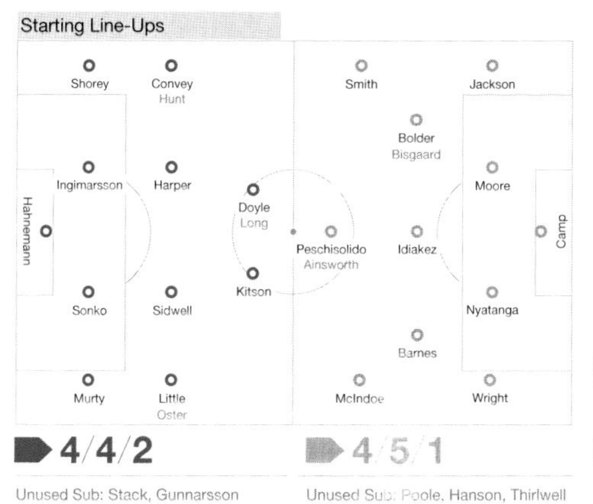

4/4/2

Unused Sub: Stack, Gunnarsson

4/5/1

Unused Sub: Poole, Hanson, Thirlwell

Championship Totals	Reading	Derby
Championship Appearances	885	538
Team Appearances	853	518
Goals Scored	100	64
Assists	97	67
Clean Sheets (goalkeepers)	40	21
Yellow Cards	59	49
Red Cards	0	2
Full Internationals	6	4

Age/Height

Reading Age
26 yrs, 2 mo

Derby County Age
26 yrs, 5 mo

Reading Height
5'11"

Derby County Height
5'10"

Match Statistics

League Table after Fixture

	Played	Won	Drawn	Lost	For	Against	Pts
1 Reading	41	28	11	2	87	26	95
2 Sheff Utd	41	23	10	8	69	42	79
3 Watford	41	20	12	9	71	49	72
4 Leeds	41	20	12	9	54	34	72
5 Crystal Palace	41	20	10	11	63	42	70
6 Preston	41	16	19	6	50	28	67
7 Wolverhampton	41	14	17	10	44	36	59
...	...	...	...	...	...	...	...
20 Derby	41	9	18	14	50	61	45

Statistics	Reading	Derby
Goals	5	0
Shots on Target	12	7
Shots off Target	6	2
Hit Woodwork	1	0
Possession %	54	46
Corners	8	5
Offsides	0	8
Fouls	10	7
Disciplinary Points	0	0

2-5 Cardiff City Reading

Championship

08.04.06

Coca-Cola
FOOTBALL
LEAGUE

Steve Sidwell savours another five-goal showing

Event Line
10 Harper / RF / OP / IA
Assist: Convey
39 Kitson / LF / OP / IA
Assist: Convey
Half time 0-2
52 Loovens / H / OG / 6Y
Assist: Kitson
65 Parry > Cooper
67 Jerome / RF / OP / 6Y
Assist: Koumas
68 Long > Kitson
73 Purse
75 Hunt > Convey
80 Parry / H / C / IA
Assist: Koumas
87 Doyle / H / OP / 6Y
Assist: Hunt
89 Gunnarsson > Oster
90 Harper / RF / OP / IA
Assist: Hunt
Full time 2-5

Any fears that the champions would take their foot off the pedal in the final few fixtures were fast dispelled as Steve Coppell's ruthless side fired five more at Cardiff.

Determined to prolong the visitors' euphoric mood, Bobby Convey cut a 10th minute ball back to James Harper who began the scoring from 12 yards out. Nicky Shorey's outswinging cross landed at Dave Kitson's feet ten yards out and with relaxed confidence he calmly passed into the right corner for 2-0.

Early in the second half Kitson hurried Glenn Loovens into a misguided header which nestled in the top corner of his own goal, but Jason Koumas charged Shorey's clearance down to allow Cameron Jerome to pull one back and a sun-soaked Ninian Park sniffed an unexpected comeback when Paul Parry headed home to make it 3-2.

But with three minutes left Stephen Hunt's excellent cross found Kevin Doyle's head to restore the two-goal advantage and then Harper completed his first brace in Reading colours with a low 20 yard drive, making it five on the afternoon and 10 against the Bluebirds in 2005/6.

Quote

Steve Coppell

At 3-0 we had the game won, but to Cardiff's credit they fought back and we needed to go up a gear.

Championship Milestone

10

James Harper's second goal was his tenth in the Championship.

Venue: Ninian Park
Attendance: 11,866
Capacity: 20,000
Occupancy: 59%

Referee: A.R.Leake - 05/06
Matches: 33
Yellow Cards: 75
Red Cards: 4

Cardiff City
Reading

Form Coming into Fixture

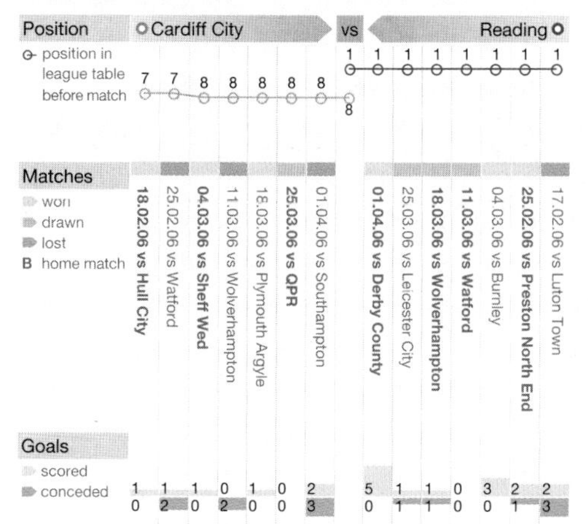

Position
Cardiff City
vs
Reading
position in league table before match
7 7 8 8 8 8 8
8
1 1 1 1 1 1 1 1
Matches
won
drawn
lost
B home match
18.02.06 vs Hull City
25.02.06 vs Watford
04.03.06 vs Sheff Wed
11.03.06 vs Wolverhampton
18.03.06 vs Plymouth Argyle
25.03.06 vs QPR
01.04.06 vs Southampton
01.04.06 vs Derby County
25.03.06 vs Leicester City
18.03.06 vs Wolverhampton
11.03.06 vs Watford
04.03.06 vs Burnley
25.02.06 vs Preston North End
17.02.06 vs Luton Town
Goals
scored
conceded
1 1 1 0 1 0 2
0 2 0 2 0 0 3
5 1 1 0 3 2 2
0 1 1 0 0 1 3

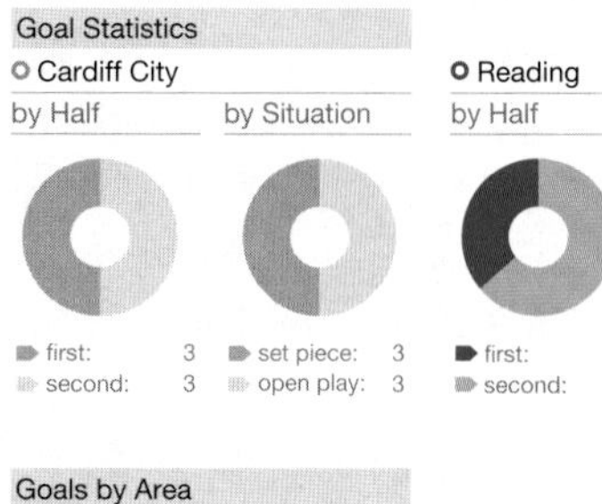

Goal Statistics
Cardiff City
by Half
by Situation
first: 3
second: 3
set piece: 3
open play: 3

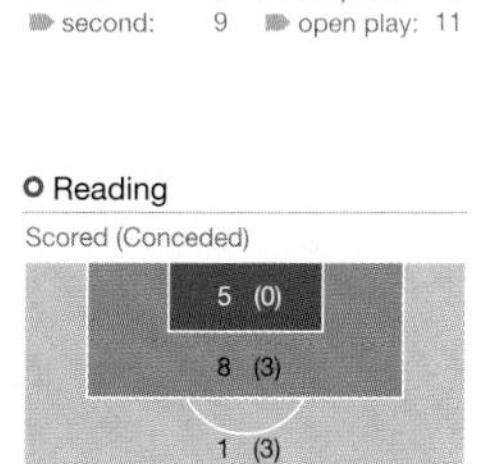

Reading
by Half
by Situation
first: 5
second: 9
set piece: 3
open play: 11

Goals by Area

Cardiff City
Scored (Conceded)
2 (3)
4 (4)
0 (0)

Reading
Scored (Conceded)
5 (0)
8 (3)
1 (3)

Team Statistics

Starting Line-Ups

Ledley
Koumas
Loovens
Boland
Alexander
Jerome
Doyle
Thompson
Kitson
Long
Purse
Scimeca
Ardley
Cooper
Parry
Oster
Gunnarsson
Murty
Sidwell
Sonko
Hahnemann
Harper
Ingimarsson
Convey
Hunt
Shorey

4/4/2

Unused Sub: Barker, Cox, Whitley, Ndumbu-Nsungu

4/4/2

Unused Sub: Stack, Makin

Championship Totals	Cardiff	Reading
Championship Appearances	526	889
Team Appearances	466	821
Goals Scored	68	107
Assists	61	77
Clean Sheets (goalkeepers)	19	41
Yellow Cards	42	62
Red Cards	3	1
Full Internationals	5	7

Age/Height

Cardiff City Age
27 yrs

Reading Age
26 yrs, 2 mo

Cardiff City Height
5'11"

Reading Height
5'11"

Match Statistics

League Table after Fixture

		Played	Won	Drawn	Lost	For	Against	Pts
●	1 Reading	42	29	11	2	92	28	98
●	2 Sheff Utd	42	24	10	8	72	44	82
↑	3 Leeds	42	20	13	9	54	34	73
↓	4 Watford	41	20	12	9	71	49	72
↑	5 Preston	42	17	19	6	52	28	70
↓	6 Crystal Palace	42	20	10	12	63	44	70
●	7 Wolverhampton	42	14	18	10	46	38	60
●	8 Cardiff	42	16	11	15	56	53	59
●	9 Norwich	42	16	8	18	51	60	56

Statistics	Cardiff	Reading
Goals	2	5
Shots on Target	8	6
Shots off Target	8	6
Hit Woodwork	0	0
Possession %	51	49
Corners	8	2
Offsides	3	7
Fouls	10	9
Disciplinary Points	4	0

1-1 Leeds United / Reading

Championship

15.04.06

KYOCERA

John Oster keeps things simple at Elland Road

Event Line

Half time 0-0

47 Hulse / RF / OP / 6Y
Assist: Derry

64 Hunt > Oster

76 Graham > Hulse

78 Long > Doyle

83 Moore > Bakke

83 Gunnarsson > Murty

85 Hunt / H / OP / 6Y
Assist: Ingimarsson

86 Beckford > Healy

Full time 1-1

Substitute Stephen Hunt ruined Leeds' distant hopes of a top two finish with an 85th minute equaliser that stunned Elland Road and kept alive Reading's hopes of beating Sunderland's 105-point record.

Jonathan Douglas and Shaun Derry had merely warmed Marcus Hahnemann's palms with rare first half strikes, but Rob Hulse struck two minutes after the interval to give Leeds the lead. Derry impressively cut the ball back from the byline and the former West Brom striker neatly tapped home at the near post.

Hulse's head was put to use at the other end when clearing John Oster's floated cross from underneath his own crossbar, but the Whites hero lost a little respect when disgracefully diving inside the box in a feeble attempt to win a penalty.

After substitute Shane Long instinctively volleyed just too high the points seemed destined to stay in Yorkshire, but when Brynjar Gunnarsson's floated far post cross was headed back across goal by Ivar Ingimarsson, Hunt scrappily bundled it past Paul Butler on the line for a close range leveller.

Quote

Wally Downes

We don't want to lose until the end of the season. If we get the record great, but the target is to be unbeaten.

Venue:	Elland Road	Referee:	M.R.Halsey - 05/06	**Leeds United**
Attendance:	24,535	Matches:	32	**Reading**
Capacity:	40,204	Yellow Cards:	48	
Occupancy:	61%	Red Cards:	6	

Form Coming into Fixture

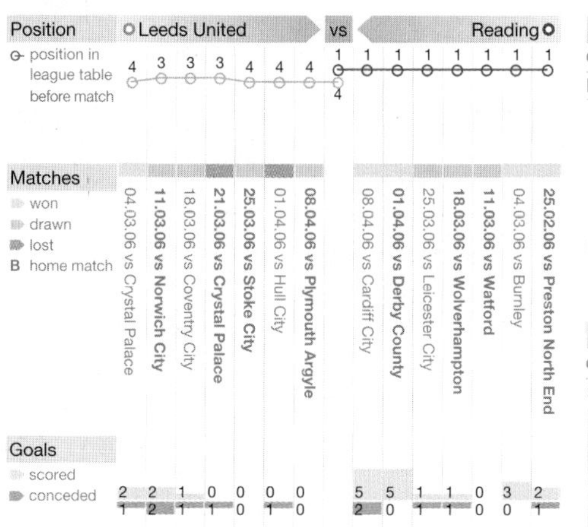

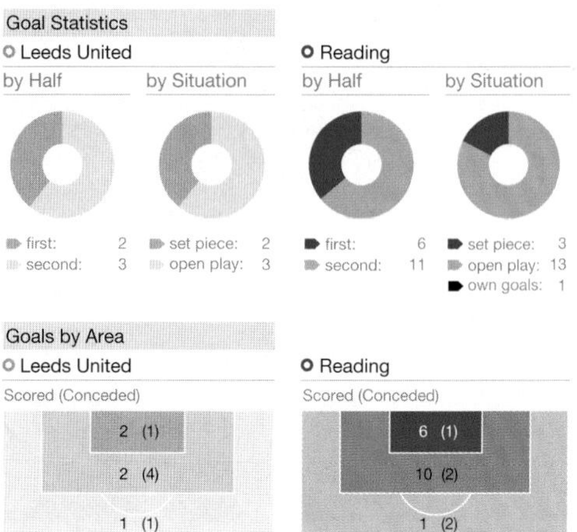

Team Statistics

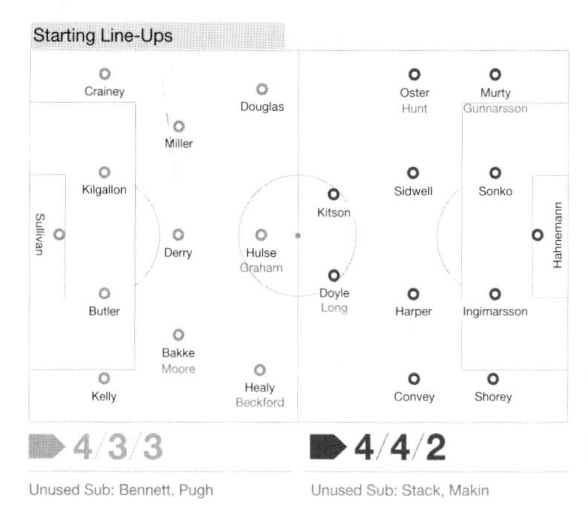

4/3/3

4/4/2

Unused Sub: Bennett, Pugh

Unused Sub: Stack, Makin

Championship Totals	Leeds	Reading
Championship Appearances	659	903
Team Appearances	582	835
Goals Scored	55	111
Assists	51	82
Clean Sheets (goalkeepers)	24	41
Yellow Cards	88	62
Red Cards	5	1
Full Internationals	8	7

Age/Height

Leeds United Age: 27 yrs, 2 mo

Reading Age: 26 yrs, 2 mo

Leeds United Height: 5'11"

Reading Height: 5'11"

Match Statistics

League Table after Fixture

		Played	Won	Drawn	Lost	For	Against	Pts
1	Reading	43	29	12	2	93	29	99
2	Sheff Utd	43	25	10	8	73	44	85
3	Watford	43	20	14	9	73	51	74
4	Leeds	43	20	14	9	55	35	74
5	Preston	43	18	19	6	54	29	73
6	Crystal Palace	43	20	11	12	65	46	71
7	Wolverhampton	43	14	19	10	47	39	61
8	Cardiff	43	16	11	16	56	54	59
9	Luton	43	16	8	19	62	64	56

Statistics	Leeds	Reading
Goals	1	1
Shots on Target	3	2
Shots off Target	5	3
Hit Woodwork	0	0
Possession %	48	52
Corners	4	4
Offsides	4	3
Fouls	11	10
Disciplinary Points	0	0

3-1 Reading / Stoke City

Championship

17.04.06

Stephen Hunt congratulates goalscorer John Halls

Event Line
25 Sidwell / H / IFK / 6Y
Assist: Ingimarsson
Half time 1-0
46 Rooney > Kopteff
51 Gallagher > Sweeney
54 Dobson > Sidwell
56 Doyle / RF / P / IA
Assist: Doyle
59 Rooney / LF / OP / 6Y
62 Halls / RF / OP / 6Y
Assist: Hunt
64 Golbourne > Shorey
71 Henry > Bangoura
71 Cox > Doyle
Full time 3-1

With neither team relying on the result, Steve Coppell took a rare opportunity to rest his first team heroes in the League and those that stepped into their sizeable shoes shone to stride confidently to three more points and breach the 100-points barrier.

Skipper Graeme Murty was rested and stand-in captain Ivar Ingimarsson boasted an early assist when curling a well-taken free-kick into Steve Sidwell's untraced path, and the midfielder headed home a simple chance for the lead.

After the interval Kevin Doyle's pace frightened Carl Hoefkens into an untidy drag back and the referee pointed to the penalty spot. Murty was not named amongst the substitutes so his search for his first goal in more than five years was prolonged as Doyle comfortably dispatched the spotkick.

Paul Gallagher's excellent cross somehow ricocheted off Ingimarsson's head, the right post and Graham Stack's left leg to allow Adam Rooney to tap home and halve the deficit, but almost immediately league debutant John Halls stroked Stephen Hunt's deep cross past Steve Simonsen to secure the victory.

Quote

Steve Coppell

People talk about the prestige of beating records, but prestige never bought me dinner in a restaurant - it's winning games that does that.

Championship Milestone

75

Steve Sidwell made his 75th appearance in the Championship.

Venue:	Madejski Stadium	Referee:	S.W.Mathieson - 05/06
Attendance:	22,119	Matches:	28
Capacity:	24,200	Yellow Cards:	55
Occupancy:	91%	Red Cards:	3

Form Coming into Fixture

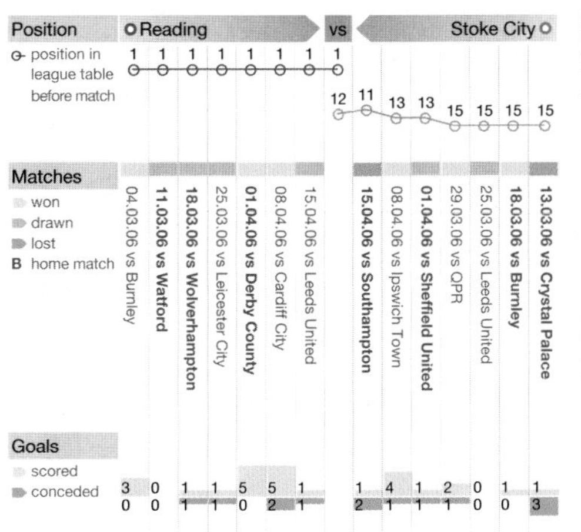
Position
Reading
vs
Stoke City
position in league table before match
1 1 1 1 1 1 1 1
12 11 13 13 15 15 15 15
Matches
won
drawn
lost
B home match
04.03.06 vs Burnley
11.03.06 vs Watford
18.03.06 vs Wolverhampton
25.03.06 vs Leicester City
01.04.06 vs Derby County
08.04.06 vs Cardiff City
15.04.06 vs Leeds United
15.04.06 vs Southampton
08.04.06 vs Ipswich Town
01.04.06 vs Sheffield United
29.03.06 vs QPR
25.03.06 vs Leeds United
18.03.06 vs Burnley
13.03.06 vs Crystal Palace
Goals
scored
conceded
3 0 1 1 5 5 1 1 4 1 2 0 1 1
0 0 1 1 0 2 1 2 1 1 1 0 0 3

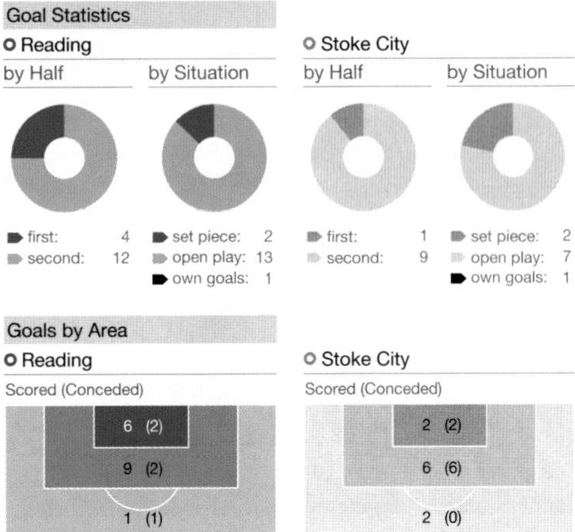
Goal Statistics
Reading
by Half
by Situation
first: 4
second: 12
set piece: 2
open play: 13
own goals: 1
Stoke City
by Half
by Situation
first: 1
second: 9
set piece: 2
open play: 7
own goals: 1
Goals by Area
Reading
Scored (Conceded)
6 (2)
9 (2)
1 (1)
Stoke City
Scored (Conceded)
2 (2)
6 (6)
2 (0)

Team Statistics

Starting Line-Ups
Shorey
Golbourne
Hunt
Sidwell
Dobson
Ingimarsson
Stack
Gunnarsson
Doyle
Cox
Sonko
Halls
Makin
Long
Kopteff
Rooney
Hoefkens
Russell
Duberry
Bangoura
Henry
Junior
Simonsen
Hill
Brammer
Sweeney
Gallagher
Dickinson

4/3/3

Unused Sub: Hahnemann, Kitson

4/5/1

Unused Sub: de Goey, Broomes

Championship Totals	Reading	Stoke
Championship Appearances	577	565
Team Appearances	446	537
Goals Scored	59	34
Assists	51	36
Clean Sheets (goalkeepers)	9	25
Yellow Cards	48	75
Red Cards	4	7
Full Internationals	3	4

Age/Height

Reading Age	Stoke City Age
24 yrs, 6 mo	24 yrs, 10 mo

Reading Height	Stoke City Height
5'11"	6'

Match Statistics

League Table after Fixture

		Played	Won	Drawn	Lost	For	Against	Pts
● 1	Reading	44	30	12	2	96	30	102
● 2	Sheff Utd	43	25	10	8	73	44	85
● 3	Watford	44	21	14	9	75	52	77
↑ 4	Preston	44	19	19	6	56	29	76
↓ 5	Leeds	43	20	14	9	55	35	74
● 6	Crystal Palace	44	20	12	12	65	46	72
● 7	Wolverhampton	44	14	19	11	47	41	61
...		...	...	...	...	...	...	...
↓ 13	Stoke	44	16	7	21	49	61	55

Statistics	Reading	Stoke
Goals	3	1
Shots on Target	4	3
Shots off Target	4	5
Hit Woodwork	0	0
Possession %	55	45
Corners	3	6
Offsides	3	3
Fouls	8	16
Disciplinary Points	0	0

1-1 Sheffield Wednesday ○ Reading ○

Championship

22.04.06

SIMEK
20
KITSON
12
plusnet

▶ Dave Kitson finds the net at Hillsborough

Event Line
5 ○ ⇄ Whelan > Hills
34 ● ⚽ Kitson / RF / OP / IA
Assist: Oster
Half time 0-1
59 ○ ⚽ MacLean / RF / P / IA
Assist: Simek
64 ● ⇄ Hunt > Convey
64 ● ⇄ Gunnarsson > Sidwell
65 ○ ⇄ Burton > Best
69 ● ▪ Kitson
72 ● ⇄ Long > Kitson
75 ○ ⇄ Tudgay > McGovern
87 ○ ▪ Spurr
Full time 1-1

Steve Coppell's champions had to hang onto a priceless point at Hillsborough as the Royals battled hard to keep their points record alive.

Excellent work between Kevin Doyle and John Oster saw the latter pick out Dave Kitson inside the box, and the striker soundly swept his 10 yard effort wide of Scott Carson for a deserved lead. Kitson was convinced he'd doubled it two minutes into the second half but his sweetly struck volley was harshly disallowed for offside.

The home team almost equalised in a mad scramble that Leon Best failed to turn home at two attempts, but when American full-back Frankie Simek was tripped by Bobby Convey in the area, Steve MacLean stepped up to fire Wednesday level from the spot.

Marcus Hahnemann had to deny MacLean the winner soon after and as time ran out, the home side pushed for an unexpected victory and with the final move Deon Burton's powerful header was brilliantly nodded off the line by Oster. The draw meant that a final day win against QPR would seal the 106 points record-breaking target.

Quote

Kevin Dillon

The record is important, but for me the main thing is our unbeaten run. We've only lost once away and once at home.

Venue: Hillsborough
Attendance: 27,307
Capacity: 39,859
Occupancy: 69%

Referee: L.Mason - 05/06
Matches: 31
Yellow Cards: 75
Red Cards: 2

Sheffield Wednesday
Reading

Form Coming into Fixture

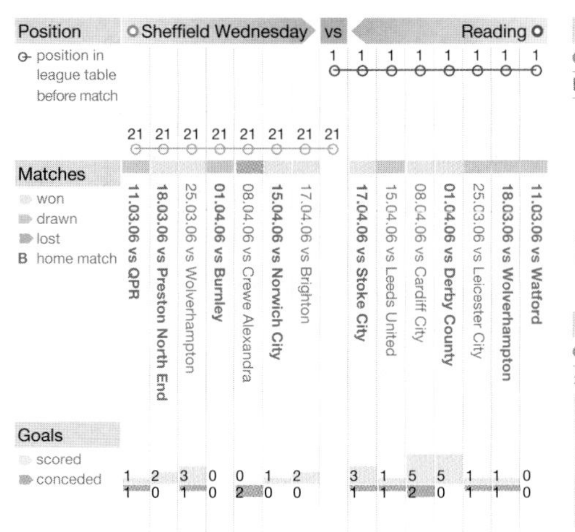
Position
Sheffield Wednesday
vs
Reading
position in league table before match
1 1 1 1 1 1 1 1
21 21 21 21 21 21 21 21
Matches
won
drawn
lost
B home match
11.03.06 vs QPR
18.03.06 vs Preston North End
25.03.06 vs Wolverhampton
01.04.06 vs Burnley
08.04.06 vs Crewe Alexandra
15.04.06 vs Norwich City
17.04.06 vs Brighton
17.04.06 vs Stoke City
15.04.06 vs Leeds United
08.04.06 vs Cardiff City
01.04.06 vs Derby County
25.03.06 vs Leicester City
18.03.06 vs Wolverhampton
11.03.06 vs Watford
Goals
scored
conceded
1 2 3 0 0 1 2
1 0 1 0 2 0 0
3 1 5 5 1 1 0
1 1 2 0 1 1 0

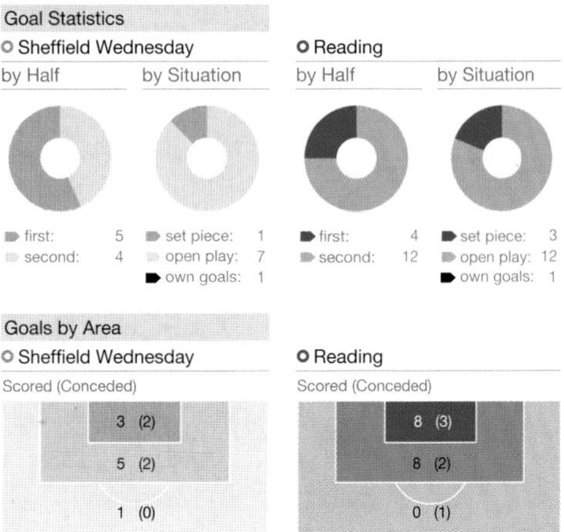
Goal Statistics
Sheffield Wednesday
by Half
by Situation
first: 5
second: 4
set piece: 1
open play: 7
own goals: 1
Reading
by Half
by Situation
first: 4
second: 12
set piece: 3
open play: 12
own goals: 1
Goals by Area
Sheffield Wednesday
Scored (Conceded)
3 (2)
5 (2)
1 (0)
Reading
Scored (Conceded)
8 (3)
8 (2)
0 (1)

Team Statistics

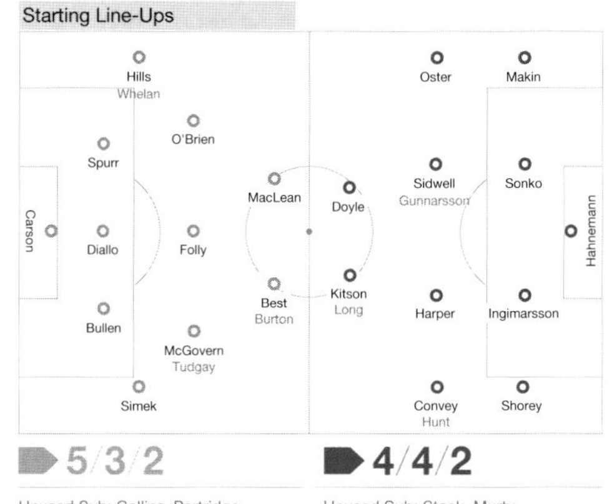
Starting Line-Ups
Hills
Whelan
O'Brien
Spurr
Carson
Diallo
Folly
Bullen
McGovern
Tudgay
Simek
MacLean
Best
Burton
Doyle
Kitson
Long
Oster
Makin
Sidwell
Gunnarsson
Sonko
Hahnemann
Harper
Ingimarsson
Convey
Hunt
Shorey
5/3/2
4/4/2

Unused Sub: Collins, Partridge

Unused Sub: Stack, Murty

Championship Totals	Sheff Wed	Reading
Championship Appearances	380	890
Team Appearances	258	788
Goals Scored	24	114
Assists	24	86
Clean Sheets (goalkeepers)	4	41
Yellow Cards	41	59
Red Cards	1	2
Full Internationals	2	6

Age/Height

Sheffield Wednesday Age: **24 yrs, 9 mo**

Reading Age: **26 yrs, 4 mo**

Sheffield Wednesday Height: **5'11"**

Reading Height: **5'11"**

Match Statistics

League Table after Fixture

		Played	Won	Drawn	Lost	For	Against	Pts
● 1	Reading	45	30	13	2	97	31	103
● 2	Sheff Utd	45	25	12	8	75	46	87
● 3	Watford	45	22	14	9	77	53	80
↑ 4	Leeds	45	21	15	9	57	36	78
↓ 5	Preston	45	19	20	6	57	30	77
● 6	Crystal Palace	45	21	12	12	67	47	75
● 7	Wolverhampton	45	15	19	11	48	41	64
...		...	...	...	...	...	...	...
● 21	Sheff Wed	45	12	13	20	37	52	49

Statistics	Sheff Wed	Reading
Goals	1	1
Shots on Target	9	4
Shots off Target	3	3
Hit Woodwork	0	0
Possession %	44	56
Corners	3	10
Offsides	9	4
Fouls	8	11
Disciplinary Points	4	4

2-1 Reading ○ Queens Park Rangers ○

Championship

30.04.06

■ Graeme Murty revels in his moment of glory

Event Line
40 ● ⚽ Kitson / RF / OP / 6Y
Assist: Oster
Half time 1-0
46 ○ ⇄ Cole > Jones P
61 ● ⇄ Hunt > Oster
68 ○ ⇄ Jones R > Bailey
72 ○ ⚽ Furlong / LF / IFK / IA
Assist: Jones R
84 ● ⚽ Murty / RF / P / IA
Assist: Shorey
85 ● ⇄ Gunnarsson > Convey
85 ● ⇄ Long > Doyle
Full time 2-1

Steve Coppell led his side to the highest-ever points tally in English football history with goal-starved captain Graeme Murty's 84th minute penalty earning the final fairytale points.

QPR were hoping to wreck Reading's grand designs on a blockbuster finale and Marcus Hahnemann had to save Lee Cook's swerving effort with his legs before Richard Langley headed a glorious opportunity over.

But before the break, John Oster did well to stab Bobby Convey's deep cross into Dave Kitson, who converted from close range for 1-0. But without the cushion of a second goal, Rangers continued to threaten and 18 minutes before the end Paul Furlong stroked past Marcus Hahnemann to rewrite the script and equalise.

Desperate not to miss out on making history, Stephen Hunt almost restored the lead with an amazing overhead kick that was tipped over by Jake Cole. But when Nicky Shorey's cross struck Langley's arm in the area, the scene was set for Murty!

Shrugging off enormous pressure, the Royals captain buried his spotkick to emphatically end his goal drought and earn Reading's 106th point of 2005/6.

Quote

Steve Coppell

It's true we fell one short of achieving 100 goals for the season, but that's not really going to spoil my break when I am sitting on the beach sinking a few beers.

Championship Milestone

■ 150

Graeme Murty's goal was his first in the Championship and the 150th scored in the competition by Reading.

Venue:	Madejski Stadium	Referee:	D.Drysdale - 05/06
Attendance:	23,156	Matches:	29
Capacity:	24,200	Yellow Cards:	98
Occupancy:	96%	Red Cards:	7

Reading
Queens Park Rangers

Form Coming into Fixture

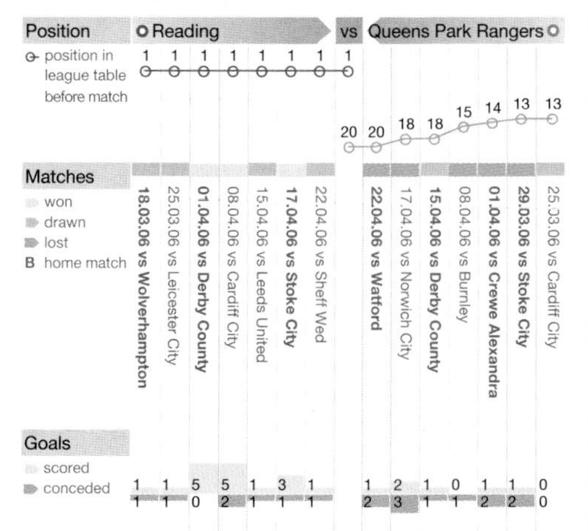

Position
Reading
vs
Queens Park Rangers
position in league table before match
1 1 1 1 1 1 1 1
20 20 18 18 15 14 13 13
Matches
won
drawn
lost
B home match
18.03.06 vs Wolverhampton
25.03.06 vs Leicester City
01.04.06 vs Derby County
08.04.06 vs Cardiff City
15.04.06 vs Leeds United
17.04.06 vs Stoke City
22.04.06 vs Sheff Wed
22.04.06 vs Watford
17.04.06 vs Norwich City
15.04.06 vs Derby County
08.04.06 vs Burnley
01.04.06 vs Crewe Alexandra
29.03.06 vs Stoke City
25.33.06 vs Cardiff City
Goals
scored
conceded
1 1 5 5 1 3 1
1 1 0 2 1 1 1
1 2 1 0 1 1 0
2 3 1 1 2 2 0

Goal Statistics

Reading

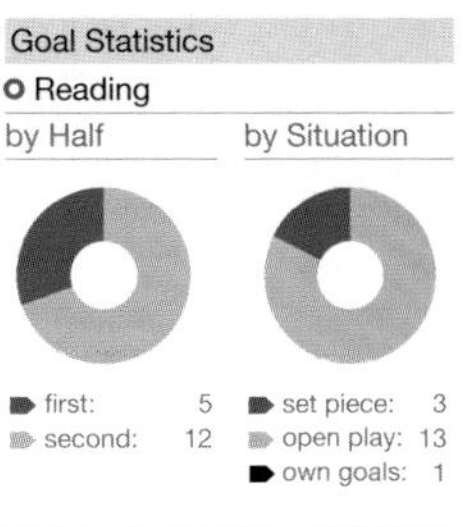

by Half
by Situation
first: 5
second: 12
set piece: 3
open play: 13
own goals: 1

Queens Park Rangers

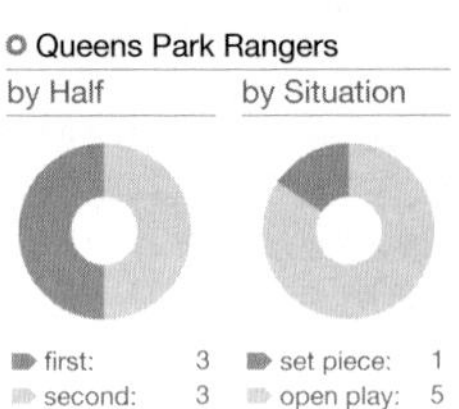

by Half
by Situation
first: 3
second: 3
set piece: 1
open play: 5

Goals by Area

Reading

Scored (Conceded)

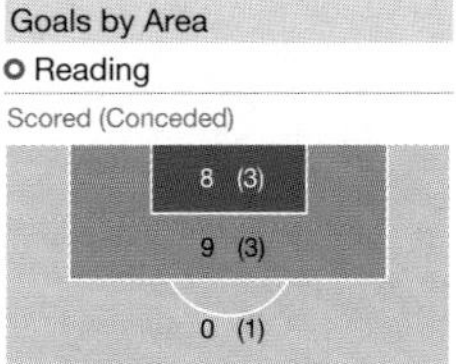

8 (3)
9 (3)
0 (1)

Queens Park Rangers

Scored (Conceded)

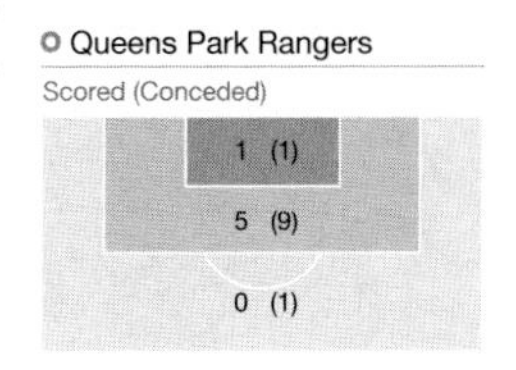

1 (1)
5 (9)
0 (1)

Team Statistics

Starting Line-Ups

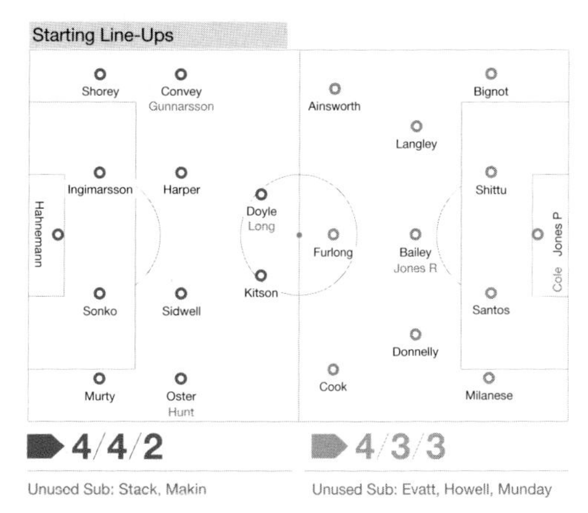

Shorey
Convey
Gunnarsson
Ingimarsson
Harper
Hahnemann
Doyle
Long
Kitson
Sonko
Sidwell
Murty
Oster
Hunt
Ainsworth
Langley
Furlong
Bailey
Jones R
Donnelly
Cook
Bignot
Shittu
Jones P
Cole
Santos
Milanese

4/4/2

Unused Sub: Stack, Makin

4/3/3

Unused Sub: Evatt, Howell, Munday

Championship Totals	Reading	QPR
Championship Appearances	938	593
Team Appearances	870	546
Goals Scored	115	60
Assists	87	63
Clean Sheets (goalkeepers)	41	9
Yellow Cards	63	79
Red Cards	1	5
Full Internationals	7	4

Age/Height

Reading Age

26 yrs, 3 mo

Queens Park Rangers Age

27 yrs, 11 mo

Reading Height

5'11"

Queens Park Rangers Height

6'

Match Statistics

League Table after Fixture

		Played	Won	Drawn	Lost	For	Against	Pts
● 1	Reading	46	31	13	2	99	32	106
● 2	Sheff Utd	46	26	12	8	76	46	90
● 3	Watford	46	22	15	9	77	53	81
↑ 4	Preston	46	20	20	6	59	30	80
↓ 5	Leeds	46	21	15	10	57	38	78
● 6	Crystal Palace	46	21	12	13	67	48	75
● 7	Wolverhampton	46	16	19	11	50	42	67
...		...	...	...	...	...	...	...
↓ 21	QPR	46	12	14	20	50	65	50

Statistics	Reading	QPR
Goals	2	1
Shots on Target	6	8
Shots off Target	6	7
Hit Woodwork	0	0
Possession %	49	51
Corners	9	6
Offsides	6	2
Fouls	14	12
Disciplinary Points	0	0

End of Season Review

www.readingfc.co.uk
RECORD BREAKING

KYOCERA KYOCERA KYOCERA
Coca-Cola Coca-Cola Coca-Cola Coca-Cola
THE HEXAGON

When the players took to the field for the opening game of the season against Plymouth Argyle on Saturday 6th August 2005, even the most optimistic Reading supporter could never have imagined the success that lay ahead. And when Argyle snatched a late winner to ruin Leroy Lita's goalscoring debut, dreams of promotion seemed very distant.

After that opening day 2-1 defeat, a quick response was imperative and just three days later the Royals got their first victory with a 2-0 success at Brighton & Hove Albion thanks to Glen Little's first goal in 15 months and Dave Kitson's powerful header.

The opening week of the season came to an impressive end with a 3-0 victory at Preston, with Lita scoring two splendid goals after latching onto excellent passes from Bobby Convey, and Little heading home Nicky Shorey's deep cross.

After a disappointing first season in English football, American winger Convey was beginning to shine and produced an outstanding performance in the following week's 5-0 thrashing of ten-man Millwall. Convey opened the scoring with a brilliant solo effort and added a free-kick before Kitson's penalty and headers from midfielders James Harper and Steve Sidwell completed the rout.

The first cup fixture of the season resulted in a 3-1 extra time victory over Swansea in the first round of the Carling Cup, and the unbeaten run was stretched to five with a hard-fought game of few chances at Watford that fully merited its 0-0 scoreline.

August ended with a game of mixed emotions at Madejski Stadium as Lita's opener was followed by Irishman Kevin Doyle coming off the bench to nod home his first Reading goal for a 2-1 victory over Burnley, but injuries to three important players – Shorey, Sidwell and Kitson – took the gloss off the win.

Those injuries gave summer signings Doyle, Chris Makin and Brynjar Gunnarsson the chance to shine, and they took that opportunity in a highly entertaining 1-1 draw at Coventry's new Ricoh Arena, where Doyle opened the scoring and Marcus Hahnemann performed heroics before Robert Page bundled home a late equaliser for the Sky Blues.

Back in Berkshire, the visit of Crystal Palace had absolutely everything. Doyle's impressive run and shot gave Reading a 1-0 lead, but Palace bounced back with goals either side of the interval by Andrew Johnson and Clinton Morrison. As the action flowed from end to end, Lita's astonishing overhead kick levelled matters before Palace keeper Gabor Kiraly saved penalties from Lita and a re-take by Little. But the Royals weren't to be denied, as Ibrahima Sonko thundered home a late header to secure a 3-2 win.

After the excitement of the Palace game, Steve Coppell's men were brought quickly back down to earth with the visit of Crewe, who put up a good fight before another central defender became the matchwinner as Ivar Ingimarsson's late header from John Oster's cross squeezed over the line for the only goal.

Oster's free-kick provided a 1-0 Carling Cup victory over Luton, and another impressive victory followed at Norwich as Harper fired home the only goal and Dean Ashton missed a last minute penalty.

The unbeaten run was further stretched with a battling 0-0 draw at rain-soaked Southampton before a clash of the top two against Sheffield United at Madejski Stadium. In an exciting game, Gunnarsson was the hero by bagging his first two Reading goals, the second of which secured a 2-1 victory with a deft header from Sekou Baradji's cross.

After a two-week international break, action resumed with an impressive 2-0 home win against Ipswich as Richard Naylor's own goal and Doyle's header secured the points. The Royals then made it 13 League games without defeat with a 1-1 draw at Hull thanks to Little's late header, before Kitson returned to the starting line-up to fire home the only goal from the penalty spot at Stoke.

Two more Kitson goals saw off an understrength Sheffield United in the Carling Cup, before a richly entertaining game with Leeds ended in a 1-1 draw as the visitors fought back well to cancel out Gunnarsson's opener. 'Yorkshire Week' concluded with a comfortable 2-0 home win against Sheffield Wednesday as Glenn Whelan put through his own net and Kitson was again on target, and another victory followed as Ingimarsson bulleted home a brilliant header at QPR after Harper's opener had been cancelled out by Lee Cook.

5
24
Hfs
LOANS

Hull City were the next victims of the Reading juggernaut as goals from Convey, Doyle and Little secured a 3-1 home victory. Steve Coppell's team were now unbeaten in a club record 18 League games, and it soon became 19 with a mightily impressive demolition of Ipswich at Portman Road on 22nd November. Sidwell, Lita and Doyle were all on target in a 3-0 victory that took the Royals to the top of the Coca-Cola Championship, a position they weren't to relinquish for the remainder of the season.

Plymouth were the only team to have defeated Reading, but the Pilgrims were unable to repeat the trick at Home Park as Little's sublime volley and Doyle's close-range strike sealed another victory, but the Royals were then handed a rare taste of defeat as the Carling Cup run came to an end with a 3-0 defeat at Highbury against a Reyes-Van Persie inspired Arsenal.

That loss seemed to have no ill effects though, as Luton were swept aside 3-0 at Madejski Stadium with goals from Sidwell, Kitson and Doyle, and the following week Kitson bagged a hat-trick in a 5-1 thrashing of Brighton as a Charlie Oatway own goal and Stephen Hunt's first strike for the Royals completed the scoring.

Moving towards Christmas, Sidwell's ferocious volley and Doyle's well-placed drive at Millwall secured an eighth consecutive League victory, and on Boxing Day Coppell's side produced one of their best performances of the season to defeat Wolves 2-0 at Molineux as Kitson and Convey hit the target.

Back at Madejski Stadium, Doyle and Gunnarsson found the net to defeat Leicester, before a real threat to the long unbeaten run came on New Year's Eve at Derby, where young Irishman Shane Long came to the rescue by heading home his first Reading goal in the 88th minute to snatch a 2-2 draw from the jaws of defeat.

2006 began with a bang as braces from Sidwell and Kitson added to a Sonko header to emphatically defeat Cardiff 5-1, and the FA Cup campaign kicked off at West Brom where Doyle's late penalty secured a deserved replay. Against Coventry, Hahnemann was called upon to make two world-class saves before two more goals from Kitson led to a 2-0 victory, and in the cup replay with WBA, Lita came to the fore with a stunning hat-trick to book a fourth round place in a 3-2 extra time thriller.

Back in the League, Harper's thunderbolt from 20 yards rescued a point at Crystal Palace after Andrew Johnson's penalty opener, before the fourth round of the Cup saw the visit of Birmingham City when Long netted again but David Dunn gave the Premiership side a replay. Before the return trip to St Andrews, the Royals fired home eight goals in two games to defeat Norwich (4-0) and Crewe (4-3) as Shorey curled home his first two of the season, Lita bagged another three, Sidwell scored in both games and Convey notched another brilliant solo effort against the Canaries.

Up in Birmingham for the cup replay, a young Reading team were unfortunate to be defeated 2-1 despite Hunt's fine volley, but there was a quick return to winning ways in the League as first half goals by strike partners Lita and Doyle saw off the challenge of Southampton at Madejski Stadium.

The eagerly anticipated rematch with second-placed Sheffield United took place on Valentine's Day, and there really was no love lost in a gruelling 1-1 draw that saw Bruce Dyer strike first only for Kitson to level almost immediately, and then home keeper Paddy Kenny ensured a fair draw with a brilliant save from Kitson's late penalty.

Then, after 33 games and more than six months, the unthinkable happened...a League defeat! The amazing, record-breaking run finally came to an end on a bitterly cold night at Luton, with the Hatters running out 3-2 winners despite Doyle scoring in the first and last minutes.

Normal service resumed the following weekend with a 2-1 home victory over Preston thanks to Sidwell's bundled opener and Lita's clinical winner, and more Lancashire opposition were dispatched when Convey's screamer, Sonko's header and Kitson's tap-in defeated Burnley at Turf Moor – although the victory was overshadowed by Lita suffering a broken ankle.

The mathematical reality of promotion was now looming large, even if celebrations were made to wait with successive hard-fought home draws against Watford (0-0) and Wolves (1-1). But then, on 25th March 2006, it was time to make some history.

Leicester were the opponents on a day that will never be forgotten, although ironically results elsewhere meant that the scoreline at Walkers Stadium was actually irrelevant. For the record, Doyle headed home in the final stages to secure a 1-1 draw, and ten

WE'RE
UP
Coca-Cola
FOOTBALL
LEAGUE
KYOCERA

minutes later the Royals were in dreamland as our place in the Premiership was confirmed.

Back home at Madejski Stadium, April Fools Day provided more memories to cherish as the Football League Championship was sealed. Second half goals from Harper, Doyle, Oster and Long (2) provided a 5-0 thrashing of Derby, sparking a joyous pitch invasion and unforgettable scenes of celebration.

Having already secured promotion and the title, attention now turned to Sunderland's single season points record of 105, and another big step was taken towards that milestone with a 5-2 battering of Cardiff at Ninian Park thanks to Harper (2), Doyle, Kitson and a Glen Loovens own goal.

The following week Hunt's late leveller in a 1-1 draw at Leeds ended the Whites' hopes of automatic promotion, and two days later on Easter Monday Steve Coppell used 'squad rotation' and was rewarded with a 3-1 victory over Stoke thanks to goals from Sidwell, Doyle and debutant John Halls.

The season's final away game was a hard-fought 1-1 draw at Sheffield Wednesday where Kitson's goal was cancelled out by Steve MacLean's penalty, and the stage was set for the final game of the season.

QPR were the visitors to Madejski Stadium, and the Royals needed maximum points to take their season tally to 106 and thereby set a new Football League record. Everything was going to plan when Kitson swept his side into the lead, only for Paul Furlong to fire a shock leveller. But now it was time for an unbelievable season to enter the realms of fantasy...

With five minutes remaining, Shorey's cross struck an arm and referee Darren Drysdale pointed to the spot. Up stepped Graeme Murty, the Reading skipper who had failed to score for more than five years. With a place in the record books up for grabs, Murty hid his nerves to smash an unstoppable penalty kick into the top right corner, sparking scenes of unrestrained joy around Madejski Stadium.

The remainder of the weekend was a blur as Murty received the Football League trophy, the players embarked on a champagne-soaked lap of honour and returned the following day for an open-top bus tour around Reading with an estimated 80,000 people celebrating...the Royals were champions!

Final Championship Table 2005/06

Pos	Team	P	W	D	L	F	A	GD	PTS
1	**Reading**	**46**	**31**	**13**	**2**	**99**	**32**	**67**	**106**
2	Sheffield Utd	46	26	12	8	76	46	30	90
3	Watford	46	22	15	9	77	53	24	81
4	Preston	46	20	20	6	59	30	29	80
5	Leeds United	46	21	15	10	57	38	19	78
6	Crystal Palace	46	21	12	13	67	48	19	75
7	Wolves	46	16	19	11	50	42	8	67
8	Coventry City	46	16	15	15	62	65	-3	63
9	Norwich City	46	18	8	20	56	65	-9	62
10	Luton Town	46	17	10	19	66	67	-1	61
11	Cardiff City	46	16	12	18	58	59	-1	60
12	Southampton	46	13	19	14	49	50	-1	58
13	Stoke City	46	17	7	22	54	63	-9	58
14	Plymouth	46	13	17	16	39	46	-7	56
15	Ipswich Town	46	14	14	18	53	66	-13	56
16	Leicester City	46	13	15	18	51	59	-8	54
17	Burnley	46	14	12	20	46	54	-8	54
18	Hull City	46	12	16	18	49	55	-6	52
19	Sheffield Wed	46	13	13	20	39	52	-13	52
20	Derby County	46	10	20	16	53	67	-14	50
21	QPR	46	12	14	20	50	65	-15	50
22	Crewe	46	9	15	22	57	86	-29	42
23	Millwall	46	8	16	22	35	62	-27	40
24	Brighton	46	7	17	22	39	71	-32	38

Player Profiles

PUMA
PUMA

KYOCERA

1 Marcus Hahnemann
Goalkeeper

Player Profile

US international goalkeeper Marcus Hahnemann joined on a free transfer in August 2002 after leaving top flight Fulham. Born in Seattle, Marcus arrived in England in June 1999 and joined the Cottagers from Colorado Rapids for £80,000. After just four appearances at Fulham and loan spells at Rochdale and Reading he then made the permanent move to Berkshire, becoming an integral part of the Royals' team and a firm favourite with supporters.

During the 2005/6 promotion campaign Marcus regularly pulled off outstanding saves to keep an impressive tally of 22 clean sheets, also earning a richly deserved call-up into his national team's World Cup squad.

Player Details:

Date of Birth:	15.06.1972
Place of Birth:	Seattle
Nationality:	American
Height:	6'3"
Weight:	16st
Foot:	Right

Player Performance 05/06

League Performance

Percentage of total possible time player was on pitch — position in league table at end of month

Month:	Aug	Sep	Oct	Nov	Dec	Jan	Feb	Mar	Apr	Total
% on pitch	100%	100%	100%	100%	100%	100%	100%	100%	83%	98%
League position	2	2	2	1	1	1	1	1	1	
Team Pts:	13/18	11/15	11/15	15/15	16/18	10/12	10/15	6/12	14/18	106/138
Team Gls F:	13	6	7	12	16	12	11	5	17	99
Team Gls A:	3	3	3	2	3	2	8	2	6	32
Total mins:	540	450	450	450	540	360	450	360	450	4,050
Starts (sub):	6	5	5	5	6	4	5	4	5	45
Goals:	0	0	0	0	0	0	0	0	0	0
Assists:	0	0	0	0	0	0	1	0	0	1
Clean sheets:	4	3	2	3	4	2	1	2	1	22
Cards (Y/R):	0	0	0	0	0	0	0	0	0	0

League Performance Totals

Clean Sheets

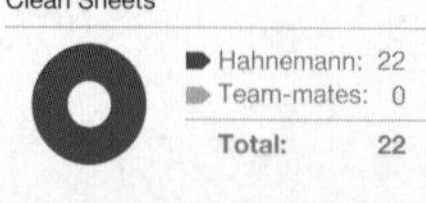

- Hahnemann: 22
- Team-mates: 0
- Total: 22

Assists

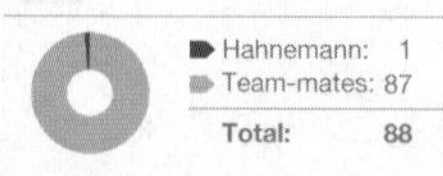

- Hahnemann: 1
- Team-mates: 87
- Total: 88

Cards

- Hahnemann: 0
- Team-mates: 38
- Total: 38

Cup Games

	Apps	CS	Cards
FA Cup	0	0	0
Carling Cup	2	1	0
Total	**2**	**1**	**0**

Career History

Career Milestones

Club Debut:

vs Wigan (H), D 1-1, Football League 1

22.12.01

Time Spent at the Club:

4 Seasons

First Goal Scored for the Club:

–

–

Full International:

USA

Championship Totals

04-06

Appearances	91
Clean Sheets	41
Assists	1
Yellow Cards	0
Red Cards	0

Clubs

Year	Club	Apps	CS
02-06	Reading	186	74
01-02	Reading	6	4
01-01	Rochdale	7	5
99-02	Fulham	4	0
	Colorado Rapids		
	Seattle Sounders		

Off the Pitch

Age:

- Hahnemann: 33 years, 11 months
- Team: 25 years, 6 months
- League: 26 years, 1 month

Height:

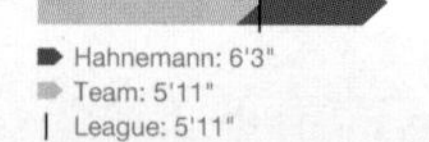

- Hahnemann: 6'3"
- Team: 5'11"
- League: 5'11"

Weight:

- Hahnemann: 16st
- Team: 12st
- League: 11st 13lb

21 Graham Stack
Goalkeeper

Player Details:

Date of Birth:	26.09.1981
Place of Birth:	Hampstead
Nationality:	Irish
Height:	6'2"
Weight:	12st 6lb
Foot:	Right

Player Profile

Goalkeeper Graham Stack joined on loan from Arsenal in the summer of 2005, before making the move permanent after Christmas. Stack had been at Highbury since joining as a schoolboy in 1998, signing as a professional in 2000. Graham became second choice stopper behind Jens Lehmann and guarded the Gunners' goal throughout a semi-final bound Carling Cup campaign whilst acting as an unused understudy during the record-breaking unbeaten title-winning season.

The former Republic of Ireland under 21 international spent the 2004/5 season on loan at Millwall before challenging Marcus Hahnemann for the goalkeeper's jersey at Reading last year.

Player Performance 05/06

League Performance

Percentage of total possible time player was on pitch

position in league table at end of month

Month:	Aug	Sep	Oct	Nov	Dec	Jan	Feb	Mar	Apr	Total
League position	2	2	2	1	1	1	1	1	1	
% on pitch	0%	0%	0%	0%	0%	0%	0%	0%	17%	2%
Team Pts:	13/18	11/15	11/15	15/15	16/18	10/12	10/15	6/12	14/18	106/138
Team Gls F:	13	6	7	12	16	12	11	5	17	99
Team Gls A:	3	3	3	2	3	2	8	2	6	32
Total mins:	0	0	0	0	0	0	0	0	90	90
Starts (sub):	0	0	0	0	0	0	0	0	1	1
Goals:	0	0	0	0	0	0	0	0	0	0
Assists:	0	0	0	0	0	0	0	0	0	0
Clean sheets:	0	0	0	0	0	0	0	0	0	0
Cards (Y/R):	0	0	0	0	0	0	0	0	0	0

League Performance Totals

Clean Sheets

Stack:	0
Team-mates:	22
Total:	**22**

Assists

Stack:	0
Team-mates:	88
Total:	**88**

Cards

Stack:	0
Team-mates:	38
Total:	**38**

Cup Games

	Apps	CS	Cards
FA Cup	4	0	0
Carling Cup	3	1	0
Total	**7**	**1**	**0**

Career History

Career Milestones

Club Debut:

vs Swansea (H), W 3-1, League Cup

23.08.05

Time Spent at the Club:

1 Season

First Goal Scored for the Club:

–

–

Full International:

–

Championship Totals

04-06

Appearances	27
Clean Sheets	9
Assists	0
Yellow Cards	0
Red Cards	0

Clubs

Year	Club	Apps	CS
05-06	Reading	8	1
04-05	Millwall	30	9
02-03	Beveren		
00-05	Arsenal	5	1

Off the Pitch

Age:

- Stack: 24 years, 8 months
- Team: 25 years, 6 months
- League: 26 years, 1 month

Height:

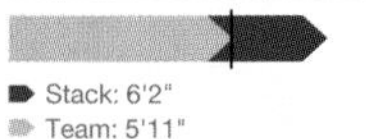

- Stack: 6'2"
- Team: 5'11"
- League: 5'11"

Weight:

- Stack: 12st 6lb
- Team: 12st
- League: 11st 13lb

2 Graeme Murty
Defence

Player Details:

Date of Birth:	13.11.1974
Place of Birth:	Saltburn
Nationality:	Scottish
Height:	5'10"
Weight:	11st 10lb
Foot:	Right

Player Profile

Reading's longest serving player signed from York City in 1998 for £700,000. He was named the fans' player of the season in both 2001/2 and 2003/4, and was appointed captain following Adie Williams' departure in November 2004.

Last season Murts skippered the Royals into the Premiership, and on the final day of the season against QPR he scored a late winner from the penalty spot, his first goal in more than five years, to secure a new Football League points record.

Graeme made his Scotland debut against Wales in February 2004, and earned two further caps against Bulgaria and Japan in May 2006.

Player Performance 05/06

League Performance

Percentage of total possible time player was on pitch — position in league table at end of month

Month:	Aug	Sep	Oct	Nov	Dec	Jan	Feb	Mar	Apr	Total
% on pitch	100%	88%	20%	100%	99%	100%	100%	100%	65%	85%
League position	2	2	2	1	1	1	1	1	1	
Team Pts:	13/18	11/15	11/15	15/15	16/18	10/12	10/15	6/12	14/18	106/138
Team Gls F:	13	6	7	12	16	12	11	5	17	99
Team Gls A:	3	3	3	2	3	2	8	2	6	32
Total mins:	540	397	90	450	536	360	450	360	353	3,536
Starts (sub):	6	5	1	5	6	4	5	4	4	40
Goals:	0	0	0	0	0	0	0	0	1	1
Assists:	1	0	0	0	0	0	0	0	1	2
Clean sheets:	4	2	0	3	4	2	1	2	1	19
Cards (Y/R):	0	1	0	0	0	1	0	1	0	3

League Performance Totals

Goals

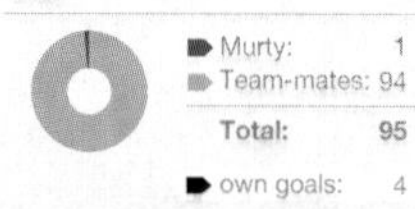

Murty:	1
Team-mates:	94
Total:	**95**
own goals:	4

Assists

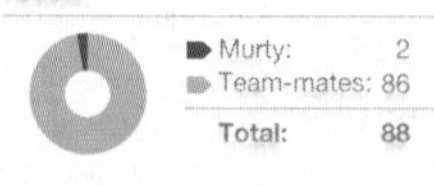

Murty:	2
Team-mates:	86
Total:	**88**

Cards

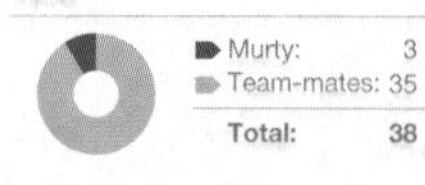

Murty:	3
Team-mates:	35
Total:	**38**

Cup Games

	Apps	Goals	Cards
FA Cup	1	0	0
Carling Cup	3	0	0
Total	**4**	**0**	**0**

Career History

Career Milestones

Club Debut:

vs Burnley (A), D 1-1, Football League 1

13.02.99

Time Spent at the Club:

8 Seasons

First Goal Scored for the Club:

vs Bristol C (H), L 1-3, Football League 1

23.03.01

Full International:

Scotland

Championship Totals

04-06

Appearances	81
Goals	1
Assists	3
Yellow Cards	5
Red Cards	0

Clubs

Year	Club	Apps	Gls
99-06	Reading	286	2
93-98	York C	144	9

Off the Pitch

Age:

- Murty: 31 years, 6 months
- Team: 25 years, 6 months
- League: 26 years, 1 month

Height:

- Murty: 5'10"
- Team: 5'11"
- League: 5'11"

Weight:

- Murty: 11st 10lb
- Team: 12st
- League: 11st 13lb

3 Nicky Shorey
Defence

Player Details:

Date of Birth:	19.02.1981
Place of Birth:	Romford
Nationality:	English
Height:	5'9"
Weight:	10st 8lb
Foot:	Left

Player Profile

Cultured left-back Nicky Shorey joined the Royals from Leyton Orient for a bargain fee of just £25,000 in February 2001.

Nicky had made just a handful of first team appearances for the O's, but showed poise and maturity beyond his years to play a key role in our 2001/2 promotion. He has received recognition from his peers by being named in the 2005/6 PFA Championship team of the year.

A quietly efficient defender who has a wonderful range of passing and loves to get forward, Nicky is also a threat from set-pieces and his sweet left foot has been responsible for some brilliant free-kick goals.

Player Performance 05/06

League Performance

Percentage of total possible time player was on pitch

position in league table at end of month

Month:	Aug	Sep	Oct	Nov	Dec	Jan	Feb	Mar	Apr	Total
% on pitch	92%	0%	80%	100%	100%	100%	100%	100%	95%	85%
League position	2	2	2	1	1	1	1	1	1	
Team Pts:	13/18	11/15	11/15	15/15	16/18	10/12	10/15	6/12	14/18	106/138
Team Gls F:	13	6	7	12	16	12	11	5	17	99
Team Gls A:	3	3	3	2	3	2	8	2	6	32
Total mins:	496	0	360	450	540	360	450	360	514	3,530
Starts (sub):	6	0	4	5	6	4	5	4	6	40
Goals:	0	0	0	0	0	1	1	0	0	2
Assists:	2	0	1	0	4	3	1	0	1	12
Clean sheets:	4	0	2	3	4	2	1	2	1	19
Cards (Y/R):	0	0	0	0	1	0	1	0	0	2

League Performance Totals

Goals

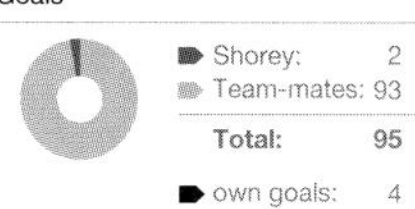

Shorey:	2
Team-mates:	93
Total:	**95**

own goals: 4

Assists

Shorey:	12
Team-mates:	76
Total:	**88**

Cards

Shorey:	2
Team-mates:	36
Total:	**38**

Cup Games

	Apps	Goals	Cards
FA Cup	1	0	0
Carling Cup	3	0	0
Total	**4**	**0**	**0**

Career History

Career Milestones

Club Debut:

vs Luton T (H), W 4-0, League Cup

21.08.01

First Goal Scored for the Club:

vs Bradford (H), W 1-0, Championship

29.10.02

Time Spent at the Club:

5.5 Seasons

Full International:

–

Championship Totals

04-06

Appearances	84
Goals	5
Assists	20
Yellow Cards	4
Red Cards	0

Clubs

Year	Club	Apps	Gls
01-06	Reading	219	9
98-01	Leyton Orient	16	0

Off the Pitch

Age:

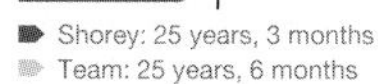

Shorey: 25 years, 3 months
Team: 25 years, 6 months
League: 26 years, 1 month

Height:

Shorey: 5'9"
Team: 5'11"
League: 5'11"

Weight:

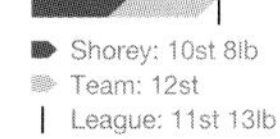

Shorey: 10st 8lb
Team: 12st
League: 11st 13lb

16 Ivar Ingimarsson
Defence

Player Profile

Ivar Ingimarsson became Steve Coppell's first signing as Reading manager when he was snapped up for £100,000 from Wolves in October 2003. He excelled in a debut victory at Sheffield United and has remained a reliable presence in the back four ever since, starting every League game in the 2005/6 title success and captaining the team on a few occasions in Graeme Murty's absence.

The Icelandic international defender first moved to English football with Brentford in 1999, joining Wolves three years later. Ivar is always a threat from set-pieces, and scored headed winners against Crewe and QPR during the 2005/6 season.

Player Details:

Date of Birth:	20.08.1977
Place of Birth:	Reykjavik
Nationality:	Icelandic
Height:	6'
Weight:	12st 7lb
Foot:	Right

Player Performance 05/06

League Performance

Percentage of total possible time player was on pitch

position in league table at end of month

Month:	Aug	Sep	Oct	Nov	Dec	Jan	Feb	Mar	Apr	Total
	100%	100%	100%	100%	100%	100%	100%	100%	100%	100%
	2	2	2	1	1	1	1	1	1	
Team Pts:	13/18	11/15	11/15	15/15	16/18	10/12	10/15	6/12	14/18	106/138
Team Gls F:	13	6	7	12	16	12	11	5	17	99
Team Gls A:	3	3	3	2	3	2	8	2	6	32
Total mins:	540	450	450	450	540	360	450	360	540	4,140
Starts (sub):	6	5	5	5	6	4	5	4	6	46
Goals:	0	1	0	1	0	0	0	0	0	2
Assists:	0	0	0	0	0	0	1	1	2	4
Clean sheets:	4	3	2	3	4	2	1	2	1	22
Cards (Y/R):	0	0	0	0	0	0	0	1	0	1

League Performance Totals

Goals

- Ingimarsson: 2
- Team-mates: 93
- **Total: 95**
- own goals: 4

Assists

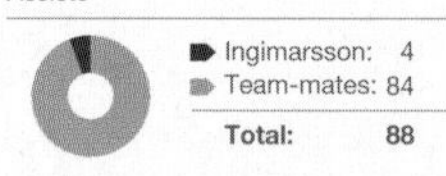

- Ingimarsson: 4
- Team-mates: 84
- **Total: 88**

Cards

- Ingimarsson: 1
- Team-mates: 37
- **Total: 38**

Cup Games

	Apps	Goals	Cards
FA Cup	3	0	0
Carling Cup	4	0	0
Total	**7**	**0**	**0**

Career History

Career Milestones

Club Debut:

vs Sheff Utd (A), W 1-2, Championship

24.10.03

First Goal Scored for the Club:

vs Cardiff (A), W 2-3, Championship

16.03.04

Time Spent at the Club:

3 Seasons

Full International:

Iceland

Championship Totals

04-06

Appearances	90
Goals	5
Assists	6
Yellow Cards	2
Red Cards	0

Clubs

Year	Club	Apps	Gls
03-06	Reading	130	7
03-03	Brighton & HA	15	0
02-03	Wolverhampton	15	2
99-02	Brentford	135	11
99-99	Torquay Utd	4	1
	IBV Vestmann		
	Valur Reykjavik		

Off the Pitch

Age:

- Ingimarsson: 28 years, 9 months
- Team: 25 years, 6 months
- League: 26 years, 1 month

Height:

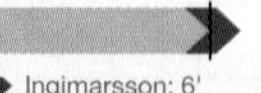

- Ingimarsson: 6'
- Team: 5'11"
- League: 5'11"

Weight:

- Ingimarsson: 12st 7lb
- Team: 12st
- League: 11st 13lb

5 Ibrahima Sonko

Defence

Player Details:

Date of Birth:	22.01.1981
Place of Birth:	Bignola
Nationality:	Senegalese
Height:	6'3"
Weight:	13st 7lb
Foot:	Right

Player Profile

Ibrahima Sonko joined on a free from Brentford in 2004. After a brief spell on the bench, he came to the fore following the departure of captain Adie Williams and has never looked back.

His form throughout the 2005/6 season was sensational, and he was rightly named in the PFA Championship team of the season. One spectacular goalline clearance against Ipswich resulted in the chant 'Sonko is Superman' ringing around Madejski Stadium on a regular basis!

Ibrahima, born in Senegal, moved to France at a young age and played for a number of clubs, including Grenoble, before his move to Brentford in 2002.

Player Performance 05/06

League Performance

Percentage of total possible time player was on pitch — position in league table at end of month

Month:	Aug	Sep	Oct	Nov	Dec	Jan	Feb	Mar	Apr	Total
% on pitch	100%	100%	100%	100%	100%	100%	100%	100%	100%	100%
League position	2	2	2	1	1	1	1	1	1	
Team Pts:	13/18	11/15	11/15	15/15	16/18	10/12	10/15	6/12	14/18	106/138
Team Gls F:	13	6	7	12	16	12	11	5	17	99
Team Gls A:	3	3	3	2	3	2	8	2	6	32
Total mins:	540	450	450	450	540	360	450	360	540	4,140
Starts (sub):	6	5	5	5	6	4	5	4	6	46
Goals:	0	1	0	0	0	1	0	1	0	3
Assists:	0	0	0	0	0	0	0	0	0	0
Clean sheets:	4	3	2	3	4	2	1	2	1	22
Cards (Y/R):	0	0	0	0	1	0	0	0	0	1

League Performance Totals

Goals

Sonko:	3
Team-mates:	92
Total:	**95**
own goals:	4

Assists

Sonko:	0
Team-mates:	88
Total:	**88**

Cards

Sonko:	1
Team-mates:	37
Total:	**38**

Cup Games

	Apps	Goals	Cards
FA Cup	2	0	1
Carling Cup	4	0	0
Total	**6**	**0**	**1**

Career History

Career Milestones

Club Debut:

vs Millwall (A), L 1-0, Championship

28.08.04

First Goal Scored for the Club:

vs Watford (H), W 3-0, Championship

26.12.04

Time Spent at the Club:

2 Seasons

Full International:

–

Championship Totals

04-06

Appearances	85
Goals	4
Assists	0
Yellow Cards	3
Red Cards	0

Clubs

Year	Club	Apps	Gls
04-06	Reading	94	4
02-04	Brentford	91	9
	Grenoble		
	St Etienne		

Off the Pitch

Age:

- Sonko: 25 years, 4 months
- Team: 25 years, 6 months
- League: 26 years, 1 month

Height:

- Sonko: 6'3"
- Team: 5'11"
- League: 5'11"

Weight:

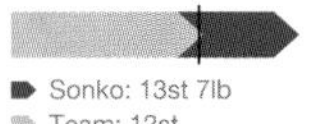

- Sonko: 13st 7lb
- Team: 12st
- League: 11st 13lb

27 Aaron Brown
Defence

Player Profile

Powerful and commanding central defender Aaron Brown signed on loan from non-league Tamworth last autumn after a successful trial period at Madejski Stadium, and penned a permanent deal in January's transfer window.

23-year old Brown moved to Tamworth from Studley in 2004 and also spent time coaching in the USA. He made his debut for the non-league England team only weeks before becoming a Royal, coming off the bench against Belgium. The towering defender was an unused substitute in League wins at Millwall and Wolves during a hectic Christmas schedule, and made nine starts for Brian McDermott's title-winning reserves.

Player Details:

Date of Birth:	23.06.1983
Place of Birth:	Birmingham
Nationality:	English
Height:	6'3"
Weight:	15st 2lb
Foot:	Right

Player Performance 05/06

League Performance

Percentage of total possible time player was on pitch

position in league table at end of month

Month:	Aug	Sep	Oct	Nov	Dec	Jan	Feb	Mar	Apr	Total
League position	2	2	2	1	1	1	1	1	1	
% on pitch	0%	0%	0%	0%	0%	0%	0%	0%	0%	0%
Team Pts:	13/18	11/15	11/15	15/15	16/18	10/12	10/15	6/12	14/18	106/138
Team Gls F:	13	6	7	12	16	12	11	5	17	99
Team Gls A:	3	3	3	2	3	2	8	2	6	32
Total mins:	0	0	0	0	0	0	0	0	0	0
Starts (sub):	0	0	0	0	0	0	0	0	0	0
Goals:	0	0	0	0	0	0	0	0	0	0
Assists:	0	0	0	0	0	0	0	0	0	0
Clean sheets:	0	0	0	0	0	0	0	0	0	0
Cards (Y/R):	0	0	0	0	0	0	0	0	0	0

League Performance Totals

Goals

Brown:	0
Team-mates:	95
Total:	**95**
own goals:	4

Assists

Brown:	0
Team-mates:	88
Total:	**88**

Cards

Brown:	0
Team-mates:	38
Total:	**38**

Cup Games

	Apps	Goals	Cards
FA Cup	0	0	0
Carling Cup	0	0	0
Total	**0**	**0**	**0**

Career History

Career Milestones

Club Debut:

–

–

First Goal Scored for the Club:

–

–

Time Spent at the Club:

0.5 Seasons

Full International:

–

Championship Totals

04-06

Appearances	0
Goals	0
Assists	0
Yellow Cards	0
Red Cards	0

Clubs

Year	Club	Apps	Gls
06-06	Bournemouth	4	0
04-06	Tamworth	41	2
	Studley		

Off the Pitch

Age:

- Brown: 22 years, 11 months
- Team: 25 years, 6 months
- League: 26 years, 1 month

Height:

- Brown: 6'3"
- Team: 5'11"
- League: 5'11"

Weight:

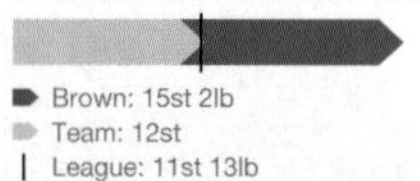

- Brown: 15st 2lb
- Team: 12st
- League: 11st 13lb

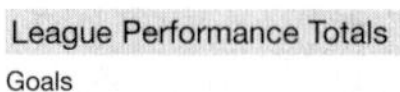

23 Chris Makin
Defence

Player Profile

An experienced and versatile full-back, Chris Makin signed in the summer of 2005 whilst the first team were on tour in Sweden. With more than 100 top flight appearances for Oldham in the early nineties, Chris has rare Royals Premiership experience. After a season-long spell with Marseille, he spent four years as Sunderland player before a £1.4m move to Ipswich Town.

After spending 2004/5 at Leicester and on loan with Derby County, Chris moved to Madejski Stadium, where he more than competently deputised for Nicky Shorey and Graeme Murty at various stages of the campaign. He ended up as the only outfield league starter not to score a goal!

Player Details:

Date of Birth:	08.05.1973
Place of Birth:	Manchester
Nationality:	English
Height:	5'11"
Weight:	12st 10lb
Foot:	Right

Player Performance 05/06

League Performance

Percentage of total possible time player was on pitch — position in league table at end of month

Month:	Aug	Sep	Oct	Nov	Dec	Jan	Feb	Mar	Apr	Total
% on pitch	8%	100%	72%	0%	0%	0%	0%	0%	33%	24%
League position	2	2	2	1	1	1	1	1	1	
Team Pts:	13/18	11/15	11/15	15/15	16/18	10/12	10/15	6/12	14/18	106/138
Team Gls F:	13	6	7	12	16	12	11	5	17	99
Team Gls A:	3	3	3	2	3	2	8	2	6	32
Total mins:	44	450	323	0	0	0	0	0	180	997
Starts (sub):	0 (1)	5	4	0	0	0	0	0	2	11 (1)
Goals:	0	0	0	0	0	0	0	0	0	0
Assists:	0	0	0	0	0	0	0	0	0	0
Clean sheets:	0	3	1	0	0	0	0	0	0	4
Cards (Y/R):	0	1	1	0	0	0	0	0	0	2

League Performance Totals

Goals

Makin:	0
Team-mates:	95
Total:	95
own goals:	4

Assists

Makin:	0
Team-mates:	88
Total:	88

Cards

Makin:	2
Team-mates:	36
Total:	38

Cup Games

	Apps	Goals	Cards
FA Cup	4	0	1
Carling Cup	3	0	0
Total	**7**	**0**	**1**

Career History

Career Milestones

Club Debut:

vs Swansea (H), W 3-1, League Cup

23.08.05

Time Spent at the Club:

1 Season

First Goal Scored for the Club:

–

–

Full International:

–

Championship Totals

04-06

Appearances	46
Goals	0
Assists	3
Yellow Cards	2
Red Cards	1

Clubs

Year	Club	Apps	Gls
05-06	Reading	19	0
05-05	Derby	13	0
04-05	Leicester	23	0
01-04	Ipswich	92	0
97-01	Sunderland	144	2
96-97	Marseille		
92-93	Wigan	15	2
91-96	Oldham	114	4

Off the Pitch

Age:

- Makin: 33 years
- Team: 25 years, 6 months
- League: 26 years, 1 month

Height:

- Makin: 5'11"
- Team: 5'11"
- League: 5'11"

Weight:

- Makin: 12st 10lb
- Team: 12st
- League: 11st 13lb

33 Scott Golbourne
Defence

LONG
24

Player Details:

Date of Birth:	29.02.1988
Place of Birth:	Bristol
Nationality:	English
Height:	5'8"
Weight:	11st 8lb
Foot:	Left

Player Profile

Talented left-back who signed for an undisclosed six-figure fee from Bristol City in January.

Scott came through the ranks at Ashton Gate to make his first team debut at just 16 in February 2005. As a City regular he scored his first career goal in a Carling Cup clash with Barnet, before the Royals stepped in.

At this year's Football League awards ceremony, Scott won the official Coca-Cola League One Apprentice of the Year award which recognised both his outstanding performances on the field and his educational achievements off it. Impressive reserves displays led to a first team substitute debut during our 3-1 win over Stoke.

Player Performance 05/06

League Performance

Percentage of total possible time player was on pitch

position in league table at end of month

Month:	Aug	Sep	Oct	Nov	Dec	Jan	Feb	Mar	Apr	Total
Position	2	2	2	1	1	1	1	1	1	
%	0%	0%	0%	0%	0%	0%	0%	0%	5%	1%
Team Pts:	13/18	11/15	11/15	15/15	16/18	10/12	10/15	6/12	14/18	106/138
Team Gls F:	13	6	7	12	16	12	11	5	17	99
Team Gls A:	3	3	3	2	3	2	8	2	6	32
Total mins:	0	0	0	0	0	0	0	0	26	26
Starts (sub):	0	0	0	0	0	0	0	0	0 (1)	0 (1)
Goals:	0	0	0	0	0	0	0	0	0	0
Assists:	0	0	0	0	0	0	0	0	0	0
Clean sheets:	0	0	0	0	0	0	0	0	0	0
Cards (Y/R):	0	0	0	0	0	0	0	0	0	0

League Performance Totals

Goals

Golbourne:	0
Team-mates:	95
Total:	**95**
own goals:	4

Assists

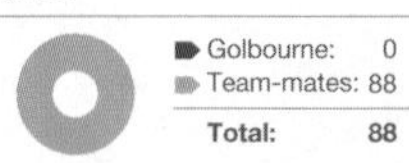

Golbourne:	0
Team-mates:	88
Total:	**88**

Cards

Golbourne:	0
Team-mates:	38
Total:	**38**

Cup Games

	Apps	Goals	Cards
FA Cup	0	0	0
Carling Cup	0	0	0
Total	**0**	**0**	**0**

Career History

Career Milestones

Club Debut:

vs Stoke (H), W 3-1, Championship

17.04.06

Time Spent at the Club:

0.5 Seasons

First Goal Scored for the Club:

–

–

Full International:

–

Championship Totals

04-06

Appearances	1
Goals	0
Assists	0
Yellow Cards	0
Red Cards	0

Clubs

Year	Club	Apps	Gls
06-06	Reading	1	0
05-06	Bristol City	15	1

Off the Pitch

Age:

- Golbourne: 18 years, 3 months
- Team: 25 years, 6 months
- League: 26 years, 1 month

Height:

- Golbourne: 5'8"
- Team: 5'11"
- League: 5'11"

Weight:

- Golbourne: 11st 8lb
- Team: 12st
- League: 11st 13lb

26 Curtis Osano
Defence

Player Profile

A young, robust defender, last season Curtis Osano successfully progressed through the Academy and reserve team ranks to make his first team bow.

Comfortable at the back or in midfield, Kenyan-born Curtis came off the bench towards the end of a gruelling 3-2 FA Cup home win over West Brom in January and made an impressive start to his Royals career on the right side of midfield.

He made little further impression as he suffered with injury towards the end of the 2005/6 campaign, but returned to fitness to head home the opening goal in the final reserves game of the season, a 3-0 win at Gillingham.

Player Details:

Date of Birth:	08.03.1987
Place of Birth:	Kenya
Nationality:	English
Height:	6'1"
Weight:	13st 10lb
Foot:	Right

Player Performance 05/06

League Performance

Percentage of total possible time player was on pitch

position in league table at end of month

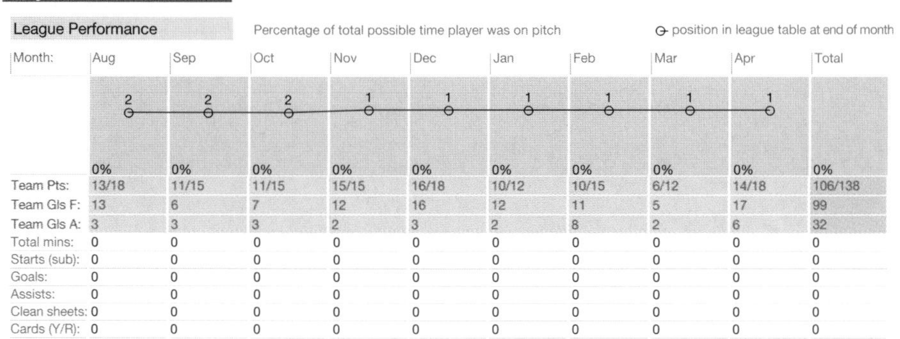

Month:	Aug	Sep	Oct	Nov	Dec	Jan	Feb	Mar	Apr	Total
League position	2	2	2	1	1	1	1	1	1	
% on pitch	0%	0%	0%	0%	0%	0%	0%	0%	0%	0%
Team Pts:	13/18	11/15	11/15	15/15	16/18	10/12	10/15	6/12	14/18	106/138
Team Gls F:	13	6	7	12	16	12	11	5	17	99
Team Gls A:	3	3	3	2	3	2	8	2	6	32
Total mins:	0	0	0	0	0	0	0	0	0	0
Starts (sub):	0	0	0	0	0	0	0	0	0	0
Goals:	0	0	0	0	0	0	0	0	0	0
Assists:	0	0	0	0	0	0	0	0	0	0
Clean sheets:	0	0	0	0	0	0	0	0	0	0
Cards (Y/R):	0	0	0	0	0	0	0	0	0	0

League Performance Totals

Goals

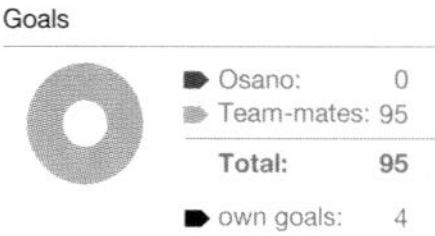

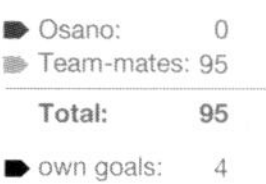

- Osano: 0
- Team-mates: 95
- **Total: 95**
- own goals: 4

Assists

- Osano: 0
- Team-mates: 88
- **Total: 88**

Cards

- Osano: 0
- Team-mates: 38
- **Total: 38**

Cup Games

	Apps	Goals	Cards
FA Cup	1	0	0
Carling Cup	0	0	0
Total	**1**	**0**	**0**

Career History

Career Milestones

Club Debut:

vs West Brom (H), W 3-2, FA Cup

17.01.06

Time Spent at the Club:

1 Season

First Goal Scored for the Club:

–

–

Full International:

–

Championship Totals

04-06

Appearances	0
Goals	0
Assists	0
Yellow Cards	0
Red Cards	0

Clubs

Year	Club	Apps	Gls
05-06	Reading	1	0

Off the Pitch

Age:

- Osano: 19 years, 2 months
- Team: 25 years, 6 months
- League: 26 years, 1 month

Height:

- Osano: 6'1"
- Team: 5'11"
- League: 5'11"

Weight:

- Osano: 13st 10lb
- Team: 12st
- League: 11st 13lb

14 John Halls
Defence

Player Details:

Date of Birth:	14.02.1982
Place of Birth:	Islington
Nationality:	English
Height:	6'
Weight:	11st
Foot:	Right

Player Profile

Former Arsenal trainee who signed from Stoke City midway through the 2005/6 season after the Royals fought off competition from a number of clubs.

A former Arsenal youth teammate of Steve Sidwell, Graham Stack and James Harper, John can play in the centre of defence or at right-back, and recorded nearly 100 first team appearances during his time at the Britannia Stadium.

John has made just one League appearance for the Royals, and marked his debut with a well-taken goal against his former club Stoke City in a 3-1 victory at Madejski Staduim towards the end of the season.

Player Performance 05/06

League Performance — Percentage of total possible time player was on pitch; position in league table at end of month

Month:	Aug	Sep	Oct	Nov	Dec	Jan	Feb	Mar	Apr	Total
League position	2	2	2	1	1	1	1	1	1	
% time on pitch	0%	0%	0%	0%	0%	0%	0%	0%	17%	2%
Team Pts:	13/18	11/15	11/15	15/15	16/18	10/12	10/15	6/12	14/18	106/138
Team Gls F:	13	6	7	12	16	12	11	5	17	99
Team Gls A:	3	3	3	2	3	2	8	2	6	32
Total mins:	0	0	0	0	0	0	0	0	90	90
Starts (sub):	0	0	0	0	0	0	0	0	1	1
Goals:	0	0	0	0	0	0	0	0	1	1
Assists:	0	0	0	0	0	0	0	0	0	0
Clean sheets:	0	0	0	0	0	0	0	0	0	0
Cards (Y/R):	0	0	0	0	0	0	0	0	0	0

League Performance Totals

Goals

- Halls: 1
- Team-mates: 94
- **Total: 95**
- own goals: 4

Assists

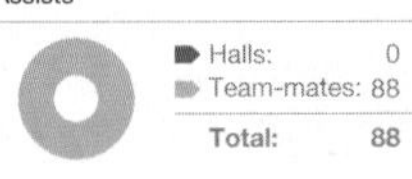

- Halls: 0
- Team-mates: 88
- **Total: 88**

Cards

- Halls: 0
- Team-mates: 38
- **Total: 38**

Cup Games

	Apps	Goals	Cards
FA Cup	2	0	0
Carling Cup	0	0	0
Total	**2**	**0**	**0**

Career History

Career Milestones

Club Debut:
vs Birmingham (H), D 1-1, FA Cup
28.01.06

First Goal Scored for the Club:
vs Stoke (H), W 3-1, Championship
17.04.06

Time Spent at the Club:
0.5 Seasons

Full International:
–

Championship Totals

04-06	
Appearances	36
Goals	3
Assists	1
Yellow Cards	5
Red Cards	2

Clubs

Year	Club	Apps	Gls
06-06	Reading	3	1
03-06	Stoke	74	2
02-03	Beveren		
02-02	Colchester Utd	6	0
00-03	Arsenal	3	0

Off the Pitch

Age:
- Halls: 24 years, 3 months
- Team: 25 years, 6 months
- League: 26 years, 1 month

Height:
- Halls: 6'
- Team: 5'11"
- League: 5'11"

Weight:

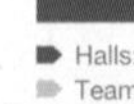

- Halls: 11st
- Team: 12st
- League: 11st 13lb

6 Brynjar Gunnarsson
Midfield

Player Details:

Date of Birth:	16.10.1975
Place of Birth:	Reykjavik
Nationality:	Icelandic
Height:	6'1"
Weight:	11st
Foot:	Right

Player Profile

Midfielder Brynjar Gunnarsson, who also plays in the centre of defence or at right-back, joined from Watford for £150,000 at the start of the 2005/6 season having been admired for some time by Steve Coppell.

The hard-working Icelandic international, who captained his country on a number of occasions, first came to English football by becoming Stoke City's record signing in 1999.

A tremendously consistent performer during the 2005/6 season, and also popped up with a few goals including a dramatic late winner against table-topping rivals Sheffield United at Madejski Stadium.

Player Performance 05/06

League Performance

Percentage of total possible time player was on pitch — position in league table at end of month

Month:	Aug	Sep	Oct	Nov	Dec	Jan	Feb	Mar	Apr	Total
% on pitch	0%	100%	99%	0%	40%	30%	26%	88%	24%	43%
League position	2	2	2	1	1	1	1	1	1	
Team Pts:	13/18	11/15	11/15	15/15	16/18	10/12	10/15	6/12	14/18	106/138
Team Gls F:	13	6	7	12	16	12	11	5	17	99
Team Gls A:	3	3	3	2	3	2	8	2	6	32
Total mins:	0	450	444	0	214	109	118	317	129	1,781
Starts (sub):	0	5	5	0	2 (3)	1 (1)	1 (2)	4	1 (4)	19 (10)
Goals:	0	0	3	0	1	0	0	0	0	4
Assists:	0	0	0	0	0	0	0	0	0	0
Clean sheets:	0	3	2	0	1	1	0	2	0	9
Cards (Y/R):	0	1	1	0	1	0	0	2	0	5

League Performance Totals

Goals

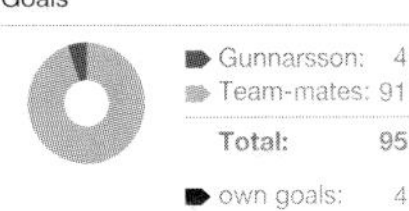

- Gunnarsson: 4
- Team-mates: 91
- Total: 95
- own goals: 4

Assists

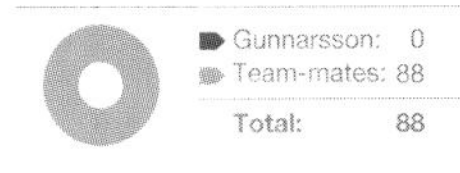

- Gunnarsson: 0
- Team-mates: 88
- Total: 88

Cards

- Gunnarsson: 5
- Team-mates: 33
- Total: 38

Cup Games

	Apps	Goals	Cards
FA Cup	4	0	1
Carling Cup	1	0	1
Total	5	0	2

Career History

Career Milestones

Club Debut:

vs Swansea (H), W 3-1, League Cup

23.08.05

First Goal Scored for the Club:

vs Sheff Utd (H), W 2-1, Championship

01.10.05

Time Spent at the Club:

1 Season

Full International:

Iceland

Championship Totals

04-06

Appearances	65
Goals	7
Assists	3
Yellow Cards	11
Red Cards	1

Clubs

Year	Club	Apps	Gls
05-06	Reading	34	4
04-05	Watford	43	3
04-04	Stoke C	3	0
03-04	Nottm Forest	14	0
99-03	Stoke C	158	19
	Orgryte IS		

Off the Pitch

Age:

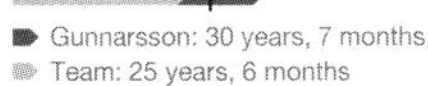

- Gunnarsson: 30 years, 7 months
- Team: 25 years, 6 months
- League: 26 years, 1 month

Height:

- Gunnarsson: 6'1"
- Team: 5'11"
- League: 5'11"

Weight:

- Gunnarsson: 11st
- Team: 12st
- League: 11st 13lb

15 James Harper
Midfield

Player Profile

Hugely energetic and talented midfielder James Harper signed from Arsenal for an undisclosed fee in February 2001, and promptly scored the opening goal on his debut against Rotherham.

James cemented his place in the side during the 2002/3 season, displaying a wonderful range of passing to 'boss' games from the centre of midfield, and was named the fans' player of the season at the end of that play-off campaign.

He has now passed 200 appearances for the club, and enjoyed his best goalscoring return in 2005/6 with seven strikes. Many observers feel that his style of play will be perfectly suited to the Premiership.

Player Details:

Date of Birth:	09.11.1980
Place of Birth:	Chelmsford
Nationality:	English
Height:	5'10"
Weight:	10st
Foot:	Right/Left

Player Performance 05/06

League Performance

Percentage of total possible time player was on pitch — position in league table at end of month

Month:	Aug	Sep	Oct	Nov	Dec	Jan	Feb	Mar	Apr	Total
% on pitch	100%	100%	100%	100%	81%	100%	100%	100%	83%	95%
League position	2	2	2	1	1	1	1	1	1	
Team Pts:	13/18	11/15	11/15	15/15	16/18	10/12	10/15	6/12	14/18	106/138
Team Gls F:	13	6	7	12	16	12	11	5	17	99
Team Gls A:	3	3	3	2	3	2	8	2	6	32
Total mins:	540	450	450	450	437	360	450	360	450	3,947
Starts (sub):	6	5	5	5	5 (1)	4	5	4	5	44 (1)
Goals:	1	1	0	1	0	1	0	0	3	7
Assists:	0	0	0	0	0	0	0	0	0	0
Clean sheets:	4	3	2	3	4	2	1	2	1	22
Cards (Y/R):	0	0	0	0	0	0	0	1	0	1

League Performance Totals

Goals
- Harper: 7
- Team-mates: 88
- **Total: 95**
- own goals: 4

Assists
- Harper: 0
- Team-mates: 88
- **Total: 88**

Cards
- Harper: 1
- Team-mates: 37
- **Total: 38**

Cup Games

	Apps	Goals	Cards
FA Cup	3	0	0
Carling Cup	3	0	1
Total	**6**	**0**	**1**

Career History

Career Milestones

Club Debut:
vs Rotherham (H), W 2-0, Football League 1
03.03.01

First Goal Scored for the Club:
vs Rotherham (H), W 2-0, Football League 1
03.03.01

Time Spent at the Club:
5.5 Seasons

Full International:
–

Championship Totals

04-06	
Appearances	86
Goals	10
Assists	1
Yellow Cards	5
Red Cards	0

Clubs

Year	Club	Apps	Gls
01-06	Reading	226	16
00-01	Cardiff City	3	0
00-01	Arsenal	0	0

Off the Pitch

Age:

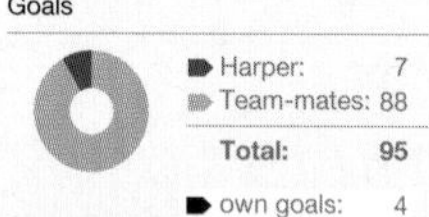

- Harper: 25 years, 6 months
- Team: 25 years, 6 months
- League: 26 years, 1 month

Height:

- Harper: 5'10"
- Team: 5'11"
- League: 5'11"

Weight:

- Harper: 10st
- Team: 12st
- League: 11st 13lb

4 Steven Sidwell
Midfield

Player Profile

Steve Sidwell signed for an undisclosed fee from Arsenal early in 2003, having previously played under the management of Steve Coppell during a loan spell at Brentford. An FA Youth Cup winning-captain with Arsenal, Steve is in many ways the complete midfielder – he can tackle, head, pass, run and has an exceptional eye for goal. During the 2005/6 title-winning season the former England under 21 star had his best goalscoring campaign so far, netting on ten occasions.

Voted into the PFA team of the year for 2005/6 and consistently rated as one of the best players outside the Premiership, Steve now has the chance to prove himself at the highest level.

Player Details:

Date of Birth:	14.12.1982
Place of Birth:	Wandsworth
Nationality:	English
Height:	5'10"
Weight:	11st 2lb
Foot:	Right

Player Performance 05/06

League Performance

Percentage of total possible time player was on pitch

position in league table at end of month

Month:	Aug	Sep	Oct	Nov	Dec	Jan	Feb	Mar	Apr	Total
% time on pitch	100%	0%	10%	100%	81%	70%	74%	12%	89%	62%
League position	2	2	2	1	1	1	1	1	1	
Team Pts:	13/18	11/15	11/15	15/15	16/18	10/12	10/15	6/12	14/18	106/138
Team Gls F:	13	6	7	12	16	12	11	5	17	99
Team Gls A:	3	3	3	2	3	2	8	2	6	32
Total mins:	540	0	43	450	440	251	332	43	478	2,577
Starts (sub):	6	0	0 (2)	5	5	3	4	0 (2)	6	29 (4)
Goals:	1	0	0	1	2	3	2	0	1	10
Assists:	0	0	0	0	2	0	0	0	0	2
Clean sheets:	4	0	0	3	3	0	1	0	1	12
Cards (Y/R):	3	0	0	1	1	0	0	0	0	5

League Performance Totals

Goals

Sidwell:	10
Team-mates:	85
Total:	**95**

own goals: 4

Assists

Sidwell:	2
Team-mates:	86
Total:	**88**

Cards

Sidwell:	5
Team-mates:	33
Total:	**38**

Cup Games

	Apps	Goals	Cards
FA Cup	4	0	0
Carling Cup	3	0	0
Total	**7**	**0**	**0**

Career History

Career Milestones

Club Debut:

vs Leicester (H), L 1-3, Championship

28.01.03

Time Spent at the Club:

3.5 Seasons

First Goal Scored for the Club:

vs Burnley (A), W 2-5, Championship

01.02.03

Full International:

–

Championship Totals

04-06

Appearances	77
Goals	15
Assists	4
Yellow Cards	16
Red Cards	0

Clubs

Year	Club	Apps	Gls
03-06	Reading	150	26
02-03	Brighton	12	5
02-02	Beveren		
01-02	Brentford	35	4
01-03	Arsenal	0	0

Off the Pitch

Age:

Sidwell: 23 years, 5 months
Team: 25 years, 6 months
League: 26 years, 1 month

Height:

Sidwell: 5'10"
Team: 5'11"
League: 5'11"

Weight:

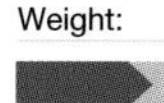

Sidwell: 11st 2lb
Team: 12st
League: 11st 13lb

17 Bobby Convey
Midfield

Player Details:

Date of Birth:	27.05.1983
Place of Birth:	Philadelphia
Nationality:	American
Height:	5'8"
Weight:	11st 6lb
Foot:	Left

Player Profile

Bobby Convey joined the Royals in July 2004 from DC United, where at the age of 16 he had become the youngest player to sign for a MLS side.

The US Young Male Athlete of 2002 almost completed a move to Tottenham in 2003, but the transfer was scuppered by the refusal of a work permit and a season later Steve Coppell snapped him up.

After adapting to the rigours of English football in his first campaign, his second season was a huge success. Bobby scored seven times in 2005/6 and created many more, playing a central role in promotion and then travelling with Bruce Arena's USA squad to the World Cup Finals.

Player Performance 05/06

League Performance

Percentage of total possible time player was on pitch — position in league table at end of month

Month:	Aug	Sep	Oct	Nov	Dec	Jan	Feb	Mar	Apr	Total
% on pitch	88%	98%	88%	85%	87%	90%	90%	97%	71%	87%
League position	2	2	2	1	1	1	1	1	1	
Team Pts:	13/18	11/15	11/15	15/15	16/18	10/12	10/15	6/12	14/18	106/138
Team Gls F:	13	6	7	12	16	12	11	5	17	99
Team Gls A:	3	3	3	2	3	2	8	2	6	32
Total mins:	474	441	395	381	469	323	404	350	382	3,619
Starts (sub):	6	5	5	5	6	4	5	4	5	45
Goals:	2	0	0	1	1	1	0	2	0	7
Assists:	3	0	1	2	0	1	4	0	3	14
Clean sheets:	3	3	2	2	2	1	1	2	0	16
Cards (Y/R):	0	0	0	0	0	0	0	1	0	1

League Performance Totals

Goals

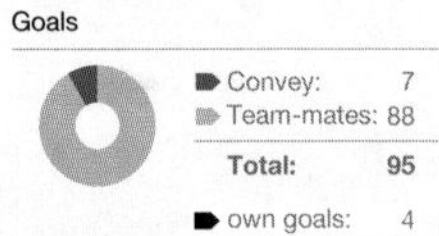

Convey:	7
Team-mates:	88
Total:	**95**
own goals:	4

Assists

Convey:	14
Team-mates:	74
Total:	**88**

Cards

Convey:	1
Team-mates:	37
Total:	**38**

Cup Games

	Apps	Goals	Cards
FA Cup	0	0	0
Carling Cup	0	0	0
Total	**0**	**0**	**0**

Career History

Career Milestones

Club Debut:

vs West Ham (A), L 1-0, Championship

10.08.04

First Goal Scored for the Club:

vs Millwall (H), W 5-0, Championship

20.08.05

Time Spent at the Club:

2 Seasons

Full International:

USA

Championship Totals

04-06

Appearances	63
Goals	7
Assists	14
Yellow Cards	1
Red Cards	0

Clubs

Year	Club	Apps	Gls
04-06	Reading	67	7
00-04	DC United		

Off the Pitch

Age:

- Convey: 23 years
- Team: 25 years, 6 months
- League: 26 years, 1 month

Height:

- Convey: 5'8"
- Team: 5'11"
- League: 5'11"

Weight:

- Convey: 11st 6lb
- Team: 12st
- League: 11st 13lb

7 Glen Little
Midfield

Player Profile

Tricky winger Glen Little signed on a 'Bosman' free transfer from Burnley in the summer of 2004, having spent a month on loan at Madejski Stadium the previous year. The former Crystal Palace trainee, who also had a brief spell in Ireland with Glentoran, was a long-time servant of the Turf Moor club before his move to Berkshire.

After a solid but unspectacular first season at Madejski Stadium, Glen was in explosive form throughout the 2005/6 campaign, dazzling opponents with his wing trickery and leading the country's assists charts thanks to a regular supply of brilliant crosses – best illustrated by a superb run and cross for Dave Kitson's opener at Wolves.

Player Details:

Date of Birth:	15.10.1975
Place of Birth:	Wimbledon
Nationality:	English
Height:	6'3"
Weight:	13st
Foot:	Right/Left

Player Performance 05/06

League Performance

Percentage of total possible time player was on pitch

position in league table at end of month

Month:	Aug	Sep	Oct	Nov	Dec	Jan	Feb	Mar	Apr	Total
% on pitch	90%	97%	82%	84%	72%	88%	60%	11%	13%	66%
League position	2	2	2	1	1	1	1	1	1	
Team Pts:	13/18	11/15	11/15	15/15	16/18	10/12	10/15	6/12	14/18	106/138
Team Gls F:	13	6	7	12	16	12	11	5	17	99
Team Gls A:	3	3	3	2	3	2	8	2	6	32
Total mins:	484	437	371	380	388	316	270	38	69	2,753
Starts (sub):	6	5	5	5	5	4	3	0 (1)	1	34 (1)
Goals:	2	0	1	2	0	0	0	0	0	5
Assists:	1	2	2	2	5	3	2	1	0	18
Clean sheets:	3	3	0	3	2	1	1	0	0	13
Cards (Y/R):	1	1	1	1	0	0	0	0	0	4

League Performance Totals

Goals

Little:	5
Team-mates:	90
Total:	**95**

own goals: 4

Assists

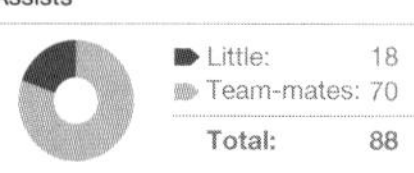

Little:	18
Team-mates:	70
Total:	**88**

Cards

Little:	4
Team-mates:	34
Total:	**38**

Cup Games

	Apps	Goals	Cards
FA Cup	1	0	0
Carling Cup	2	0	0
Total	**3**	**0**	**0**

Career History

Career Milestones

Club Debut:

vs Brighton (H), L 1-2, Championship

04.04.03

Time Spent at the Club:

2.5 Seasons

First Goal Scored for the Club:

vs Grimsby (H), W 2-1, Championship

26.04.03

Full International:

–

Championship Totals

04-06

Appearances	70
Goals	5
Assists	27
Yellow Cards	8
Red Cards	0

Clubs

Year	Club	Apps	Gls
04-06	Reading	77	5
03-03	Bolton	4	0
03-03	Reading	7	1
96-04	Burnley	282	36
95-96	Glentoran		
94-95	Crystal P	0	0

Off the Pitch

Age:

- Little: 30 years, 7 months
- Team: 25 years, 6 months
- League: 26 years, 1 month

Height:

- Little: 6'3"
- Team: 5'11"
- League: 5'11"

Weight:

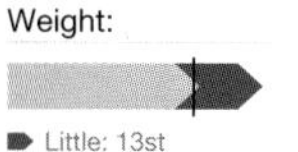

- Little: 13st
- Team: 12st
- League: 11st 13lb

10 Stephen Hunt
Midfield

Player Profile

Irishman Stephen Hunt became another of the former Brentford clan to move to Madejski Stadium with his summer 2005 transfer, reuniting with the manager he had already served at both Brentford and Crystal Palace, his first club. Most wingers are either tenacious and hard-working or creative and skilful, but Stephen possesses all those qualities and he was very unfortunate to be denied more starting appearances in his first Reading season by the brilliant form of Bobby Convey.

He still made a vital contribution to the team's runaway title success, though, generally appearing from the bench in the final stages to further demoralise already tiring defenders!

Player Details:

Date of Birth:	01.08.1981
Place of Birth:	Laois
Nationality:	Irish
Height:	5'9"
Weight:	12st 6lb
Foot:	Left/Right

Player Performance 05/06

League Performance

Percentage of total possible time player was on pitch

position in league table at end of month

Month:	Aug	Sep	Oct	Nov	Dec	Jan	Feb	Mar	Apr	Total
League position	2	2	2	1	1	1	1	1	1	
% time on pitch	12%	14%	23%	15%	28%	10%	11%	9%	39%	19%
Team Pts:	13/18	11/15	11/15	15/15	16/18	10/12	10/15	6/12	14/18	106/138
Team Gls F:	13	6	7	12	16	12	11	5	17	99
Team Gls A:	3	3	3	2	3	2	8	2	6	32
Total mins:	66	62	102	69	151	37	51	33	208	779
Starts (sub):	0 (4)	0 (3)	1 (3)	0 (5)	1 (5)	0 (2)	0 (4)	0 (4)	1 (5)	3 (35)
Goals:	0	0	0	0	1	0	0	0	1	2
Assists:	0	0	0	0	0	1	1	1	4	7
Clean sheets:	0	0	0	0	0	0	0	0	0	0
Cards (Y/R):	0	0	0	0	1	0	0	0	0	1

League Performance Totals

Goals

- Hunt: 2
- Team-mates: 93
- **Total: 95**
- own goals: 4

Assists

- Hunt: 7
- Team-mates: 81
- **Total: 88**

Cards

- Hunt: 1
- Team-mates: 37
- **Total: 38**

Cup Games

	Apps	Goals	Cards
FA Cup	4	1	0
Carling Cup	4	0	0
Total	**8**	**1**	**0**

Career History

Career Milestones

Club Debut:

vs Plymouth (H), L 1-2, Championship

06.08.05

First Goal Scored for the Club:

vs Brighton (H), W 5-1, Championship

10.12.05

Time Spent at the Club:

1 Season

Full International:

–

Championship Totals

04-06

Appearances	38
Goals	2
Assists	7
Yellow Cards	1
Red Cards	0

Clubs

Year	Club	Apps	Gls
05-06	Reading	46	3
01-05	Brentford	160	29
98-01	Crystal Palace	3	0

Off the Pitch

Age:

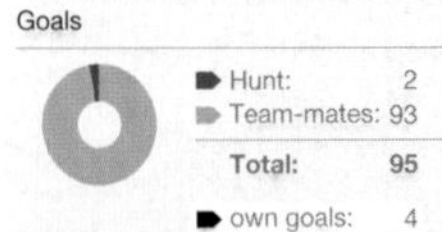

- Hunt: 24 years, 9 months
- Team: 25 years, 6 months
- League: 26 years, 1 month

Height:

- Hunt: 5'9"
- Team: 5'11"
- League: 5'11"

Weight:

- Hunt: 12st 6lb
- Team: 12st
- League: 11st 13lb

11 John Oster
Midfield

Player Profile

A free transfer signing in the summer of 2005, John Oster was one of the many Reading players who contributed fully to the record-breaking title triumph despite being confined to the subs' bench for the majority of the season. John was excellent whenever called upon, creating and scoring a number of goals despite his restricted playing time, and boss Steve Coppell regularly credited Glen Little's outstanding form to the competition for places provided by the Wales international.

John's career started at Grimsby where he became something of a club legend before a big-money move to Everton, and he later had a successful spell at Sunderland.

Player Details:

Date of Birth:	08.12.1978
Place of Birth:	Boston
Nationality:	Welsh
Height:	5'9"
Weight:	10st 9lb
Foot:	Right/Left

Player Performance 05/06

League Performance

Percentage of total possible time player was on pitch — position in league table at end of month

Month:	Aug	Sep	Oct	Nov	Dec	Jan	Feb	Mar	Apr	Total
League position	2	2	2	1	1	1	1	1	1	
% time on pitch	8%	3%	22%	16%	29%	12%	36%	77%	60%	29%
Team Pts:	13/18	11/15	11/15	15/15	16/18	10/12	10/15	6/12	14/18	106/138
Team Gls F:	13	6	7	12	16	12	11	5	17	99
Team Gls A:	3	3	3	2	3	2	8	2	6	32
Total mins:	42	13	99	70	154	44	164	277	325	1,188
Starts (sub):	0 (3)	0 (2)	0 (4)	0 (5)	1 (5)	0 (2)	2	4	4 (1)	11 (22)
Goals:	0	0	0	0	0	0	0	0	1	1
Assists:	0	1	0	1	0	0	0	1	2	5
Clean sheets:	0	0	0	0	1	0	0	1	0	2
Cards (Y/R):	1	0	0	0	0	0	1	0	0	2

League Performance Totals

Goals

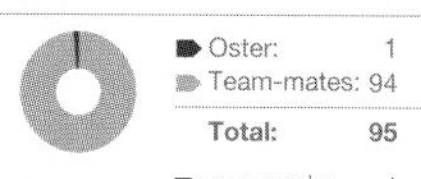

Oster:	1
Team-mates:	94
Total:	**95**
own goals:	4

Assists

Oster:	5
Team-mates:	83
Total:	**88**

Cards

Oster:	2
Team-mates:	36
Total:	**38**

Cup Games

	Apps	Goals	Cards
FA Cup	4	0	1
Carling Cup	4	1	0
Total	**8**	**1**	**1**

Career History

Career Milestones

Club Debut:
vs Brighton (A), W 0-2, Championship
09.08.05

First Goal Scored for the Club:
vs Luton (H), W 1-0, League Cup
20.09.05

Time Spent at the Club:
1 Season

Full International:
Wales

Championship Totals

04-06

Appearances	65
Goals	3
Assists	8
Yellow Cards	2
Red Cards	0

Clubs

Year	Club	Apps	Gls
05-06	Reading	41	2
05-05	Burnley	18	1
04-04	Leeds	8	1
03-03	Grimsby	7	1
02-02	Grimsby	10	5
01-01	Barnsley	2	0
99-05	Sunderland	91	6
97-99	Everton	50	3
94-97	Grimsby	25	4

Off the Pitch

Age:
- Oster: 27 years, 5 months
- Team: 25 years, 6 months
- League: 26 years, 1 month

Height:
- Oster: 5'9"
- Team: 5'11"
- League: 5'11"

Weight:
- Oster: 10st 9lb
- Team: 12st
- League: 11st 13lb

12 Dave Kitson
Forward

Player Profile

Dave Kitson joined Reading at Christmas 2003 for an initial fee of £150,000 from Cambridge United, where he had a one-in-two-games goalscoring ratio after being a late entrant into the professional game.

After breaking into the first team he quickly became a fans' favourite by scoring both goals to defeat Alan Pardew's West Ham in the former Reading boss' first game back at Madejski Stadium.

Dave has been a relentless goalscorer throughout his time at Reading, and ended the 2005/6 season as the club's leading scorer with 22 goals in all competitions – despite missing roughly a third of the campaign through injury.

Player Details:

Date of Birth:	21.01.1980
Place of Birth:	Hitchin
Nationality:	English
Height:	6'3"
Weight:	13st
Foot:	Left

Player Performance 05/06

League Performance

Percentage of total possible time player was on pitch

position in league table at end of month

Month:	Aug	Sep	Oct	Nov	Dec	Jan	Feb	Mar	Apr	Total
% on pitch	71%	0%	50%	40%	70%	64%	54%	88%	76%	57%
League position	2	2	2	1	1	1	1	1	1	
Team Pts:	13/18	11/15	11/15	15/15	16/18	10/12	10/15	6/12	14/18	106/138
Team Gls F:	13	6	7	12	16	12	11	5	17	99
Team Gls A:	3	3	3	2	3	2	8	2	6	32
Total mins:	384	0	226	180	378	230	243	315	410	2,366
Starts (sub):	5 (1)	0	2 (2)	2	4 (1)	3	3 (2)	3 (1)	5	27 (7)
Goals:	2	0	1	1	5	4	1	1	3	18
Assists:	2	0	1	1	2	0	0	0	2	8
Clean sheets:	3	0	1	1	3	1	0	1	1	11
Cards (Y/R):	1	0	0	1	1	0	1	0	1	5

League Performance Totals

Goals

Kitson:	18
Team-mates:	77
Total:	**95**
own goals:	4

Assists

Kitson:	8
Team-mates:	80
Total:	**88**

Cards

Kitson:	5
Team-mates:	33
Total:	**38**

Cup Games

	Apps	Goals	Cards
FA Cup	2	0	1
Carling Cup	3	4	2
Total	**5**	**4**	**3**

Career History

Career Milestones

Club Debut:

vs Ipswich (H), D 1-1, Championship

10.01.04

First Goal Scored for the Club:

vs Cardiff (A), W 2-3, Championship

16.03.04

Time Spent at the Club:

2.5 Seasons

Full International:

–

Championship Totals

04-06

Appearances	71
Goals	37
Assists	11
Yellow Cards	9
Red Cards	0

Clubs

Year	Club	Apps	Gls
03-06	Reading	94	46
01-03	Cambridge Utd	123	47
	Arlesey T		

Off the Pitch

Age:

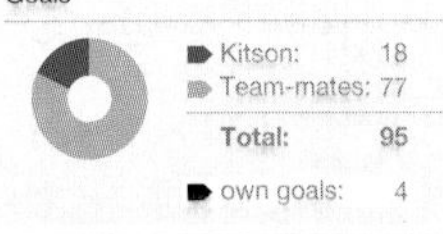

- Kitson: 26 years, 4 months
- Team: 25 years, 6 months
- League: 26 years, 1 month

Height:

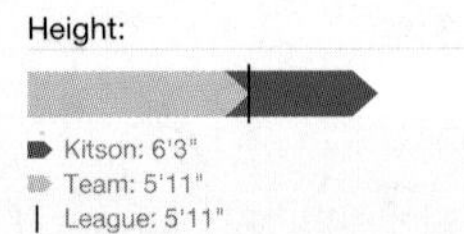

- Kitson: 6'3"
- Team: 5'11"
- League: 5'11"

Weight:

- Kitson: 13st
- Team: 12st
- League: 11st 13lb

8

Leroy Lita
Forward

Coca-Cola

Player Details:	
Date of Birth:	28.12.1984
Place of Birth:	Congo
Nationality:	English
Height:	5'7"
Weight:	11st 12lb
Foot:	Right

Player Profile

Goal machine Leroy Lita became Reading Football Club's record signing in July 2005 when he was snapped up for £1m from Bristol City.

Leroy started out as a trainee with Chelsea before moving to Ashton Gate, where he became a teenage strike sensation. He quickly attracted the attention of a number of clubs, but the Royals acted quickest to secure the England under 21 international's signature.

Leroy quickly began repaying his transfer fee with a brilliant brace at Preston in August, and reached 15 goals before his season was cruelly cut short by a broken ankle at Burnley in March.

Player Performance 05/06

League Performance

Percentage of total possible time player was on pitch — position in league table at end of month

Month:	Aug	Sep	Oct	Nov	Dec	Jan	Feb	Mar	Apr	Total
% time on pitch	98%	93%	53%	60%	11%	33%	48%	13%	0%	46%
League position	2	2	2	1	1	1	1	1	1	
Team Pts:	13/18	11/15	11/15	15/15	16/18	10/12	10/15	6/12	14/18	106/138
Team Gls F:	13	6	7	12	16	12	11	5	17	99
Team Gls A:	3	3	3	2	3	2	8	2	6	32
Total mins:	530	418	238	270	62	119	218	45	0	1,900
Starts (sub):	6	5	3	3	1	1 (2)	2 (2)	1	0	22 (4)
Goals:	4	1	0	1	0	1	4	0	0	11
Assists:	1	0	0	1	0	1	0	0	0	3
Clean sheets:	4	3	1	2	0	1	1	0	0	12
Cards (Y/R):	0	1	0	0	0	0	0	0	0	1

League Performance Totals

Goals

- Lita: 11
- Team-mates: 84
- **Total: 95**
- own goals: 4

Assists

- Lita: 3
- Team-mates: 85
- **Total: 88**

Cards

- Lita: 1
- Team-mates: 37
- **Total: 38**

Cup Games

	Apps	Goals	Cards
FA Cup	3	3	1
Carling Cup	3	1	0
Total	**6**	**4**	**1**

Career History

Career Milestones

Club Debut:
vs Plymouth (H), L 1-2, Championship
06.08.05

First Goal Scored for the Club:
vs Plymouth (H), L 1-2, Championship
06.08.05

Time Spent at the Club:
1 Season

Full International:
–

Championship Totals

04-06	
Appearances	26
Goals	11
Assists	3
Yellow Cards	1
Red Cards	0

Clubs

Year	Club	Apps	Gls
05-06	Reading	32	15
02-05	Bristol City	100	38

Off the Pitch

Age:
- Lita: 21 years, 5 months
- Team: 25 years, 6 months
- League: 26 years, 1 month

Height:

- Lita: 5'7"
- Team: 5'11"
- League: 5'11"

Weight:
- Lita: 11st 12lb
- Team: 12st
- League: 11st 13lb

9 Kevin Doyle
Forward

Player Profile

22 year old Irishman Kevin Doyle signed last summer from Cork City became the surprise of the season.

Top scorer in the Eircom League before his move, the ex-Wexford and St Patrick's forward quickly starred as he came into the Reading team and soon became indispensable.

With 18 league goals, a total only bettered by Marlon King, Kevin maintained an outstanding level of commitment, energy and creative talent in his first season in England to earn Reading's 'Player of the Season' award. He also made the international step up to gain his first cap under new Irish boss Steve Staunton.

Player Details:

Date of Birth:	18.09.1983
Place of Birth:	Wexford
Nationality:	Irish
Height:	5'11"
Weight:	12st 6lb
Foot:	Right/Left

Player Performance 05/06

League Performance

Percentage of total possible time player was on pitch — position in league table at end of month

Month:	Aug	Sep	Oct	Nov	Dec	Jan	Feb	Mar	Apr	Total
% on pitch	33%	100%	94%	99%	96%	95%	100%	100%	90%	88%
League position	2	2	2	1	1	1	1	1	1	
Team Pts:	13/18	11/15	11/15	15/15	16/18	10/12	10/15	6/12	14/18	106/138
Team Gls F:	13	6	7	12	16	12	11	5	17	99
Team Gls A:	3	3	3	2	3	2	8	2	6	32
Total mins:	180	450	424	444	521	341	450	360	486	3,656
Starts (sub):	1 (4)	5	5	5	6	4	5	4	6	41 (4)
Goals:	1	2	1	3	4	0	3	1	3	18
Assists:	0	1	1	4	1	2	1	0	1	11
Clean sheets:	0	3	1	3	4	1	1	2	0	15
Cards (Y/R):	1	1	0	1	0	0	1	0	0	4

League Performance Totals

Goals

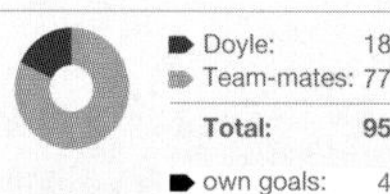

Doyle:	18
Team-mates:	77
Total:	**95**
own goals:	4

Assists

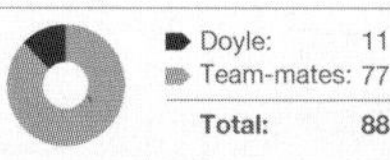

Doyle:	11
Team-mates:	77
Total:	**88**

Cards

Doyle:	4
Team-mates:	34
Total:	**38**

Cup Games

	Apps	Goals	Cards
FA Cup	3	1	0
Carling Cup	3	0	0
Total	**6**	**1**	**0**

Career History

Career Milestones

Club Debut:

vs Plymouth (H), L 1-2, Championship

06.08.05

First Goal Scored for the Club:

vs Burnley (H), W 2-1, Championship

29.08.05

Time Spent at the Club:

1 Season

Full International:

Rep. Ireland

Championship Totals

04-06

Appearances	45
Goals	18
Assists	11
Yellow Cards	4
Red Cards	0

Clubs

Year	Club	Apps	Gls
05-06	Reading	51	19
03-05	Cork C		
	St Patrick's Ath		
	Wexford		
	Adamstown		

Off the Pitch

Age:

- Doyle: 22 years, 8 months
- Team: 25 years, 6 months
- League: 26 years, 1 month

Height:

- Doyle: 5'11"
- Team: 5'11"
- League: 5'11"

Weight:

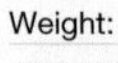

- Doyle: 12st 6lb
- Team: 12st
- League: 11st 13lb

24 Shane Long
Forward

Player Profile

Young and speedy Irish striker Shane Long partnered teammate Kevin Doyle to Madejski Stadium to sign from Cork City in July 2005.

Moving to Cork from Tipperary club St Michael's, Shane left family traditions of hurling behind and his raw talent soon proved to be a valuable asset, when in only his second Royals appearance he scored a last gasp equaliser at Derby to preserve our unbeaten run.

As 2006 unfolded the Irish under 19s striker scored in front of the home fans in a 1-1 FA Cup clash with Birmingham, before completing the season in style with two more in the 5-0 win over Derby that saw the Royals crowned champions.

Player Details:

Date of Birth:	22.01.1987
Place of Birth:	Kilkenny
Nationality:	Irish
Height:	5'10"
Weight:	11st 2lb
Foot:	Right

Player Performance 05/06

League Performance

Percentage of total possible time player was on pitch — position in league table at end of month

Month:	Aug	Sep	Oct	Nov	Dec	Jan	Feb	Mar	Apr	Total
League position	2	2	2	1	1	1	1	1	1	
% time on pitch	0%	0%	0%	0%	6%	8%	0%	8%	31%	6%
Team Pts:	13/18	11/15	11/15	15/15	16/18	10/12	10/15	6/12	14/18	106/138
Team Gls F:	13	6	7	12	16	12	11	5	17	99
Team Gls A:	3	3	3	2	3	2	8	2	6	32
Total mins:	0	0	0	0	30	30	0	29	165	254
Starts (sub):	0	0	0	0	0 (2)	0 (2)	0	0 (1)	1 (5)	1 (10)
Goals:	0	0	0	0	1	0	0	0	2	3
Assists:	0	0	0	0	0	0	0	0	0	0
Clean sheets:	0	0	0	0	0	0	0	0	0	0
Cards (Y/R):	0	0	0	0	0	0	0	0	0	0

League Performance Totals

Goals

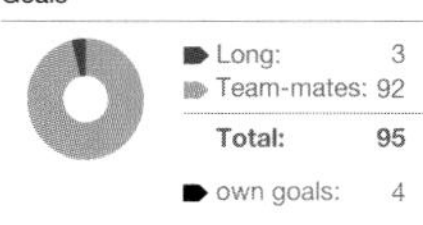

Long:	3
Team-mates:	92
Total:	**95**
own goals:	4

Assists

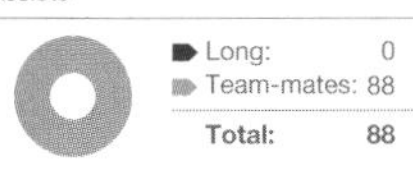

Long:	0
Team-mates:	88
Total:	**88**

Cards

Long:	0
Team-mates:	38
Total:	**38**

Cup Games

	Apps	Goals	Cards
FA Cup	4	1	1
Carling Cup	0	0	0
Total	**4**	**1**	**1**

Career History

Career Milestones

Club Debut:

vs Leicester (H), W 2-0, Championship

28.12.05

First Goal Scored for the Club:

vs Derby (A), D 2-2, Championship

31.12.05

Time Spent at the Club:

1 Season

Full International:

–

Championship Totals

04-06

Appearances	11
Goals	3
Assists	0
Yellow Cards	0
Red Cards	0

Clubs

Year	Club	Apps	Gls
05-06	Reading	15	4
04-05	Cork C		
	St Michael's		

Off the Pitch

Age:

- Long: 19 years, 4 months
- Team: 25 years, 6 months
- League: 26 years, 1 month

Height:

- Long: 5'10"
- Team: 5'11"
- League: 5'11"

Weight:

- Long: 11st 2lb
- Team: 12st
- League: 11st 13lb

31 Simon Cox
Forward

Player Details:

Date of Birth:	28.04.1987
Place of Birth:	Reading
Nationality:	English
Height:	5'10"
Weight:	10st 12lb
Foot:	Right

Player Profile

Reading-born forward Simon Cox signed his first professional contract with Reading in November 2005 at the age of 18.

Growing up in Tilehurst, at the age of eight Simon was initially spotted by Kevin Dillon while playing in the same team as the first team coach's son.

Progressing through the youth ranks and starring at Academy level, Simon can be effectively deployed both in midfield and attack, his preferred position. Last season he made six appearances for the first team as a substitute in Carling Cup, FA Cup and Coca-Cola Championship clashes and showed glimpses of his obvious talent.

Player Performance 05/06

League Performance

Percentage of total possible time player was on pitch — position in league table at end of month

Month:	Aug	Sep	Oct	Nov	Dec	Jan	Feb	Mar	Apr	Total
League position	2	2	2	1	1	1	1	1	1	
% on pitch	0%	0%	0%	0%	0%	0%	0%	0%	4%	0%
Team Pts:	13/18	11/15	11/15	15/15	16/18	10/12	10/15	6/12	14/18	106/138
Team Gls F:	13	6	7	12	16	12	11	5	17	99
Team Gls A:	3	3	3	2	3	2	8	2	6	32
Total mins:	0	0	0	0	0	0	0	0	19	19
Starts (sub):	0	0	0	0 (1)	0	0	0	0	0 (1)	0 (2)
Goals:	0	0	0	0	0	0	0	0	0	0
Assists:	0	0	0	0	0	0	0	0	0	0
Clean sheets:	0	0	0	0	0	0	0	0	0	0
Cards (Y/R):	0	0	0	0	0	0	0	0	0	0

League Performance Totals

Goals

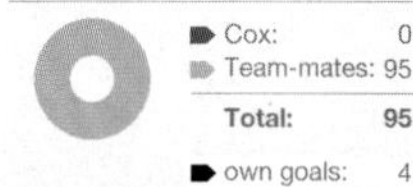

Cox:	0
Team-mates:	95
Total:	**95**
own goals:	4

Assists

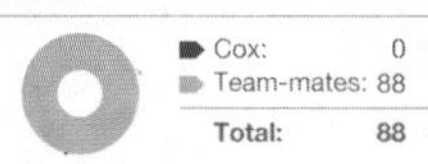

Cox:	0
Team-mates:	88
Total:	**88**

Cards

Cox:	0
Team-mates:	38
Total:	**38**

Cup Games

	Apps	Goals	Cards
FA Cup	2	0	0
Carling Cup	2	0	0
Total	**4**	**0**	**0**

Career History

Career Milestones

Club Debut:

vs Luton (H), W 1-0, League Cup

20.09.05

First Goal Scored for the Club:

–

–

Time Spent at the Club:

1 Season

Full International:

–

Championship Totals

04-06

Appearances	2
Goals	0
Assists	0
Yellow Cards	0
Red Cards	0

Clubs

Year	Club	Apps	Gls
05-06	Reading	6	0

Off the Pitch

Age:

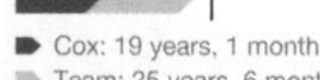

- Cox: 19 years, 1 month
- Team: 25 years, 6 months
- League: 26 years, 1 month

Height:

- Cox: 5'10"
- Team: 5'11"
- League: 5'11"

Weight:

- Cox: 10st 12lb
- Team: 12st
- League: 11st 13lb

19 Seol Ki-Hyeon

Midfield

SEOL
19

Player Profile

South Korean wide player signed from Wolves for a package worth £1.5m in July 2006. Started his career at Antwerp in Belgium, before joining Anderlecht where he stayed for three years, playing Champions League football during that time. He also starred for South Korea in the 2002 World Cup Finals in his native country, playing all six games as they reached the semi-finals. Signed for Wolves for £1.2m in August 2004, playing 76 games and scoring 10 goals. He was also involved in the 2006 World Cup Finals in Germany, appearing as a substitute in group stage games against France and Switzerland.

Sam Sodje

Defence

SODJE
18

Player Profile

Nigerian defender joined the Royals for an initial £350,000 from Brentford in July 2006. Sam was targeted by a number of clubs following two impressive seasons for the Bees. Younger brother of Nigerian international Efe, he began his English career at non-league Stevenage before moving onto Margate and then being snapped up by the Bees' then-manager Martin Allen in the summer of 2004. Went on to make 100 appearances for the West London side, earning a reputation as a scorer of goals from set-pieces by bagging 14 goals during his time at Griffin Park. Was voted into the League One team of the season for 2005/6.

The Management

WD
KYOCERA

AS
PUMA
KYOCERA
KD

John Madejski
Chairman

Coca-Cola
ROYALS

John Madejski became Chairman of Reading Football Club in 1990. He had earlier founded Thames Valley Trader in 1976 which soon became Auto Trader and earned the successful businessman his fortune.

His backing allowed the Club to move from Elm Park to Madejski Stadium in 1998 and slowly he has financed the growth and progression of Reading Football Club.

In 2000 he was awarded the OBE in recognition of his contribution to Reading Football Club and the community. He is also Deputy Lieutenant of Berkshire and was admitted as a Freeman of the Borough after leading his beloved Royals into the top tier of English football.

Nigel Howe
Chief Executive

The nephew of former England and Arsenal coach Don Howe, Nigel worked in the construction industry and initially joined Reading Football Club to oversee the building of Madejski Stadium before being appointed Chief Executive.

Nigel works closely with John Madejski, Nick Hammond and Steve Coppell to direct the Club's footballing progress, and is also responsible for the management of the Club's off-the-field activities, overseeing the work of the various behind the scenes departments.

Nigel also maintains close relationships with other associated interests such as the Royal Berkshire Conference Centre, the Millennium Madejski Hotel and London Irish.

Steve Coppell
Manager

The first person to take the Royals into the Premiership, Steve Coppell was appointed as manager of Reading Football Club in October 2003.

Steve's illustrious playing career began at Tranmere before a move to Tommy Docherty's Manchester United in 1975. The wing wizard also totted up 42 England caps before injury forced him to hang up his boots at 28 in 1983.

A youthful managerial career began with Crystal Palace where Steve catapulted the Eagles into the top flight and then to the 1990 FA Cup Final. Four spells in total at Palace and brief spells at Manchester City, Brentford and Brighton led to his appointment at Madejski Stadium.

Nick Hammond
Director of Football

Former Royals keeper Nick Hammond was named as the Club's first ever Director of Football in September 2003.

Starting out as an Arsenal apprentice, Nick spent loan spells at Bristol Rovers, Peterborough and Aberdeen before joining Swindon Town in 1987. After moving to Plymouth eight years later, a loan spell at Elm Park was made permanent when he signed for Reading for £40,000 in January 1996.

A recurrent back injury forced retirement but Nick was handed a coaching role by Alan Pardew and soon became Academy Director before taking up his current position, which sees him liaise between the football staff and management and the Board of Directors.

Kevin Dillon
First Team Coach

Sunderland-born Kevin Dillon was promoted to the position of first team coach in December 2001 under the management of Alan Pardew, helping the team gain promotion in his first season.

As a player, Kevin began with Birmingham before a spell at Portsmouth. He joined Reading from Newcastle in 1991, playing more than 100 games for the Royals, and later returned as a youth coach under the managerial duo of Jimmy Quinn and Mick Gooding.

He took over as caretaker manager after Pardew's September 2003 exit, having previously been his number two and reserve team manager, and significantly aided Steve Coppell last season in leading the Royals into the top flight.

Wally Downes
First Team Coach

PUMA

Former Brentford boss Wally Downes joined as a first team coach with the Royals in the summer of 2004, having previously worked as Steve Coppell's number two at Brentford and taken over at the Griffin Park club in 2002.

With more than 15 years as a player with Wimbledon and Sheffield United, Wally was an integral part of the Dons' 'Crazy Gang' days.

After retiring from playing, he began coaching with Crystal Palace and Brentford, and has developed into a highly respected coach who has greatly assisted Steve Coppell in building the modern-day Royals. Wally predominantly looks after defensive coaching duties at the Club.

Nigel Gibbs
First Team Coach

BM
PUMA
PUMA

Former Watford stalwart Nigel Gibbs joined the Royals coaching team during the summer of 2006, with the primary function of integrating promising young players into the first team squad. Nigel will also work closely alongside Brian McDermott to run the reserve team as we enter the Premier Reserve League for the first time. Nigel's long playing career as a full-back was spent entirely with Watford, where he became an extremely popular figure and started his coaching career by leading the Hornets' second string to the reserve league title. He left Watford in 2005 and worked with Spurs and Swansea before joining the Royals.

Brian McDermott
Reserve Team Manager & Chief Scout

Joining the Club in 2000 after the sad death of Maurice Evans, Brian McDermott was appointed as under 17s manager and Chief Scout.

As a player, the winger started out at Arsenal in the 1970's, making almost 100 appearances for the Gunners. He was named Sweden's Player of the Year during a loan spell with Norrkoping before joining Oxford in 1984.

Helping United into the top flight in 1985, he won more honours at Cardiff and Exeter before beginning his coaching career as assistant manager at Yeovil. Brian later became boss at Slough and after a short spell at Woking, he made his way to Reading where he also now takes charge of our reserves.

Jon Fearn
Head Physiotherapist

PUMA
READING FOOTBALL CLUB
EST. 1871

Jon joined the Royals in the summer of 2001 to become the Club's Head Physiotherapist.

Jon qualified as a Chartered Physiotherapist in 1991 at St Mary's Hospital in Paddington, London, before joining the NHS and working as physio for Richmond and London Welsh rugby union sides. He also worked in American Football with the London Olympians and the Great Britain squad.

After completing a masters degree in Physiotherapy at University College, he took up a position at West Ham in 1997, working as a physiotherapist for the Hammers' Academy and then first team squad for four years before the move to Reading.

Jon Goodman
Sports Scientist

PUMA
READING FOOTBA
EST. 1871

Walthamstow-born Sports Scientist Jon Goodman joined the Royals in the summer of 2005 following the departure of Niall Clark to West Ham.

The former Republic of Ireland international striker began his career at non-league Bromley before a £50,000 move to Millwall in 1990. 35 goals in just under 100 starts during four years with the Lions saw him earn a £650,000 move to Wimbledon.

A regular during the 1995/6 season, he scored six Premiership goals for the Dons but hung up his boots as the millennium neared an end to begin sports science roles with Watford amongst other clubs.

Sal Bibbo
Goalkeeping Coach

READING FOOTBALL CLUB
EST. 1871

Basingstoke-born Salvatore Bibbo has worked as the Royals' goalkeeping coach for the last two seasons, coaching our academy and first team stoppers.

His playing career began as an apprentice at Bournemouth, before spells at Crawley Town and then Sheffield United. Limited first team chances at Bramall Lane led to a loan spell at Chesterfield but after being released by the Blades in 1996, Sal impressed in pre-season to earn a contract at Reading.

Making his Royals debut at Barnsley when Bulgarian Bobby Mihailov was away on international duty, Sal kept his first Reading clean sheet two games later in a local derby with Oxford and totalled nine Royals appearances.

Ron Grant
Kit Manager

One of the longest-serving Reading staff, kit manager Ron Grant has performed duties for the Royals first team for more than ten years and celebrated his 70th birthday last autumn.

Often described as 'Mr Reading FC', his devotion to the side has been unrivalled and his attention to detail remains excellent. A reliable and very much valued member of the first team squad.

Andy Stanbury
Masseur

AS
PUMA
KYOCERA

28-year old Andy Stanbury began working at Reading as a part-time massage therapist to the first team in 2004/5.

The following summer he combined that role with the title of video technician when he took over from Mark Boddy, but is now employed as a full-time masseur at the club. He has a Sports Science degree and further qualifications in Sports Massage.

Eamonn Dolan
Academy Manager

Academy Manager Eamonn Dolan took charge of the youth system at Reading following the departure of Chelsea-bound Brendan Rodgers in 2004.

As a player, Eamonn played for Birmingham City and West Ham United but a series of serious injuries coupled with a successful fight against cancer saw him hang up his boots and begin a coaching career.

Leading cash-strapped Exeter City to great success, he quickly became highly rated before the Royals managed to prise him away from St James Park. As under 18s coach he helped clinch an impressive 3-2 FA Youth Cup win over Everton last season and is overseeing the development of a number of promising prospects.

Nas Bashir
Assistant Academy Manager

PUMA

A former youth trainee at Reading, Nas Bashir is currently our Assistant Academy Manager and coach of the under 15 and under 16 youth sides.

Formerly with the youth set-up and centre of excellence at Wycombe Wanderers, UEFA licensed coach Bashir joined in 2002/3 and continues to nurture the young talent through our Academy.

Geoff Warner
Senior Assistant Academy Manager

GW
PUMA

Having spent time as the Club's youth coach, development centre manager and assistant director of youth football, Geoff Warner is now Reading's Senior Assistant Academy Manager.

Arriving at the Club in January 2000, Geoff is one of the longest-serving members of our Academy coaching staff. He gained a great deal of experience with Crystal Palace's youth set-up, bringing through talents such as Hayden Mullins.

2006/07: The Opposition

Hfs
LOANS

Hfs
HFS
puma
puma

Arsenal

Arsenal

Nickname:	The Gunners	Telephone:	020 7704 4000
Manager:	Arsène Wenger	Ticket Office:	020 7704 4040
Chairman:	Peter Hill-Wood	Club Shop:	020 7704 4120
Website:	www.arsenal.com		

Emirates Stadium

Season Review 05/06

It was a season of mixed fortunes for an Arsenal side that grew up enormously over the course of the campaign.

Reaching the Champions League Final was a terrific achievement, with defeat to Barcelona tempered by Thierry Henry's decision to stay at the club. Prior to that, the Gunners said goodbye to Highbury by clinching fourth place at the expense of Tottenham.

Points / Position

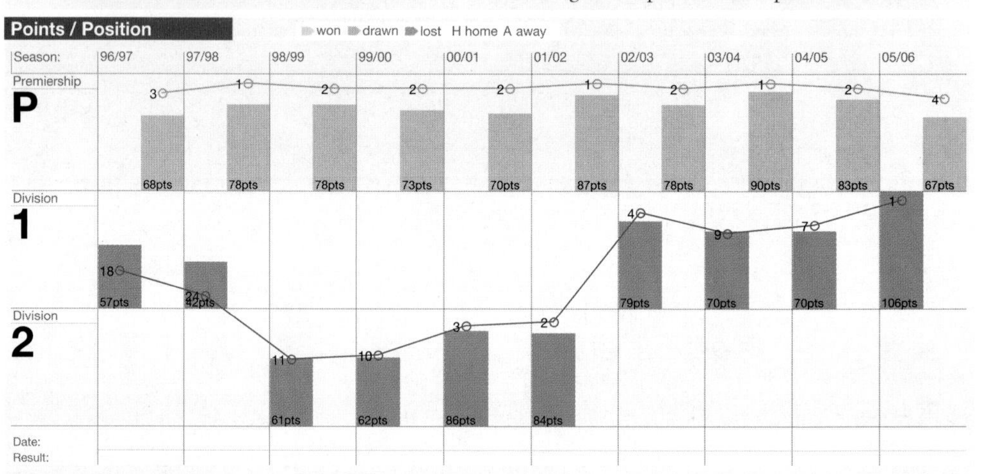

won drawn lost H home A away
Season: 96/97 97/98 98/99 99/00 00/01 01/02 02/03 03/04 04/05 05/06
Premiership
P
3 1 2 2 2 1 2 1 2 4
68pts 78pts 78pts 73pts 70pts 87pts 78pts 90pts 83pts 67pts
Division
1
18 24 4 9 7 1
57pts 42pts 79pts 70pts 70pts 106pts
Division
2
11 10 3 2
61pts 62pts 86pts 84pts
Date:
Result:

Goals 05/06

Goals by Time Period

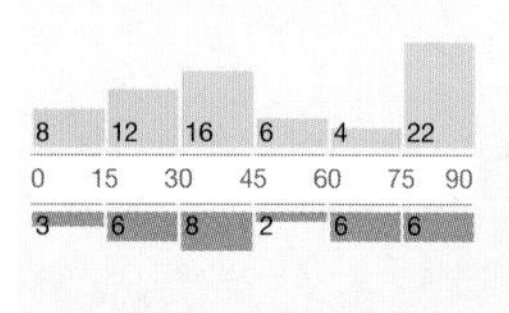

8 12 16 6 4 22
0 15 30 45 60 75 90
3 6 8 2 6 6
scored
conceded

Goals by Area

Scored (Conceded)

11 (6)

48 (21)

9 (4)

Goals by Position

Scored		Conceded	
forward:	43	forward:	10
midfield:	17	midfield:	17
defence:	6	defence:	4
own goals:	2		

Goal by Situation

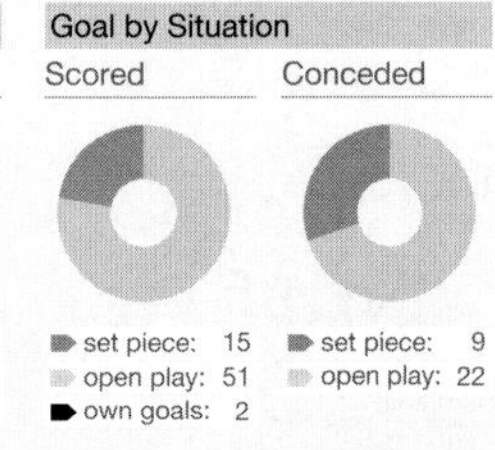

Scored		Conceded	
set piece:	15	set piece:	9
open play:	51	open play:	22
own goals:	2		

All-Time Records

Total Premiership Record

Total Matches Played	544
Total Matches Won	289
Total Matches Drawn	146
Total Matches Lost	109
Total Goals Scored	911
Total Goals Conceded	481
Total Points	1,013
Total Players Used	113

All-Time Record vs Reading

Competition	Played	Won	Drawn	Lost	For	Against
League	0	0	0	0	0	0
FA Cup	3	3	0	0	6	2
League Cup	2	2	0	0	4	0
Other	0	0	0	0	0	0
Total	**5**	**5**	**0**	**0**	**10**	**2**

Aston Villa

Nickname:	The Villans	Telephone:	0121 327 2299
Manager:	David O'Leary	Ticket Office:	0121 327 5353
Chairman:	Doug Ellis	Club Shop:	0121 326 1559
Website:	www.avfc.co.uk		

Villa Park

Season Review 05/06

It was a season of frustration at Villa Park, with many disillusioned fans calling for the heads of Manager David O'Leary and Chairman Doug Ellis.

A 3-0 Carling Cup hammering at League One side Doncaster Rovers was the low point of a campaign in which Villa finished just eight points and two places away from relegation to the Championship.

Points / Position

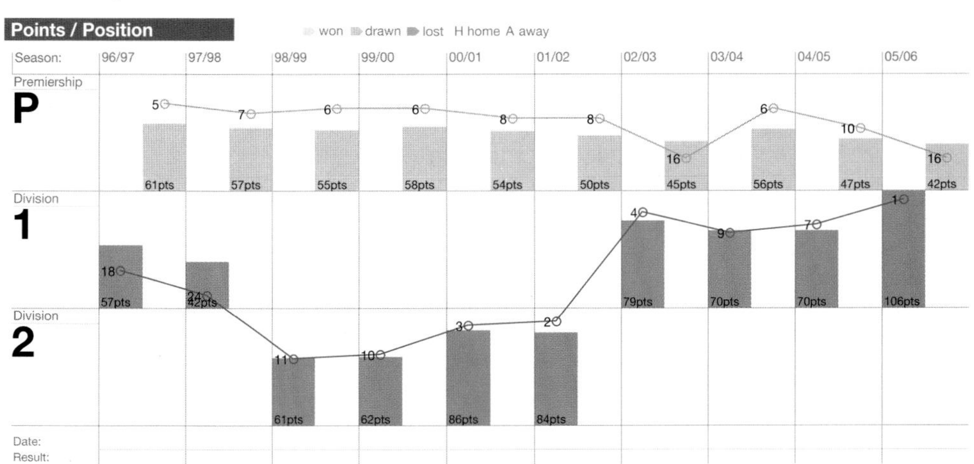

won drawn lost H home A away
Season: 96/97 97/98 98/99 99/00 00/01 01/02 02/03 03/04 04/05 05/06
Premiership P
5 7 6 6 8 8 16 6 10 16
61pts 57pts 55pts 58pts 54pts 50pts 45pts 56pts 47pts 42pts
Division 1
18 24 4 9 7 1
57pts 42pts 79pts 70pts 70pts 106pts
Division 2
11 10 3 2
61pts 62pts 86pts 84pts
Date:
Result:

Goals 05/06

Goals by Time Period

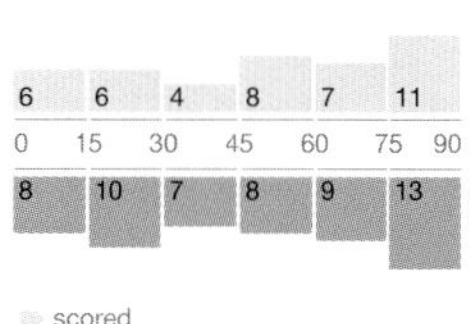

6 6 4 8 7 11
0 15 30 45 60 75 90
8 10 7 8 9 13
scored
conceded

Goals by Area

Scored (Conceded)

18 (10)
20 (36)
4 (9)

Goals by Position

Scored		Conceded	
forward:	24	forward:	33
midfield:	10	midfield:	18
defence:	7	defence:	3
own goals:	1	own goals:	1

Goal by Situation

Scored		Conceded	
set piece:	9	set piece:	21
open play:	32	open play:	33
own goals:	1	own goals:	1

All-Time Records

Total Premiership Record

Total Matches Played	544
Total Matches Won	203
Total Matches Drawn	158
Total Matches Lost	183
Total Goals Scored	668
Total Goals Conceded	632
Total Points	767
Total Players Used	120

All-Time Record vs Reading

Competition	Played	Won	Drawn	Lost	For	Against
League	4	4	0	0	11	5
FA Cup	4	2	1	1	9	4
League Cup	4	3	1	0	9	3
Other	0	0	0	0	0	0
Total	**12**	**9**	**2**	**1**	**29**	**12**

Blackburn Rovers

BLACKBURN ROVERS F.C.
ARTE ET LABORE

Nickname:	Rovers	Telephone:	08701 113 232
Manager:	Mark Hughes	Ticket Office:	08701 123 456
Chairman:	John Williams	Club Shop:	0870 042 3875
Website:	www.rovers.co.uk		

Ewood Park

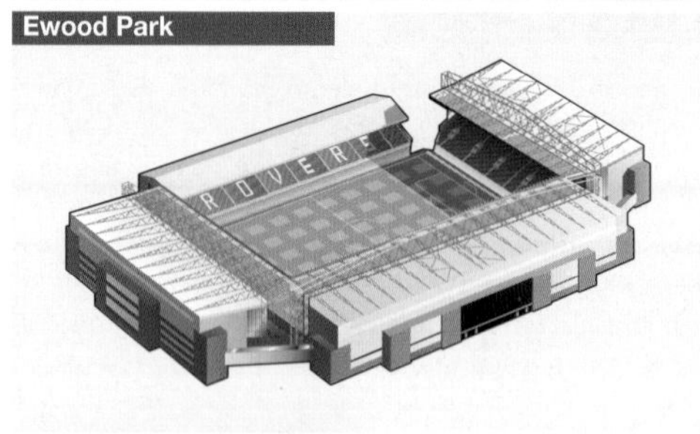
ROVERS

Season Review 05/06

Mark Hughes guided Blackburn to sixth place and UEFA Cup qualification in his first full season in charge. Despite operating with a relatively small squad, the Ewood Park outfit also reached the last four in the Carling Cup.

Craig Bellamy proved to be a shrewd acquisition, whilst the likes of Steven Reid and Morten Gamst Pedersen really shone.

Points / Position

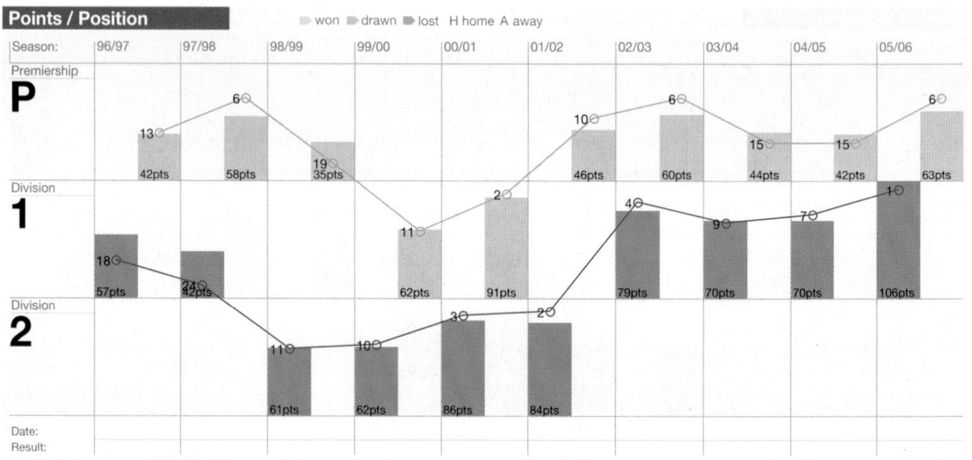
won
drawn
lost
H home A away
Season:
96/97
97/98
98/99
99/00
00/01
01/02
02/03
03/04
04/05
05/06
Premiership
P
Division
1
Division
2
13
42pts
6
58pts
19
35pts
10
46pts
6
60pts
15
44pts
15
42pts
6
63pts
18
57pts
24
42pts
11
61pts
10
62pts
11
62pts
2
91pts
3
86pts
2
84pts
4
79pts
9
70pts
7
70pts
1
106pts
Date:
Result:

Goals 05/06

Goals by Time Period

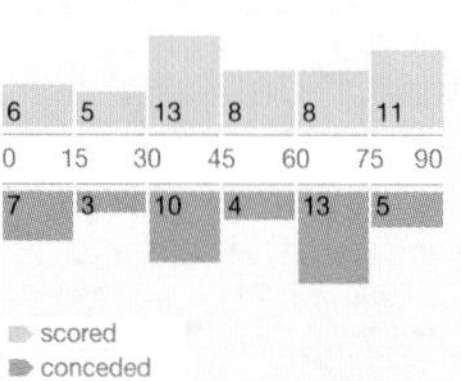
6
5
13
8
8
11
0
15
30
45
60
75
90
7
3
10
4
13
5
scored
conceded

Goals by Area

Scored (Conceded)

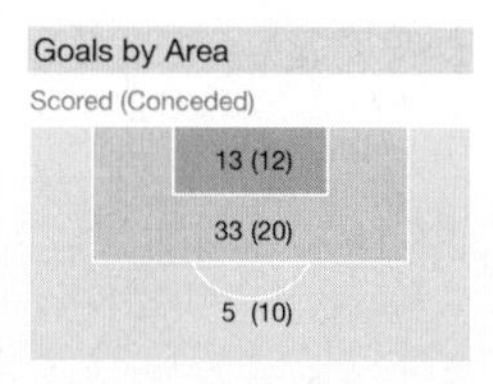
13 (12)
33 (20)
5 (10)

Goals by Position

Scored		Conceded	
forward:	26	forward:	27
midfield:	19	midfield:	14
defence:	4	defence:	0
own goals:	2	own goals:	1

Goal by Situation

Scored		Conceded	
set piece:	16	set piece:	15
open play:	33	open play:	26
own goals:	2	own goals:	1

All-Time Records

Total Premiership Record

Total Matches Played

468

Total Matches Won

190

Total Matches Drawn

125

Total Matches Lost

153

Total Goals Scored

650

Total Goals Conceded

553

Total Points

695

Total Players Used

124

All-Time Record vs Reading

Competition	Played	Won	Drawn	Lost	For	Against
League	6	1	4	1	6	8
FA Cup	1	1	0	0	2	1
League Cup	0	0	0	0	0	0
Other	0	0	0	0	0	0
Total	**7**	**2**	**4**	**1**	**8**	**9**

Bolton Wanderers

Nickname:	The Trotters
Manager:	Sam Allardyce
Chairman:	Phil Gartside
Website:	www.bwfc.co.uk

Telephone:	01204 673 673
Ticket Office:	0871 871 2932
Club Shop:	01204 673 650

Reebok Stadium

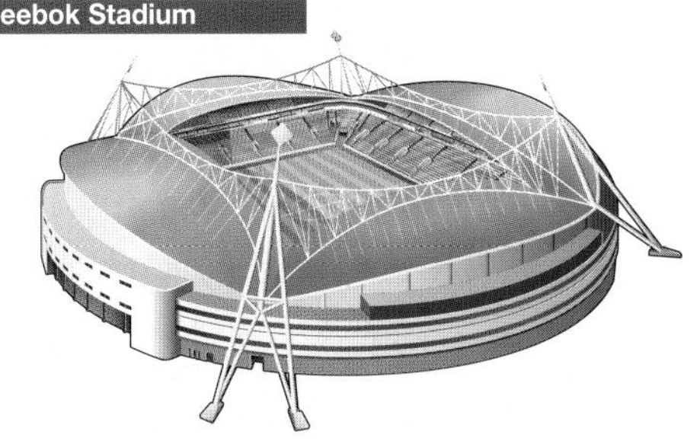

Season Review 05/06

It was another encouraging season for Bolton, with a top-half finish and European adventure to boot. Games against the likes of eventual winners Sevilla in the UEFA Cup only served to raise the profile of the club.

A disappointing end to the campaign was attributed in many quarters to the incessant speculation linking boss Sam Allardyce to the England job.

Points / Position

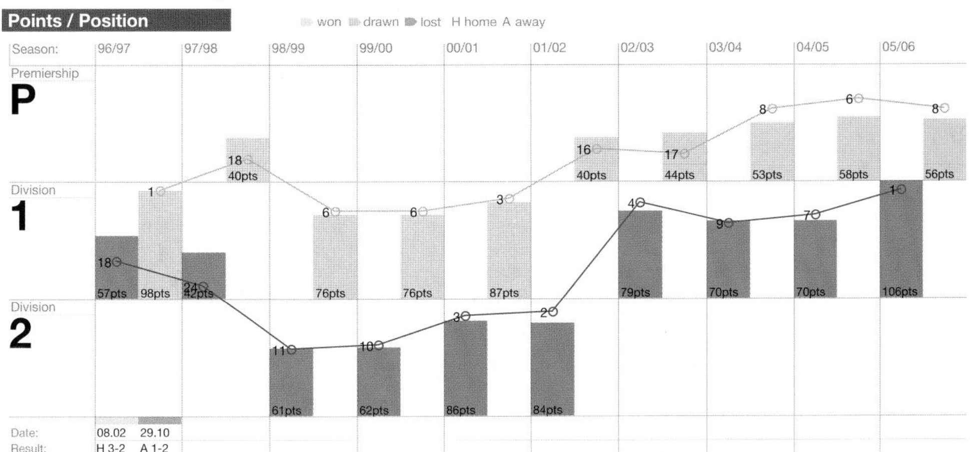
won drawn lost H home A away
Season: 96/97 97/98 98/99 99/00 00/01 01/02 02/03 03/04 04/05 05/06
Premiership
P
Division
1
Division
2
18 57pts
1 98pts
24 42pts
18 40pts
11 61pts
6 76pts
10 62pts
6 76pts
3 86pts
3 87pts
2 84pts
16 40pts
4 79pts
17 44pts
9 70pts
8 53pts
7 70pts
6 58pts
8 56pts
1 106pts
Date: 08.02 29.10
Result: H 3-2 A 1-2

Goals 05/06

Goals by Time Period

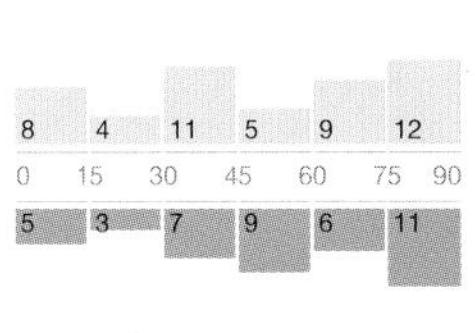
8 4 11 5 9 12
0 15 30 45 60 75 90
5 3 7 9 6 11
scored
conceded

Goals by Area

Scored (Conceded)

17 (13)

27 (25)

5 (3)

Goals by Position

Scored

- forward: 16
- midfield: 28
- defence: 3
- own goals: 2

Conceded

- forward: 23
- midfield: 15
- defence: 2
- own goals: 1

Goal by Situation

Scored

- set piece: 18
- open play: 29
- own goals: 2

Conceded

- set piece: 12
- open play: 28
- own goals: 1

All-Time Records

Total Premiership Record

Total Matches Played	266
Total Matches Won	81
Total Matches Drawn	77
Total Matches Lost	108
Total Goals Scored	311
Total Goals Conceded	386
Total Points	320
Total Players Used	109

All-Time Record vs Reading

Competition	Played	Won	Drawn	Lost	For	Against
League	18	8	3	7	24	21
FA Cup	4	2	1	1	6	4
League Cup	0	0	0	0	0	0
Other	1	1	0	0	4	3
Total	**23**	**11**	**4**	**8**	**34**	**28**

Charlton Athletic

CHARLTON
ATHLETIC

Nickname:	The Addicks	Telephone:	020 8333 4000
Manager:	Iain Dowie	Ticket Office:	020 8333 4010
Chairman:	Richard Murray	Club Shop:	020 8333 4035
Website:	www.cafc.co.uk		

The Valley

Season Review 05/06

The 2005/06 season will be remembered at Charlton as the last in Alan Curbishley's 15-year reign. A great start saw the Addicks win five of their first six league games, but they ultimately slipped to a respectable 13th place.

Darren Bent arrived from Ipswich with a bang, firing in 18 goals to finish as the leading English marksman in the Premiership.

Points / Position

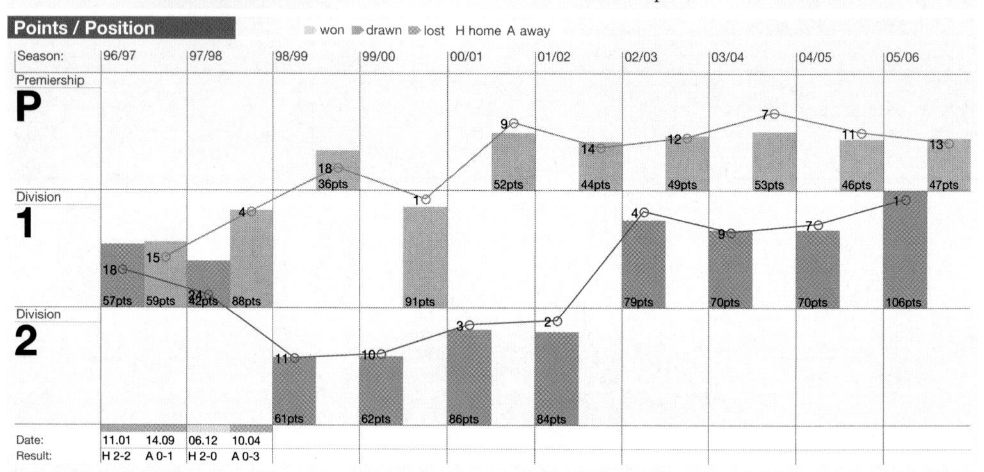

won drawn lost H home A away
Season: 96/97 97/98 98/99 99/00 00/01 01/02 02/03 03/04 04/05 05/06
Premiership
P
Division
1
Division
2
18 57pts
15 59pts
24 42pts
4 88pts
11 61pts
18 36pts
10 62pts
1 91pts
3 86pts
9 52pts
2 84pts
14 44pts
4 79pts
12 49pts
9 70pts
7 53pts
7 70pts
11 46pts
1 106pts
13 47pts
Date: 11.01 14.09 06.12 10.04
Result: H 2-2 A 0-1 H 2-0 A 0-3

Goals 05/06

Goals by Time Period

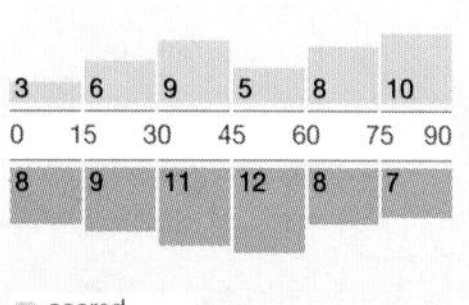

3 6 9 5 8 10
0 15 30 45 60 75 90
8 9 11 12 8 7
scored
conceded

Goals by Area

Scored (Conceded)

9 (13)

27 (35)

5 (7)

Goals by Position

Scored		Conceded	
forward:	24	forward:	29
midfield:	14	midfield:	21
defence:	2	defence:	3
own goals:	1	own goals:	2

Goal by Situation

Scored		Conceded	
set piece:	10	set piece:	15
open play:	30	open play:	38
own goals:	1	own goals:	2

All-Time Records

Total Premiership Record

Total Matches Played

266

Total Matches Won

85

Total Matches Drawn

72

Total Matches Lost

109

Total Goals Scored

308

Total Goals Conceded

382

Total Points

327

Total Players Used

74

All-Time Record vs Reading

Competition	Played	Won	Drawn	Lost	For	Against
League	28	9	8	11	33	34
FA Cup	0	0	0	0	0	0
League Cup	2	1	1	0	5	3
Other	0	0	0	0	0	0
Total	**30**	**10**	**9**	**11**	**38**	**37**

Chelsea

Nickname:	The Blues	Telephone:	0870 300 2322
Manager:	José Mourinho	Ticket Office:	0870 300 2322
Chairman:	Bruce Buck	Club Shop:	0870 300 1212
Website:	www.chelseafc.com		

Stamford Bridge

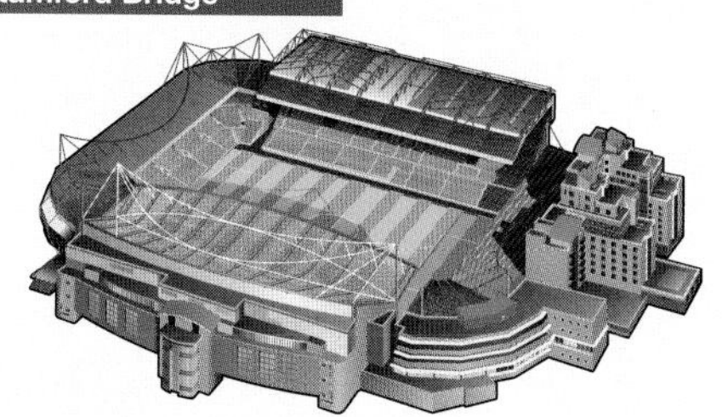

Season Review 05/06

Chelsea dominated the league season from start to finish, though they were less successful in cup competitions. Barcelona, Liverpool and Charlton ensured that José Mourinho had to be content with the Premiership and Community Shield.

John Terry and Frank Lampard were once again star performers, whilst Joe Cole found the consistency to match his abundance of skill.

Points / Position

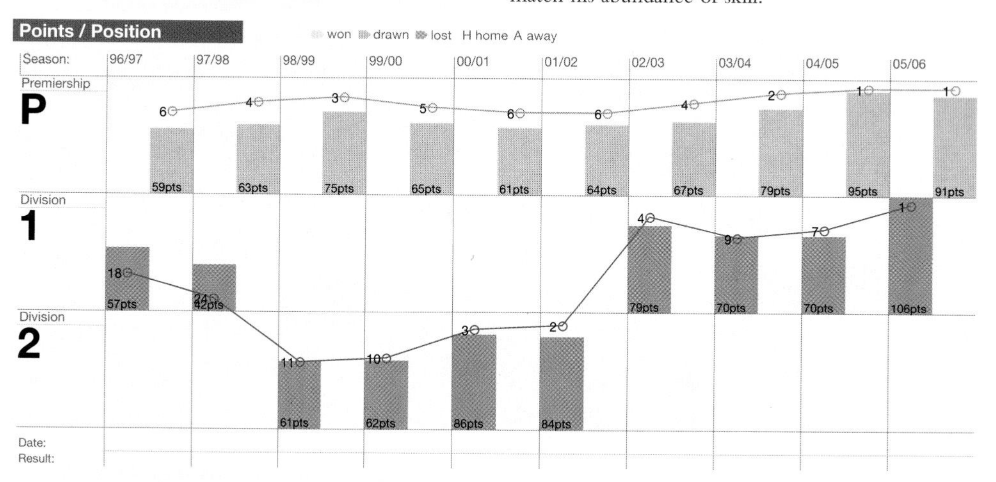

won drawn lost H home A away
Season: 96/97 97/98 98/99 99/00 00/01 01/02 02/03 03/04 04/05 05/06
Premiership
P
6 4 3 5 6 6 4 2 1 1
59pts 63pts 75pts 65pts 61pts 64pts 67pts 79pts 95pts 91pts
Division
1
18 24 4 9 7 1
57pts 42pts 79pts 70pts 70pts 106pts
Division
2
11 10 3 2
61pts 62pts 86pts 84pts
Date:
Result:

Goals 05/06

Goals by Time Period

	0–15	15–30	30–45	45–60	60–75	75–90
scored	6	11	10	12	24	9
conceded	4	3	8	3	2	2

Goals by Area

Scored (Conceded)

- 15 (5)
- 45 (17)
- 12 (0)

Goals by Position

Scored		Conceded	
forward:	24	forward:	11
midfield:	36	midfield:	9
defence:	11	defence:	2
own goals:	1		

Goal by Situation

Scored		Conceded	
set piece:	25	set piece:	10
open play:	46	open play:	12
own goals:	1		

All-Time Records

Total Premiership Record

Total Matches Played	544
Total Matches Won	261
Total Matches Drawn	147
Total Matches Lost	136
Total Goals Scored	848
Total Goals Conceded	556
Total Points	930
Total Players Used	135

All-Time Record vs Reading

Competition	Played	Won	Drawn	Lost	For	Against
League	8	3	3	2	10	10
FA Cup	3	1	2	0	5	3
League Cup	3	2	0	1	5	5
Other	0	0	0	0	0	0
Total	**14**	**6**	**5**	**3**	**20**	**18**

Everton

18
78
Everton

Nickname: The Toffees
Manager: David Moyes
Chairman: Bill Kenwright
Website: www.evertonfc.com

Telephone: 0870 442 1878
Ticket Office: 0870 442 1878
Club Shop: 0870 442 1878

Goodison Park

Season Review 05/06

Everton followed up the amazing form of their previous campaign with a mid-table finish. A return to European football brought only heartbreak, as the Toffees fell early in both the Champions League and UEFA Cup.

Nigel Martyn continued to defy his advancing years in goal, whilst James Beattie began to show what he could do at the other end.

Points / Position

won drawn lost H home A away

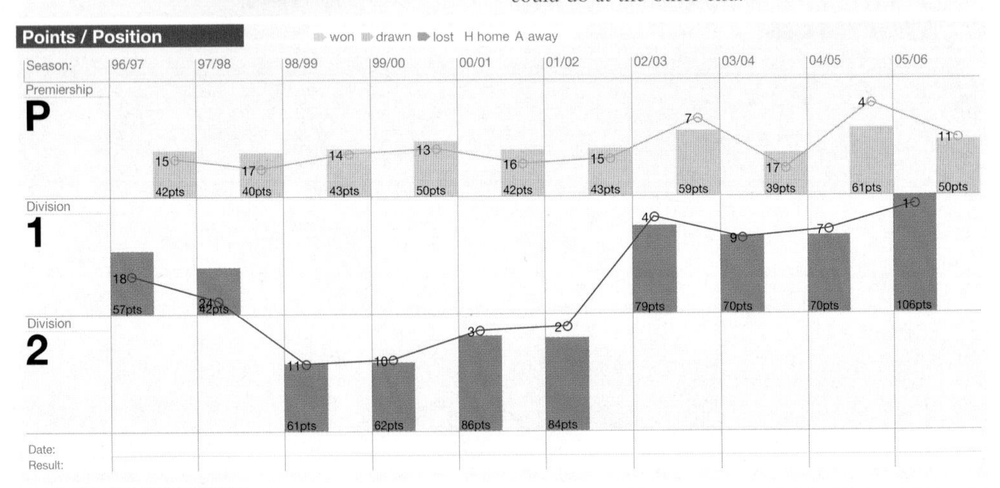

Season:
96/97
97/98
98/99
99/00
00/01
01/02
02/03
03/04
04/05
05/06
Premiership
P
15
42pts
17
40pts
14
43pts
13
50pts
16
42pts
15
43pts
7
59pts
17
39pts
4
61pts
11
50pts
Division
1
18
57pts
24
42pts
4
79pts
9
70pts
7
70pts
1
106pts
Division
2
11
61pts
10
62pts
3
86pts
2
84pts
Date:
Result:

Goals 05/06

Goals by Time Period

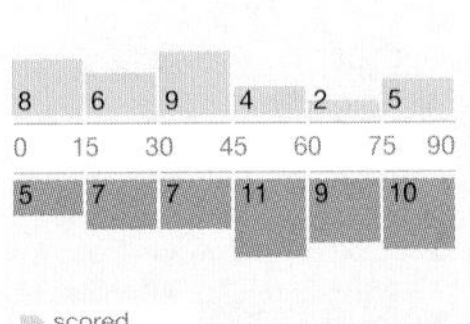

8
6
9
4
2
5
0
15
30
45
60
75
90
5
7
7
11
9
10

scored
conceded

Goals by Area

Scored (Conceded)

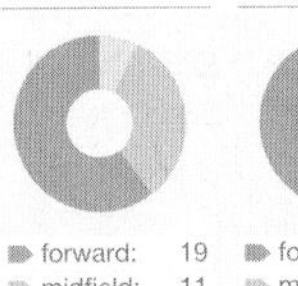

10 (12)
18 (28)
6 (9)

Goals by Position

Scored		Conceded	
forward:	19	forward:	22
midfield:	11	midfield:	17
defence:	2	defence:	7
own goals:	2	own goals:	3

Goal by Situation

Scored		Conceded	
set piece:	16	set piece:	16
open play:	16	open play:	30
own goals:	2	own goals:	3

All-Time Records

Total Premiership Record

Total Matches Played
544

Total Matches Won
177

Total Matches Drawn
146

Total Matches Lost
221

Total Goals Scored
651

Total Goals Conceded
739

Total Points
677

Total Players Used
132

All-Time Record vs Reading

Competition	Played	Won	Drawn	Lost	For	Against
League	2	2	0	0	5	2
FA Cup	0	0	0	0	0	0
League Cup	1	1	0	0	1	0
Other	0	0	0	0	0	0
Total	**3**	**3**	**0**	**0**	**6**	**2**

Fulham

Nickname:	The Cottagers
Manager:	Chris Coleman
Chairman:	Mohamed Al Fayed
Website:	www.fulhamfc.com
Telephone:	0870 442 1222
Ticket Office:	0870 442 1234
Club Shop:	0870 442 1223

Craven Cottage

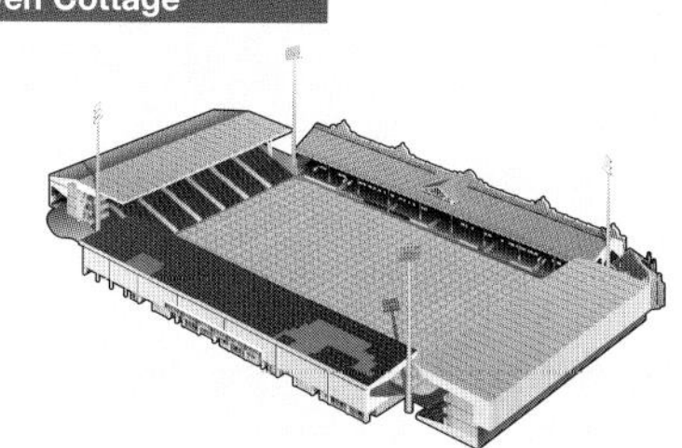

Season Review 05/06

Fulham experienced a real Jekyll and Hyde campaign, with an abysmal away record undoing much of their good work at Craven Cottage. It took Chris Coleman's team until April to win on the road, whilst they claimed 13 Premiership victories on home soil.

Luis Boa Morte excelled in his role as captain, notably scoring the only goal in a memorable win against local rivals Chelsea.

Points / Position

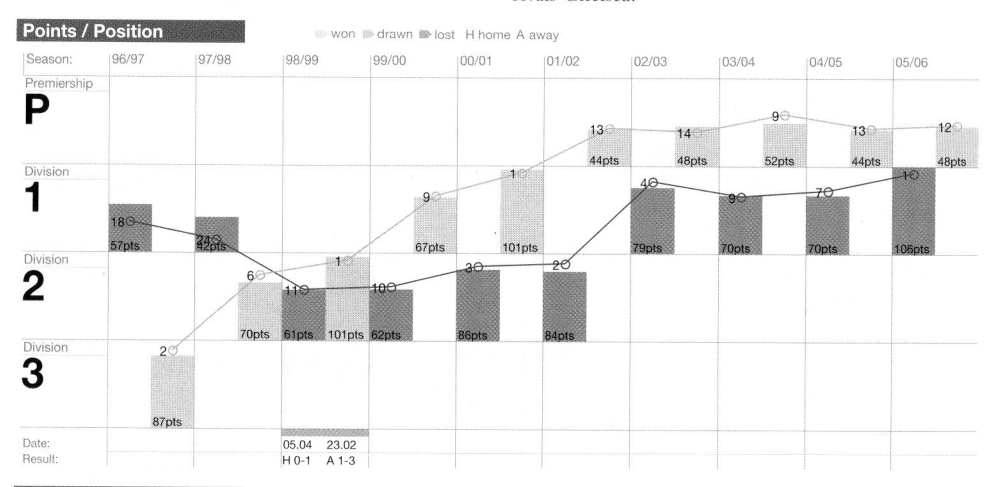
won drawn lost H home A away
Season: 96/97 97/98 98/99 99/00 00/01 01/02 02/03 03/04 04/05 05/06
Premiership
P
Division 1
Division 2
Division 3
13 44pts
14 48pts
9 52pts
13 44pts
12 48pts
18 57pts
24 42pts
9 67pts
1 101pts
4 79pts
9 70pts
7 70pts
1 106pts
6 70pts
11 61pts
1 101pts
10 62pts
3 86pts
2 84pts
2 87pts
Date: 05.04 23.02
Result: H 0-1 A 1-3

Goals 05/06

Goals by Time Period

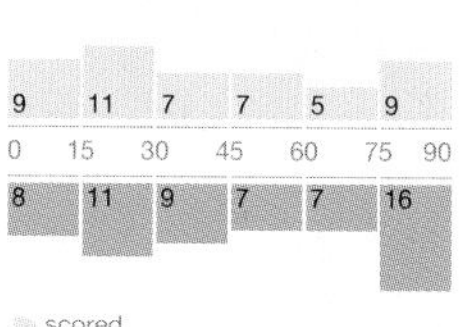
9 11 7 7 5 9
0 15 30 45 60 75 90
8 11 9 7 7 16
scored
conceded

Goals by Area

Scored (Conceded)

5 (15)
39 (34)
4 (9)

Goals by Position

Scored		Conceded	
forward:	30	forward:	26
midfield:	16	midfield:	17
defence:	1	defence:	9
own goals:	1	own goals:	6

Goal by Situation

Scored		Conceded	
set piece:	15	set piece:	18
open play:	32	open play:	34
own goals:	1	own goals:	6

All-Time Records

Total Premiership Record

Total Matches Played
190

Total Matches Won
63

Total Matches Drawn
47

Total Matches Lost
80

Total Goals Scored
229

Total Goals Conceded
258

Total Points
236

Total Players Used
60

All-Time Record vs Reading

Competition	Played	Won	Drawn	Lost	For	Against
League	28	11	7	10	37	33
FA Cup	4	2	2	0	3	1
League Cup	5	1	3	1	5	6
Other	0	0	0	0	0	0
Total	**37**	**14**	**12**	**11**	**45**	**40**

Liverpool

Nickname:	The Reds	Telephone:	0151 263 2361
Manager:	Rafael Benítez	Ticket Office:	0870 444 4949
Chairman:	David Moores	Club Shop:	0870 066 7036
Website:	www.liverpoolfc.tv		

Anfield

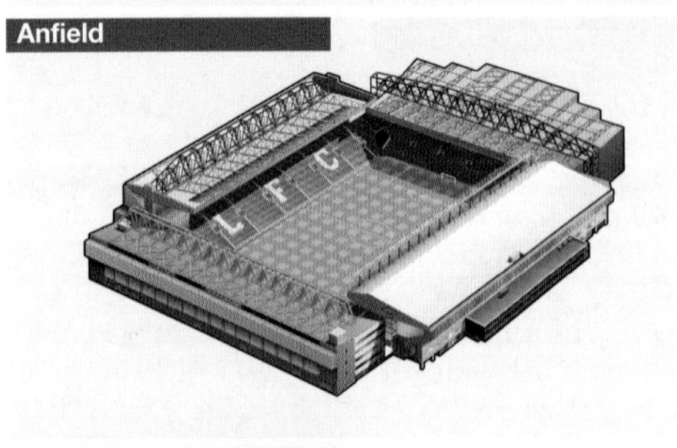

Season Review 05/06

Liverpool added both the UEFA Super Cup and FA Cup to their trophy collection, with captain Steven Gerrard winning the PFA Player of the Year award.

A clear improvement was also evident in the league, as Rafael Benitez's team finished 24 points better off than 12 months previously. In fact, only Champions Chelsea could boast a better defensive record than the Merseysiders.

Points / Position

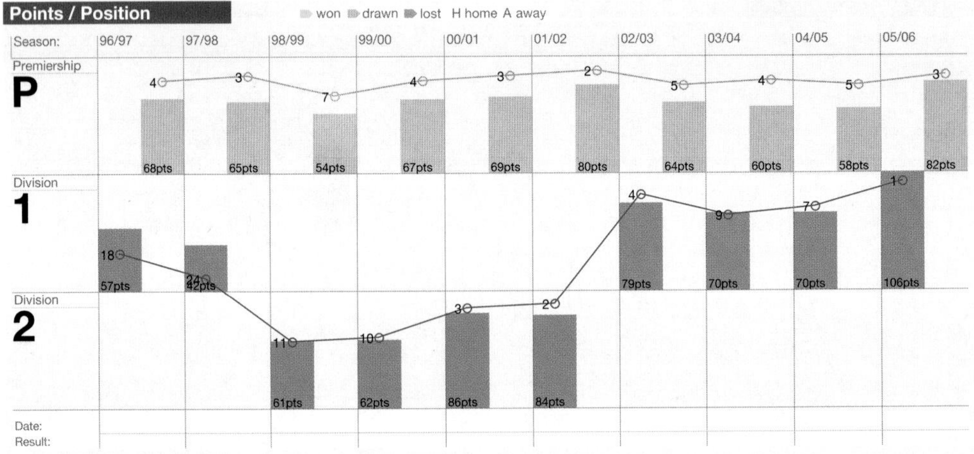

won drawn lost H home A away
Season: 96/97 97/98 98/99 99/00 00/01 01/02 02/03 03/04 04/05 05/06
Premiership
P
4 68pts
3 65pts
7 54pts
4 67pts
3 69pts
2 80pts
5 64pts
4 60pts
5 58pts
3 82pts
Division
1
18 57pts
24 42pts
4 79pts
9 70pts
7 70pts
1 106pts
Division
2
11 61pts
10 62pts
3 86pts
2 84pts
Date:
Result:

Goals 05/06

Goals by Time Period

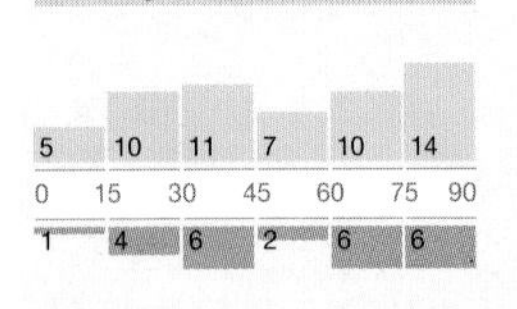

5 10 11 7 10 14
0 15 30 45 60 75 90
1 4 6 2 6 6

scored
conceded

Goals by Area

Scored (Conceded)

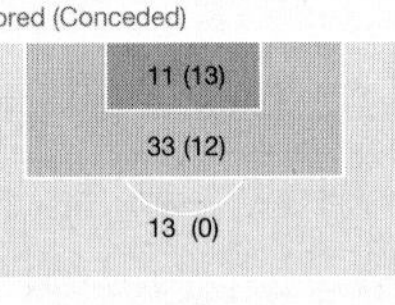

11 (13)
33 (12)
13 (0)

Goals by Position

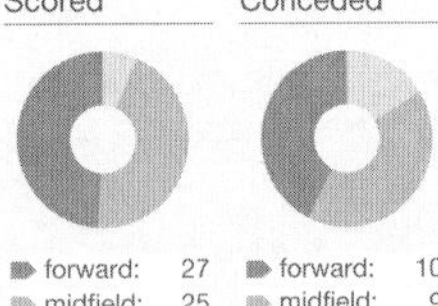

Scored		Conceded	
forward:	27	forward:	10
midfield:	25	midfield:	9
defence:	3	defence:	4
own goals:	2	own goals:	2

Goal by Situation

Scored		Conceded	
set piece:	14	set piece:	6
open play:	41	open play:	17
own goals:	2	own goals:	2

All-Time Records

Total Premiership Record

Total Matches Played	544
Total Matches Won	265
Total Matches Drawn	136
Total Matches Lost	143
Total Goals Scored	868
Total Goals Conceded	552
Total Points	931
Total Players Used	108

All-Time Record vs Reading

Competition	Played	Won	Drawn	Lost	For	Against
League	0	0	0	0	0	0
FA Cup	0	0	0	0	0	0
League Cup	0	0	0	0	0	0
Other	0	0	0	0	0	0
Total	**0**	**0**	**0**	**0**	**0**	**0**

Manchester City

Nickname:	The Citizens	Telephone:	0870 062 1894
Manager:	Stuart Pearce	Ticket Office:	0870 062 1894
Chairman:	John Wardle	Club Shop:	0870 062 1894
Website:	www.mcfc.co.uk		

City of Manchester Stadium

Season Review 05/06

It was largely a season of disappointment for the blue half of Manchester. Stuart Pearce's team made an encouraging start to the campaign, but lost nine of their final 10 games to slide down the table.

There was still reason for optimism, however, with the continued emergence of talented youngsters such as Micah Richards and Stephen Ireland.

Points / Position

won drawn lost H home A away

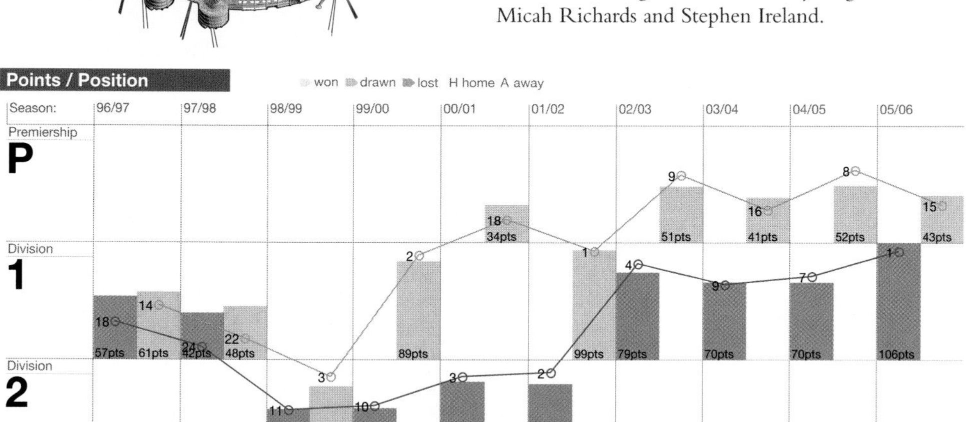

Season:
96/97
97/98
98/99
99/00
00/01
01/02
02/03
03/04
04/05
05/06
Premiership
P
Division
1
Division
2
18 57pts
14 61pts
22 42pts
24 48pts
11 61pts
3 82pts
10 62pts
2 89pts
3 86pts
18 34pts
2 84pts
1 99pts
4 79pts
9 51pts
9 70pts
16 41pts
7 70pts
8 52pts
1 106pts
15 43pts

Date:	15.10	03.05	24.02	18.10	27.03	24.10
Result:	H 2-0	A 2-3	H 3-0	A 0-0	H 1-3	A 1-0

Goals 05/06

Goals by Time Period

	0–15	15–30	30–45	45–60	60–75	75–90
scored	8	6	7	4	9	9
conceded	6	5	13	6	7	11

Goals by Area

Scored (Conceded)

9 (8)

30 (34)

4 (6)

Goals by Position

Scored		Conceded	
forward:	23	forward:	24
midfield:	14	midfield:	19
defence:	6	defence:	5

Goal by Situation

Scored		Conceded	
set piece:	9	set piece:	16
open play:	34	open play:	32

All-Time Records

Total Premiership Record

Total Matches Played	354
Total Matches Won	103
Total Matches Drawn	101
Total Matches Lost	150
Total Goals Scored	413
Total Goals Conceded	482
Total Points	410
Total Players Used	126

All-Time Record vs Reading

Competition	Played	Won	Drawn	Lost	For	Against
League	12	6	2	4	18	12
FA Cup	4	2	2	0	12	1
League Cup	2	1	1	0	3	2
Other	0	0	0	0	0	0
Total	**18**	**9**	**5**	**4**	**33**	**15**

Manchester United

Nickname: The Red Devils
Manager: Sir Alex Ferguson
Owner: Malcolm Glazer
Website: www.manutd.com

Telephone: 0870 442 1994
Ticket Office: 0870 442 1994
Club Shop: 0870 111 8107

Old Trafford

Season Review 05/06

A Carling Cup triumph and second place in the Premiership would be seen as success at most clubs, but not at Manchester United. In fact, Sir Alex Ferguson's charges never genuinely threatened Chelsea's grip on the title.

The performances of Wayne Rooney continued to win him admirers across the globe, with Edwin van der Sar providing calm assurance in goal.

Points / Position

won drawn lost H home A away

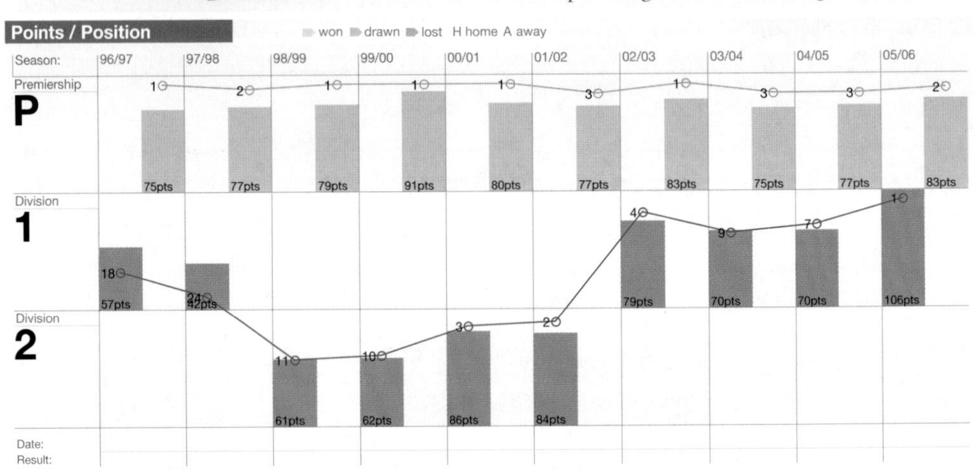

Season: 96/97 97/98 98/99 99/00 00/01 01/02 02/03 03/04 04/05 05/06
Premiership P
1 75pts
2 77pts
1 79pts
1 91pts
1 80pts
3 77pts
1 83pts
3 75pts
3 77pts
2 83pts
Division 1
Division 2
Date:
Result:

Goals 05/06

Goals by Time Period

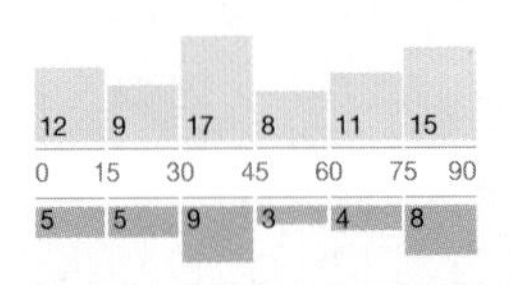

12 9 17 8 11 15
0 15 30 45 60 75 90
5 5 9 3 4 8

scored
conceded

Goals by Area

Scored (Conceded)

18 (11)
46 (17)
8 (6)

Goals by Position

Scored

- forward: 45
- midfield: 18
- defence: 5
- own goals: 4

Conceded

- forward: 13
- midfield: 16
- defence: 5

Goal by Situation

Scored

- set piece: 17
- open play: 51
- own goals: 4

Conceded

- set piece: 14
- open play: 20

All-Time Records

Total Premiership Record

Total Matches Played
544

Total Matches Won
339

Total Matches Drawn
126

Total Matches Lost
79

Total Goals Scored
1,057

Total Goals Conceded
489

Total Points
1,143

Total Players Used
99

All-Time Record vs Reading

Competition	Played	Won	Drawn	Lost	For	Against
League	0	0	0	0	0	0
FA Cup	10	5	4	1	20	9
League Cup	0	0	0	0	0	0
Other	0	0	0	0	0	0
Total	**10**	**5**	**4**	**1**	**20**	**9**

Middlesbrough

MIDDLESBROUGH
FOOTBALL CLUB
19
86

Nickname:	Boro	Telephone:	0870 421 1986
Manager:	Gareth Southgate	Ticket Office:	0870 421 1986
Chairman:	Steve Gibson	Club Shop:	0870 421 1986
Website:	www.mfc.co.uk		

Riverside Stadium

Season Review 05/06

An unforgettable season at the Riverside saw Boro struggle in the league but thrive in cup competitions. Victories against FC Basle and Steaua Bucharest resulted in a UEFA Cup Final appearance, whilst an FA Cup Semi-Final was also reached.

Following weeks of intense speculation, manager Steve McClaren was finally unveiled as the successor to Sven-Goran Eriksson as England boss in May.

Points / Position

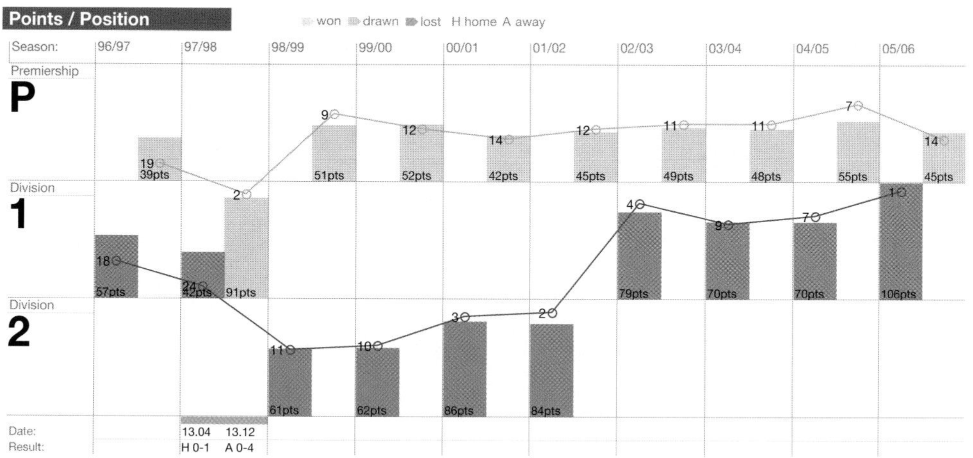

won drawn lost H home A away
Season:
96/97
97/98
98/99
99/00
00/01
01/02
02/03
03/04
04/05
05/06
Premiership
P
Division
1
Division
2
19 39pts
9 51pts
12 52pts
14 42pts
12 45pts
11 49pts
11 48pts
7 55pts
14 45pts
2 91pts
18 57pts
24 42pts
4 79pts
9 70pts
7 70pts
1 106pts
11 61pts
10 62pts
3 86pts
2 84pts
Date:
Result:
13.04 13.12
H 0-1 A 0-4

Goals 05/06

Goals by Time Period
6 6 11 7 9 9
0 15 30 45 60 75 90
5 12 4 9 13 15
scored
conceded
Goals by Area
Scored (Conceded)
9 (9)
33 (37)
6 (12)
Goals by Position
Scored
Conceded
forward: 31
midfield: 10
defence: 6
own goals: 1
forward: 34
midfield: 18
defence: 4
own goals: 2
Goal by Situation
Scored
Conceded
set piece: 18
open play: 29
own goals: 1
set piece: 18
open play: 38
own goals: 2

All-Time Records

Total Premiership Record

Total Matches Played	422
Total Matches Won	131
Total Matches Drawn	123
Total Matches Lost	168
Total Goals Scored	506
Total Goals Conceded	582
Total Points	516
Total Players Used	132

All-Time Record vs Reading

Competition	Played	Won	Drawn	Lost	For	Against
League	12	4	6	2	17	8
FA Cup	0	0	0	0	0	0
League Cup	1	1	0	0	1	0
Other	0	0	0	0	0	0
Total	**13**	**5**	**6**	**2**	**18**	**8**

Newcastle United

Nickname: The Magpies
Manager: Glenn Roeder
Chairman: Freddy Shepherd
Website: www.nufc.co.uk

Telephone: 0191 201 8400
Ticket Office: 0191 261 1571
Club Shop: 0191 201 8426

St James' Park

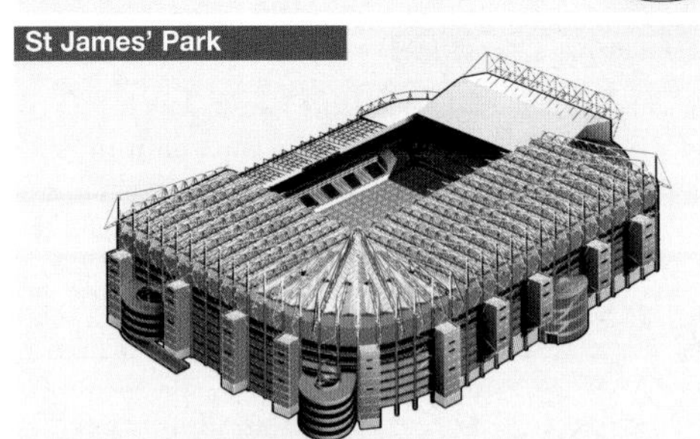

Season Review 05/06

Glenn Roeder was the toast of Tyneside as he led Newcastle from a position of adversity to InterToto Cup qualification. The team collected 32 points from 15 games under the former West Ham boss, thus earning him the job on a permanent basis.

Alan Shearer finally hung up his boots, bowing out of competitive action with a goal in the 4-1 triumph at arch-rivals Sunderland.

Points / Position

won drawn lost H home A away

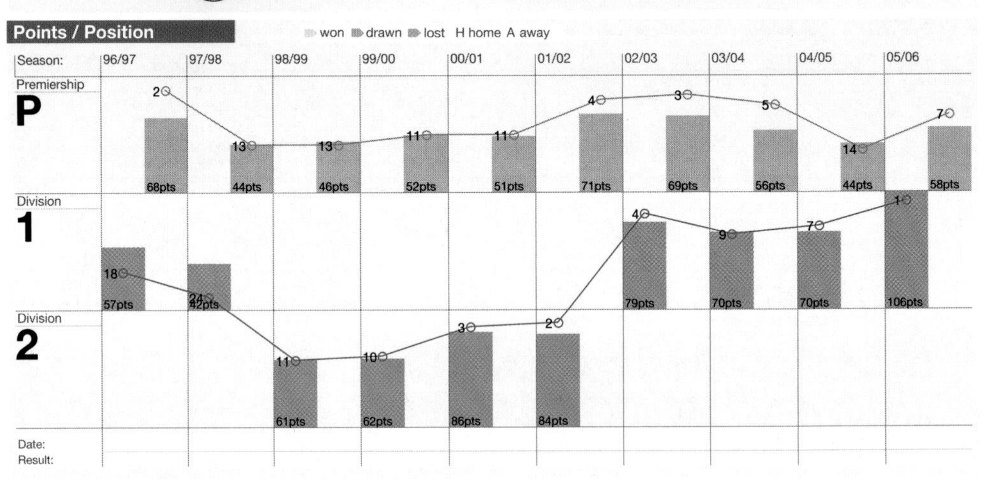

Season: 96/97 97/98 98/99 99/00 00/01 01/02 02/03 03/04 04/05 05/06
Premiership
P
2 68pts
13 44pts
13 46pts
11 52pts
11 51pts
4 71pts
3 69pts
5 56pts
14 44pts
7 58pts
Division
1
18 57pts
24 42pts
4 79pts
9 70pts
7 70pts
1 106pts
Division
2
11 61pts
10 62pts
3 86pts
2 84pts
Date:
Result:

Goals 05/06

Goals by Time Period

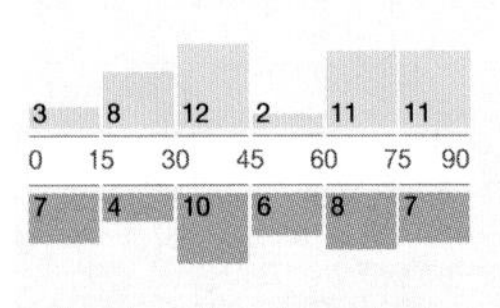

3 8 12 2 11 11
0 15 30 45 60 75 90
7 4 10 6 8 7
scored
conceded

Goals by Area

Scored (Conceded)

9 (9)
31 (26)
7 (7)

Goals by Position

Scored		Conceded	
forward:	28	forward:	25
midfield:	16	midfield:	13
defence:	2	defence:	2
own goals:	1	own goals:	2

Goal by Situation

Scored		Conceded	
set piece:	17	set piece:	9
open play:	29	open play:	31
own goals:	1	own goals:	2

All-Time Records

Total Premiership Record

Total Matches Played	502
Total Matches Won	218
Total Matches Drawn	132
Total Matches Lost	152
Total Goals Scored	761
Total Goals Conceded	606
Total Points	786
Total Players Used	125

All-Time Record vs Reading

Competition	Played	Won	Drawn	Lost	For	Against
League	0	0	0	0	0	0
FA Cup	4	3	1	0	13	5
League Cup	2	1	0	1	5	3
Other	0	0	0	0	0	0
Total	**6**	**4**	**1**	**1**	**18**	**8**

Portsmouth

Portsmouth FC

Nickname:	Pompey	Telephone:	02392 731 204
Manager:	Harry Redknapp	Ticket Office:	0871 230 1898
Chairman:	Milan Mandaric	Club Shop:	02392 778 552
Website:	www.pompeyfc.co.uk		

Fratton Park

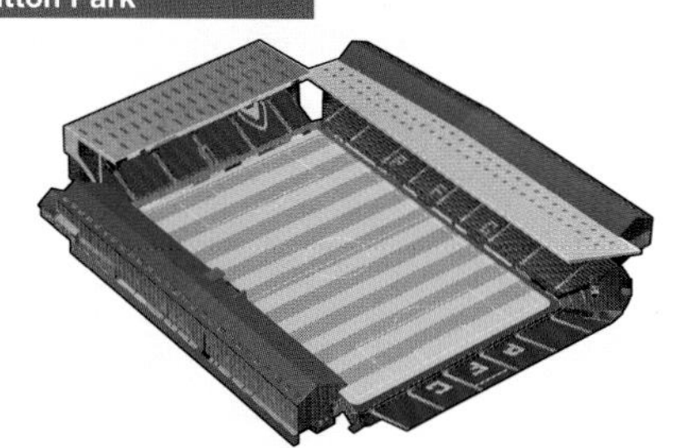

Season Review 05/06

Portsmouth seemed destined to be relegated for much of the season, but were saved by a combination of Alexandre Gaydamak's millions and the nous of returning manager Harry Redknapp.

Having picked up just 18 points from their first 28 games, an astonishing turnaround in form saw the South Coast club collect a further 20 to beat the drop with a match to spare.

Points / Position

won drawn lost H home A away

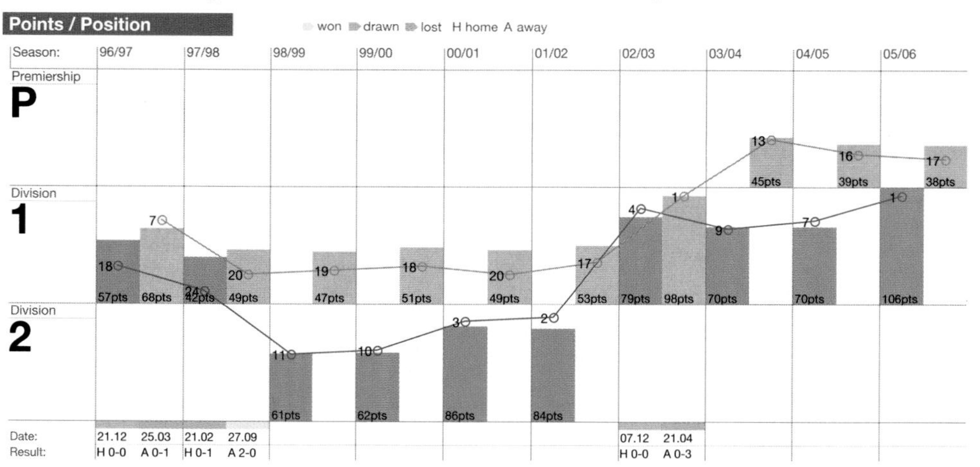

Season: 96/97 97/98 98/99 99/00 00/01 01/02 02/03 03/04 04/05 05/06
Premiership
P
Division
1
Division
2
13 16 17
45pts 39pts 38pts
7 1 4 9 7 1
18 20 19 18 20 17 24
57pts 68pts 42pts 49pts 47pts 51pts 49pts 53pts 79pts 98pts 70pts 70pts 106pts
11 10 3 2
61pts 62pts 86pts 84pts
Date: 21.12 25.03 21.02 27.09 07.12 21.04
Result: H 0-0 A 0-1 H 0-1 A 2-0 H 0-0 A 0-3

Goals 05/06

Goals by Time Period

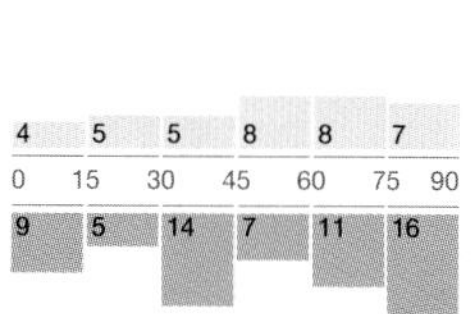

4 5 5 8 8 7
0 15 30 45 60 75 90
9 5 14 7 11 16

scored
conceded

Goals by Area

Scored (Conceded)

11 (11)

16 (45)

10 (6)

Goals by Position

Scored		Conceded	
forward:	15	forward:	31
midfield:	21	midfield:	23
defence:	0	defence:	5
own goals:	1	own goals:	3

Goal by Situation

Scored		Conceded	
set piece:	14	set piece:	18
open play:	22	open play:	41
own goals:	1	own goals:	3

All-Time Records

Total Premiership Record

Total Matches Played
114

Total Matches Won
32

Total Matches Drawn
26

Total Matches Lost
56

Total Goals Scored
127

Total Goals Conceded
175

Total Points
122

Total Players Used
64

All-Time Record vs Reading

Competition	Played	Won	Drawn	Lost	For	Against
League	34	15	12	7	45	25
FA Cup	4	2	0	2	5	4
League Cup	0	0	0	0	0	0
Other	0	0	0	0	0	0
Total	**38**	**17**	**12**	**9**	**50**	**29**

Sheffield United

Nickname: The Blades
Manager: Neil Warnock
Chairman: Derek Dooley
Website: www.sufc.co.uk

Telephone: 0870 787 1960
Ticket Office: 0870 787 1799
Club Shop: 0870 442 8705

Bramall Lane

Season Review 05/06

Having been in the top-two for most of the season, few could argue that Sheffield United deserved to win promotion. Ten wins from the opening 11 games of the campaign laid the foundations for success.

Manager Neil Warnock continued to court controversy on the touchline, getting into a war of words with Norwich's Nigel Worthington and being sent to the stands against Leeds.

Points / Position

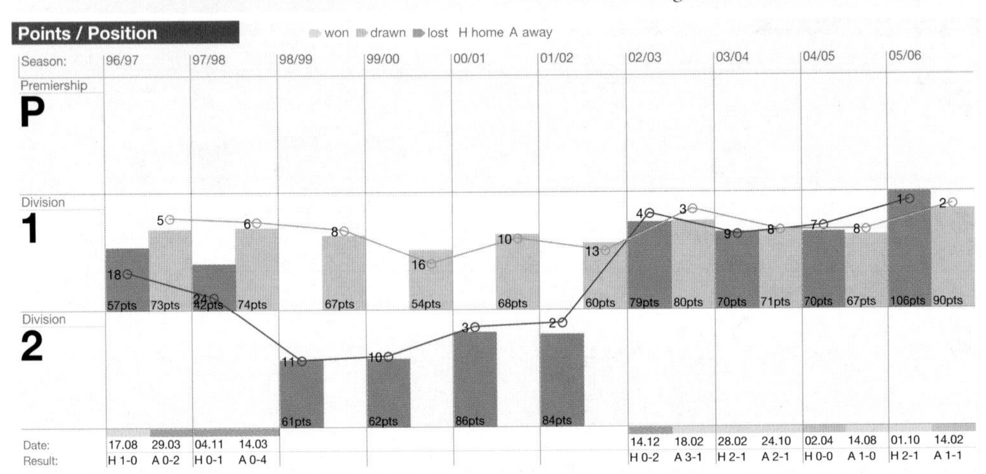

won drawn lost H home A away
Season: 96/97 97/98 98/99 99/00 00/01 01/02 02/03 03/04 04/05 05/06
Premiership
P
Division
1
Division
2
18 5 24 6 11 8 10 16 3 10 2 13 4 3 9 8 7 8 1 2
57pts 73pts 42pts 74pts 61pts 67pts 62pts 54pts 86pts 68pts 84pts 60pts 79pts 80pts 70pts 71pts 70pts 67pts 106pts 90pts
Date: 17.08 29.03 04.11 14.03 14.12 18.02 28.02 24.10 02.04 14.08 01.10 14.02
Result: H 1-0 A 0-2 H 0-1 A 0-4 H 0-2 A 3-1 H 2-1 A 2-1 H 0-0 A 1-0 H 2-1 A 1-1

Goals 05/06

Goals by Time Period

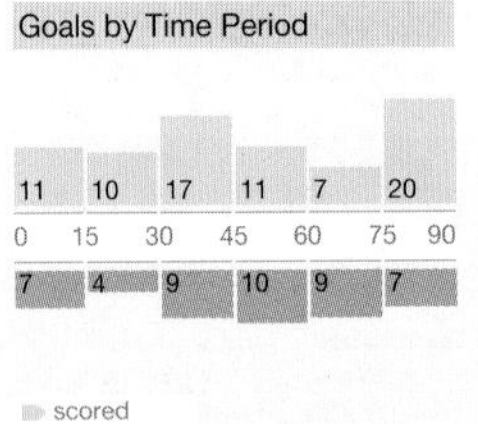

11 10 17 11 7 20
0 15 30 45 60 75 90
7 4 9 10 9 7

scored
conceded

Goals by Area

Scored (Conceded)

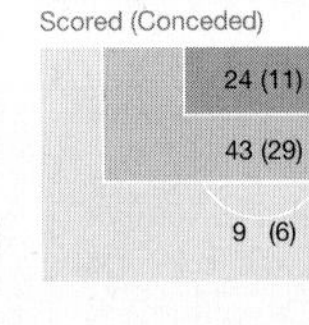

24 (11)
43 (29)
9 (6)

Goals by Position

Scored		Conceded	
forward:	36	forward:	29
midfield:	25	midfield:	14
defence:	12	defence:	1
own goals:	3	own goals:	2

Goal by Situation

Scored		Conceded	
set piece:	24	set piece:	15
open play:	49	open play:	29
own goals:	3	own goals:	2

All-Time Records

Total Premiership Record

Total Matches Played
84

Total Matches Won
22

Total Matches Drawn
28

Total Matches Lost
34

Total Goals Scored
96

Total Goals Conceded
113

Total Points
94

Total Players Used
34

All-Time Record vs Reading

Competition	Played	Won	Drawn	Lost	For	Against
League	28	10	6	12	36	29
FA Cup	1	1	0	0	1	0
League Cup	1	0	0	1	0	2
Other	0	0	0	0	0	0
Total	**30**	**11**	**6**	**13**	**37**	**31**

Tottenham Hotspur

TOTTENHAM HOTSPUR

Nickname: Spurs
Manager: Martin Jol
Chairman: Daniel Levy
Website: www.tottenhamhotspur.com

Telephone: 0870 420 5000
Ticket Office: 0870 420 5000
Club Shop: 020 8365 5042

White Hart Lane

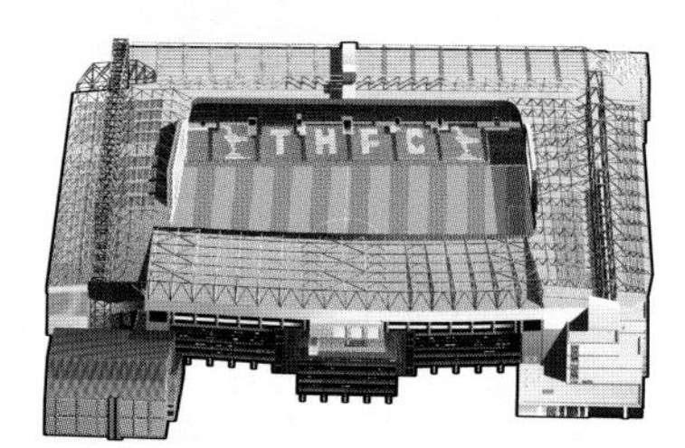

THFC

Season Review 05/06

Despite being pipped to Champions League qualification by their great rivals Arsenal on the final day of the season, Spurs could still look back on a campaign in which they made tremendous progress.

Manager Martin Jol was unafraid to put his faith in youth, allowing the likes of Aaron Lennon and Michael Dawson to shine.

Points / Position

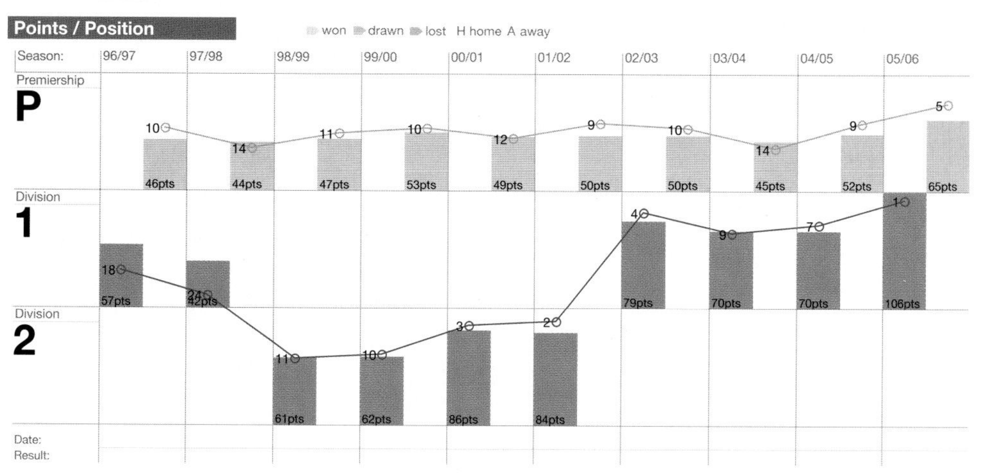

won
drawn
lost
H home A away
Season:
96/97
97/98
98/99
99/00
00/01
01/02
02/03
03/04
04/05
05/06
Premiership
P
Division
1
Division
2
18
57pts
24
42pts
11
61pts
10
62pts
3
86pts
2
84pts
4
79pts
9
70pts
7
70pts
1
106pts
10
46pts
14
44pts
11
47pts
10
53pts
12
49pts
9
50pts
10
50pts
14
45pts
9
52pts
5
65pts
Date:
Result:

Goals 05/06

Goals by Time Period

	0–15	15–30	30–45	45–60	60–75	75–90
scored	4	5	11	10	12	11
conceded	7	8	5	5	5	8

0 15 30 45 60 75 90

scored
conceded

Goals by Area

Scored (Conceded)

11 (9)
37 (23)
5 (6)

Goals by Position

Scored

- forward: 36
- midfield: 12
- defence: 4
- own goals: 1

Conceded

- forward: 17
- midfield: 14
- defence: 7

Goal by Situation

Scored

- set piece: 15
- open play: 37
- own goals: 1

Conceded

- set piece: 10
- open play: 28

All-Time Records

Total Premiership Record

Total Matches Played
544

Total Matches Won
195

Total Matches Drawn
143

Total Matches Lost
206

Total Goals Scored
716

Total Goals Conceded
732

Total Points
728

Total Players Used
139

All-Time Record vs Reading

Competition	Played	Won	Drawn	Lost	For	Against
League	6	2	2	2	14	11
FA Cup	5	2	1	2	7	6
League Cup	0	0	0	0	0	0
Other	0	0	0	0	0	0
Total	**11**	**4**	**3**	**4**	**21**	**17**

Watford

Nickname:	The Hornets	Telephone:	0870 111 1881
Manager:	Adrian Boothroyd	Ticket Office:	0870 111 1881
Chairman:	Graham Simpson	Club Shop:	01923 496 005
Website:	www.watfordfc.co.uk		

Vicarage Road

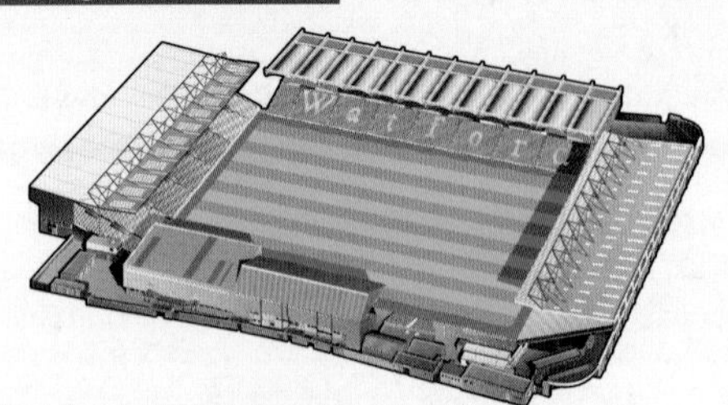

Season Review 05/06

Watford were the surprise package of the Championship, finishing third and going on to gain promotion through the Play-Offs.

Success was built around a belief instilled in his players by ultra-confident young boss Aidy Boothroyd. The likes of Marlon King and Matthew Spring were given a new lease of life, whilst Ashley Young and Jay DeMerit blossomed into stars.

Points / Position

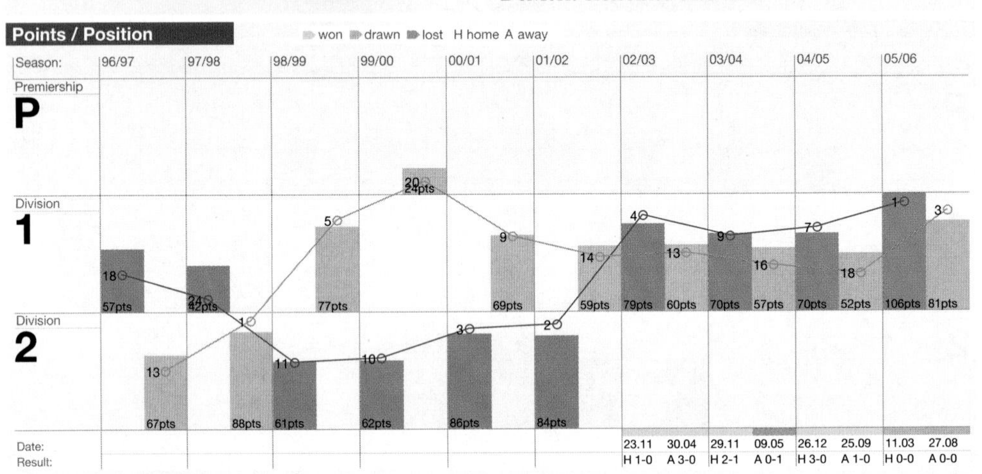

won drawn lost H home A away
Season: 96/97 97/98 98/99 99/00 00/01 01/02 02/03 03/04 04/05 05/06
Premiership
P
Division
1
Division
2
18 57pts
13 67pts
24 42pts
1 88pts
5 77pts
11 61pts
10 62pts
20 24pts
3 86pts
9 69pts
2 84pts
14 59pts
4 79pts
13 60pts
9 70pts
16 57pts
7 70pts
18 52pts
1 106pts
3 81pts
Date: 23.11 30.04 29.11 09.05 26.12 25.09 11.03 27.08
Result: H 1-0 A 3-0 H 2-1 A 0-1 H 3-0 A 1-0 H 0-0 A 0-0

Goals 05/06

Goals by Time Period

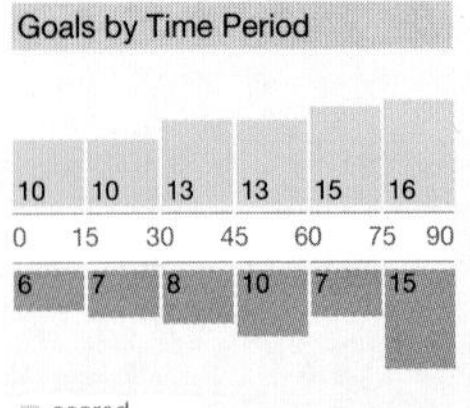

10 10 13 13 15 16
0 15 30 45 60 75 90
6 7 8 10 7 15
scored
conceded

Goals by Area

Scored (Conceded)

23 (13)

35 (34)

19 (6)

Goals by Position

Scored		Conceded	
forward:	36	forward:	23
midfield:	31	midfield:	21
defence:	8	defence:	6
own goals:	2	own goals:	3

Goal by Situation

Scored		Conceded	
set piece:	24	set piece:	18
open play:	51	open play:	32
own goals:	2	own goals:	3

All-Time Records

Total Premiership Record

Total Matches Played	38
Total Matches Won	6
Total Matches Drawn	6
Total Matches Lost	26
Total Goals Scored	35
Total Goals Conceded	77
Total Points	24
Total Players Used	32

All-Time Record vs Reading

Competition	Played	Won	Drawn	Lost	For	Against
League	86	34	16	36	117	133
FA Cup	5	2	1	2	9	7
League Cup	11	5	3	3	22	12
Other	0	0	0	0	0	0
Total	**102**	**41**	**20**	**41**	**148**	**152**

West Ham United

WEST HAM UNITED

Nickname:	The Hammers
Manager:	Alan Pardew
Chairman:	Terence Brown
Website:	www.whufc.com

Telephone:	020 8548 2748
Ticket Office:	0870 112 2700
Club Shop:	020 8548 2730

Upton Park

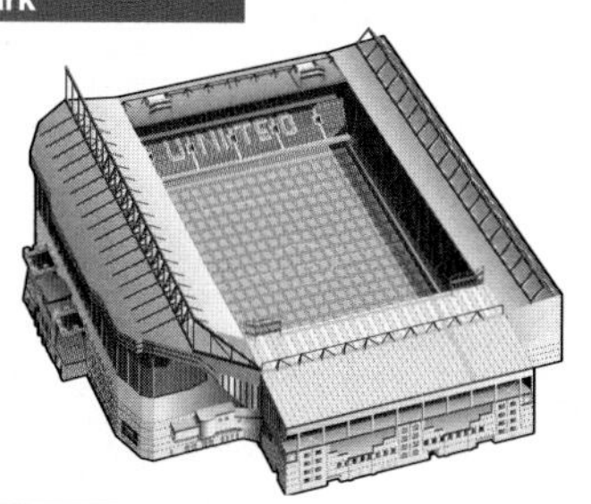

Season Review 05/06

West Ham enjoyed a memorable return to the top-flight, finishing ninth and reaching the FA Cup Final. The Hammers came within four minutes of lifting the trophy, but were ultimately undone by some magic from Liverpool's Steven Gerrard.

Manager Alan Pardew won over his many critics with a stylish brand of attacking football firmly in keeping with the traditions of the club.

Points / Position

won drawn lost H home A away

Season:	96/97	97/98	98/99	99/00	00/01	01/02	02/03	03/04	04/05	05/06
West Ham United	P 14, 42pts	P 8, 56pts	P 5, 57pts	P 9, 55pts	P 15, 42pts	P 7, 53pts	P 18, 42pts	1: 4, 74pts	1: 6, 73pts	P 9, 55pts
Reading	1: 18, 57pts	1: 24, 42pts	2: 11, 61pts	2: 10, 62pts	2: 3, 86pts	2: 2, 84pts	1: 4, 79pts	1: 9, 70pts	1: 7, 70pts	1: 1, 106pts

Premiership **P** · Division **1** · Division **2**

Date:	03.04	13.09	12.03	10.08
Result:	H 2-0	A 0-1	H 3-1	A 0-1

Goals 05/06

Goals by Time Period

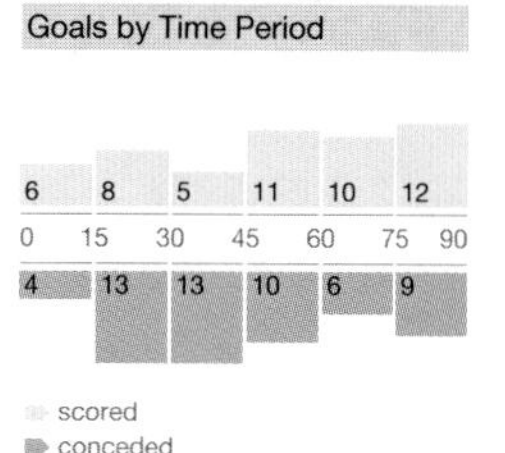
6
8
5
11
10
12
0
15
30
45
60
75
90
4
13
13
10
6
9

scored
conceded

Goals by Area

Scored (Conceded)

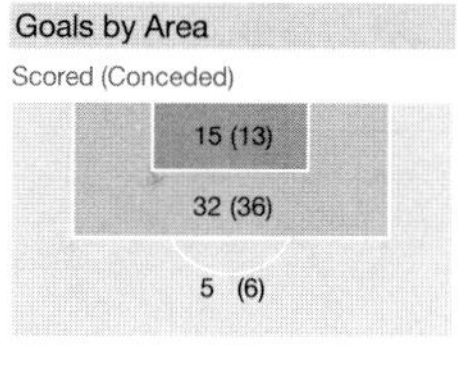
15 (13)
32 (36)
5 (6)

Goals by Position

Scored		Conceded	
forward:	29	forward:	33
midfield:	14	midfield:	17
defence:	5	defence:	5
own goals:	4		

Goal by Situation

Scored		Conceded	
set piece:	13	set piece:	14
open play:	35	open play:	41
own goals:	4		

All-Time Records

Total Premiership Record

Total Matches Played
426

Total Matches Won
148

Total Matches Drawn
111

Total Matches Lost
167

Total Goals Scored
514

Total Goals Conceded
590

Total Points
555

Total Players Used
142

All-Time Record vs Reading

Competition	Played	Won	Drawn	Lost	For	Against
League	4	2	0	2	3	5
FA Cup	0	0	0	0	0	0
League Cup	1	0	1	0	0	0
Other	0	0	0	0	0	0
Total	**5**	**2**	**1**	**2**	**3**	**5**

Wigan Athletic

Nickname: The Latics
Manager: Paul Jewell
Chairman: Dave Whelan
Website: www.wiganlatics.co.uk

Telephone: 01942 774 000
Ticket Office: 0870 112 2552
Club Shop: 01942 216 945

JJB Stadium

Season Review 05/06

Wigan surprised pundits and supporters alike by finishing in the top half of the table. A trip to Cardiff in the Carling Cup Final also served to highlight just how far the club had come in such a short space of time.

The platform for success was built early in the season, with Paul Jewell's men amassing 25 points from their first 11 Premiership matches.

Points / Position

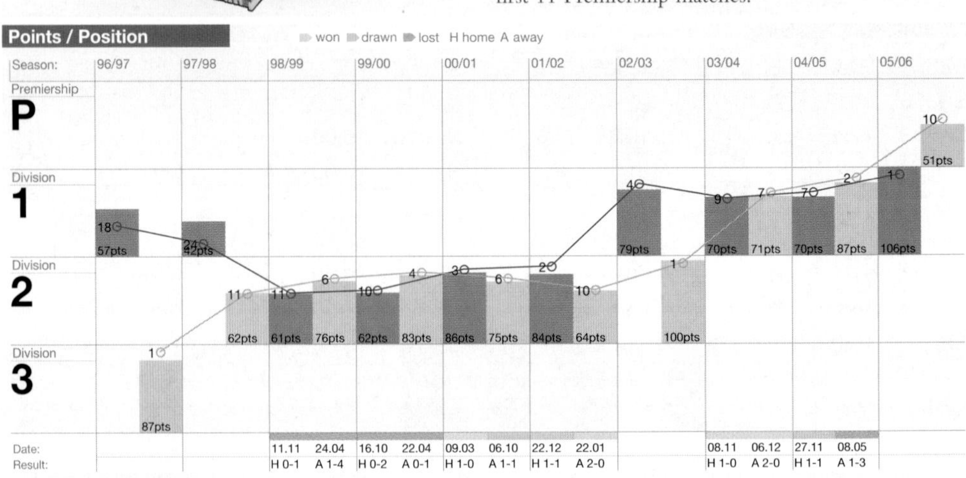

won drawn lost H home A away
Season: 96/97 97/98 98/99 99/00 00/01 01/02 02/03 03/04 04/05 05/06
Premiership P
Division 1
Division 2
Division 3
18 57pts
24 42pts
1 87pts
11 62pts
11 61pts
6 76pts
10 62pts
4 83pts
3 86pts
6 75pts
2 84pts
10 64pts
4 79pts
1 100pts
9 70pts
7 71pts
7 70pts
2 87pts
1 106pts
10 51pts
Date: 11.11 24.04 16.10 22.04 09.03 06.10 22.12 22.01 08.11 06.12 27.11 08.05
Result: H 0-1 A 1-4 H 0-2 A 0-1 H 1-0 A 1-1 H 1-1 A 2-0 H 1-0 A 2-0 H 1-1 A 1-3

Goals 05/06

Goals by Time Period

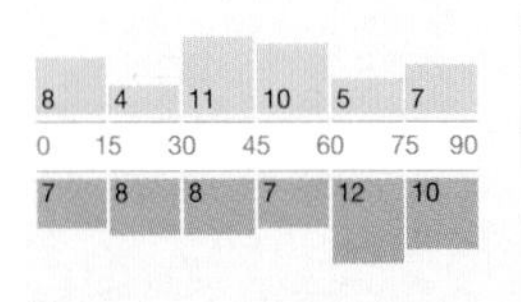

8 4 11 10 5 7
0 15 30 45 60 75 90
7 8 8 7 12 10

scored
conceded

Goals by Area

Scored (Conceded)

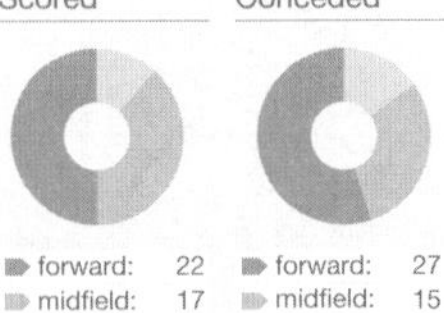

12 (15)
27 (31)
6 (6)

Goals by Position

Scored		Conceded	
forward:	22	forward:	27
midfield:	17	midfield:	15
defence:	5	defence:	8
own goals:	1	own goals:	2

Goal by Situation

Scored		Conceded	
set piece:	16	set piece:	16
open play:	28	open play:	34
own goals:	1	own goals:	2

All-Time Records

Total Premiership Record

Total Matches Played
38

Total Matches Won
15

Total Matches Drawn
6

Total Matches Lost
17

Total Goals Scored
45

Total Goals Conceded
52

Total Points
51

Total Players Used
25

All-Time Record vs Reading

Competition	Played	Won	Drawn	Lost	For	Against
League	30	12	7	11	38	34
FA Cup	0	0	0	0	0	0
League Cup	0	0	0	0	0	0
Other	2	0	1	1	1	2
Total	**32**	**12**	**8**	**12**	**39**	**36**

2006/07: The Fixtures

BARCLAYS
PREMIERSHIP

DATE	KO	v	OPPONENT
AUGUST			
Sat 19	**15:00**	**H**	**Middlesbrough**
Wed 23	19:45	A	Aston Villa
Sat 26	15:00	A	Wigan Athletic
SEPTEMBER			
Mon 11	**20:00**	**H**	**Man City**
Sat 16	15:00	A	Sheffield Utd
Sat 23	**17:15**	**H**	**Man Utd**
OCTOBER			
Sun 1	15:00	A	West Ham
Sat 14	**17:15**	**H**	**Chelsea**
Sun 22	**16:00**	**H**	**Arsenal**
Sat 28	15:00	A	Portsmouth
NOVEMBER			
Sat 4	15:00	A	Liverpool
Sun 12	**13:30**	**H**	**Tottenham**
Sat 18	**15:00**	**H**	**Charlton**
Sat 25	15:00	A	Fulham
DECEMBER			
Sat 2	**15:00**	**H**	**Bolton**
Wed 6	19:45	A	Newcastle
Sat 9	15:00	A	Watford
Sat 16	**15:00**	**H**	**Blackburn**
Sat 23	**15:00**	**H**	**Everton**
Tue 26	13:00	A	Chelsea
Sat 30	15:00	A	Man Utd
JANUARY			
Mon 1	**15:00**	**H**	**West Ham**
Sat 13	15:00	A	Everton
Sat 20	**15:00**	**H**	**Sheffield Utd**
Tue 30	**20:00**	**H**	**Wigan Athletic**
FEBRUARY			
Sat 3	15:00	A	Man City
Sat 10	**15:00**	**H**	**Aston Villa**
Sat 24	15:00	A	Middlesbrough
MARCH			
Sat 3	15:00	A	Arsenal
Sat 17	**15:00**	**H**	**Portsmouth**
Sat 31	15:00	A	Tottenham
APRIL			
Sat 7	**15:00**	**H**	**Liverpool**
Mon 9	15:00	A	Charlton
Sat 14	**15:00**	**H**	**Fulham**
Sat 21	15:00	A	Bolton
Sat 28	**15:00**	**H**	**Newcastle**
MAY			
Sat 5	**15:00**	**H**	**Watford**
Sun 13	15:00	A	Blackburn

Log on to www.readingfc.co.uk for the most up-to-date fixture list